Intersectionality in Femin
and Queer Movements

Examining the ways in which feminist and queer activists confront privilege through the use of intersectionality, this edited collection presents empirical case studies from around the world to consider how intersectionality has been taken up (or indeed contested) by activists in order to expose and resist privilege.

The volume sets out three key ways in which intersectionality operates within feminist and queer movements: it is used as a collective identity, as a strategy for forming coalitions, and as a repertoire for inclusivity. The case studies presented in this book then evaluate the extent to which some, or all, of these types of intersectional activism are used to confront manifestations of privilege. Drawing upon a wide range of cases from across time and space, this volume explores the difficulties with which activists often grapple when it comes to translating the desire for intersectionality into a praxis which confronts privilege.

Addressing inter-related and politically relevant questions concerning how we apply and theorise intersectionality in our studies of feminist and queer movements, this timely edited collection will be of interest to students and scholars from across the social sciences and humanities with an interest in gender and feminism, LGBT+ and queer studies, and social movement studies.

Elizabeth Evans is Reader in Politics at Goldsmiths, University of London. She researches feminist activism and theory, intersectionality, and political representation and is the author of two books, the most recent compares third-wave feminisms in Britain and the US.

Éléonore Lépinard is Associate Professor in Gender Studies at the University of Lausanne. Her research focuses on feminist movements and theory, gender and law, intersectionality, and gender and political representation.

Routledge Advances in Feminist Studies and Intersectionality

Routledge Advances in Feminist Studies and Intersectionality is committed to the development of new feminist and pro-feminist perspectives on changing gender relations, with special attention to:

- Intersections between gender and power differentials based on age, class, dis/abilities, ethnicity, nationality, racialisation, sexuality, violence, and other social divisions.
- Intersections of societal dimensions and processes of continuity and change: culture, economy, generativity, polity, sexuality, science, and technology;
- Embodiment: Intersections of discourse and materiality, and of sex and gender.
- Transdisciplinarity: intersections of humanities, social sciences, and medical, technical, and natural sciences.
- Intersections of different branches of feminist theorising, including historical materialist feminisms, postcolonial and anti-racist feminisms, radical feminisms, sexual difference feminisms, queer feminisms, cyber feminisms, post-human feminisms, and critical studies on men and masculinities.
- A critical analysis of the travelling of ideas, theories, and concepts.
- A politics of location, reflexivity, and transnational contextualising that reflects the basis of the Series framed within European diversity and transnational power relations.

Core editorial group

Professor Jeff Hearn (managing editor; Örebro University, Sweden; Hanken School of Economics, Finland; University of Huddersfield, UK)
Dr Kathy Davis (Institute for History and Culture, Utrecht, The Netherlands)
Professor Anna G. Jónasdóttir (Örebro University, Sweden)
Professor Nina Lykke (managing editor; Linköping University, Sweden)
Professor Elżbieta H. Oleksy (University of Łódź, Poland)
Dr Andrea Pető (Central European University, Hungary)
Professor Ann Phoenix (Institute of Education, University of London, UK)
Professor Chandra Talpade Mohanty (Syracuse University, USA)

Rethinking Transnational Men
Beyond, Between and Within Nations
*Edited by Jeff Hearn, Marina Blagojević and
Katherine Harrison*

Being a Man in a Transnational World
The Masculinity and Sexuality of Migration
Ernesto Vasquez del Aguila

Love
A Question for Feminism in the Twenty-First Century
Edited by Anna G. Jónasdóttir and Ann Ferguson

The Politics of Recognition and Social Justice
Transforming Subjectivities and New Forms
of Resistance
Edited by Maria Pallotta-Chiarolli and Bob Pease

Writing Academic Texts Differently
Intersectional Feminist Methodologies and the Playful
Art of Writing
Edited by Nina Lykke

Gender, Globalization, and Violence
Postcolonial Conflict Zones
Edited by Sandra Ponzanesi

Gendered Tropes in War Photography
Mothers, Mourners, Soldiers
Marta Zarzycka

Assisted Reproduction Across Borders
Feminist Perspectives on Normalizations, Disruptions and
Transmissions
Edited by Merete Lie and Nina Lykke

Rethinking Ethnic Masculinities
Intersections and New Directions
*Edited by Josep M. Armengol, Marta Bosch-Vilarrubias, Àngels Carabí
and Teresa Requena Pelegrí*

Visualizing Difference
Performative Audiencing in the Intersectional Classroom
Elżbieta Oleksy

Intersectionality in Feminist and Queer Movements

Confronting Privileges

Edited by Elizabeth Evans
and Éléonore Lépinard

Routledge
Taylor & Francis Group
LONDON AND NEW YORK

First published 2020
by Routledge
2 Park Square, Milton Park, Abingdon, Oxon OX14 4RN

and by Routledge
52 Vanderbilt Avenue, New York, NY 10017

Routledge is an imprint of the Taylor & Francis Group, an informa business

First issued in paperback 2021

British Library Cataloguing-in-Publication Data
A catalogue record for this book is available from the British Library

Library of Congress Cataloging-in-Publication Data
A catalog record has been requested for this book

ISBN: 978-0-367-25785-9 (hbk)
ISBN: 978-1-03-208440-4 (pbk)
ISBN: 978-0-429-28985-9 (ebk)

Typeset in Times New Roman
by Apex CoVantage, LLC

Printed in the United Kingdom
by Henry Ling Limited

Contents

Contributors

Petra Ahrens is Guest Professor in Comparative Politics and Gender and Diversity at University of Antwerp and Senior Researcher for EUGenDem at Tampere University.

Abbie Bonane is a PhD candidate in the Department of Politics and International Relations at Goldsmiths, University of London.

Daniela Cherubini is Assistant Professor of Sociology of Culture at the Ca' Foscari University of Venice, Italy, and Senior Researcher in the ERC project "DomEQUAL. A global approach to paid domestic work and global inequalities".

Emmanuelle David is a PhD candidate at Sciences Po Bordeaux (LAM) and University of Lausanne (CRAPUL).

Elizabeth Evans is Reader in Politics in the Department of Politics and International Relations at Goldsmiths, University of London.

Giulia Garofalo Geymonat is Assistant Professor of Sociology at the Ca' Foscari University of Venice and Senior Researcher in the ERC project "DomEQUAL. A global approach to paid domestic work and global inequalities".

Beatrice Halsaa is a political scientist and Professor Emeritus at the Centre for Gender Research at the University of Oslo.

Nayia Kamenou is a VC2020 Lecturer in the School of Applied Social Sciences at De Montfort University, Leicester.

Alexie Labelle is a PhD candidate in the Department of Political Science at the University of Montreal and is affiliated with the Centre de recherche sur les politiques et le développement social (CPDS).

Marie Laperrière is a PhD candidate at the Department of Sociology at Northwestern University.

Éléonore Lépinard is Associate Professor in Gender Studies and Social Sciences at the Université de Lausanne.

Zakiya Luna is Assistant Professor of Sociology and Feminist Studies at University of California, Santa Barbara.

Sabrina Marchetti is Associate Professor of Sociology at the Ca' Foscari University of Venice and PI of the ERC Project "DomEQUAL. A global approach to paid domestic work and global inequalities".

Maria Martin de Almagro is a Marie Curie postdoctoral fellow at the Department of Politics and International Studies at the University of Cambridge and Assistant Professor in International Affairs at Vesalius College, VUB, Brussels.

Petra Meier is Professor in Politics and Dean of the Faculty of Social Sciences at University of Antwerp.

Lucile Quéré is a PhD candidate in Gender Studies at the University of Lausanne and visiting doctoral student at the Department of Politics and International Relations at Goldsmiths, University of London.

Pauline Stoltz is a political scientist and associate professor at the FREIA Centre for Gender Research and the Department of Politics and Society at Aalborg University, Denmark.

Christel Stormhøj is a sociologist and associate professor at the Centre for Gender, Power and Diversity and the Department of Social Sciences and Business at Roskilde University.

Sofia Strid is Associate Professor in Gender Studies at the Unit of Gender Studies and Sociology, Örebro University, Sweden, and one of three Directors of the GEXcel International Collegium for Advanced Transdisciplinary Gender Studies.

Mieke Verloo is Professor in Comparative Politics and Inequality Issues at the Department of Political Sciences, Institute for Management Research, Radboud University, Nijmegen, the Netherlands, and Permanent Non-residential Fellow at the IWM, Institute for Human Sciences in Vienna.

Confronting privileges in feminist and queer movements

Elizabeth Evans and Éléonore Lépinard

In the fall of 2014 a new feminist collective, called Mwasi, self-designated as intersectional and Afro-feminist, was created in Paris. This event marked the first time, in France, that the term intersectionality was appropriated as a feminist identity. This does not mean that forms of what we would now designate as intersectional feminism did not previously exist in France. Indeed, the history of Black women's activism in France, and in many other European countries, is still to be retrieved from social erasure and ignorance by archival research, but we do know that Black women's collectives existed in France in the early 1980s (Coppet forthcoming; Ohene-Nyako 2018). What was new about Mwasi was, among other things, its claiming of its intersectional identity and its use of intersectionality as a tool to analyse its members' experience of oppression and marginalisation (Mwasi Collectif Aforéministe 2018, 2019; Larcher 2017). The occurrence of the term intersectionality in the French context in 2014 can be seen as somewhat belated, given the proliferation of intersectionality in activism and academia in the last decade (Davis 2008). Its relatively late emergence is testimony to both the resistance to take account of race, racism, and intersectionality within French activism (Lépinard, this volume) and the crucial role that intersectionality can play in the emergence and development of new forms of feminist activism which aim to represent the needs and interests of multiply-marginalised women, especially with respect to race. Indeed, as this volume illustrates, both in Europe and in North and Latin America, intersectionality has become a crucial frame to make visible and take into account structural racism in feminist activism and discourses.

Pride marches have historically been a critical and high-profile form of LGBT+[1] social movement activism around the world (Johnston 2007). Despite criticisms of the rainbow flag for its Euro-centric universalism (see Wallerstein 2006) as well as for its uses in neoliberal branding (Brenner et al. 2012), it remains an iconic symbol of Pride (Cain 2018). Therefore, the 2017 decision taken by Philadelphia Pride to update the flag to include two new colours – brown and black – was significant. As part of their 'More Color, More Pride' campaign, their decision to include brown and black visually signified the movement's inclusion of people of colour, as well as their opposition to racism within the LGBT+ movement. The decision to add the two new colours elicited a backlash amongst some queer activists who argued that the flag already symbolised unity and should not be racialised.[2] However, taking the lead from Philadelphia, other Pride initiatives sought to include the two new colours. The resistance to changing the rainbow flag, through appeals to a pre-existing universalism, helps illuminate how social movements often struggle to adopt inclusive intersectional politics and recognise difference and privilege. These are themes explored throughout this book, as authors consider the difficulties with which privileges are exposed, and confronted, within feminist and queer movements.

While these examples are recent, they belong to a long list of campaigns, groups, and movements spanning more than three decades, especially in the US, which have used 'explicitly intersectional strategies' (Hancock 2016, p. 4). However, what we have been witnessing more recently is a proliferation and a dissemination of intersectionality in activists' and organisations' discourses, well beyond the US context, as well as beyond those organisations and movements with links to Black feminism and feminism of colour. This proliferation has brought with it fears that the activist roots of intersectionality, and the centrality of Black women's experiences in its conceptualisation, and project of social justice might be forgotten in the process (Crenshaw 2011; Alexander-Floyd 2012; Jordan-Zachery 2013; Hancock 2016; Mügge et al. 2018). Whilst the term has been picked up, heralded, and sometimes dismissed, it does not hold the same meaning in all contexts and for all actors; as Kathy Davis suggested in her critical appraisal of the success of 'intersectionality' in academia, likening it to a 'buzzword' (2008). For Davis, the embrace of the term, in feminist theorising and beyond, may be due to the fact that the concept holds a promise to solve an enduring dilemma of feminism and feminist theory, that of thinking through differences and inequalities between women. However, the histories of feminist movements have shown that how this question of differences and power asymmetries may be answered varies greatly (Mohanty, Russo, and Torres 1991).

While there is debate about what intersectionality may mean in feminist and queer activist practices and discourses, there is broad agreement at the theoretical level about what the concept designates, both as it was articulated by Kimberlé Crenshaw (Crenshaw 1989, 1991) and as it was theorised, under other concepts and terms, before she coined the term. Ange-Marie Hancock defines intersectionality as a conceptualisation of what she calls 'ontological complexity,' which rests on the premise that 'analytical categories like "race", "gender", "class" and the hegemonic practices associated with them (racism, sexism, classism to which imperialism and homophobia certainly could be added) are mutually constitutive, not conceptually distinct' (Hancock 2016, p. 71; see also Collins 1990). Importantly this refutes the idea of a primary category: categories are co-constructed, and therefore cannot be artificially separated. How does this conceptual definition translate in terms of activist practices? Intersectionality has its roots in activism, as a project of social justice that makes visible multiply-marginalized groups (Crenshaw 1991; Hancock 2016); however, the ways in which intersectionality may take form in each given context cannot be predicted. It is for this very reason that intersectional theorists have warned about the risk of mis-appropriation and co-optation of intersectionality, in particular with respect to its historical project of racial justice. As Ange-Marie Hancock notes, 'race [is] a central analytic element that cannot be jettisoned without inflicting fatal violence on the integrity of intersectionality's intellectual project' (Hancock 2016, p. 13).

The variety of uses, and mis-uses, of intersectionality by activists and the ways in which they hold up to the social justice project of intersectionality are at the centre of this volume's inquiry. Importantly, while the development of intersectionality, as a theory and an activist practice, is rooted in feminism, we explore in this volume both feminist and queer movements. We conceive of these movements in a broad and inclusive fashion, including cases, such as the domestic workers' movement, which take labour and working conditions as their principle focus of analysis and claim-making but in a way that clearly intersects with gender. Considering intersectionality across different types of movements, and this is a first illustration of the variety of uses of intersectionality, the issues that pertain to the domain of intersectionality – power asymmetries within activists' constituencies based on racial, class, sexual, or able bodied/minded privilege and political analyses taking into account the interlocking nature of systems of oppression – have not unfolded along similar lines, but there has been cross-fertilisation of the debates going on, on the one hand in feminist movements and on the other hand in queer movements.

Historically, the question of 'differences' has been deployed differently in feminist and LGBT+ movements. Analysing the American LGBT movement from the 70s to the 90s, Elizabeth Armstrong notes that whilst the question of diversity within the movement spurred conflicts, this diversity was celebrated in LGBT organisations and not deemed to be threatening to the movement's unity, contrary to what happened in the feminist movement in the US over the same period (Armstrong 2002). This valorisation of a diverse movement was, Armstrong contends, the result of the focus on individual emancipation (and the connected commodification of individual sexual pleasure). Conversely, one could suggest that the insistence on collective rather than individual emancipation, in Western (white majority) feminist movements, fuels a suspicion of diversity because differences are perceived as divisive and as a threat to a unitary vision of identity.

Today, however, things have changed, and queer movements are more critically engaged in dynamics of power that go well beyond a celebration of diversity. In queer movements, the concept of homonationalism is the main analytical frame which has been used and promoted to critically assess power and exclusion. Coined by Jasbir Puar (2007), the term identified the pinkwashing of homosexuality by Israeli authorities, with the complicity of LGBT actors, as a way to depict the Palestinians as hostile to sexual diversity. Puar's theorisation is focused on contexts of war and imperialism, during which a suppression of queerness, and a promotion of some gay rights in the name of patriotism, occurs (Puar 2007, p. XII). The term has been widely used beyond its initial context as a way to describe, in particular in Europe, the instrumentalisation of LGBT rights, such as gay marriage, by far-right and conservative governments in order to portray immigrant communities as backwards, hostile to gay rights, and therefore in need of either ejection or reformation (Mepschen, Duyvendak, and Tonkens 2010). The framing of homonationalism tends to centre the analysis on race, migration, and colonialism, leaving aside other grounds of inequalities, power, and privilege within queer communities and activism (see Bonane, this volume).

Conversely, in feminist movements the recent debates over intersectionality have mainly been spurred by critical activism of feminists of colour (Townsend-Bell 2011; Bassel and Emejulu 2017; Joly and Wadia 2017). In line with historical precedent in which women of colour activism has challenged white feminist organisation assumptions and practices (Lorde 1984; Amos and Parmar 1984; Anzaldúa and Moraga 1983), the salience of race and racism is central to the dynamics of contemporary feminist intersectional politics. However, this salience does not go uncontested, especially in Europe, which is one focus of this book. There has been debate about the opportunity, and desirability, to present intersectional theories and practices that do not place race centrally in their analysis, but rather insist on class (Lutz, Herrera Vivar, and Supik 2011). However, as this volume documents, in activists' practices race is situated centrally in their concern when they use the term intersectionality and claim it as a tool, a strategy, or an identity. This inevitably also raises questions, especially when other systems of oppression, such as ableism, tend to be sidelined in feminist discourses and practices (Inckle 2015, see also chapter by Evans, this volume).

Hence, while framing may differ between feminist and queer movements, they tend to centre the analysis on race, broadly understood as encompassing issues of migration, citizenship, religion, and colonialism. Queer movements increasingly use the concept of intersectionality to address race and racism as well as other issues, such as biphobia and the inclusion of trans* people in the movement. Reciprocally, some feminist movements have adopted the term femonationalism coined by Sara Farris as a way to identify and oppose the instrumentalisation of women's rights for xenophobic and conservative political agendas which target migrants, refuges, and their offspring (Farris 2017).

Recognising that feminist and queer movements differ amongst and between themselves in terms of their approach to intersectionality and privilege, the remainder of this chapter reviews, synthesises, and categorises the key approaches and tensions which arise when activists engage with these ideas. How do they frame modes of activism and which forms of difference are considered politically salient? We begin by setting out the three main dimensions of intersectionality that dominate scholarly studies and social movement tactics. We then link these three dimensions to privilege and explore how the latter operates within social movement contexts. We finish by considering how social movement actors incorporate intersectional praxis in order to (try to) confront privilege.

Intersectionality in social movements: identity, inclusivity, and privilege

As the concept of intersectionality flourishes within feminist and queer movements discourse, it has become a signifier for multiple concerns, identities, and conflicts. In many contexts, feminist and queer movements address, and struggle, with the meaning and the realisation of intersectionality. Indeed, in any social movement, appeals to solidarity or interest claims based on one identity alone privilege the dominant/majority group at the expense of minority, multiply-marginalized groups (Crenshaw 1991; Strolovitch 2007) and therefore promote forms of what Myra Marx Ferree and Silke Roth have termed exclusionary solidarity (Ferree and Roth 1998, p. 629). Hence, identifying the social conditions required for a successfully inclusive movement or coalition, as well as recognising the need for different types of intersectional praxis, according to different contexts, are two critical aims for those interested in exploring intersectionality and social movements (Cho, Crenshaw, and McCall 2013).

The 'need' or 'desire' for more intersectionality is common across feminist and queer discourse, although it is not always met with concrete practices that would bring about the desired change. We can distinguish three main uses of intersectionality in feminist and queer discourse. Many organisations deploy the term as a new identity signifier, defining themselves as intersectional, claiming 'intersectional feminism,' and thus constituting what has been termed 'identity based intersectional movements' (Broad-Wright 2017). Here, the term intersectionality supports the constitution of new forms of feminist and queer collective identities and signals their difference from other organisations. Such an intersectional identity can sustain processes of dis-identification (Reger 2015) with other parts of the movement in order to claim a feminist or queer identity at the intersection of gender and race, or gender and religion for example, that may not be represented in other feminist or queer organisations (Chun, Lipsitz, and Shin 2013; Luna 2016; Tungohan 2016; Larcher 2017; chapter by Labelle, this volume).

Another important use of intersectionality is to claim it as a prerequisite and a strategy for successful coalitions (Weldon 2006; Cole 2008; Giraud and Dufour 2010). Here, attention to intersectional issues translates into coalitional practices which foster the representation and participation of multiply-marginalized groups within the coalition. For example, in a broad transnational coalition such as the World March of Women 2000 and successive iterations, specific practices were put in place to ensure the representation of women from the Global South (Giraud and Dufour 2010; Giraud 2015). A third use of intersectionality is made by feminist and queer organisations who summon it as a strategy to ensure inclusivity and to confront persisting privileges within their organisations and practices (Terriquez 2015; Laperrière and Lépinard 2016; Tormos 2017). Intersectionality is in this case used as a synonym for inclusivity, drawing attention to the composition of social movement organisations to contest the under-representation of multiply-marginalized groups of feminists within organisations and to signal oneself as an organisation or movement that is inclusive of various differences (e.g. the 'Feminism of the 99%' and chapter by Stoltz, Halsaa, and Stormhøj, this volume). However, this discourse is often non-performative: while intersectionality is used as a good to be desired, and the absence of it is lamented, many organisations display feelings of distress at how to go about achieving the desired change (Ward 2008; Reger 2012; Evans 2016; Schuster 2016).

As these three types of discursive repertoires show, being intersectional, or claiming intersectionality, has become a way to signal new feminist identities, as well as reflecting the shift in feminism's goals, from gender identities and inequalities to differences, inequalities, and privileges. Claiming intersectionality is also a way to confront persisting patterns of marginalisation within feminist and queer organisations. Whether, and how, these claims of inclusivity translate into actual practices that transform the composition of those movements, which have been criticised for prioritising the needs, identities, and interests of those who are not multiply-marginalized and tend to dominate their constituency, is a matter for empirical inquiry and opens up a wide field of investigation (Strolovitch 2007; Townsend-Bell 2011; Lépinard 2014; Evans 2015).

Indeed, when is intersectionality achieved within an organisation or a movement that claims to be inclusive? Is it a process, a challenge, or an objective that can be measured and reached? Perceptions of the intersectional nature of a movement vary (see Luna, this volume) and are linked in important and different ways to participation, representation, and claim-making: the participation of multiply-marginalized actors, their representation within an organisation's ranks, and a discursive and political attention to the ways in which gender and sexuality intersect with other axes of oppression all combine to influence the degree to which a movement or organisation can be considered intersectional. Hence, while intersectionality has become a central way to define and analyse feminist and queer movements, determining how to measure or capture when, where, how, whether, and why intersectionality has been achieved, attained, or performed, remains an open, and debatable, question.

The extant literature on intersectionality in social movements has explored the three main ways in which it is practiced: intersectionality as a collective identity for social movement organisations; intersectionality as the basis for coalition between social movement organisations; and intersectionality as a collective repertoire and strategy for organisations which aim to be inclusive. We review here how this expanding scholarship has contributed to our understanding of feminist and queer movements' dynamics.

Intersectionality as collective identity

Research on intersectionality in feminist movements has emphasised how multiply-marginalised groups of women organise around an intersectional identity, both as a need to 'organise one's own,' as Benita Roth has underlined (2004), and as a result of obstacles to inclusion within dominant movements which prioritise gender identity over other axes of identity and marginalisation (Anderson-Bricker 1999; Roth 2004; Springer 2005; Predelli and Halsaa 2012; Chun et al. 2013; Bassel and Emejulu 2017). These important studies look at how the experience of multiple marginalisation, of what Kimberlé Crenshaw would call 'structural intersectionality,' leads to the need and desire to self-organise in order to represent oneself. In a context in which, as Crenshaw described in her analysis of organisations fighting violence against women (Crenshaw 1991), the needs of multiply-marginalised women are rendered invisible in feminist discourses and political platforms, self-organisation become a necessity: a central strategy to access representation and promote a project of social justice that is adequate to the group's needs. Thus, intersectional feminist and queer organisations occupy 'strategic group positions' (Chun et al. 2013), which imply that they develop activist repertoires focusing on interlocking oppressions rather than on single-axis claims, thereby enabling them to engage with multiple stakeholders (Tungohan 2016).

The logic of self-organising was well described by Black feminists and feminists of colour in the 1970s and 1980s, as they theorised the need for intersectionality at the conceptual *and* the activist level (Combahee River Collective 1982; Anzaldúa and Moraga 1983; Collins 1990). Research which analyses how multiply-marginalized groups, especially feminist and queer ones, claim intersectionality as an identity, and as a collective action strategy, reminds us of the activist roots of the concept and its continuing relevance for social movement practices (Collins 2012; Hancock 2016; Broad-Wright 2017). In this literature, intersectionality is often understood as a given, something achieved through the very intersectional identity of the activists themselves. In other words, organisations are considered intersectional because they organise around an intersectional identity. Intersectionality thus provides a rationale for self-organisation and separatism, in order to be represented within the broader movement (Lépinard 2014).

However, interpreting intersectionality as a social movement identity risks essentialising the identities of multiply-marginalised groups. Indeed, various scholars have identified that self-organisation based on a multiply-marginalised identity, such as Black feminist, Afro-feminist, queer of colour, Muslim feminist, or disabled feminist, is not the 'natural' product of an identity but is also work performed by activists to create solidarity and a sense of identity: political identities are never 'pure' and do not exist prior to mobilisation (Lugones 1994; Mohanty 2003). They are rather the product of politicisation, a process which closely resembles coalitions across differences (Cole 2008; Cole and Luna 2010; Carastathis 2013; Broad-Wright 2017). The question of inclusivity, and attentiveness to other differences than the ones that support the identity of the organisation, thus remains an issue also for movements organised around an intersectional identity (Springer 2005; Luna 2016, 2017). Here we see that studying intersectionality from the perspective of an organisation's or a movement's identity can in fact be articulated alongside the two other principal approaches to intersectionality, that is as a strategy for coalition and a repertoire for inclusivity. For example, Ethel Tungohan shows how Filipina migrant grassroots activists in Canada claim an intersectional identity and, more importantly, use intersectionality as a normative framework to elaborate their actions (Tungohan 2016).

Conversely, Celeste Montoya argues that while multiply-marginalised groups self-organised around intersectional identities in the US Occupy movement – Women Occupy Wall Street, People of Colour Caucuses, Queering OWS – and made interventions vis-à-vis the rest of the movement, they did not adopt intersectional practices internally, thereby replicating single-axes approaches that were not conducive to broader coalitions (Montoya 2019). In a similar vein, Daniela Cherubini, Giulia Garofalo Geymonat, and Sabrina Marchetti show in their chapter on Colombia and Ecuador that while organisations promoting domestic worker's rights build complex identities on the intersection of gender, race, and class, when they pursue inclusivity, as well as when they make alliances in the contexts of coalitions, their strategies may differ: in some circumstances, they will privilege only one axis of domination (class) in their efforts to build a large coalition front, while in others they will maintain their focus on the intersection of the three, either applying 'multiple' or 'intersectional' approaches (Hancock 2007).

Coalitional intersectionality

A second approach explores how intersectionality is used as a strategy to build and sustain coalitions. Inclusive coalitions are usually (implicitly) defined as coalitions in which there is descriptive and substantive representation of minority and multiply-marginalised women; or as coalitions which, despite internal dissent and differences among women, manage to achieve substantial political gains (Weldon 2006; Giraud and Dufour 2010; Giraud 2015). Studies focusing on coalitions examine the intersectional discourses and practices that coalitions adopt to work across differences (Weldon 2006; Cole 2008; Cole and Luna 2010; Townsend-Bell 2011). This literature on intersectional coalitions delineates various factors that foster coalitions or encourage separatism. Among the factors that might foster intersectional coalition politics, a recurring theme is the acknowledgement, under various institutional forms, of power relationships amongst participants in the coalition. S. Laurel Weldon, for example, shows that norms of inclusivity in the successful transnational coalition she studied included a commitment to descriptive representation and separate organisations of disadvantaged groups (Weldon 2006). Similarly, Isabelle Giraud shows that the representation of young women in the World Women's March was ensured, in line with Weldon's analysis, by separate organising and formal descriptive representation (Giraud 2015). Meanwhile, Marie Laperrière and Éléonore Lépinard show how the Québécois coalition for women's rights used intersectionality as a way to identify, and attempt to redress, the political marginalisation of migrant and Québécois Native women in the movement (Laperrière and Lépinard 2016). Elizabeth Cole argues that power differentials, often expressed by asymmetrical access to resources and funding, need to be addressed directly for a coalition to sustain collaborative work (Cole

2008). Indeed, Barbara E. Smith identifies that a first necessary (but not in and of itself sufficient) step in maintaining a feminist coalition across the 'great racial divide' amongst working women in the US South, was the involvement of all participants in anti-racism consciousness-raising groups (Smith 1995). By contrast, failure to acknowledge power relations was one of the reasons advanced by US feminists of colour who refused to engage in coalitional politics with white feminists (Nelson 2003; Roth 2004).

While acknowledging power relations is a critical part of forging successful intersectional coalitions, other factors, which are external to movement dynamics, will also foster or impede intersectional coalitions. Here studies are attentive to how context shapes opportunities for intersectional coalition. For example, Philip Ayoub demonstrates that adversarial contexts, such as the aftermath of the financial crisis, may in fact encourage transnational LGBT+ movements to be more intersectional (Ayoub 2019). In this volume, Nayia Kamenou also shows how the structure of political opportunities opened up by the process of European integration in Cyprus led to the promotion of more intersectional coalitions by LGBTIQ actors. Comparative work on coalitions can help highlight how the history of engagement with racial difference in a movement, and the presence of hegemonic narratives about race, for example, condition how a coalition will address issues of racial privilege and inequalities. Comparing Québec and France, Éléonore Lépinard shows how the Québécois women's rights coalition had to engage early on in reflections about racial privileges in its relations to Québécois indigenous women's organisations. Attentiveness to racial inequalities was also encouraged by official policies on multiculturalism. Contrastingly in France, the national women's rights coalition historically did not engage with the question of race, and the official colour-blind public policy discourse delegitimised considerations of racial inequalities. These two radically different contexts led to diverging coalition efforts: in Québec intersectionality became a prominent concern for the coalition, which was not the case in France (Lépinard 2014, 2020).

Intersectionality as a repertoire for inclusivity

Finally, a third approach to intersectionality in feminist and queer movements, and in social movements in general, look at intersectionality as a strategy and repertoire used by organisations to address issues of inclusivity and solidarity (Tormos 2017). Here there is an overlap with intersectionality as a coalition practice since analyses are also attentive to intersectionality as a discourse and a tool geared towards inclusivity. However, studies in this last approach are focused on organisations themselves rather than coalitions which are, by nature, more temporary and focused on specific claims. In the case of feminist and queer organisations, the challenges raised by intersectionality are often framed as identifying exclusionary processes, ensuring inclusion of marginalised groups, and therefore changing activists' practices.

Research in this vein conceives of intersectionality as a repertoire or a practice, used by activists to transform their organisation. Jill Irvine, Sabine Lang, and Celeste Montoya differentiate various ways in which intersectionality is used by organisations to increase capacity, find voice, form alliances, and act politically (Irvine, Lang, and Montoya 2019). For each of these practices, they identify how resources, funding, discursive repertoires, and practices of translation (Doerr 2018) facilitate descriptive and substantive representation that are crucial to intersectional solidarity, as well as to forging alliances, a form of intersectional practice *par excellence*. Laperrière and Lépinard study another example in Québec where grassroots women's rights centres use intersectionality to increase attentiveness to the specific oppression lived by migrant women. Intersectionality is in this case a discursive repertoire to increase 'consciousness' about inequalities and processes of exclusion within organisations (2016). Similarly, studying student activism in the UK, Elizabeth Evans finds that a discursive commitment to intersectionality is at the heart of attempts to raise awareness about specific issues (e.g. period poverty) with intersectionality often used heuristically to refer to an accepted and normalised approach to inclusivity and social justice (2016). Meanwhile Dara Strolovitch finds that affirmative advocacy strategies, which concentrate on substantive and descriptive representation of marginalised groups within an organisation's constituency, lead to the reallocation of resources (2007).

The implementation and success of these strategies to enact forms of 'intersectional solidarity' (Lépinard 2014; Tormos 2017) depend in part upon two key factors which we explore in this book. The first is the *type of organisation* that engages – or shies away from – intersectional politics. While more established and hierarchical organisations may intuitively seem less able to reform their focus on a single-axis identity (i.e. gender), informality and lack of hierarchy may also produce forms of exclusion (Staggenborg 2015). Indeed, Slutwalks, which present themselves as demonstrations open to all women (and often men as well) willing to publicly oppose violence against women and the shaming of women's sexuality, tend to reproduce boundaries, along age/generation (Reger 2015), as well as along racial identities (Mercier 2016). The first part of this volume engages in this type of analysis by reviewing various types of movements and organisations, assessing whether, when, where, why, and how intersectionality is adopted.

The second is the *range of identities* that form the basis for mobilisation, and the extent to which they also provide different opportunities to engage with intersectional praxis. As we explore in the second part of this volume, identities which intersect with gender or sexuality also raise different possibilities of intersectional politics: while in some contexts attentiveness to race may appear today as a prerequisite to intersectional feminist practice, disability does not trigger similar discourses and commitments (Erevelles 2011). Similarly, some markers of difference and privilege, such as Europeanness, make sense very differently depending on the context.

Intersectionality and privilege

In this volume, we assess discourses and practices of intersectionality in feminist and queer organisations and movements with a specific focus on how claims and uses of intersectionality as an identity, a guiding principle in an organisation or coalition, contribute, or not, to challenging privilege. Indeed, confronting and challenging privileges is a central aim of intersectionality, both as a concept which unveils social processes of invisibilisation and as a project of social justice (Crenshaw 1989; Carastathis 2013; Hancock 2016). Focusing on how discourses and practices of intersectionality contribute to the confrontation of privileges therefore provides an interesting vantage point from which to analyse and assess what intersectionality, as a political imperative which redefines what it means to be 'truly' feminist or queer, does to social movement organisations. How is the discourse of intersectionality used to unveil privileges? What are the privileges identified by intersectional feminist and queer critiques in a given context? How can reference to intersectionality guide discourses and practices which aim at challenging and undoing privileges? Is intersectionality always used to confront privileges? Or can it be claimed without calling into question privileges, asymmetries, and inequalities within organisations and movements? And finally, what is it used for exactly?

We explore how intersectional discourses and practices address issues of privilege for various feminist and queer movements in different contexts underpinned by two main research questions. The first part of this volume questions how forms of activism and modalities of organising impact social movement organisations' ability and willingness to adopt intersectional repertoires that challenge privilege. Are some ways of organising – grassroots community centres vs. umbrella organisations or coalitions for example – more conducive to adopting intersectionality as a core organisational principle? The second part of the volume is devoted to a second, interrelated, question, that is, how do various forms of intersectionality lead to different types of collective mobilisation and organising repertoires? In other words, which forms of difference tend to be considered as more salient in feminist and queer activism? And which relations of marginalisation, axes of disempowerment, receive less attention under the label 'intersectionality'?

The concept of privilege is inherent to intersectionality theorising. Black feminists and feminist of colour theorising intersectionality, and previously under other names, consistently challenged white privilege within the US feminist movement, identifying how privilege and ignorance framed dominant feminist discourses and resulted in the exclusion of many feminist subjects (Anzaldúa and Moraga 1983; Davis 1983; Lorde 1984). Kimberlé Crenshaw's seminal article is focused on the workings of what can be called relative privilege in each subgroup she studies: Blacks and women (Crenshaw 1989). Indeed, her metaphor of individuals mounted on each other's shoulders, with the relatively privileged – white women or Black men – on top of the others illustrates the dynamics of privilege which is premised on the additional weight that those at the bottom are carrying. As a social justice project designed to make visible groups which have been made invisible, intersectionality aims to name and challenge privilege, especially when those privileges have benefited from social invisibility by parading as universal – think whiteness.

However, while challenging privilege is obviously one aim of intersectional politics, the question of the nature of privilege, and of how it/they can be contested by intersectional repertoires and strategies remain to be fully explored. Part of this book is thus to better understand the term 'privilege' and how it fits within intersectional organising and analysis.

Conceptualising privilege

Despite the significant impact that intersectionality has had upon gender studies (Davis 2008), privilege, which is usually taken to be intimately associated with ideas surrounding power, oppression, and inequality, has received relatively little by way of academic attention. In this section of the chapter we review the extant literature on privilege, exploring the ways in which it is approached and understood by scholars working across a range of intellectual traditions. We argue that privilege is a critical tool by which to analyse intersectionality and patterns of marginalisation, not least because it allows us to properly identify and name dynamics of power. The focus on privilege is important to fully excavate systemic and structural inequalities, and to understand them within historic, social, and economic contexts. Whilst the term privilege is common within intersectional analysis, it is not always defined. Indeed, it is often expected to stand for itself. However, examining how we understand the term privilege, and the conceptual work we expect it to do, is an important part of both scholarly and/or activist intersectional praxis.

Etymological study of the word privilege reveals its foundation in legal terminology: the word derives from the Latin *privus* (private) and *legis* (laws), and a *privilegium* was a decree which exempted an individual from the normal requirements of the law (Kruks 2005). This etymology is important because it reminds us that privilege is as much about embodying the norm (and the universal) as about escaping it. Post-enlightenment, the idea of privilege became somewhat tainted as universal ideals of humanism raised serious questions regarding the privileges associated with birthrights. Whilst revolutions took up the challenge of dismantling *some* forms of privilege, particularly those associated with the divine right of kings, other forms of privilege were enabled to spread, and to flourish. Indeed, colonial powers actively sought to spread and naturalise various forms of privilege, especially those pertaining to race, gender, and sexuality (McClintock 2013). Campaigns for the expansion of suffrage in the West revealed the extent to which many *within* marginalised groups who received gender-, class-, and race-based privileges, e.g. white women, were willing to pursue legal changes that would only be of benefit to people like themselves.

More broadly, the advent of twentieth-century civil rights movements saw attempts by individuals to dismantle their own privileges (Hurtado 1996), whilst at the same time articulating the ways in which different forms of privilege related directly to 'structural differentiations' that entrenched inequalities, disparities, and forms of oppression (Kruks 2005). This legacy of privilege, viewed as being inextricably linked to debates about equality, inequality, and power, has had a strong purchase amongst 'progressives' (Kruks 2005); concomitantly, it is also clear that the term is frequently deployed without any specificity, and moreover, it is often elided with 'power' (McIntosh 2012) which occludes its conceptual and practical use.

Amongst scholars and activists, privilege is broadly understood as referring to 'unearned' advantages or benefits which society grants to individuals and specific groups, based on prized or aspirational identity characteristics or categories, for example white privilege or male privilege (Allen 1975; McIntosh 1992). Most who use the term privilege do so in recognition of its structural and systemic foundations (Kruks 2005; Harris 2016); identifying how different forms of privilege produce and naturalise inequalities and oppression (Utrata 2011; Van Amsterdam 2013). The benefits afforded to privileged groups typically go unnoticed by those who are privileged, as Bob Pease notes, 'not being aware of privilege is an important aspect of having it' (p. 9); although others stress the active role that privileged groups and actors play in continuing to normalise and sustain systems of privilege (Leonardo 2004; Bhopal 2018). Indeed, this tension between passive and agentic interpretations of privilege is an issue for activists seeking to pursue an intersectional praxis. Surveying the existing literature on privilege reveals a plethora of different approaches, emphases, and interpretations, which we have grouped under the following interconnected categories which are most relevant to students of intersectionality in social movements: epistemic, productive, relational, and institutional.

Epistemic privilege

For those researching and writing about privilege, the question of our own subjectivity and role in the knowledge-production process raises important questions about epistemological privilege, both in terms of who is producing the knowledge but also regarding who is the object under study (Castañeda 2001). For some, a process of self-interrogation is a critical way in which to dismantle our own complicities with matrices of oppression and domination (Ferguson 1998; Carastathis 2013). However, reflexivity about privilege and its epistemic implications is difficult. Indeed, an important aspect of how epistemic privilege works is precisely through what some critical race scholars have called an *epistemology of ignorance* (Sullivan and Tuana 2007). Indeed, as these authors suggest, the epistemic privilege entailed by whiteness is one of ignorance: actively ignoring how one's own social position is premised on the othering or exploitation of others, and importantly, ignoring the very privileges to which one is entitled due to her whiteness. This lack of awareness of one's own privilege, which is the very manifestation of privilege itself, makes self-interrogation a complex and often failed process. Kruks observes that 'working on oneself' could result in such overwhelming guilt that any further engagement with broader issues is inhibited (2005). This translates in a common manifestation in social movements when privileged activists express anger and/or resentment and feel 'accused' of having privilege (Pease 2010). Sarita Srivastava describes such conflictual dynamics linked to racial privilege in the Canadian feminist movement, which point to resistances to unsettling privileges, especially around race, by using emotions as a resistance strategy on the part of white feminists, focusing discussion on their emotional states rather than on the practical changes demanded by their non-white fellow activists (Srivastava 2006). Hence, whilst feminists have long sought to deal with some of these epistemological and political problems (hooks 2000), identifying and reflecting upon situational subjectivities remains challenging for both scholars and/or activists alike. Several chapters in this volume speak to this issue, showing how epistemic privilege works and frames movements' claims and feminist and queer practices. For example, in her chapter Éléonore Lépinard describes how whiteness and the ignorance of privilege it entails shaped responses by French feminist organisations to pressing intersectional issues such as the prohibition of Islamic veiling in public schools and of full veiling in public spaces in France.

Productive

One of the most important features of privilege is that it is productive. By that we mean that it produces, and reproduces, systemic forms of oppression. The majority of scholars writing on, or around, privilege identify the material effects of privilege in relation to a wide range of structural forms of oppression, including racism, sexism, homophobia, classism, or some combination of these (Black and Stone 2005). Moreover, other studies use the privilege framework to examine more specific themes, such as body size (Van Amsterdam 2013), single parenthood (Utrata 2011), student protests (Chen 2011), or same-sex marriage (Ammaturo 2014). The material effects of privilege permeate, and indeed are foundational to, economic systems and social policies, especially those related to health, education, and criminal justice (Bhopal 2018). It is in some respects the productive nature of privilege which makes it such an integral part of intersectional analysis, and in particular the acknowledgement of, and resistance to, injustice (Collins and Bilge 2016). A number of chapters in this volume highlight and analyse the productive nature of privilege, for instance Marie Laperrière's chapter explores the ways in which organisers within the anti-violence movement produce and reproduce racist narratives by failing to acknowledge or confront their own racial privilege. Indeed, as she argues, this becomes a stumbling block to the achievement of intersectional praxis, despite the explicitly articulated desire to undertake intersectional activism.

Relational

Privilege is of course relational. Acknowledging this is even more important when considering privilege alongside, and as part of, an intersectional framework. Scholars such as Aida Hurtado define relational privilege as a frame by which to understand an individual or a group's proximity, and importance, to white male privilege (1996, p. 12). For Hurtado, therefore, we can only really grasp the complexity of privilege when we understand the ways in which gender, race, and class intertwine during the 'allocation' of privilege by any given society. Just as we understand and grasp the idea of intersecting identities within broader matrices of oppression (Collins 1990), so too must we understand how identities interact so as to create privilege. If privilege is relational, it is also contextual: relations are embedded in social contexts and their intersections vary. In her chapter on LGBTIQ politics in Cyprus, Nayia Kamenou shows how the process of access to the EU has introduced and stabilised new forms of privilege among LGBTIQ activists, with Europeanness, and the privileges it carries in comparison to the Republic of Cyprus which acceded to the EU, becoming a new norm for LGBTIQ activists.

Institutional

More recent engagement with the idea of privilege has explored the ways in which it is institutionalised, whether that is in the make-up of legislatures or the leadership teams within organisations, or in terms of approaches to public policy (Bhopal 2018; Romero 2018). Indeed, both the visible and invisible operation of privilege permeates both formal and informal institutions, sustained by normalised and normative approaches to equality and meritocracy. Critical race theorists have long identified the mutable and numerous ways in which whiteness and white male privilege underpin the institutions at the heart of liberal democracies (Crenshaw 1991; Bonilla-Silva 2006). The institutionalisation of privileges is in some respects part of the reason why we are unable to name privilege when we see it because it permeates the very fabric of our society. Privileges are codified, for example through laws governing who can run for office; but privileges are also evident in the numerous unwritten rules which shape our society, for instance in social norms regarding care and reproductive work. In their chapter about the feminist Nordiskt forum, a major feminist manifestation held in Malmö, Sweden, Pauline Stoltz, Beatrice Halsaa, and Christel Stormhøj show how perceptions of privilege and criticisms about the organisation of this feminist event as reproducing privileges, concentrated on institutionalised privileges. Access to financial resources and the ability to be part of the organising committee were perceived as privileging already privileged feminists, in terms of their status and economic resources, and an alternative feminist festival was organised to make alternative and intersectional voices more visible. While this 'Feministiskt' festival also benefited from public resources and became in itself an institution, it was free of charge, contrary to the Nordiskt Forum, and endorsed an intersectional discourse, two dimensions perceived as challenging the structure of privilege which characterised the other event. In their chapter which explores domestic workers' organisations, Daniela Cherubini, Giulia Garofalo Geymonat, and Sabrina Marchetti detail the challenge to institutional privileges embedded in the social division of work (the divide between productive and reproductive labour) and the social distribution of reproductive work between genders, classes, and racialised social groups.

These four types of privilege are not mutually exclusive and often work in conjunction to inscribe and reinscribe dominant discourses, networks, and organisational repertoires which results in patterns of marginalisation. Intersectionality, as a theory and as a social movement tool and strategy is, we argue, one way in which these privileges can be revealed and contested. In the final section of this introduction we provide an overview of the various chapters in this volume identifying how, and how effectively, activists have engaged with intersectional repertoires to resist privilege.

Intersectionality as a tool to confront privilege?

Thus far, we have provided an overview of the ways in which intersectionality operates within social movement spaces, highlighting in particular its use as a collective identity, its function in forming coalitions, and how it can be deployed as a repertoire for inclusivity. We have also delineated four key approaches towards, and manifestations of, privilege: epistemic, productive, relational, and institutional. Unpacking how privilege is produced, expressed, and reproduced through a variety of social processes helps focus our analytical attention to these various dimensions when analysing how intersectionality may, or may not, contribute to actually challenge or dismantle those privileges.

We now introduce the chapters presented in this volume, which analyse the numerous ways in which intersectionality operates within feminist and queer movements in order to challenge and dismantle privilege as it appears in its various guises. The following chapters all provide empirical case studies of feminist and queer movements from around the world. They take the use of, and approaches towards, intersectionality in feminist and queer organisations as their starting point to identify and unpack the various tensions that arise through different modalities of organising as well as in relation to different intersections. Indeed, activists and organisations can use intersectionality to challenge normative assumptions which underpin privileges – about ableism and racism, for example – to claim for specific representation and to reject tokenism, or to impose specific political priorities and organisational modalities for coalitions. However, while repertoires of intersectionality are discursively deployed, they do not always perform the desired outcomes.

The first section of the volume includes chapters which explore different forms of movement organising and the ways in which intersectional politics are played out differently depending on the type of organising that structures activists' practices and reflections on intersectionality. The chapters move from large movements and organisations – transnational and national coalitions – to more micro-practices and small groups expressing activism through less studied means, such as self-help and artistic practices. This section thus spans a wide range of activist practices and shows that intersectional challenges, in particular those relating to institutional and epistemic privileges, are raised and formulated in different terms for each context of activism. Maria Martin de Almagro's chapter, which opens this section, argues that transnational feminist networks operating in post-conflict societies have overlooked intersectionality, instead relying upon strategic essentialism as a means by which to advocate for gender justice. Her research concentrates on the activities of the two main transnational feminist campaigns in the Democratic Republic of Congo (DRC) and finds that they play an active role, as brokers, in producing discursive and symbolic borders and boundaries which reinforce existing privileges. This case study, therefore, illustrates not only the limitations of transnational feminist networks operating in post-conflict societies to engage with intersectionality but also their agentic role in *producing* and reproducing forms of privilege.

Zakiya Luna explores the complex and versatile use of the concept of intersectionality in the context of the 2017 Women's Marches, with a focus on the US. She shows that what activists might mean by 'intersectionality' varies greatly and is dependent on their location: the local context in which the march took place for them and their own trajectory of politicisation. In this perspective, while some commentators insisted on the intersectional nature of the marches, meaning here the diversity of the constituency which attended, for some activists the marches were not perceived as particularly intersectional. For some respondents surveyed in Luna's research, intersectionality designates the need for more diversity within feminism and a priority that should be given to consideration of racism and racial issues in the mobilisation. Intersectionality is therefore used as a discourse to challenge *relational and institutional privilege*, but when mentioned by participants, it is often in order to lament its absence. While heralded as an organising principle of the marches, depending on the context, intersectionality is not always 'visible' to participants. However, exceptions exist, such as a march in Winnipeg, Canada, in which organisational tactics were used to challenge privilege, putting in front of events indigenous and racialised women.

In Chapter 3, Petra Ahrens and Petra Meier compare the extent to which institutional feminisms in Belgium and Germany have (successfully or otherwise) sought to engage with intersectionality. They take as their principal focus the national women's umbrella organisations, emphasising the role that histories play in determining whether, how, in what ways, and why organisations take up intersectional discourse and repertoires. They approach their comparison by focusing on elements of representation – in particular the extent to which the groups are descriptively representative or substantively representative of a wide range of women and women's issues. The historical methods they adopt is a critical tool for uncovering and charting the existence of *institutional privileges* and the difficulties with which they can be confronted within historic organisations.

Sofia Strid and Mieke Verloo examine in Chapter 4 the policies against gender-based violence in the UK, Sweden, and the Netherlands. The authors look at how knowledge about gender-based violence is produced by feminist movements and feminist policies in the three countries and show how definitions of gender-based violence generally tend to limit the issue to domestic violence, thereby producing forms of *epistemic privilege*. This lack of engagement with intersectionality in policy framing reproduces privilege, and when there is a consideration for intersectionality, as is the case in the Netherlands, it leads to a hypervisibility of violence against migrant women and a culturalisation of the issue, rather than an analysis of how interlocking systems of oppression combine to structure gender-based violence.

In Chapter 5, Emmanuelle David explores the turn towards intersectional activism in Morocco, arguing that activists have adopted and adapted intersectional discourse in order to better suit their needs. The ways in which Moroccan feminists appropriate and adapt intersectionality offers an important insight into not only the ways in which intersectionality travels but also its use as a collective identity which helps form and sustain new generations of feminist activists. The process of self-identifying as intersectional feminists has also helped reveal *relational privileges* – specifically male privilege within social justice activism and class privilege amongst second-wave or 'institutional' feminists in Morocco. An intersectional lens, therefore, helps younger feminists in Morocco reveal relational privileges and contest them by engaging in new creative modes of activism.

In the last chapter of this section, Lucile Quéré analyses the gynaecological self-help movement in France, revealing how activists' desire for intersectionality cannot always overcome *relational privilege*. The case study demonstrates that even when activists use intersectionality to create a collective identity and to pursue a repertoire of inclusion, processes of marginalisation and exclusion are revealed through *relational* and *epistemic privileges*. Indeed, Quéré identifies the difficulty of performing intersectionality even when strategies have been put in place to create a collective identity. The affective dimensions of non-performativity are thus laid bare through the frustration articulated by activists who have been unable to overcome or resist certain forms of privilege.

The second section explores the ways in which a range of differences and privileges is taken into consideration, or not, by feminist and queer movements when they claim to implement intersectional tactics and practices. The section starts with disability and then moves to several chapters about race, and closes with the question of generation/age, which is seldom analytically addressed, while it is a difference which is very present in activists' discourses. Each of the several chapters focusing on race look to a particular instantiation of the particular nexus of racial relations: nationalism, whiteness, race and class, and religion. Hence, six chapters offer different perspectives on how race is problematised and addressed with an intersectional perspective and as it is articulated with other social relations of privilege such as class and religion. In Chapter 7, Elizabeth Evans analyses the extent to which disabled women and disability-related issues are included within the UK women's movement. She identifies that despite attempts on the part of feminist organisations, especially newer groups, to use intersectionality as a form of collective identity and as a means by which to achieve inclusion, disabled women do not feel included. Evans argues that the forms of marginalisation experienced by disabled women are produced by ableist privilege. In this case, the desire for intersectionality, and for inclusivity, is insufficient to tackle *epistemic* and *productive* forms of privilege. Non-disabled women are assumed to be the default feminist subject, whilst ableist privilege produces forms of activism that are (literally) inaccessible for disabled feminists.

Chapter 8 by Nayia Kamenou explores intersectional politics in the LGBTIQ movement in Cyprus. Looking at Greek-Cypriot and Turkish-Cypriot activists, Kamenou focuses on how exclusions along ethnic differences and gender conformity (cis/trans) are performed within the movement. She shows how the process of accession to the EU has helped LGBTIQ activists to advance their political agenda, but has also tended to bolster forms of homonationalism, as Europeanness has become a valuable commodity for Greek Cypriots. However, she also shows that forms of intersectional attention can emerge and challenge the problematic association between nationalism and queer activism and the *relational privilege* of European identity it helps sustain. Hence, Kamenou's chapter highlights the continuing importance of nationality and nation, as well as cis-identity, as grounds of privilege and exclusion in queer movements.

Éléonore Lépinard identifies feminist whiteness as a key explanation for resistance to intersectionality within French feminist organisations, in Chapter 9. In this study, white feminists both produce and reinforce *epistemic privilege* by making feminism white; an active process wherein non-white women, especially Muslim women, are constructed as other. Lépinard argues that the process of ignoring race, and specifically whiteness, in the pursuit of the universal feminist subject acts as a method to maintain racial privilege. In this case study, therefore, we see failure to engage in intersectional activism result in the othering of non-white women and the establishment of *relational privileges* that are presented as a normalised manifestation of feminist politics.

Alexie Labelle's chapter explores whiteness within Québec's LGBTQ movement. Labelle identifies how approaches to intersectionality have reinforced relational privilege in LGBTQ organisations through a tokenistic approach to inclusion, which she contrasts with the autonomous organising 'at the margins' which works to resist and contest white privilege. Whilst intersectionality is often invoked to suggest a collective identity, this case reveals the ways in which institutional white privilege amongst Québec's LGBTQ organisations serves to undermine attempts at solidarity. Institutional privilege manifests itself within the specifically tokenistic approach to inclusion demonstrated by some organisations who sought to diversify by recruiting non-white executive board members. Indeed, this case underscores the importance of self-organising for marginalised groups as critical to the project of contesting privilege.

In Chapter 11, Marie Laperrière analyses the intersections between race, gender, and class in Chicago's anti-violence movement, finding that epistemic and productive privileges limit the extent to which activists can achieve intersectional praxis. Laperrière argues that despite an explicitly articulated commitment to intersectionality and to intersectional theory, racialised narratives of violence continue to have a purchase on white anti-violence activists, who are thus unable (or unwilling) to interrogate or confront relational privileges. Again, we see the limitations of the desire for intersectionality as a repertoire for inclusion, as it comes into conflict with systemic and historic manifestations of privilege. The case study also highlights the ways in which intersectionality can be deployed to demonstrate expertise, thus producing its own forms of epistemic privilege.

Comparing movements for the rights of domestic workers in Ecuador and Colombia, Daniela Cherubini, Giulia Garofalo Geymonat, and Sabrina Marchetti show how organisations representing domestic workers in both contexts used intersectionality differently, albeit always with some success. In Ecuador, activists recognised the interlocking nature of oppression and the role that gender and class, in addition to race, play in the inequalities that weigh on domestic workers. While they articulate these three dimensions in their own discourse, as they lobby their government to ratify the ILO 'Convention No. 189 on decent work for domestic workers,' they privileged alliances based on class and the promotion of labour rights. On the contrary, in Colombia, activists engaged in the campaign for equal wage used their intersectional identities, as Afro-Colombian women domestic workers to articulate demands rooted in a feminist analysis of the care economy, thereby promoting a discourse in the public sphere in which gender, race, and class were always present. In this case, intersectionality became a successful way to challenge epistemic and institutional privilege, by articulating a new frame to understand the interlocking nature of oppression lived by paid domestic workers around the notion of 'care economy.'

In Chapter 13, Abbie Bonane explores the rise of autonomous queer Muslim activism in the UK, partly as a response to the lack of visibility given to queer Muslims by the mainstream civil society organisation, Stonewall. Abbie Bonane situates this development within a homonationalist context in which Islam as a religion and Muslim individuals are considered antithetical to LGBT+ rights and LGBT+ equality. Such a context renders the very idea of the queer Muslim as an impossibility. The chapter reveals how and when Stonewall have sought to address issues of Islamophobia, as well as their important role in helping support the autonomous organising of groups set up specifically by and for queer Muslims. This chapter demonstrates the ways in which homonormative assumptions privilege certain 'non-threatening' LGBT+ identities, which results in the exclusion and marginalisation of others within the movement.

The final empirical case study, by Pauline Stoltz, Beatrice Halsaa, and Christel Stormhøj, looks back at a major feminist event: the *Nordiskt Forum Malmö* held in Malmö, Sweden, in 2014, and the 'counter' festival, the *Feministiskt Festival*, which was held simultaneously but organised by a different set of actors. The Nordiskt Forum, as a major event in Scandinavia, encountered the usual issues of representation and inclusivity, and was thus criticised as overwhelmingly white and privileged because of its institutional sources of funding. On the contrary, the Feministiskt Festival portrayed itself as intersectional and inclusive and was free of charge thanks to the support of the City of Malmö. Here the discourse of intersectionality was used to challenge *institutional privilege* reproduced by the Nordiskt Forum. The authors ask whether the difference of generation may explain the diverging patterns of discourse and organisation of the two events with respect to intersectionality: with an older generation of feminists that can be labelled 'rights oriented' or state feminists focused on a single-axis perspective, and a younger generation located in the context of neoliberalism and conservativism, self-defining itself as practicing intersectional feminism and multiple-axes analyses.

This introductory chapter has set out the two intertwined frameworks which we use to explore feminist and queer movements in this book: (1) intersectionality, as collective identity, coalitional strategy, and a repertoire for inclusion; and (2) epistemic, productive, relational, and institutional forms of privilege. The chapters draw upon examples from across time and space to illustrate the difficulties with which social movement actors realise their desire to achieve or perform intersectionality, and the extent to which they are able (or willing) to identify, analyse, and confront privilege(s).

Notes

1 We use the term queer in this volume and introduction as an umbrella term which recognises the lived realities of those who have been marginalised and demonised, politically, materially, and culturally, because they do not conform to heteronormative and/or cis-normative assumptions. We also use the term LGBT+, as do some of our authors, to refer to specific movements or organisations.
2 White, Nadine. 2019. "Black and Brown Colours Added to LGBT Flag by Manchester Pride." *Huffington Post*, January 16. www.huffingtonpost.co.uk/entry/manchester-pride-calls-for-greater-inclusion-in-lgbt-community-by-adding-black-and-brown-colours-to-flag_uk_5c3dd0a0e4b0922a21d8954f [accessed 10 June 2019]

References

Alexander-Floyd, Nikol G. 2012. "Disappearing Acts: Reclaiming Intersectionality in the Social Sciences in a Post – Black Feminist Era." *Feminist Formations* 24 (1): 1–25.

Allen, Theodore William. 1975. *Class struggle and the Origin of Racial Slavery: The Invention of the White Race*. New York: New England Free Press.

Ammaturo, Francesca Romana. 2014. "The Right to a Privilege? Homonormativity and the Recognition of Same-Sex Couples in Europe." *Social and Legal Studies* 23 (2): 175–194.

Amos, Valerie, and Pratibha Parmar. 1984. "Challenging Imperial Feminism." *Feminist Review* 17: 3–19.

Anderson-Bricker, Kristin. 1999. "'Triple Jeopardy': Black Women and the Growth of Feminist Consciousness in SNCC, 1964–1975." In *Still Lifting, Still Climbing: African American Women's Contemporary Activism*, edited by Kimberly Springer, 49–69. New York, NY: New York University Press.

Anzaldúa, Gloria, and Cherrie Moraga, eds. 1983. *This Bridge Called My Back: Radical Writings by Women of Color* (2nd ed.). New York, NY: Kitchen Table, Women of Color Press.

Armstrong, Elizabeth A. 2002. *Forging Gay Identities: Organizing Sexuality in San Francisco, 1950–1994*. Chicago, IL: University of Chicago Press.

Ayoub, Phillip M. 2019. "Intersectional and Transnational Alliances during Times of Crisis: The European LGBT Movement." In *Gendered Mobilizations and Intersectional Challenges: Contemporary Social Movements in Europe and North America*, edited by Jill Irvine, Sabine Lang, and Celeste Montoya. London; New York, NY: Rowman & Littlefield.

Bassel, Leah, and Akwugo Emejulu. 2017. *Minority Women and Austerity: Survival and Resistance in France and Britain*. Bristol, UK: Policy Press.

Bhopal, Kalwant. 2018. *White Privilege: The Myth of a Post-Racial Society*. Bristol: Policy Press.

Black, Linda L. and David Stone. 2005. 'Expanding the Definition of Privilege: The Concept of Social Privilege.' *Journal of Multicultural Counselling and Development* 33(4): 243–255.

Bonilla-Silva, Eduardo. 2006. *Racism Without Racists: Color-Blind Racism and the Persistence of Racial Inequality in the United States*. New York: Rowman & Littlefield.

Brenner, Neil, Marcuse, Peter and Mayer, Margit. eds. 2012. *Cities for People, Not for Profit: Critical Urban Theory and the Right to the City*. London and New York: Routledge.

Broad-Wright, Kendal. 2017. "Social Movement Intersectionality and Re-Centring Intersectional Activism." *Atlantis: Critical Studies in Gender, Culture & Social Justice* 38 (1): 41–53.

Cain, Patricia. 2018. *Rainbow Rights*. New York: Routledge.

Carastathis, Anna. 2013. "Identity Categories as Potential Coalitions." *Signs: Journal of Women in Culture and Society* 38 (4): 941–965.

Castañeda, Claudia. 2001. "The Child as a Feminist Figuration: Towards a Politics of Privilege." *Feminist Theory* 2(1): 29–52.

Cho, Sumi, Kimberlé Williams Crenshaw, and Leslie McCall. 2013. "Toward a Field of Intersectionality Studies: Theory, Applications, and Praxis." *Signs: Journal of Women in Culture and Society* 38 (4): 785–810.

Chen, Chris. 2011. "We Have All Become Students of Color Now." The California Student Movement and the Rhetoric of Privilege." *South Atlantic Quarterly* 110(2).

Chun, Jennifer Jihye, George Lipsitz, and Young Shin. 2013. "Intersectionality as a Social Movement Strategy: Asian Immigrant Women Advocates." *Signs: Journal of Women in Culture and Society* 38 (4): 917–940.

Cole, Elizabeth R. 2008. "Coalitions as a Model for Intersectionality: From Practice to Theory." *Sex Roles* 59 (5–6): 443–453.

Cole, Elizabeth R., and Zakiya Luna. 2010. "Making Coalitions Work: Solidarity Across Difference within US Feminism." *Feminist Studies* 36 (1): 71–98.

Collins, Patricia Hill. 1990. *Black Feminist Thought: Knowledge, Consciousness, and the Politics of Empowerment* (1st ed.). Boston, MA: Unwin Hyman.

Collins, Patricia Hill. 2012. *On Intellectual Activism*. Philadelphia, PA: Temple University Press.

Collins, Patricia Hill, and Sirma Bilge. 2016. *Intersectionality*. Cambridge: Polity.

Combahee River Collective. 1982. "A Black Feminist Statement." In *All the Women Are White, All the Blacks Are Men, But Some of Us Are Brave*, edited by Gloria Hull, Patricia Bell, and Barbara Smith. Old Westbury, NY: Feminist Press.

Coppet, Victoire. Forthcoming. "Un féminisme Noir en France dans les années 1970? Eléments socio-historiques en vue d'une analyse politico-philosophique." *Les Cahiers du genre*.

Crenshaw, Kimberlé Williams. 1989. "Demarginalizing the Intersection of Race and Sex: A Black Feminist Critique of Antidiscrimination Doctrine, Feminist Theory and Antiracist Politics." *University of Chicago Legal Forum* 139: 139–168.

Crenshaw, Kimberlé Williams. 1991. "Mapping the Margins: Intersectionality, Identity Politics, and Violence Against Women of Color." *Stanford Law Review* 43 (6): 1241–1299.

Crenshaw, Kimberlé Williams. 2011. "Postscript." In *Framing Intersectionality: Debates on a Multi-Faceted Concept*, edited by Helma Lutz, M. T. Herrera Vivar, and Linda Supik, 221–233. Farnham, UK: Ashgate.

Davis, Angela Y. 1983. *Women, Race, & Class*. New York, NY: Vintage.

Davis, Kathy. 2008. "Intersectionality as Buzzword: A Sociology of Science Perspective on What Makes a Feminist Theory Successful." *Feminist Theory* 9 (1): 67–85.

Doerr, Nicole. 2018. *Political Translation: How Social Movement Democracies Survive*. Cambridge, UK: Cambridge University Press.

Erevelles, Nirmala. 2011. *Disability and Difference in Global Contexts*. New York: Palgrave.

Evans, Elizabeth. 2015. *The Politics of Third Wave Feminisms: Neoliberalism, Intersectionality, and the State in Britain and the US*. New York, NY: Palgrave Macmillan.

Evans, Elizabeth. 2016. "Intersectionality as Feminist Praxis in the UK." *Women's Studies International Forum* 59: 67–75.

Farris, Sara R. 2017. *In the Name of Women's Rights: The Rise of Femonationalism*. Durham, NC: Duke University Press.

Ferguson, Ann. 1998. "Resisting the Veil of Privilege: Building Bridge Identities as an Ethico-Politics of Global Feminisms." *Hypatia* 13(3): 95–113.

Ferree, Myra Marx, and Silke Roth. 1998. "Gender, Class, and the Interaction Between Social Movements: A Strike of West Berlin Day Care Workers." *Gender & Society* 12 (6): 626–648.

Giraud, Isabelle. 2015. "Intégrer La Diversité Des Oppressions Dans La Marche Mondiale Des Femmes." *L'Homme et La Société* 4: 95–112.

Giraud, Isabelle, and Pascale Dufour. 2010. *Dix Ans de Solidarité Planétaire: Perspectives Sociologiques Sur La Marche Mondiale Des Femmes*. Montréal: Éditions du Remue-ménage.

Hancock, Ange-Marie. 2007. "When Multiplication Doesn't Equal Quick Addition: Examining Intersectionality as a Research Paradigm." *Perspectives on Politics* 5(1): 63–79.

Hancock, Ange-Marie. 2016. *Intersectionality: An Intellectual History*. Oxford: Oxford University Press.

Harris, Treviene A. 2016. "Privilege." *Critical Quarterly* 58(3): 100–102.

hooks, bell. 2000. *Feminist Theory: From Margin to Center*. New York: Pluto Press.

Hurtado, Aida. 1996. *The Color of Privilege: Three Blasphemies on Race and Feminism.* Ann Arbor, MI: University of Michigan Press.

Inckle, Kay. 2015. "Debilitating Times: Compulsory Ablebodiedness and White Privilege in Theory and Practice." *Feminist Review* 111 (1): 42–58.

Irvine, Jill, Sabine Lang, and Celeste Montoya. 2019. "Introduction: Gendered Mobilization and Intersectional Challenges." In *Gendered Mobilizations and Intersectional Challenges: Contemporary Social Movements in Europe and North America*, edited by Jill Irvine, Sabine Lang, and Celeste Montoya. London; New York, NY: Rowman & Littlefield.

Johnston, Lynda. 2007. *Queering Tourism: Paradoxical Performances of Gay Pride Parades.* New York: Routledge.

Joly, Danièle, and Khursheed Wadia. 2017. *Muslim Women and Power.* Basingstoke: Palgrave.

Jordan-Zachery, Julia. 2013. "Now You See Me, Now You Don't: My Political Fight Against the Invisibility/Erasure of Black Women in Intersectionality Research." *Politics, Groups, and Identities* 1 (1): 101–109.

Kruks, Sonia. 2005. "Simone de Beauvoir and the Politics of Privilege." *Hypatia* 20 (1): 178–205.

Laperrière, Marie, and Éléonore Lépinard. 2016. "Intersectionality as a Tool for Social Movements: Strategies of Inclusion and Representation in the Québécois Women's Movement." *Politics* 36 (4): 374–382.

Larcher, Silyane. 2017. " 'Nos vies sont politiques ! ' L'afroféminisme en France ou la riposte des petites-filles de l'Empire." *Participations* 19 (3): 97–127.

Leonardo, Zeus. 2004. "The Color of Supremacy: Beyond the Discourse of White Privilege." *Educational Philosophy and Theory* 36 (2): 137–152.

Lépinard, Éléonore. 2014. "Doing Intersectionality: Repertoires of Feminist Practices in France and Canada." *Gender & Society* 28 (6): 877–903.

Lépinard Éléonore. 2020. *Feminist Trouble. Intersectional Politics in PostSecular Times.* New York, London: Oxford University Press.

Lorde, Audre. 1984. *Sister Outsider: Essays and Speeches.* New York, NY: Crossing Press.

Lugones, María. 1994. "Purity, Impurity, and Separation." *Signs: Journal of Women in Culture and Society* 19 (2): 458–479.

Luna, Zakiya. 2016. "'Truly a Women of Color Organization': Negotiating Sameness and Difference in Pursuit of Intersectionality." *Gender & Society* 30 (5): 769–790.

Luna, Zakiya. 2017. "Who Speaks for Whom? (Mis)Representation and Authenticity in Social Movements." *Mobilization: An International Journal* 22 (4): 435–450.

Lutz, Helma, M. T. Herrera Vivar, and Linda Supik, eds. 2011. *Framing Intersectionality: Debates on a Multi-Faceted Concept.* Farnham, UK: Ashgate.

McClintock, Anne. 2013. *Imperial Leather: Race, Gender, and Sexuality in the Colonial Contest.* New York, NY: Routledge.

McIntosh. Peggy. 1992. "White Privilege Unpacking the Invisible Knapsack." In *Multiculturalism*, edited by Anna May Filor, 30–36. New York, NY: NYSCEA.

McIntosh, Peggy. 2012. "Reflections and Future Directions for Privilege Studies." *Journal of Social Issues*, 68(1): 194–206.

Mepschen, Paul, Jan Willem Duyvendak, and Evelien H. Tonkens. 2010. "Sexual Politics, Orientalism and Multicultural Citizenship in the Netherlands." *Sociology* 44 (5): 962–979.

Mercier, Élisabeth. 2016. "Sexualité et Respectabilité Des Femmes: La SlutWalk et Autres (Re) Configurations Morales, Éthiques et Politiques." *Nouvelles Questions Féministes* 35 (1): 16–31.

Mohanty, Chandra Talpade. 2003. *Feminism Without Borders: Decolonizing Theory, Practicing Solidarity.* Durham, NC: Duke University Press.

Mohanty, Chandra Talpade, Ann Russo, and Lourdes Torres, eds. 1991. *Third World Women and the Politics of Feminism.* Bloomington, IN: Indiana University Press.

Montoya, Celeste. 2019. "From Identity Politics to Intersectionality? Identity-Based Organizing in the Occupy Movement." In *Gendered Mobilizations and Intersectional Challenges: Contemporary Social Movements in Europe and North America,* edited by Jill Irvine, Sabine Lang, and Celeste Montoya. London ; New York, NY: Rowman & Littlefield.

Mügge, Liza, Celeste Montoya, Akwugo Emejulu, and S. Laurel Weldon. 2018. "Intersectionality and the Politics of Knowledge Production." *European Journal of Politics and Gender* 1 (1): 17–36. https://doi.org/info:doi/10.1332/251510818X15272520831166

Mwasi Collectif Afroféministe. 2018. *Afrofem.* Paris: Syllepse.

Mwasi Collectif Afroféministe. 2019. "Those Who Fight for Us Without Us Are Against Us: Afrofeminist Activism in France." In *To Exist Is to Resist,* edited by Akwugo Emejulu and Francesca Sobande, 46–62. London: Pluto Press.

Nelson, Jennifer. 2003. *Women of Color and the Reproductive Rights Movement.* New York, NY: New York University Press.

Ohene-Nyako, Pamela. 2018. "Black Women's Transnational Activism and the World Council of Churches." *Open Cultural Studies,* 3: 219–231.

Pease, Bob. 2010. *Undoing Privilege.* London: Zed Books.

Predelli, Line Nyhagen, and Beatrice Halsaa. 2012. *Majority-Minority Relations in Contemporary Women's Movements: Strategic Sisterhood.* Houndmills, Basingstoke: Palgrave Macmillan.

Puar, Jasbir K. 2007. *Terrorist Assemblages: Homonationalism in Queer Times.* Durham, NC: Duke University Press.

Reger, Jo. 2012. *Everywhere and Nowhere: Contemporary Feminism in the United States.* New York, NY: Oxford University Press.

Reger, Jo. 2015. "The Story of a Slut Walk: Sexuality, Race, and Generational Divisions in Contemporary Feminist Activism." *Journal of Contemporary Ethnography* 44 (1): 84–112.

Romero, Mary. 2018. *Introducing Intersectionality.* Cambridge: Polity Press.

Roth, Benita. 2004. *Separate Roads to Feminism: Black, Chicana, and White Feminist Movements in America's Second Wave.* Cambridge, UK: Cambridge University Press.

Schuster, Julia. 2016. "Intersectional Expectations: Young Feminists' Perceived Failure at Dealing With Differences and Their Retreat to Individualism." *Women's Studies International Forum* 58 (September): 1–8. https://doi.org/10.1016/j.wsif.2016.04.007

Smith, Barbara Ellen. 1995. "Crossing the Great Divides: Race, Class, and Gender in Southern Women's Organizing, 1979–1991." *Gender & Society* 9 (6): 680–696.

Springer, Kimberly. 2005. *Living for the Revolution: Black Feminist Organizations, 1968–1980.* Durham, NC: Duke University Press.

Srivastava, Sarita. 2006. "Tears, Fears and Careers: Anti-Racism and Emotion in Social Movement Organizations." *The Canadian Journal of Sociology* 31 (1): 55–90.

Staggenborg, Suzanne. 2015. "Event Coalitions in the Pittsburgh G20 Protests." *The Sociological Quarterly* 56 (2): 386–411.

Strolovitch, Dara Z. 2007. *Affirmative Advocacy: Race, Class, and Gender in Interest Group Politics*. Chicago, IL: University of Chicago Press.

Sullivan, Shannon, and Nancy Tuana, eds. 2007. *Race and Epistemologies of Ignorance*. Albany, NY: State University of New York Press.

Terriquez, Veronica. 2015. "Intersectional Mobilization, Social Movement Spillover, and Queer Youth Leadership in the Immigrant Rights Movement." *Social Problems* 62 (3): 343–362.

Tormos, Fernando. 2017. "Intersectional Solidarity." *Politics, Groups, and Identities* 5 (4): 707–720. https://doi.org/10.1080/21565503.2017.1385494

Townsend-Bell, Erica. 2011. "What Is Relevance? Defining Intersectional Praxis in Uruguay." *Political Research Quarterly* 64 (1): 187–199.

Tungohan, Ethel. 2016. "Intersectionality and Social Justice: Assessing Activists' Use of Intersectionality Through Grassroots Migrants' Organizations in Canada." *Politics, Groups, and Identities* 4 (3): 347–362.

Utrata, Jennifer. 2011. "Youth Privilege: Doing Age and Gender in Russia's Single Mother Families." *Gender and Society* 25 (5): 616–641.

Van Amsterdam, Noortje. 2013. "Big Fat Inequalities, Thin Privilege: An Intersectional Perspective on 'Body Size'." *European Journal of Women's Studies* 20 (2): 155–169.

Wallerstein, Immanuel. 2006. *European Universalism: The Rhetoric of Power*. London: New Press.

Ward, Jane. 2008. *Respectably Queer: Diversity Culture in LGBT Activist Organizations*. Nashville: Vanderbilt University Press.

Weldon, S. Laurel. 2006. "Inclusion, Solidarity, and Social Movements: The Global Movement Against Gender Violence." *Perspectives on Politics* 4 (1): 55–74.

Intersectionality and social movement organising

Chapter 1

Borders, boundaries, and brokers

The unintended consequences of strategic essentialism in transnational feminist networks

Maria Martin de Almagro

Introduction

In May 2017, women activists from the eastern part of the Democratic Republic of Congo (DRC) travelled to the capital, Kinshasa, in an effort to join forces with feminist organisations in the city to give a push to their campaign for the implementation of measures to ensure women's participation in politics and the implementation of the newly drafted Parity Law. The initiative, which started as a campaign of 15 women's organisations from North Kivu, South Kivu, and Kinshasa for the modification of the electoral law, became, over a matter of two years, an established feminist 'social movement that is here to stay.'[1] During the months leading up to the elections of 2018, the movement launched its online 'Electoral Clinique' and a WhatsApp group to help women candidates win elections by offering training modules and information; and the campaign received funding and help from the United Nations Organisation Stabilisation Mission in the DRC (MONUSCO) to advocate for gender parity before local chiefs and to publish a report on the participation of women in the elections.[2] Ultimately, slogans such as 'debout Congolaises' (Rise up, Congolese women!) as well as the name of the movement, Rien Sans les Femmes (Nothing Without the Women), have helped rally a diversity of women and international activists around a unitary vision of collective identity, thus sustaining a coalition of diverse groups of women activists that would on their own lack the numbers and support to achieve their goals. Strategic essentialising around the figure of *the* Congolese woman has created a collective of more than 60 different women's organisations coming from opposite corners of a country the size of Western Europe. There now exists an extensive grassroots community, which maintains visibility and close contact with international organisations, donors, and NGOs in the country, as well as successfully advocating for gender parity in all of its forms, from the increase of the number of women as local chiefs to the organisation of workshops on positive masculinities.

Since the Women's Conferences in the 1970s and 1980s, international and local NGOs, human rights activists, and social movements have played a key role in convincing policymakers of the need to put gender mainstreaming and gender equality on the agenda (Brown Thompson 2002; Coomaraswamy 1997; Bunch

1990; Marx-Ferree and Tripp 2006). The activists and strategies put forward by transnational networks of women's organisations are considered by the literature to be successful case studies of the growing influence that non-governmental organisations (NGOs) and civil society organisations (CSOs) have on the emergence, diffusion, and institutionalisation of gender norms (Brown Thompson 2002; Keck and Sikkink 1998; Moghadam 2005). These networks work across countries in order to negotiate with reluctant governments and localise international norms. In order to do so, they collaborate with local and national women's organisations, building coalitions and opening up windows of opportunity for local women (Joachim 2007; Zwingel 2017). One of the success stories of this trend is the creation of the Women, Peace and Security Agenda of the United Nations Security Council, which, since the year 2000, has seen the birth of a battery of eight resolutions, 79 National Action Plans, and 11 Regional Action Plans for the implementation of the agenda.[3] This agenda has had a very positive impact on women's rights in post-conflict countries, and local women's movements have used it as a tool to advocate for better policies at home (McLeod 2015).

Nevertheless, the extraordinary success of global gender norms has not always resulted in implementation at the national level in post-conflict countries. Activists and scholars alike have claimed that the global discourse, and even the creation of National Action Plans, has not resulted in tangible improvements in women's lives (Reeves 2012; Martin de Almagro and Ryan 2019). This gap becomes all the more evident when reading statistics on the implementation of the Women, Peace and Security agenda in the Global Study for the implementation of Resolution 1325 conducted by UNWOMEN in 2015 (Coomaraswamy 2015), which shows that while there have been advancements in civil and political rights, advocacy, and implementation, work on the Women, Peace and Security agenda has not brought results regarding socio-economic emancipation for women. I argue that this failure is partly due to the ways in which transnational campaigns for local implementation have downplayed and disguised intersectionality and internal dissent in order to achieve substantial political gains (Weldon 2006; Townsend-Bell 2011). Despite the origins of the Women, Peace and Security agenda in the transformative work of the transnational network of the Women's International League for Peace and Freedom (WILPF), which advocated for a comprehensive understanding of gender security and gender justice, the transnational feminist advocacy campaigns for its implementation have been based on a strategic essentialising of the woman-in-conflict (Cook 2016). This strategic essentialising fails to bring sustainable results because it does not pay attention to the ways in which women's different embodied experiences of conflict are based not only on gender, but also on broader power relationships and on the sustained post-war intersectional privileges that are (re)produced by the way in which transnational advocacy campaigns work.

The notion of intersectionality was first used in 1989 by Kimberlé Crenshaw when she tried to make visible the legal invisibility of multiple dimensions of oppression experienced by female black workers of General Motors. Since then, intersectionality has become one of the most used terms in academia to address multiple and interdependent identities and inequalities (Brah and Phoenix 2004;

Bilge 2010). Feminist movements also invoke the term to claim that they represent all those who identify as women, in all their diversity (Weldon 2008, p. 217; Evans 2016), and scholars have started to study what intersectionality means for social movements, how it is practiced (Evans and Lépinard, this volume), and with what consequences (see, for example, Bassel and Emejulu 2010, 2014; Chun, Lipsitz, and Shin 2013; Lépinard 2014; Townsend-Bell 2011; Laperrière and Lépinard 2016). This literature has analysed the challenges in forging coalitions between diverse groups of women (Fominaya 2010; Rolandsen Agustín 2013; Townsend-Bell 2011; Weldon 2006) and the contradictory goals that feminist movements pursue when implementing intersectionality (Laperrière and Lépinard 2016).

In this chapter, I contribute to this new field of research by examining how transnational women's movements in post-conflict countries hide intersectionality and privilege amongst its members as a way, first, to produce the figure of the 'real local woman' and build bridges between the international and the native, and second, as a means to gain space in the overcrowded development and peace-building market. However, ignoring differences amongst women and how ethnicity, class, gender, and sexuality are historically constituted might compromise the very same emancipatory potential that transnational networks could offer. This chapter contributes not only to social movement scholarship, but also to feminist peacebuilding literature that challenges the simplistic understandings of the 'woman' in conflict (Cook 2016; Bjarnegård and Melander 2017). Postcolonial feminist writing on peacebuilding is fairly well developed, but the exploration of intersectionality within women's movements in relation to peacebuilding remains under-explored and under-theorised. With this opening in mind, this chapter seeks to challenge the conceptual delinking of intersectionality and feminism in transnational women's networks by unpacking the centrality of strategic essentialising.

Methods

The empirical data is derived of a period of biographical interviews and participant observation of an advocacy campaign conducted by the transnational network Rien Sans les Femmes in May 2017 in Kinshasa, DRC. I also draw on data gathered from several periods of research in the Great Lakes area on gender and peacebuilding. I documented the campaign using a field notebook, my camera, and a series of informal conversations with participants, activists, and policymakers. For this specific research, I interviewed 25 activists who were part of the Rien Sans les Femmes campaign or were working for other activist initiatives developed by UNWOMEN in Kinshasa. Half of these women came from the Kivus, in the eastern part of the country, just for this particular week of advocacy, while the other half were living in Kinshasa. The participants were identified through snowballing technique, but also through direct observation of the advocacy activities that took place during that week, and all were granted anonymity. The semi-structured interviews had a duration of 60 to 90 minutes, were recorded and then transcribed, and then coded using NVivo12. Participants were asked to comment on the reasons why they joined a women's movement, the type of advocacy strategies that they considered useful and the ones which were not, as well as the aims they hoped to attain with the campaign. All of the participants had a university degree and came from families where education of women and girls was considered important. All of them had a full-time position either as activists working for a civil society organisation or as lawyers, teachers, or businesswomen.

The structure of the chapter is as follows. In the next section, I situate my contribution within the debate regarding inclusion and difference in post-conflict social movements. Drawing upon the transnational advocacy campaign Nothing Without the Women in the Democratic Republic of Congo, I propose a conceptual grid around *borders*, *boundaries*, and *brokers* as co-constitutive pillars that define the construction of a social movement, showing how a postcolonial feminist lens can change the way we look at transnational advocacy networks, collective identities, and everyday practices. Using this framework, one can better understand how and when privilege emerges or is (re)produced in transnational organising and the way in which strategic essentialism is used. Firstly, ideological boundaries draw attention to the heteronormative gendered peace constructions that drive the framing of the campaigns. These boundaries determine what it is possible to claim for. Secondly, brokers are those individuals who use strategic essentialism and link international and local activists, providing access to information and resources. With regard to the third pillar on borders, I make a case for considering the political economy of transnational activism in post-conflict spaces where the materiality of scarcity and lack of access to basic goods and services dominates much of the relations between locals and internationals.

Intersectionality, difference, and transnational feminist advocacy in post-conflict contexts

Critical peace and conflict studies scholars have done an important job pushing practitioners to work with local civil society in conflict-affected societies and interrogating the normative universal assumptions of liberal peacebuilding. Wallis and Richmond (2017) illustrate that local knowledge is now taken seriously by policymakers and that international organisations have been transitioning from liberal peace approaches towards hybrid modes of peace. Indeed, major donors and all official Western development assistance now massively fund local civil society support in peacebuilding and state building (OECD 2010), and transnational advocacy networks often coalesce with local social movements in order to put pressure on reluctant national governments or to promote the rights of marginalised populations. Nevertheless, this support can also (re)produce historically constituted local power dynamics and privilege, enabling some local activists who speak English, live in the capital city, and already have a wide transnational professional network to participate in transnational advocacy networks and transnational peacebuilding initiatives, while preventing others from joining.

My argument is that although transnational advocacy networks are supposed to bring inclusiveness in post-conflict contexts, they risk essentialising the intersectional identities of multiply-marginalised groups of activists. This risk is because they understand inclusivity through the binary lens of including the local and the international and disregard the important historical constitution of social and political privileges in the post-conflict societies – of which the international participation has been a key part, as it distributes resources, power, and attention (Iniguez de Heredia 2018).

In other words, this understanding of inclusivity has a particular understanding of what constitutes local civil society and valid knowledge and experience, forgetting other local representations that do not conform to this understanding and further excluding those. This argument resonates with Randazzo's claim regarding post-liberal peacebuilding approaches that risk exercising discrimination and normalisation in their quest to emancipate the local (2016). This situation is rather unfortunate, since empirical studies have found the local to be as diverse as the international and also divided along intersectional lines of gender, ethnicity, social class, and other power structures (Belloni 2012; Orjuela 2003). Understanding this diversity and paying attention to how intersectional social categories determine who is part of an advocacy campaign and who is not can reveal the multidimensional dynamics at work that go beyond the binary understanding of the international as compliance-seeker and the local as producing indigenous alternatives (Heathershaw 2013; Autesserre 2010; Richmond 2010; Boege, Brown, and Clements 2009; Englebert and Tull 2008; Mac Ginty 2008; Mac Ginty and Sanghera 2012; Mac Ginty and Richmond 2016; Suhrke 2007; Pouligny 2005). In this chapter, I propose a three-legged conceptual framework to study transnational advocacy networks through international lenses that promises not only to reveal subjectivities present and absent in the network, but also to shed light on the potential for structural change that these advocacy campaigns can bring about.

In the following section I demonstrate how the attempts of a transnational campaign to represent Congolese women may have reproduced, albeit unintentionally, a sanitised picture of the local women as a singular monolithic abstraction that does not take into account the coloniality of international interventions and the historical and economic dynamics that shape who is and who is not part of transnational advocating. That is, in their efforts to ensure inclusivity and confront inequalities, transnational networks end up reinforcing them through their organisational practices. This evidence, in turn, demonstrates how transnational networks effect and reproduce distribution of privileges in the social and political hierarchies in the society where the campaign is taking place.

Campaigning for women's rights in the Democratic Republic of Congo

Over the past decades, conflict-related sexual and gender-based violence (SGBV) in the Democratic Republic of Congo has received a high degree of media and policy attention (Eriksson Baaz and Stern 2013; Meger 2016). Activists, celebrities, and international politicians such as Margot Wallstrom labelled the DRC 'the rape capital of the world' (Wallstrom 2010). The ensuing declarations by heads of state in the region, such as the Goma declaration on the eradication of sexual violence and the eradication of impunity in the Great Lakes region, as well as the Kampala declaration on sexual and gender-based violence in 2011, have projected a clear story of local black men perpetrating rape against women in a war driven by conflict minerals. Not only has this focus eclipsed other forms of gender-based violence (Mertens and Myrttinen 2019), but it has also encouraged transnational feminist organising around the implementation of the Women, Peace and Security agenda to focus only on actions regarding protection of women and girls from SGBV, leaving aside any campaign for the participation of women in peacebuilding, governance, and the security sector.

Although very successful at increasing legal and judicial attention to sexual violence crimes (including numerous prosecutions in the east), scholars, practitioners, and activists have critiqued these campaigns as they ignore female agency and reproduce the dominant female victim subject (Freedman 2015; Lake 2018; Martin de Almagro 2018b); fail to address the structural, historical, and local context in which sexual violence takes place (Eriksson Baaz and Stern 2013; Mertens and Pardy 2017); and have not succeeded at representing the varied gendered experiences of women and men, as well as other gender identities (Dolan 2010). The feminist campaign of Rien Sans les Femmes (Nothing Without the Women – RSLF) was born out of these critiques, under the hybrid initiative of the international NGOs International Alert and Kvinna till Kvinna as well as several women's organisations in eastern Congo. Acting as brokers, the two international NGOs invited the leaders of 30 Congolese civil society organisations to a workshop in March 2015 in order to study how to promote the Women, Peace and Security agenda's third pillar in the DRC and establish initiatives on political participation and representation (Martin de Almagro 2018b).

The result of this meeting was the launch of the RSLF campaign, that first sought to advocate for the enactment of the Parity Law recognising the importance of women's participation in governmental structures and more broadly in all aspects of public life, and second, requested a revision of the electoral law so that all electoral lists would be required to respect parity. Marches were organised in the east of the country in Bukavu, Uvira, and Goma, gaining popular support. The marches served not only as an advocacy and visibility tool, but also as a way to set up a counter-narrative to that of women as victims, reclaim agency, and mark distance from the transnational feminist campaign on countering sexual violence (Martin de Almagro 2018b, p. 325). Furthermore, during the last week of May 2017, representatives of the movement from Goma and Bukavu joined forces in Kinshasa with the capital's representatives in order to organise a series of advocacy activities at the national level. In all of these events, the transnational network used a master frame in opposition to the dominant narrative of women as victims of SGBV, and rather highlighted the idea that having women in political office was a condition *sine qua non* for a successful bottom-up approach to peace.

The international outcry on the emergency of the SGBV situation in the DRC aided the mobilisation of women and of international women's organisations and

NGOs who served as brokers of connections between previously unconnected actors; for example, a grassroots women's group and an international funding institution such as UNWOMEN. However, the shortcomings of a campaign focused on women as victims of SGBV also led to the fracture of the advocacy work on the Women, Peace and Security agenda and bolstered emerging local voices calling for women's increased presence in public spaces and in leadership roles. In other words, two clusters of local and international women's rights activists had now formed and were competing for funds, media attention, and issue coverage on implementation of the Women, Peace and Security agenda in Kinshasa: those who focused on prevention of SGBV and protection of women and girls from SGVB and those who, in de facto opposition, focused on participation of women in peacebuilding and post-conflict governance. As I argue elsewhere (Martin de Almagro 2018b), these clusters of local and international actors joined forces to develop a series of advocacy initiatives in what I label a 'hybrid club.' These clubs are characterised as spaces where differences amongst actors are minimised through strategic essentialism (Spivak 1996). That is, although there is consciousness that the activists conforming the transnational network are highly different in terms of origin, race, class, sexuality, and gender, they engage in a process of homogenising their public image and discourse[4] with the intention of projecting a common homogeneous identity to help make their cause visible and universal. This strategy works to do two things: first, to create the subject position of 'the local Congolese woman' with her needs and thoughts, as well as to determine what gender security is, how to achieve it, and who should be in charge of achieving it; and second, to convince donors and policymakers that their claims and topic of mobilisation – and not the claims of the competitor – are those of the majority of the population.

Apart from a discourse constructed upon the figure of the local woman, as a victim or as the agent able to bring sustainable peace, there are material and embodied elements that work to reinforce group identification and to undermine differences, such as, for example, dress. When in May 2017 the RSLF movement introduced a report on the challenges of the Parity Law to the international donors at the Swedish Embassy, all the women participating in the campaign wore dresses made of cloth that read 'RSLF.' If the dresses served to constitute a visual trait of collective identity, the introductory speech of one of the international NGO representatives on the need for equal representation of women in politics as key for peace worked to differentiate this transnational feminist network from the rest. In their strategic approach vis-à-vis international donors, the crucial point is not to highlight and celebrate the diversity of members of RSLF, but rather its collective and transnational character. What is more, this differentiation is hidden or portrayed as needed. Conversely, at another advocacy meeting with the members of the Congolese parliament, it was only the Congolese women who wore the RSLF clothes and who spoke about women as agents of sustainable peace. The aim was to show not only unity amongst Congolese women, but also that this advocacy campaign was rather not transnational, but truly Congolese.

In sum, it is precisely their need to differentiate from other transnational networks, which also claim universality by the very nature of their content,[5] and to demonstrate the unity of Congolese women – in order to attract attention from international donors and national authorities alike – that works to hide privilege and inequalities within the network and disguises the many differences among the locals, sometimes even more than between local and international actors. In the next section, I use a tripartite conceptual grid to show, first, that there are still a lot of similarities between the two main transnational feminist networks in the DRC, and second, that privilege and inequalities inside advocacy networks can be revealed if we look at their brokers, the discursive boundaries about what is possible to advocate for, and the borders or the limitations of who is allowed in.

Revealing privilege through brokers, boundaries, and borders

In this section, I unpack the social, material, and epistemological mechanisms of mobilisation through which collective identity and strategic essentialising are possible in the two main transnational feminist campaigns in DRC: the brokers with authority and legitimacy to create alliances, the discursive or symbolic boundaries produced by these brokers, and the borders constituted by the material hierarchies that prevent certain activists from participating in transnational advocacy. I argue that this three-legged conceptual framework reveals how privilege operates to organise transnational networks. As does Rottenberg, I understand privilege as a relation vis-à-vis dominant norms (2018, p. 125). It is therefore not an individual, fixed characteristic that one activist within the network possesses. In particular, privilege is precisely constituted through a coalescing of various *intersecting* and hierarchical categories of identity (race, class, gender, ethnicity, religion, etc.). It is not that privilege results from the alignment of different categories of identity, such as race and gender; rather, this alignment has to enable the subject to accumulate the most social and cultural capital (Rottenberg 2018, p. 126). As exemplified with the case of RSLF and the campaign for ending SGBV, when one specific category such as class is considered as a site of privilege, the individuals and groups who are privileged in that sense tend to render it invisible. Second, when an activist is positioned as being privileged with respect to one category, such as class, s/he will try to bring to the fore other categories in relation to which s/he is not privileged. In sum, privilege operates through a system of hiding – in our case class and sometimes race – and showing of categories – gender in our case study – which ends up strengthening existing social hierarchies.

Brokers

As highlighted in the previous section, international actors and NGOs rapidly arrived in the DRC after the end of the Second Congo War in 2003 and served as brokers of connections between what were small women's associations and international organisations and funds. For example, Solange, the leader of the small association in South Kivu, Causes des Femmes Congolaise du Sud-Kivu pour la Paix, recalls having been approached by international NGOs and offered a platform – the opportunity to participate in international training sessions that facilitate the exchange of information and ideas and are funded by the international members of their network.[6] Soon a group of local brokers or 'interstitial elites' emerged (Swidler and Watkins 2009). The local broker speaks several languages, including English and French, and she has studied at university and has international friends. While no comprehensive data exists that can shed light on the type of women who founded and led these brokering associations, my data suggests that most come from a particular background and socio-economic status, while they represent wider local experiences of conflict and peace of their broader membership in the international arena. In other words, while ordinary women form grassroots organisations and carry out informal advocacy activities at a local, village level, larger and better-connected domestic associations or NGOs start to connect these ordinary women with international organisations and NGOs. Nevertheless, the fact that only a certain type of woman is able to participate in the campaign while representing 'the Congolese woman' – and the almost wholesale invisibility of other gender identities, non-heteronormative ways of being, ethnicities, and socio-economic privileges – hides the constraints this process puts on what constitutes agency and victimhood.

Ultimately, there is a clear division between those brokers who receive training, professionalise, and give speeches to the international community or the Congolese Parliament and those grassroots activists about whom these brokers speak. This division also points again to a fundamental issue: class. While the subject position of the woman victim of SGBV – the one the activists campaign for, as 'she is the one that suffers the most from war'[7] – is that of the lower classes, the subject position of the woman politician is linked to the elites taking part in the campaign: 'we would like to be as numerous on the political parties' lists as the men are.'[8]

In particular, many of these organisations formed to access socio-economic rights for women, such as access to land and resources that would enable women to secure a livelihood for themselves and their families after war (multiple interviews), but these claims were transformed into a broader framework of either political and economic empowerment or a framework on individualised attention to women victims of SGBV. In other words, the distinctive social locations of individuals within the network – as brokers or at the margins – also have important epistemological implications. As Stoetzel and Yuval-Davis point out, imagination and knowledge are situated and social positioning as brokers shapes knowledge, imagination, and the material realities that accompany knowledge-production processes (2002, p. 316). It is therefore essential to pay attention to how epistemological boundaries are drawn in the design of a transnational advocacy master frame and how urban, middle-, and upper-class concerns determine what gender security is and what will be advocated for.

Epistemological boundaries

If transnational activism seems to have overcome borders through a sense of universal sisterhood, in both cases – RSLF and the transnational network on ending SGBV – still, epistemological boundaries remain when advocating for the implementation of the Women, Peace and Security agenda. Strongly Western-inspired norms of individual victimhood and individual agency have been introduced, calling for men and women to become leaders or agents of change, at times with little regard for the material and structural constraints of people's lives. For example, the campaigns for the implementation of the first two Ps of the agenda – prevention of violence and protection of women and girls from violence – have become specifically prevention of SGBV by local black men towards women. There is not much on the master frame about conflict prevention more broadly (Kirby 2015). The subject position of women here is that of victims of this particular kind of violence, but for those doing the advocating, it is also that of agents of change in efforts to combat sexual violence against women and girls.

The discursive boundaries erase any challenge to the dynamics of war or to the political economy of post-war reconstruction, which render so many of these women, including those doing the advocating, insecure. In particular, SGBV projects in which local NGOs and civil society work together with international organisations reinforce perspectives of female victimhood and individual agency, once they recover and start participating in women's economic empowerment and female entrepreneurship programmes.[9] As the sub-section on borders demonstrates below, the risk here is double. First, the advocacy discourses on women's economic empowerment resonate with colonial practices in their reproduction of existing states of vulnerability and inequality (Mertens and Myrttinen 2019). Second, these discourses forget how 'violent masculinities may be emerging in response to deep structural issues such as histories of colonialism or centre/periphery tensions which can privilege older city elites over younger men at the margins' (Duriesmith 2017).

The case of RSLF is similar in that a liberal normative project based on individual women's agency as political leaders is constructed as legitimate, while at the same time being detached from the broader structure of national and global politics that determine which women will be able to exercise that agency. The network takes into account class and socio-economic differences as it advocates for the end of the provision in the Electoral Code that requires electoral candidates to have a secondary school diploma or a university degree, depending on the election, as well as the end of the provision regarding payment for the filing of a candidature.[10] However, these petitions do not give any indication that more substantial reforms will be sought, thus settling for the mere inclusion of women through quotas rather than guaranteeing the transformation of political institutions or their mode of governing in order to ensure meaningful participation of a diversity of women.

This scene is reminiscent of Nancy Fraser's two contrasting approaches to remedying injustice: the first one is an affirmative approach, by which unjust situations are corrected 'without disturbing the underlying framework that generates them.' The second is a transformative approach, in which remedies are set up in order to correct unjust situations 'precisely by restructuring the underlying generative framework' (1997, p. 23). According to Fraser, only an approach that addresses three types of injustices – socio-cultural, political, and economic – can be transformative. Recognition of difference through 'revaluing disrespected identities' can remedy socio-cultural injustice, while better representation of women and their interests in terms of decision-making rules and procedures designed to claim justice can address political injustice. Finally, 'redistributing income, re-organising the division of labour' can help achieve economic justice. Re-evaluating disrespected and marginalised identities and recognising that women experience war in a different way is at the core of transnational initiatives on prevention of SGBV and protection of women and girls from SGBV. The RSLF network focuses on representation of women in decision-making rules and procedures. Nevertheless, none of them advocate for economic redistribution in a way that prevents structural violence and privilege from perpetuating gender inequalities. The fact that redistribution is silenced only makes sense if viewed from a historicist perspective, one that takes into account patterns of privilege, accumulation, and dispossession underpinning power relations within the DRC but also within transnational feminist networks.

Borders (material hierarchies and limits)

The idea of universal sisterhood serves to divert attention from the realities of massive inequality and poverty that fuel violent conflict and gender-based violence. Indeed, none of the campaigns are able to fundamentally shift the masculinist and militarist attitudes that are at the core of women's lack of access to resources and economic independence, and rather serve as testing grounds for internationally led norms to address gender inequality and insecurity, such as the Women, Peace and Security agenda. For example, 60 percent of women in the DRC live below the poverty line, and although they are the ones doing the majority of the agricultural work, they are forced to rely on men to access land. To the contrary, as argued by Mertens and Myrttinen (2019), the sexual politics and dynamics that underpin imperial power continue as undercurrents in contemporary interventions aimed at addressing sexual violence in conflict settings. Although the campaign for political participation overcomes the limits of the frame on victimhood and sexual violence, the RSLF network also disregards the important historical constitution of social and political hierarchies in Congolese society, which the transnational feminist activities are also a part of (see also Iniguez de Heredia 2018).

Ultimately, this situation also leaves the direction of knowledge production within transnational feminist networks unchanged: while grassroots activists bring empirical knowledge and practical knowledge only, the theorisation and proposal of a master frame comes from the international members of the campaign and local brokers. Neoliberal understandings of what constitutes a 'proper' way of working towards ending violence echo colonial-era interventions. As McLeod rightfully puts it, 'realizing the diversity of local and international allows a deeper consideration of what knowledge counts and why it matters, and the ways in which certain knowledge is privileged' (McLeod 2015, pp. 14–15). Furthermore, paying attention to the ways in which the type of knowledge that comes from experiencing the world from a marginalised position is masked is important (Haraway 1988; Harding 1991), because it can give us hints as to why implementation of the Women, Peace and Security agenda has been advocated in certain ways – implementation of gender quotas or protection and prevention of sexual and gender-based violence – and not in others. The issue here is not about acknowledging that women, and rural women in particular, do not have the material possibilities to participate in electoral processes, but rather to provide spaces that take into account the way these intersectional inequalities have prevented those women from critically engaging and that offer opportunities to those marginalised to now lead the way forward in the implementation of the agenda.

Concluding remarks: revealing the silences

In this chapter, I offered a three-legged conceptual framework for studying transnational feminist networks that goes beyond a fixed approach to intersectionality and understands privilege in a historical, evolving, and relational way. The framework enables the researcher to uncover the mechanisms by which strategic essentialism is enacted and intersectionality is hidden. The consequences of these mechanisms are twofold: first, there are limits as to who can be part of the transnational feminist network; second, the structures underpinning the socio-economic status quo remain untouched. Making privilege visible enables us to understand why strategic essentialising can be beneficial to reach international ears but tends to exclude those whose experiences do not fit and those who do not have the material capacity to access transnational networks.

Although I consider that the work these transnational advocacy networks are doing critical and extremely important, and I am not equating their campaigns with efforts to maintain colonialism or neoliberal peace agendas, I argue that their strategic essentialism prevents activists from taking into account the gendered complexities of lived realities in DRC (Hollander 2014; Lake 2018). Moreover, it prevents them from taking seriously international or external resistances to their gender equality work, coming from a variety of sites (Martin de Almagro 2018a), and working through them rather than ignoring and/or tacitly accommodating them (Ratele 2015; Mertens and Myrttinen 2019). A postcolonial feminist framework that focuses on revealing privilege can highlight the processes of material distribution and authority, where the transnational element may prioritise new claims of authority and willingness to redistribute but without destabilising the internal power dynamics of the network. The interwoven brokers, borders, and boundaries result in advocacy work related to the politics of representation – bringing more female bodies to the negotiation table and to politics and government – as well as the politics of recognition – how war and violence is gendered. The boundaries around what is possible to advocate for encompass a privatised politics of representation and recognition of individual harms, but it is all disconnected from systematic critique and materialist histories of colonialism, capitalism, and heteropatriarchy (Mohanty 2013, p. 972).

The representation and recognition discourse that is easily disconnected from its material causes and consequences does enable the appropriation of feminism by the neoliberal peacebuilding project and the depoliticisation of the notion of difference. This disjuncture, in turn, obscures how privilege is (re)produced in transnational movements, from efforts to implement the Women, Peace and Security agenda in post-war countries, to the #MeToo movement of those who can afford to reveal past abuses, and the white, middle-class dominated Women's March in the US. This trend follows with Donna Murdock's (2003) analysis of how neoliberal institutions and states rely on NGOs to provide work on an uncritical notion of gender that does not problematise power relations and cannot advocate for social transformation. It follows, then, that materialities of feminist transnationalism come in a diversity of shapes and have ambivalent implications for thinking about meaningful ways to engage with activists from the Global South and broaden agency. In sum, the strategic essentialising in transnational feminist networks cannot challenge or redistribute power internally or externally, and it certainly does not destabilise the status quo. Until redistribution of wealth and resources becomes key in transnational feminist networks, there will be no bonding among women that transcends class (hooks 2000, p. 61).

Notes

1 Speech delivered by one member of the movement during a presentation at the Swedish embassy in the DRC in May 2017.
2 "Rapport finale de l' Observatoire de la parité sur l'implication de la femme dans les elections." *Debout Congolaises!* https://deboutcongolaises.org/rapport-final-de-lobservatoire-de-la-parite-sur-limplication-de-la-femme-dans-les-elections/ [accessed 18 July 2019].
3 As of December 2018.
4 I use discourse here interchangeably with mobilisation master frame.
5 I thank Eléonore Lépinard for pointing out the fact that the very nature of the claims of a campaign can also produce an idea of homogeneity and universality.
6 Fieldwork notes, 17 May 2017.
7 Interview 4, member of RSLF, 17 May 2017, Kinshasa.
8 Interview 6, 19 May 2017.
9 Interview 8, UNWOMEN staff member, 18 May 2017, Kinshasa.
10 See the Electoral Code. "Loi Electorale No. 17/013 du 24 décembre 2017 modifiant et complétant la loi No. 06/006 du 09 mars 2006 portant organisation des élections présidentielle, legislatives, provincials, urbaines, municipals et locales telle que modifiée à ce jour." www.ceni.cd/assets/bundles/documents/La%20loi%20%c3%a9lectorale%20du%2024%20d%c3%a9cembre%2020170002.pdf [accessed 24 June 2019].

References

Autesserre, Severine. 2010. *The Trouble With the Congo: Local Violence and the Failure of International Peacebuilding*. Cambridge, UK: Cambridge University Press.

Bassel, Leah, and Akwugo Emejulu. 2010. "Struggles for Institutional Space in France and the United Kingdom: Intersectionality and the Politics of Policy." *Politics & Gender* 6 (4): 517–544.

Bassel, Leah, and Akwugo Emejulu. 2014. "Solidarity Under Austerity: Intersectionality in France and the United Kingdom." *Politics & Gender* 10 (1): 130–136.

Belloni, Roberto. 2012. "Hybrid Peace Governance: Its Emergence and Significance." *Global Governance* 18 (1): 21–38.

Bilge, Sirma. 2010. "Beyond Subordination vs. Resistance: An Intersectional Approach to the Agency of Veiled Muslim Women." *Journal of Intercultural Studies* 31 (1): 9–28.

Bjarnegård, Elin, and Erik Melander. 2017. "Pacific Men: How Attitudes to Gender Equality Explain Hostility." *The Pacific Review* 30 (4): 478–493.

Boege, Volker, M. Anne Brown, and Kevin P. Clements. 2009. "Hybrid Political Orders, Not Fragile States." *Peace Review* 21 (1): 13–21.

Brah, Avtar, and Ann Phoenix. 2004. "Ain't I a Woman? Revisiting Intersectionality." *Journal of International Women's Studies* 5 (3): 75–86.

Brown Thompson, Karen. 2002. "Women's Rights Are Human Rights." In *Restructuring World Politics: Transnational Social Movements, Networks and Norms*, edited by Sanjeev Khagram, et al. Minneapolis, MN: University of Minnesota Press.

Bunch, Charlotte. 1990. "Women's Rights as Human Rights: Towards a Re-Vision of Human Rights." *Human Rights Quarterly* 12: 486–498.

Chun, Jennifer Jihye, George Lipsitz, and Young Shin. 2013. "Intersectionality as a Social Movement Strategy: Asian Immigrant Women Advocates." *Signs: Journal of Women in Culture and Society* 38 (4): 917–940.

Cook, Sam. 2016. "The 'Woman-in-Conflict' at the UN Security Council: A Subject of Practice." *International Affairs* 92 (2): 353–372.

Coomaraswamy, Radhika. 1997. "Reinventing International Law: Women's Rights as Human Rights in the International Community." *Commonwealth Law Bulletin* 23 (3–4): 1249–1262.

Coomaraswamy, Radhika. 2015. "Preventing Conflict, Transforming Justice, Securing the Peace: A Global Study on the Implementation of United Nations Security Council Resolution 1325." Report from UN Women.

Dolan, Chris. 2010. *"War Is Not Yet Over": Community Perceptions of Sexual Violence and Its Underpinnings in Eastern DRC*. London: International Alert.

Duriesmith, David. 2017. "Engaging Men and Boys in the Women, Peace and Security Agenda: Beyond the 'Good Men' Industry." LSE Women, Peace and Security Working Paper Series.

Englebert, Pierre, and Denis M. Tull. 2008. "Post-Conflict Reconstruction in Africa: Flawed Ideas About Failed States." *International Security* 32 (4): 106–139.

Eriksson Baaz, Maria, and Maria Stern. 2013. *Sexual Violence as a Weapon of War? Perceptions, Prescriptions, Problems in the Congo and Beyond*. London: Zed Books.

Evans, Elizabeth. 2016. "Intersectionality as Feminist Praxis in the UK." *Women's Studies International Forum* 59: 67–75.

Fominaya, Christina Flecher. 2010. "Creating Cohesion from Diversity: The Challenge of Collective Identity Formation in the Global Justice Movement." *Sociological Inquiry* 80 (3): 377–404.

Fraser, Nancy. 1997. *Justice Interruptus: Critical Reflections on the "Post-socialist" Condition*. New York, NY: Routledge.

Freedman, Jane. 2015. *Gender, Violence and Politics in the Democratic Republic of Congo*. London: Routledge.

Haraway, Donna. 1988. "Situated Knowledges: The Science Question in Feminism and the Privilege of Partial Perspective." *Feminist Studies* 14 (3): 575–599.

Harding, Sandra. 1991. *Whose Knowledge? Whose Science? Thinking from Women's Lives*. Ithaca, NY: Cornell University Press.

Heathershaw, John. 2013. "Towards Better Theories of Peacebuilding: Beyond the Liberal Peace Debate." *Peacebuilding* 1 (2): 275–282.

Hollander, Theo. 2014. "Men, Masculinities, and the Demise of a State: Examining Masculinities in the Context of Economic, Political, and Social Crisis in a Small Town in the Democratic Republic of the Congo." *Men and Masculinities* 17 (4): 417–439.

hooks, bell. 2000. *Feminist Theory: From Margin to Center*. New York, NY: Pluto Press.

Iniguez de Heredia, M. 2018. "The Conspicuous Absence of Class and Privilege in the Study of Resistance in Peacebuilding Contexts." *International Peacekeeping* 25 (3): 325–348.

Joachim, Jutta. 2007. *Agenda Setting, the UN, and NGOs: Gender Violence and Reproductive Rights*. Washington, DC: Georgetown University Press.

Keck, Margaret, and Katharine Sikkink. 1998. *Activists Beyond Borders: Advocacy Networks in International Politics*. Ithaca, NY: Cornell University Press.

Kirby, Paul. 2015. "Ending Sexual Violence in Conflict: The Preventing Sexual Violence Initiative and Its Critics." *International Affairs* 91 (3): 457–472.

Lake, Milli. 2018. *Strong NGOs and Weak States: Pursuing Gender Justice in the Democratic Republic of Congo and South Africa*. Cambridge, UK: Cambridge University Press.

Laperrière, Marie, and Eléonore Lépinard. 2016. "Intersectionality as a Tool for Social Movements: Strategies of Inclusion and Representation in the Québécois Women's Movement." *Politics* 36 (4): 374–382.

Lépinard, Eléonore. 2014. "Doing Intersectionality: Repertoires of Feminist Practices in France and Canada." *Gender & Society* 28 (6): 877–903.

Mac Ginty, Roger. 2008. "Indigenous Peace-making Versus the Liberal Peace." *Cooperation and Conflict* 43 (2): 139–163.

Mac Ginty, Roger, and Gurchathen Sanghera. 2012. "Hybridity in Peacebuilding and Development: An Introduction." *Journal of Peacebuilding & Development* 7 (2): 3–8.

Mac Ginty, Roger, and Oliver Richmond. 2016. "The Fallacy of Constructing Hybrid Political Orders: A Reappraisal of the Hybrid Turn in Peacebuilding." *International Peacekeeping* 23 (2): 219–239.

Martin de Almagro, Maria. 2018a. "Lost Boomerangs, the Rebound Effect and Transnational Advocacy Networks: A Discursive Approach to Norm Diffusion." *Review of International Studies* 44 (4): 672–693.

Martin de Almagro, Maria. 2018b. "Hybrid Clubs: A Feminist Approach to Peacebuilding in the Democratic Republic of Congo." *Journal of Intervention and Statebuilding* 12 (3): 319–334.

Martin de Almagro, Maria, and Caitlin Ryan. 2019. "Subverting Economic Empowerment: Towards a Postcolonial-Feminist Framework on Gender (in) Securities in Post-war Settings." *European Journal of International Relations* 25 (4): 1059–1079.

Marx-Ferree, Myra, and Aili Mari Tripp, eds. 2006. *Global Feminism: Transnational Women's Activism, Organizing, and Human Rights*. New York, NY: New York University Press.

McLeod, Laura. 2015. "A Feminist Approach to Hybridity: Understanding Local and International Interactions in Producing Post-Conflict Gender Security." *Journal of Intervention and Statebuilding* 9 (1): 48–69.

Meger, Sara. 2016. "The Fetishization of Sexual Violence in International Security." *International Studies Quarterly* 60 (1): 149–159.

Mertens, Charlotte, and Henri Myrttinen. 2019. "'A Real Woman Waits' – Heteronormative Respectability, Neo-Liberal Betterment and Echoes of Coloniality in SGBV Programming in Eastern DR Congo." *Journal of Intervention and Statebuilding* 1–22.

Mertens, Charlotte, and Maree Pardy. 2017. "'Sexurity' and Its Effects in Eastern Democratic Republic of Congo." *Third World Quarterly* 38 (4): 956–979.

Moghadam, Valentine M. 2005. *Globalizing Women: Transnational Feminist Networks*. Baltimore, MD: Johns Hopkins University Press.

Mohanty, Chandra Talpade. 2013. "Transnational Feminist Crossings: On Neoliberalism and Radical Critique." *Signs* 38 (4): 967–991.

Murdock, Donna F. 2003. "Neoliberalism, Gender, and Development: Institutionalizing 'Post-Feminism' in Medellín, Colombia." *Women's Studies Quarterly* 31 (3-4): 129–153.

OECD. 2010. *Aid Predictability: Survey on Donors' Forward Spending Plans 2010–2012*. www.oecd.org/dac/financing-sustainable-development/development-finance-topics/2010-Report-on-Aid-Predictability.pdf [accessed 19 June 2019].

Orjuela, Camilla. 2003. "Building Peace in Sri Lanka: A Role for Civil Society?" *Journal of Peace Research* 40 (2): 195–212.

Pouligny, Béatrice. 2005. "Civil Society and Post-Conflict Peacebuilding: Ambiguities of International Programmes Aimed at Building 'New' Societies." *Security Dialogue* 36 (4): 495–510.

Randazzo, Elisa. 2016. "The Paradoxes of the 'Everyday': Scrutinising the Local Turn in Peace Building." *Third World Quarterly* 37 (8): 1351–1370.

Ratele, Kopano. 2015. "Working Through Resistance in Engaging Boys and Men Towards Gender Equality and Progressive Masculinities." *Culture, Health & Sexuality* 17 (2): 144–158.

Reeves, Audrey. 2012. "Feminist Knowledge and Emerging Governmentality in UN Peacekeeping." *International Feminist Journal of Politics* 14 (3): 348–369.

Richmond, Oliver P. 2010. "Resistance and the Post-Liberal Peace." *Millennium: Journal of International Studies* 38 (3): 665–692.

Rolandsen Agustín, L. 2013. *Gender, Equality, Intersectionality, and Diversity in Europe*. New York, NY: Palgrave Macmillan.

Rottenberg, Catherine. 2018. *The Rise of Neoliberal Feminism*. New York, NY: Oxford University Press.

Spivak, Gayatri Chakravorty. 1996. "Subaltern Studies: Deconstructing Historiography." In *The Spivak Reader*, edited by Donna Landry and Gerald MacLean, 203–236. London: Routledge.

Stoetzel, Marcel, and Nira Yuval-Davis. 2002. "Standpoint Theory, Situated Knowledge and the Situated Imagination." *Feminist Theory* 3 (3): 315–333.

Suhrke, Astri. 2007. "Reconstruction as Modernisation: The 'Post-Conflict' Project in Afghanistan." *Third World Quarterly* 28 (7): 1291–1308.

Swidler, Ann, and Susan Cotts Watkins. 2009. "'Teach a Man to Fish': The Sustainability Doctrine and Its Social Consequences." *World Development* 37 (7): 1182–1196.

Townsend-Bell, E. 2011. "What Is Relevance? Defining Intersectional Praxis in Uruguay." *Political Research Quarterly* 64 (1): 187–199.

Wallis, Joanne, and Oliver Richmond. 2017. "From Constructivist to Critical Engagements With Peacebuilding: Implications for Hybrid Peace." *Third World Thematics: A TWQ Journal* 2 (4): 422–445.

Wallstrom, Margot. 2010. "Ending Sexual Violence: From Recognition to Action." Speech delivered at the Women and War UNSCR1325 Tenth Anniversary Conference, Washington, DC, November 3.

Weldon, Laurel. 2006. "Inclusion, Solidarity and Social Movements: The Global Movement Against Gender Violence." *Perspectives on Politics* 4 (1): 55–74.

Weldon, Laurel. 2008. "Intersectionality." In *Politics, Gender, and Concepts: Theory and Methodology*, edited by G. Goertz and A. G. Mazur, 193–218. New York, NY: Cambridge University Press.

Zwingel, Suzanne. 2017. "Women's Rights Norms as Content-in-Motion and Incomplete Practice." *Third World Thematics: A TWQ Journal* 2 (5): 675–690.

Chapter 2

Location matters

The 2017 women's marches as intersectional imaginary[1]

Zakiya Luna

Within a week of the election of Donald J. Trump as the 45th US president, a woman in Hawaii posted a Facebook event with the suggestion of 'another march.' She had participated in the 2004 March for Women's Lives in Washington DC; thus, she was eager to participate in another protest event. The idea spread quickly with thousands of people expressing interest in what would eventually become 600 'sister' marches throughout the world occurring on 22 January 2017, the day after Trump's inauguration. The marches captured the attention of onlookers, activists, politicians, news organisations, and researchers alike. To some people these marches represented a new era in protest, whereas for others it appeared to be the same women's movement, just with some new phrases invoked, such as 'intersectional feminism.' While much is up for debate about the marches, one fact remains uncontested: the marches occurred in different locations. Focusing on location as both a physical and conceptual space allows us to interrogate how intersectionality is conceptualised and practiced in social movements. To that end, this chapter draws on a multisite survey of participants in various marches to consider how participants at different marches articulated intersectionality within different march locations and how this presumed a subject of 'the' women's movement.

In the remainder of the chapter, I discuss literatures on the role of location in social movements, how imagination operates for movements, and the growing scholarship on the women's marches so far. Then I move to results, comparing how respondents at different marches identified the presence or absence of intersectionality based on their perception of the march's apparent demographics or inclusivity of issues. Finally, I conclude with implications. This chapter adds to our understanding of how the concept of intersectionality 'travels' across time and space and how different social actors perceived it based on their own social location. This chapter adds to the growing body of scholarship that attends to different manifestations of intersectionality in practice and the implications for movements.

The location of intersectionality

Location connotes many things, including physical space, which movement scholars take as a given but has important implications: 'A spatial analysis offers conceptual tools that enable us to conceptualize the relationships between social inequality, social justice, and the materiality of space' (Twine and Gardener 2013, p. 6). Different cities have different demographics for myriad reasons, including histories of segregation and its contemporary reproduction (Krysan and Bader 2009; Lipsitz 2009; Bonilla-Silva 2015; Saito 2015). Further, cities have different political histories, infrastructure for protest, and receptivity towards claims made by protesters, which Burciaga and Martinez (2017) identify as the *localised political context*. Rather than there being *one* political opportunity structure that applies equally to all locations, there is a variety of political opportunity structures. This suggests that cities, towns, and rural areas are not the same, all protest groups are not received the same in one location, and thus organising strategies will not necessarily be the same. Yet, for the Women's March, the action the protesters were to take was to be the same across location: gather as a collective to protest as or for women.

Location also connotes social location, or where a person falls in a social order. Sociologists have long noted that a person's social location influenced their view of society: as Du Bois famously wrote about the 'Negro' in the US., a white supremacist nation, who had held 'a double-consciousness, this sense of always looking at one's self through the eyes of others' (Du Bois 1903, p. 3). Decades later, feminist theorists pointed out that the basic approaches of sociological research emerged from the experience of men, thereby ignoring or at least only partially providing insights into the experiences of women (Smith 1974). Thus,

> If we begin from the world as we actually experience it, it is at least possible to see that we are located and that what we know of the other is conditional upon that location as part of a relation comprehending the other's location also.
>
> (Smith 1974, p. 12)

Patricia Hill Collins (1990) deepened the idea of standpoint with attention to and theorising about an explicitly Black feminist standpoint. To refer to one's standpoint means to reflect on one's own position with a set of oppressions and privileges. Standpoint theorists presume that a person's location influences how she experiences the world. In the physical world, if we are located in one spot, we see a particular view of a scene. But if we stand opposite of that spot, we have a different view of the scene. It is the same material scene but our location influences what part of the scene appears closest, or most salient, to us. Similarly, people interpret the world through different lenses. In a self-reflexive situated analysis, Canadian social worker Hulko (2009) starts with how her status as a White lesbian affects her experience in different countries. Then she turns to re-analyse data from her own prior studies in which research participants discussed experiences of immigration and how they were perceived in countries that have different racial orders. Thus, she shows how intersectionality manifests differently over time and space within an individual's life.

An increasing number of scholars of movements have drawn explicit attention to the role of the capacious idea of intersectionality as it is deployed and attempted by movements in both the US and globally. Kimberlé Crenshaw's (1991) early articulation of intersectionality included attention to political intersectionality, or how movements address the needs of their constituents who could be served by multiple movements. Scholars such as Roberts and Jesudason (2013) began attending to what they referred to as movement intersectionality as demonstrated by the bringing together of representatives of seemingly somewhat opposed movements – reprogenetics (reproductive genetics) advocates and disability rights activists, who were at times at odds on issues such as abortion. Other scholars are paying attention to women of colour–led social movement organising (Brown et al. 2017; Luna 2016), or how the concept of intersectionality is articulated or fails to hold salience for women's organisations in other countries (Lépinard 2014). Terriquez and colleagues' research (Terriquez 2015; Terriquez, Brenes, and Lopez 2018) on undocumented youth's activism offers the idea of intersectionality as a master frame, which draws on ideas proposed by Snow and Benford (1992). These scholars all highlight different ways that intersectionality operates in movement practice.

Movements and imagination

Imagination in a general sense involves thinking about a possibility that is not currently in front of you. Movement work involves imagining a future where there is a different set of relationships, different models of distributing resources, a different configuration of people in positions of power, and the like. For some people, the imagined future is a return to a prior model, whereas for others the imagined future is the creation of a new model. Considering that participating in protest is not a statistically normative activity, some participants only have images in their mind from mass media. In the US., common news images include those around Martin Luther King Junior's birthday or grainy black-and-white images of US Civil Rights protest, which also appeared in newspapers. This could include movies that include protest (e.g. *Norma Rae, Forrest Gump, Milk, Selma*) or any stock image of protest such as the common image of protesters yelling and otherwise engaging in confrontative tactics. Prior to the women's marches there have been protests visible in media both traditional (e.g. television and newspaper) and social (e.g. Facebook, Twitter). These included protests related to the Tea Party (2009), Wisconsin Capitol protest (2011), Tehrir Square (2011), Occupy Wall Street (2011), and Black Lives Matter (2013 to now), among others. So, for these marches,people could have envisioned images that include prior protest in which they participated or those of other people's participation, whether from media stories that cover actual experience or media that represent such experiences.

For self-identified progressives, the maintenance of an explicitly radical imagination poses continual challenges. As Breines (1980) suggested, creating movement structures that reflect the imagined society activists are proposing produces a form of prefigurative politics. This is easier said than practiced. In reflecting on the coalescing and eventual dissolution of a radically minded university-based group, some remaining participants (Zielińska, Kowzan, and Prusinowska 2011) wrote about their experience. When surveying fellow participants, activist-researchers found that imagination of the possibilities for change shift over the life of a campaign. The actual experience of *participating* in protest left participants with different lessons – and feelings – about the movement's process and future possibilities for working in coalition. Yet imagination is critical as it provides activists hope for the future, whether for Black radical movements (Kelley 2002) fighting for freedom or movements by other minority groups (Anderson 2016; DelaRosa 2018).

Research on feminist activism highlights how contemporary feminists, particularly educated White feminists, know they are supposed to be concerned with racial/ethnic diversity. Interviews with younger feminists active in the 1990s demonstrated that they understood 'second-wave' feminism had a tainted image of racial exclusivity, so their feminism needed to pay attention to racial diversity (Reger 2017). More recent research in New Zealand (Schuster 2016) found that interviewees shared 'intersectional expectations' that feminism consider perspectives of different women and that women of relative privilege have a responsibility to ensure they do not impose their worldview on women with less privilege. In the formally bicultural context of New Zealand, feminists of European descent used 'intersectionality' as a synonym for 'inclusivity' whether of specific social issues or specific groups. They knew that 'good' feminism included other perspectives, but in practice their organisations remained unable to attract feminists of colour, who largely preferred their own feminist spaces. Consequently, feminists of European descent relied on an individualistic approach to feminism that subtly evaded the challenge of producing intersectional collective efforts.

Evans (2016) concludes that even though high-profile UK feminists and political commentators debated the utility of 'intersectionality,' for a younger generation of activists who populate universities, intersectionality has become normalised, as proposed by Cho, Crenshaw, and McCall (2013). In a survey of campus feminist groups in the United Kingdom, Evans also found that intersectionality was being used to highlight inclusion, with campus activists sometimes going further by 'at times using it as a proxy for safe and inclusive spaces' (Evans 2016, p. 71). Even though their student organisations did not have high levels of racial diversity and at times elided discussions of class status, a key point of contention in the UK context, the organisations engaged in public education about intersectionality and 'were keen to discuss its implications, its complexity and how best to translate it from theory to praxis' (Evans 2016, p. 73). Ultimately, theoretical knowledge of the importance of intersectionality or imagining feminist movements that welcome a diversity of bodies and perspectives cannot guarantee the production of this diversity in practice.

Marches as research phenomenon

The women's marches also serve as their own research phenomenon. They have been the focus of multiple academic journals including a *Gender, Place and Culture* special issue in 2017 and a *Mobilisation* symposium in 2018. As some researchers have noted, the march was touted as an important moment in the historical trajectory of protest as well 'construction of social memory for the future' (Kitch 2018, p. 120). This 'social memory' is of the type that will, ironically, become part of media representations of what protest is 'supposed' to look like. Various sources highlight people's multiple imagined ideas of what these marches would be: official positions listed in the march principles, people's personal blogs discussing why they would (not) march, news stories in which people were quoted and prior experience.

The Women's March organisers articulated a desire for intersectional praxis as demonstrated in the various configurations of leadership and the stated claim to be 'a women-led movement bringing together people of all genders, ages, races, cultures, political affiliations, disabilities and backgrounds in our nation's capital on January 21, 2017, to affirm our shared humanity and pronounce our bold message of resistance and self-determination.' Assumedly people were marching because they either identified as women in some way or were in support of women. However, the imagined community of 'women' was up for negotiation as views on abortion (Bosman 2017; Eberstadt 2017) and the role of genitalia (Wrenn 2018) became a marker of who fits within the boundaries of the group. This collective identity (Taylor and Whittier 1992) was not simply a matter of people being conscious that they were participating in a Women's March. Rather, negotiation of the boundaries of 'a' women's movement continued across march locations and within participant's own understanding of how a Women's March event *should* look, based on their own images of protest.

Some researchers have argued that the Women's March of DC offered a useful example of intersectional mobilising across issues (Fisher, Dow, and Ray 2017). One study of a sample of women's marches and related events found that while 40 percent began organising about two weeks after Donald Trump's election, giving them about eight weeks of preparation, about the 20 percent of marches only began planning within one week of their March occurrence (Beyerlein et al. 2018). Since effective organising rests on developing long-term relationships (Han 2014), one week of preparation would pose difficulty to mobilising a diverse set of protesters if those networks were not already developed. Qualitative analyses offered nuanced perspective of the feeling of the DC march and others. One author-participant observed that of the official speakers at DC only one referred to historical events in the women's movement and instead focused on the accomplishments of men, the Civil Rights movement, and the contemporary Black Lives Matter movement. Thus,

Despite the attendance of several activists from the second wave of the American women's rights movement, few references were made to those 1970s protests. Thus, the official ceremony was a diverse pageant that nevertheless downplayed its grounding in the continuous social and political history of the American women's movement.

(Kitch 2018, p. 122)

That racial diversity and proximity to racial justice concerns were understood as the marker of the 'correct' way to engage in feminist praxis was perhaps best demonstrated in the imagery of the Women's March posters. Although the official DC logo that multiple marches used was of three silhouettes of faces rather than a specific representation, the popular 'We the People' posters Shepard Fairey produced were decidedly representational. The four images were of indigenous women and women (or girls) of colour – there were no images of White women.[2] These posters appeared throughout the DC march even if the women who they were to represent did not. For example, researchers interested in surveying Black women who attended the Washington DC march noted difficulty in physically finding Black women to survey (Bunyasi and Smith 2018).

Two Canadian professors who attended a local march reflected on the racial demographics of that march in an article title that conveys the main point: ' "It Definitely Felt Very White": Race, Gender, and the Performative Politics of Assembly at the Women's March in Victoria, British Columbia' (Rose-Redwood and Rose-Redwood 2017). More specifically, when reflecting on the posters they saw; the researchers observed many phrases. They noted,

'and we saw pink signs everywhere saying, 'More Women in Positions of Power,' 'Women's Rights Are Human Rights,' and 'This Is What Feminism Looks Like.' If this is really what feminism 'looks like,' we both thought, it seems like quite a white affair.

(Rose-Redwood and Rose-Redwood 2017)

The first author, a Black woman, felt like she and her daughter became a spectacle for picture taking by White protesters who wanted to document their participation. Documenting racial minorities' presence can be read as an attempt by White protesters to demonstrate they are participating in an 'authentically' diverse women's movement, engaging literally in what I have discussed in another paper as proximity practices (Luna 2017). The authors later questioned whether the audience of primarily White-appearing women would show the same level of support for marches explicitly focused on indigenous women and women of colour. Thus, the material realities of march locations alongside the embodied experience of marchers combine to create an intriguing analyses of a 'shared' protest experience.

Data and methods

This chapter draws on data from the Mobilizing Millions project's first-wave survey of 2017 Women's March participants. I serve as the principal investigator and three other faculty collaborated with me on developing the first phase of the project. This included development and distribution of a survey (Luna, Kulick, and Chatillon 2017) and participant observation at marches. Our interests included understanding motivations in participation, networks, and organisations and how movements engage with formal politics (e.g. elections). The survey asked basic questions such as which march the respondent attended and if they had voted in the 2018 US presidential election. The survey also included questions that allowed for write-in answers, such as, 'What are the most important reasons you came to this march?' 'How is this march similar to and/or different from other marches you have attended?' and 'Is there anything new that you have learned or seen here?'

An initial set of research teams were on the ground at various 2017 women's Marches in the United States: Austin, Boston, Los Angeles, Oakland, Philadelphia, Portland, St. Louis, and Washington DC. This included other faculty and graduate students, over 30 undergraduate students and interested community members who volunteered to be on site at different places. The online survey was distributed via emails collected at eight march locations and social media recruitment (e.g. postings on hundreds of march Facebook pages.) Over 3,000 people responded, with the majority identifying as White women who marched in the US. This chapter focuses on responses in which the people specifically wrote in a response that referred to intersectionality or its variants (e.g. 'intersectional'). Notably, none of the survey questions included the word 'intersectionality,' therefore respondents had to produce the phrase or variant on their own, which about two percent did.

As other scholars note (Schuster 2016), people's perspectives can be informed by the idea of intersectionality without referring to it, but for the purposes of this analysis, I limited my focus. The responses chosen for this chapter each offered more information about how the respondent thought about 'intersectionality' in that the response included more than an isolated reference to it. For example, one survey respondent answered, 'I've learned there is a need for intersectionality discussions.' In a binary analysis, this response would count as presence of intersectionality. However, for a more nuanced analysis such as the one I am presenting in this chapter, this text (or any other part of the write-in responses) does not offer insight into the respondent's interpretation of the meaning of intersectionality or why there would be a need for intersectionality discussions.

Connecting to locations

Early observations of the marches noted some commonalities, including that there were many more participants than expected, levels of confusion about what events were happening when, and people having difficulty getting to where they were 'supposed' to be (Luna et al. 2017). As an example of how location matters to protest participation in different ways, the first response to our survey came on 21 January 2017 at 6:20 am. This response was possible because, quite simply, of location: the respondent lived in Edinburgh, Scotland, United Kingdom, and had participated in the march there (named WMW Sister March: Edinburgh!). Thus, by the time this survey was first distributed via social media in the US (East Coast morning), she had already participated in a march, whereas the US protests had not yet begun. She was born in 1996 and self-identified as 'queer.' She had learned about the march through social media. In response to the questions about the most important reasons to march, she replied,

> For all those who could not be *there*. For equality for all. To show that there is *no place* for hate and that we will not lie down quietly. Because I'm *abroad right now* and want a way to be *connected to my country*.'
>
> (emphasis added)

In a 44-word response she referred to location four different times: 'there' (at the protest), 'no place' (not allowable in a symbolic space), 'abroad right now' (her present geography), and 'connected to my country' (a geographical location which is physically distant but to which she imagines she will feel connected through participating in a common activity). Her response highlights how location can matter in multiple senses of the word.

Similar prior experiences, different takes

The Women's March on Austin focused on the state capitol. Two respondents who attended this march had previously participated in protests events including for, in their terms, gay and lesbian rights and Black Lives Matter. Both noted that the 2017 Women's March was larger than many other protests they had previously attended. Since they had participated in other protests, they had crowd sizes against which to measure this. While they agreed on the magnitude of the march, they perceived the Austin Women's March differently. An older White woman (40) saw the Austin march as 'by far the largest and the most intersectional,' whereas a younger White woman (27) saw the Austin march as 'mostly attended by white feminists with a pretty superficial interest (if any) in intersectionality.' The second comment about intersectionality was not under the question where we asked respondents to reflect on the march in comparison to other marches. Rather, her answer about intersectionality came after the survey question that asked, 'Is there anything new that you have learned or seen here [at the March].' The respondent replied, 'no, not particularly,' then, by way of explanation, put her comment including a reflection on intersectionality. Noticeably, she acknowledged that her march was not only composed of fellow White women. In her thinking, the other attendees were not interested in intersectionality and therefore she did not learn anything, implying that she was already familiar with the gender-based claims many other attendees were making.

Different prior experience, different takes

The Atlanta, Georgia, march was renamed the Atlanta March for Social Justice and Women. The march was to start at the Center for Civil and Human Rights and go to the state capitol.[3] A White respondent in her 30s who brought her child to the march did not list having participated in any prior marches. She reflected on her lessons learned from the experience: 'I am seeing the need to be a lot more intersectional in my life and speak out when I am relatively privileged to do so, even if it's scary!' She identifies intersectionality as something she can do more of in her life. This respondent acknowledges emotions and embodied experience that can be present when vocalising concerns: fear and discomfort can be 'scary.' Yet, she also identifies the need to vocalise as only required when she is 'relatively privileged to do so.' This implies that a responsibility applies in situations when she feels she has power. As Evans and Lépinard (this volume) note, privilege is relational and 'relations are embedded in social contexts and their intersections vary.' Her solution was to focus on *individual* actions ('my life'). While this is a useful way to consider the importance of vocalising concerns and reiterates the importance of context and audience, the response leaves out any reference to groups or collectivity. Yet, we know group position influences an individual's position. For example, in the US, scholars from a range of disciplines have documented how Whiteness offers many benefits and 'wages' translating to continued advantage in the economic sector and otherwise (Roediger 1999; Lipsitz 2009). Thus, in any situation she was likely to *continually* occupy a position of relative privilege, whether or not she recognised her racial privilege.

In contrast to the prior respondent's individualised answer, a White woman in her early 40s answered with a response that addressed collectivity or lack thereof. Her previous protest experience included that against the Persian Gulf war and in support of Black Lives Matter. To her, the Atlanta 2017 march, while larger, was 'less organised.' In reflecting on her march experience, she referred to both national and local context. She wrote,

> I think the leadership of women like Linda Sarsour was critical, but for many it was clear that intersectionality wasn't even part of their thinking. And it was painful to watch. I think sharing guidelines about how to engage, and even having some pre march meetings to have some conversations before the March could have created a greater sense of unity the day of the March.

She observed the development of the DC women's march as indicated by referencing of Linda Sarsour, who had become a co-organiser of the Women's March in Washington DC. The respondent identified feeling emotionally connected to how that organising played out, finding it 'painful.' Since this respondent did not participate in the DC march, her language suggests a level of emotional investment in the public space of feminist discourse. This respondent also suggested multiple solutions to the problems she identified: march participants meeting with each other before the march and having guidelines. The solution was to act at a group level and learn to 'engage.' More specifically she wanted pre-march meetings at which potential protesters would be able to talk with each other. She imagined that having meetings and conversations would necessarily produce a 'sense of unity.' Part of what this respondent appeared to desire was creation of a collective identity beyond that of a broad category of 'women.'

As a practical matter, reviewing guidelines would be a lower-level investment for participants than attending meetings. What is interesting is that the Atlanta March website *did* include various resources for marchers, including guidelines.[4] The organiser's page included pictures of people holding signs that explained 'whyimarch.' From these pictures, the Atlanta March organisers appeared to be a multiracial, multireligious, multiage, multigender group. The website's 'Guide to a Safe and Meaningful March' contained a list of guidelines. These included 'Be kind,' 'Be respectful,' 'Be positive,' and 'Be safe.' Being 'kind' included welcoming people and reaching out to others. However, the next line made a large claim: 'Marchers are all here for the same reason: social justice and unity.' The need to be respectful was explained as, 'We all come from different backgrounds and experiences and have one thing in common: the desire to work together to create safe, inclusive communities and government.' Under the explanation of what it means to 'be positive,' the site explained, 'We are mad, sad, disappointed and everything in between, but we want to put positive, hope filled messages out into the community during this march.' While march guidelines encouraged marchers to 'be yourself,' marchers would not be allowed to wear face coverings (we could imagine masks, etc.). Creativity was urged, but was again emphasised as needing to reflect a specific type of message. Specifically, the examples of being creative were to 'write a positive slogan or chant.'

After a reminder to leave pets behind (service animals welcome) was the final guideline. It reminded protesters to 'Be the change you want to see in the world. Our children and youth are watching us and will be joining us. Let us fill them with hope and positive messages. They are our future.' The guideline drew on a famous quote attributed to non-violence proponent Mahatma Ghandi, who Martin Luther King Jr. cited as an inspiration. The guideline implies marchers should behave in a certain way for a semi-imagined audience of children who compose an imagined future. The guidelines construct young people as empty vessels waiting to be filled with 'hope and positive messages,' as if they could not have their own feelings or responses to the activity. This Atlanta survey respondent's desire to have marchers meet before to talk to create unity presumed all perspectives could have been contained satisfactorily. Reading these guidelines, we can imagine that even if Atlanta marchers had met previously in formal meetings, they would have been discouraged from expressing what had already been presented as 'negative emotions' in favour of appearing as a united, cohesive protest group. While there is much to be gained from hope and positivity, these guidelines suggest that the appropriate way to engage in protest is to channel feeling 'mad, sad, disappointed' into feeling 'positive.' The guidelines subtly present feeling 'mad,' which connotes anger, as bad and positivity as good. By presenting these emotions as mutually exclusive, the guidelines discouraged expressions of 'negative' feelings. The insistence on kindness and positivity also appear particularly gendered, encouraging women to behave properly no matter how unjust they feel the circumstances.

What appears to matter most in these respondents' interpretation of the march is their own standpoints. If we interpreted the Austin responses as an issue of age and different generational expectations, Atlanta would challenge that assumption. These two Atlanta respondents only differed in age by 10 years, but articulated different experiences. One woman appears to be excited and in an early learning stage about intersectionality. The other more familiar with intersectionality appeared disappointed – she understood intersectionality as being about different ways of thinking and going beyond thought to how people 'engage.' These Atlanta respondents both emphasised embodying theories in practice, but they interpreted intersectionality in different ways.

Imagining other intersections

A White respondent in her early 30s noted many motivations for attending a Chicago march, including 'women's rights, immigrant/refugee rights, and civil rights broadly defined (POC, LGBTQ, freedom of speech/press, etc.) demonstrate that Trump does not have a mandate.' This suggested motivations to support both broad issues and express concern about a specific threat (new president). This Chicago respondent had previously attended an immigrant's rights rally and explicitly identified the Women's March as 'much larger, more demographically diverse, [with] many different causes represented.' The described conditions of the march did not teach her anything about protest; thus, she replied to the survey question about learning with a reflection, 'No, I can't say that [I learned]. Aside from being larger in both scale and scope, it also felt like many of the activist groups I have been around.' Her comment indicated that the specific 'activist groups' with which she was familiar were, contradictorily, similar to the Women's March protest event that was, from her own description, 'more demographically diverse, [with] many different causes represented' in comparison to the activist space with which she was familiar. Her refection on intersectionality of the march indicated where the gap existed for her: 'I wish that workers' rights were considered as equal of an "intersectional" issue as others that were included in the marches.' So, for her the similarity between these types of events likely stemmed from a seeming *lack* of attention to a particular intersection, namely labour, which could also connote class. If we consider intersectionality in Crenshaw's term of political intersectionality, then it also implores us to consider representing different types of movements in a space.

Embodied reflexivity as intersectional praxis

The reflections on intersectionality extended to participants outside the US., which points to how the discourse has travelled beyond the USA borders, where the concept was first developed. The one respondent who answered about the Winnipeg Women's March reflected on various aspects of the march, identity, and intersectional praxis. She was 60 years old and in answering the demographic question about race added,

> I am a Jewish person of Ashkenazi (European) descent. In many situations I am 'White,' but when this question of identity comes up I identify more with my own ethnicity and the immigrant experience of my ancestors than I do with 'white settler' or 'white colonialist' identities.

The level of detail in her response indicated she was grappling with the various complexities of race, ethnicity, and nation at a structural level and personal level. She had participated in many events: 'International women's day, indigenous issues, Pride, protest entry to war in Iraq (we succeeded on this issue in Canada), protest nuclear weapons, environmental issues, etc.' Writing an 'etc.' indicated that she could not name all her prior event participation. Indeed, in another fill-in answer she referred to protests in the 1980s. Thus, she had extensive experience with protest, which provided her many examples of comparison.

In answering the question on how the Winnipeg event differed from the other protests in which the respondent had participated, she wrote one of the longest responses to any of the questions. In almost 500 words (13 sentences), she offered an analysis that provided specific examples of what she felt was attention to privilege and intersectionality, and how her own social location influenced her experience. She wrote:

> One difference that stands out for me is how overt the awareness of privilege was among the organizers. Our premarch rally was held indoors, and the MC [emcee or master of ceremonies] asked able-bodied people to go up to the balconies and leave room right in front of the stage for people with disabilities. After the rally, people with 'privilege' – I forget the exact phrasing that was used – were asked to wait until indigenous and other people – again I forget the exact phrase used – exited the building first so the march was lead [sic] by them. I was surprised to notice that I found this challenging – food for thought. (BTW [by the way], I am hard of hearing, an 'invisible disability' but it was not too difficult for me to find a place to hear, but not see the speeches – it was great actually that we were such a large crowd that most of us could not see the stage.)

A few things are notable in this response. She is attuned to the idea of 'privilege.' She begins by describing a rally that occurred before the event, which offered an opportunity for logistical coordination and brief creation of collective identity. The rally organisers structured the event to consider different social groups – the emcee explicitly asked people to create physical space to prioritise people with disabilities' ability to view the stage. Then indigenous people (and possibly other historically marginalised groups) were placed at the front of the march. This required both forethought on the part of the rally organisers and agreement by people with 'privilege' to stay in their physical place in the back. This respondent was likely not the only person of the thousands who found it 'challenging' to wait their 'turn.' Of course, historically, indigenous people and people of colour have waited their 'turn' for access to rights that White people have been granted automatically. She was also able to articulate how she was specifically socially located within this space as someone whose own disability – hearing – would have been an exact reason to join the crowd closer to the stage. Yet, she recognised that her presence would have felt disconcerting for other people, as she did not appear to have a disability. Further, as demonstrated in her response to the question regarding race, she noted feeling closer to an immigrant experience than that of 'settler' or 'coloniser,' yet she is read as belonging to the latter, thus the appropriate location for her is also behind the indigenous people who were to lead the march.

Her response then shifted to considering the broader ways the Winnipeg march differed, with specific reference to intersectionality. She wrote:

> The intersectionality, the multiple areas of focus, and our attempt to march with one eye on local and national Canadian issues and the other on American and global problems, made this march challenging but also exhilarating. It was truly thrilling to know we were marching at the same time as people all over the world.[5]

She draws attention to how location mattered, offering four examples of contexts to which she paid attention: 'local' (presumably Winnepegian or Manitobian), Canadian, American, where American stands in for the US (since technically Canada is part of North America), and 'global' equalling all other locations.

She also draws attention to how the specificity of her physical location, in her mind, did not diminish the experience and indeed enhanced it, since 'we were marching at the same time.' Her reference to simultaneous marches was an imagining. The marches had different start times even within the same time zone and occurred all over the world, thus there was both simultaneity and discontinuity. Still, this respondent's point was that it *felt* like people were marching at the same time, thereby giving her a feeling of 'thrilling' connection.

Discussion and conclusion

Based on prior research, it would be surprising if everyone within a specific march and across the 2017 marches articulated the same experience. This would not be a march but more of a cult gathering. The size of the 2017 protest marches surprised people the world over, and while this was a consistent theme in both of the survey responses, media reports, and some recent studies on those marches, the insistence on focusing on the size of the marches at different locations obscures some key concerns of participants.

The idea of presence, the idea of existing together, across time and space, was enough for some respondents to feel connected to an imagined community of diverse women, whereas for others it was not enough to produce a sense of soli-darity. In both cases they have imagined a unity among the massive category of 'women' that does not exist. The perceived quantity of protestors or quantity of issues present at a specific march did not automatically translate to perception of quality of participation. Some respondents' dissatisfaction seemed to stem from a disconnection between quantity and quality: without knowing the many others in the street, the quantity of possible connections did not make up for lack of quality in these connections. While they recognised there were large numbers of people at the march who were ostensibly there to participate in the same event, various respondents questioned the motives of other participants. Interestingly, they could very well have been perceived by *others* as 'low-quality' participa-tors – at a march there are few ways to know people's internal motivation. Cues would include signs, clothing, and the many accessories people wore to signal their motivation. But not everyone chooses to express in those ways.

Considering the age ranges of the respondents, this is not a clean story of politi-cal generations (Whittier 1997), where younger respondents were more aware of intersectionality or its lack thereof. Indeed, one of the most cogent analyses of march dynamics and observations of intersectional praxis came from a respondent in her 60s. There could be many reasons for this, including her self-identification as someone occupying liminal identity space: her Ashkenazi roots provided her with a different narrative of her social locations – one as connected to Europe and rejecting colonial Whiteness, while presenting as White. Further, experienc-ing physical deterioration of her hearing to an extent she felt it disabled her also contributed to her feeling that she belonged to a social group – people with dis-abilities – but in a way that others would not view her as such. How individuals make sense of intersectionality, and how this differs based on someone's own social location, is the crux of these different reflections on experiences at what was ostensibly the same march in each place.

The discourse of intersectionality has been normalised in feminist academic spaces, many parts of the US women's movement, and other movements. This discourse was visible in various official Women's March materials and state-ments by representatives. Yet, for participants in the streets in various places, what it meant and was imagined to look like in relation to their own social loca-tion and experience varied. The Atlanta respondent who referred to being able to 'do' intersectionality in her life constructed it as a skill or practice. While her answer was focused on individuals and presumed people can leverage inter-sectionality at will, considering what it looks like to individuals remains use-ful. Depending upon the participant, intersectionality was imagined as a set of identities, interest areas, or nebulous space. Further, 'intersectionality' could be named by the absence of how that participant imagined an appropriately 'intersectional' march would look. These respondents were all White identified, and while some spoke of 'privilege,' what that meant to them clearly varied. The diversity of responses even among this small sample has implications for academics and organisers.

While scholars certainly have many ideas about what intersectionality means in terms of movements, it is interesting to see how individuals who participate in protest conceptualise intersectionality, to the degree they do. Even if we take as a given that the Washington DC Women's March offered a good example of intersectional praxis – a debatable assertion – we still have the reality of trickle-down intersectionality, or of intersectional diffusion, that cannot reach all spaces equally. Further, the responses suggest the social location within specific bodies affects the embodied experience of intersectionality. Staying at theoretical means ignoring the visceral experiences of oppression or privilege with which people contend in movements. No detail is too small in how people interpret an experience and its success at producing what an individual interprets as meeting their intersectional expectations.

Starting from a clear image of what form of intersectionality is being attempted in any movement or specific protest event would be a good, albeit undoubtedly challenging, starting place. Doing so means from the beginning participants can assess beforehand whether their individual image matches the collective one and whether to move forward rather than feeling disappointed after the fact. Helping people work within and across and capitalise on intersectionality in its varied images increases possibilities for bringing these images closer together in productive tension, which is the promise and reality of intersectionality in practice to bring collective liberation across movement sectors.

Notes

1 Please direct correspondence to Zakiya Luna, Department of Sociology, University of California, Santa Barbara, CA 93106-9430, zluna@soc.ucsb.edu. Prior versions of this chapter were presented at the Pacific Sociological Association 90th annual meeting, Third Mobilization-SDSU conference on Social Movements and Nonviolent Protest, and the Council for European Studies 26th Annual Conference of Europeanists. Thank you to the volume editors, Éléonore Lépinard and Elizabeth Evans, for their feedback, enthusiasm, and encouragement. Thank you to the many enthusiastic volunteers across sites who distributed fliers and collected emails for the survey on the ground. In addition, thank you to the UCSB undergraduates who participated in the project through the Faculty Research Assistance Program and students of faculty collaborators who posted recruitment notices on hundreds of Facebook pages.
2 Shepard Fairey is a US artist best known for producing then-Senator Barack Obama's multicolour "Hope" and "Change" posters for his first presidential campaign. https://obeygiant.com/obama/
3 Atlanta has a long history of civil rights activism. It hosts the Martin Luther King Jr. Center for Nonviolent Social Change. In 2007, the Atlanta organisation also hosted the first U.S. Social Forum, which was modelled after the World Social Forum, started in 2001 'by organizations and social movements that were self summoned and mobilized for a huge meeting in Porto Alegre, in opposition to the neoliberalism represented by the World Economic Forum' (see https://wsf2018.org/en/english-world-social-forum-2018/).
4 As of the writing of this chapter, the website for the 2017 event was still available at https://atlantamarch.com/.

5 The rest of her response included discussion of her experience with police, including awareness of differences in police treatment of protesters engaged in G8 and Black Lives Matter protests.

References

Anderson, SaVonne. 2016. "Radical Imagination Is a Necessary, Sustaining Force of Black Activism." *Mashable*. https://mashable.com/2016/02/28/black-activism-radical-imagination/ [accessed 30 May 2019].

Beyerlein, Kraig, Peter Ryan, Aliyah Abu-Hazeem, and Amity Pauley. 2018. "The 2017 Women's March: A National Study of Solidarity Events." *Mobilization: An International Quarterly* 23 (4): 425–449.

Bonilla-Silva, Eduardo. 2015. "The Structure of Racism in Color-Blind, 'Post-Racial' America." *American Behavioral Scientist* 59 (11): 1358–1376.

Bosman, Julie. 2017. "In Rust Belt Town, March Draws Shrugs and Cheers from Afar." *New York Times*, January 22, 1–14.

Breines, Wini. 1980. "Community and Organization: The New Left and Michels' 'Iron Law'." *Social Problems* 27 (4): 419–429.

Brown, Melissa, Rashawn Ray, Ed Summers, and Neil Fraistat. 2017. "#SayHerName: A Case Study of Intersectional Social Media Activism." *Ethnic and Racial Studies* 40 (11): 1831–1846. https://doi.org/10.1080/01419870.2017.1334934

Bunyasi, Tehama Lopez, and Candis Watts Smith. 2018. "Get in Formation: Black Women's Participation in the Women's March on Washington as an Act of Pragmatic Utopianism." *The Black Scholar* 48 (3): 4–16.

Burciaga, Edelina M., and Lisa M. Martinez. 2017. "How Do Political Contexts Shape Undocumented Youth Movements? Evidence from Three Immigrant Destinations." *Mobilization: An International Quarterly* 22 (4): 451–471.

Cho, Sumi, Kimberlé Williams Crenshaw, and Leslie McCall. 2013. "Toward a Field of Intersectionality Studies: Theory, Applications, and Praxis." *Signs* 38 (4): 785–810.

Collins, Patricia Hill. 1990. *Black Feminist Thought: Knowledge, Consciousness, and the Politics of Empowerment*. Boston, MA: Unwin Hyman.

Crenshaw, Kimberlé. 1991. "Mapping the Margins: Intersectionality, Identity Politics, and Violence Against Women of Color." *Stanford Law Review* 43 (6): 1241–1299.

DelaRosa, Tony. 2018. "Lessons of 'Radical Imagination': What the Filipinx Community Can Learn from the Black Community." *Asian American Policy Review* 28: 83–89.

Du Bois, William Edward Burghardt. 1903. *The Souls of Black Folk: Essays and Sketches*. Chicago, IL: A. C. McClurg & Company.

Eberstadt, Mary. 2017. "How the Abortion Debate Rocked Progressivism." *Time*, February 6, 32–32.

Evans, Elizabeth. 2016. "Intersectionality as Feminist Praxis in the UK." *Women's Studies International Forum* 59: 67–75.

Fisher, Dana R., Dawn M. Dow, and Rashawn Ray. 2017. "Intersectionality Takes it to the Streets: Mobilizing Across Diverse Interests for the Women's March." *Science Advances* 3 (9): eaao1390.

Han, Hahrie. 2014. *How Organizations Develop Activists: Civic Associations and Leadership in the 21st Century*. Oxford, UK: Oxford University Press.

Hulko, Wendy. 2009. "The Time- and Context-Contingent Nature of Intersectionality and Interlocking Oppressions." *Affilia* 24 (1): 44–55.

Kelley, Robin D. G. 2002. *Freedom Dreams: The Black Radical Imagination*. Boston, MA: Beacon Press.

Kitch, Carolyn. 2018. "'A Living Archive of Modern Protest': Memory-Making in the Women's March." *Popular Communication* 16 (2): 119–127.

Krysan, Maria, and Michael D. M. Bader. 2009. "Racial Blind Spots: Black-White-Latino Differences in Community Knowledge." *Social Problems* 56 (4): 677–701.

Lépinard, Éléonore. 2014. "Doing Intersectionality Repertoires of Feminist Practices in France and Canada." *Gender & Society* 28 (6): 877–903.

Lipsitz, George. 2009. *The Possessive Investment in Whiteness: How White People Profit from Identity Politics, Revised and Expanded Edition*. Philadelphia, PA: Temple University Press.

Luna, Zakiya. 2016. "'Truly a Women of Color Organization' Negotiating Sameness and Difference in Pursuit of Intersectionality." *Gender & Society* 30 (5): 769–790.

Luna, Zakiya. 2017. "Who Speaks for Whom? (Mis) Representation and Authenticity in Social Movements." *Mobilization: An International Quarterly* 22 (4): 435–450.

Luna, Zakiya, Kristen Barber, Selina Gallo-Cruz, Kelsy Kretschmer, and Chandra Russo. 2017. "Mobilizing Millions-Women's March Participants Survey Wave 1." Unpublished Survey.

Luna, Zakiya T., Alex Kulick, and Anna Chatillon. 2017. "Why Did Millions March? A View from the Many Women's Marches." *The Society Pages-Sociological Images*. https://thesocietypages.org/socimages/2017/02/15/why-did-millions-march-a-view-from-the-many-womens-marches/ [accessed 17 April 2017].

Reger, Jo. 2017. "Finding a Place in History: The Discursive Legacy of the Wave Metaphor and Contemporary Feminism." *Feminist Studies* 43 (1): 193–221.

Roberts, Dorothy, and Sujatha Jesudason. 2013. "Movement Intersectionality." *Du Bois Review: Social Science Research on Race* 10 (2): 313–328.

Roediger, David R. 1999. *The Wages of Whiteness: Race and the Making of the American Working Class*. New York, NY: Verso.

Rose-Redwood, CindyAnn, and Reuben Rose-Redwood. 2017. "'It Definitely Felt Very White': Race, Gender, and the Performative Politics of Assembly at the Women's March in Victoria, British Columbia." *Gender, Place & Culture* 24 (5): 645–654.

Saito, Leland. 2015. "From Whiteness to Colorblindness in Public Policies Racial Formation and Urban Development." *Sociology of Race and Ethnicity* 1 (1): 37–51.

Schuster, Julia. 2016. "Intersectional Expectations: Young Feminists' Perceived Failure at Dealing With Differences and Their Retreat to Individualism." *Women's Studies International Forum* 58: 1–8.

Smith, Dorothy E. 1974. "Women's Perspective as a Radical Critique of Sociology." *Sociological Inquiry* 44 (1): 7–13.

Snow, David A., and Robert D. Benford. 1992. "Master Frames and Cycles of Protest." In *Frontiers in Social Movement Theory*, edited by A. D. Morris and C. M. Mueller, 133-155. New Haven, CT: Yale University Press.

Taylor, Verta, and Nancy E. Whittier. 1992. "Collective Identity in Social Movement Communities: Lesbian Feminist Mobilization." In *Frontiers in Social Movement Theory*, edited by A. D. Morris and C. M. Mueller, 104-129. New Haven, CT: Yale University Press.

Terriquez, Veronica. 2015. "Intersectional Mobilization, Social Movement Spillover, and Queer Youth Leadership in the Immigrant Rights Movement." *Social Problems* 62 (3): 343–362.

Terriquez, Veronica, Tizoc Brenes, and Abdiel Lopez. 2018. "Intersectionality as a Multi-purpose Collective Action Frame: The Case of the Undocumented Youth Movement." *Ethnicities* 18 (2): 260–276.

Twine, France Winddance, and Bradley Gardener. 2013. *Geographies of Privilege*. London: Routledge.

Whittier, Nancy. 1997. "Political Generations, Micro-Cohorts, and the Transformation of Social Movements." *American Sociological Review* 62 (5): 760–778.

Wrenn, Corey. 2018. "Pussy Grabs Back: Bestialized Sexual Politics and Intersectional Failure in Protest Posters for the 2017 Women's March." *Feminist Media Studies* 1–19.

Zielińska, Małgorzata, Piotr Kowzan, and Magdalena Prusinowska. 2011. "Social Movement Learning: From Radical Imagination to Disempowerment?" *Studies in the Education of Adults* 43 (2): 251–267.

Chapter 3

Changing core business? Institutionalised feminisms and intersectionality in Belgium and Germany

Petra Ahrens and Petra Meier

Introduction

While the institutionalisation of feminism in state institutions and other social movements – for instance, the LGBTQI movement – and the different foci that result are well researched (Beckwith 2013; McBride and Mazur 2013), we know astonishingly little about institutionalised non-state organisations originating from these movements – such as national women's umbrella organisations. In this chapter we concentrate on such women's organisations, often presented as successors of the first-wave women's movements, and ask to what extent they rely on intersectionality as a repertoire of inclusivity and a strategy for coalition building (Evans and Lépinard, this volume). Throughout recent decades, research on intersectional aspects of mobilisation (or the lack thereof; cf. Crenshaw 1991; Nyhagen Predelli and Halsaa 2012) has grown in importance and has illustrated the failures and successes of women's or feminist movements in becoming more inclusive (Bassel and Emejulu 2014; Mohanty 2003; Irvine, Lang, and Montoya 2019; Lépinard 2014), but again without paying much attention to national women's umbrella organisations.

We set intersectionality as a precondition to substantively represent the complexity of gender equality, to avoid marginalising more vulnerable groups, and to build a larger and more sustainable movement (Irvine et al. 2019). In other words, without an intersectional approach, women's organisations stick to the 'Oppression Olympics' (Yuval-Davis 2012), lose impact due to their limited scope, and, in the long run, might be less able to represent equality issues. Notwithstanding this claim, we did not expect to find much evidence of intersectional practices and repertoires. In fact, we have found that intersectionality is at best used as a rhetorical tool and in non-performative ways in the national women's umbrella organisations.

In our analysis we examine the two Belgian Women's Councils (Conseil des Femmes Francophones de Belgique and Vrouwenraad) and the National Council of German Women's Organisations (Deutscher Frauenrat: DFR). Women's umbrella organisations are important for a variety of reasons. Political institutions such as governments and parliaments accept them as the main representatives of women's interests and have established their participation in policymaking by inviting them as experts to hearings, meetings, and public consultations. This participation in policy makes them a likely node for norm diffusion in two directions: from civil society to politics and vice versa. Furthermore, they have the potential to mobilise for gender equality policies by organising their members as a visible public pressure group. Finally, they are a crucial connection between the national and the supranational level, because they form the national coordination of the European Women's Lobby (EWL), the biggest supranational women's organisation in the European Union (EU), with the possibility of influencing supranational policies that return to the national level through hard or soft law. Our perspective includes examining their possible institutional privilege in participating in policymaking. Women's organisations mark their territory by defining who can become a member and at what cost, by structuring policy positions, by forging compromise positions (possibly) at the cost of those with less power or resources in the organisation, and by acting as primary contact for invitation by state institutions and other stakeholders. Due to their long history and position, women's umbrella organisations have been recognised as core actors on behalf of women's interests and posit privileged institutional access in the form of advisory roles.

Belgium and Germany are good cases for examining intersectionality in women's organisations: they have long-standing social movements founded in the wake of first-wave feminism. Both movements are nowadays organised in overarching umbrella organisations, bringing together many different groups and initiatives in countries with an increasingly diverse population. With our chapter we contribute to the research on intersectionality in movements by investigating the often-neglected traditional women's organisations as core civil society actors and policymakers (Irvine et al. 2019; Lépinard 2014). Understanding the historical context and its impact on the desire (and ability) of women's organisations to pursue intersectional praxis is utterly important.

Our 'thick description' aims to trace how far these organisations are able to challenge their own internal power relations by adopting intersectional praxis. We distinguish between descriptive aspects of intersectionality (office staff, member organisations) and substantive aspects that would mean 'doing intersectionality' (policy papers, hearings, conferences), to identify specific forms of privilege and marginalisation and the extent to which intersectionality becomes visible in their organisational structure and intersectional claims appear in their output.

What do we mean when we say 'women's movement' as opposed to a 'feminist movement'? We follow Beckwith (2013) in that a women's movement may refer to any women-led movement organising around gendered identity while it is not part of state institutions. Feminist movements, instead, also pursue the goal of changing gendered hierarchies and improving the status of women (McBride and Mazur 2013). Thus, we see the national women's umbrella organisations as stemming from a tradition of women's but not necessarily feminist movements.

Explaining women's movements' engagement with intersectionality

Why do women's organisations adopt (or not) an intersectional perspective? Literature suggests different explanatory perspectives for women's movements' success (and failures) regarding institutionalisation, privileged positions in policymaking, and their engagement with intersectional aspects. In comparing French and Canadian women's movements, Lépinard (2014, pp. 898–899) shows that they exhibit not one single but four different repertoires in dealing with intersectionality – intersectional recognition, gender first, individual recognition, and intersectional solidarity – of which some seem more apt to foster the project of an inclusive feminist political agenda than others. Intersectional recognition resembles well what Crenshaw (1991) defined as structural and political intersectionality; intersectional solidarity leads to converting minority women's specific claims into existing feminist vocabulary, while the other two repertoires engage with differences and diversity in a less comprehensive way. Lépinard (2014, pp. 881–885) emphasises the advantages of comparative analysis in carving out conditions favouring or impeding intersectionality and proposes to distinguish between single-axis and dual-axis as well as between advocacy and service-oriented movements. In this chapter, we look at single-axis advocacy women's umbrella organisations and explore two different national contexts.

Not only different repertoires, but also women's movements' different historical paths, top-down and bottom-up pressures, and political opportunity structures influence the different ways in which women's organisations engage with intersectionality. The *long history* and connected specific national context of women's organisations make it likely that some intersectional aspects would be picked up more than others, thereby often privileging the needs of majority groups over those of minority groups (Marx Ferree 2012; Nyhagen Predelli and Halsaa 2012; Strolovitch 2007). Historical institutionalism allows addressing such developments by asking about path dependencies in institutionalising women's organisations.

National women's umbrella organisations comprise a broad variety of different member organisations, and this *bottom-up* approach shapes their common ground, their common identity. How are conflicts between member organisations solved and whose position is privileged and whose dismissed? Will different intersections – for instance Catholic-bourgeois vs. LGBTQI vs. domestic workers – clash, or can conflicts be mediated and dissolved (Wiercx 2011; Verloo 2006; Yuval-Davis 2012)?

Likewise, norm diffusion from the supranational level can pressure organisations *top-down* into engaging with intersectional aspects. The Belgian and German women's umbrella organisations are all members of the EWL. Founded in 1990, the EWL is the biggest supranational women's umbrella organisation with national women's umbrella organisations and – more recently – other supranational civil society organisations as members. The EWL receives public funding, has privileged access to several EU committees, expert groups, and hearings, and has also often been criticised as being exclusionary and solely representing the interests of white, middle-class, well-educated heterosexual women (Ahrens 2019; Strid 2014). Stubbergaard (2015) has emphasised recent changes towards more intersectionality, for instance, in the EWL's creation of the European Network of Migrant Women and upholding strong ties with it, but not with the European Forum of Muslim Women; one of the reasons for this decision being the clear 'gender-first' approach of the EWL. Nevertheless, we would expect that an opening up of the EWL to intersectionality on the supranational level would exert pressure on national members to pay more attention to intersectionality as well (see, for Germany, Marx Ferree 2012, p. 210).

Finally, social movement theory suggests that the national *political opportunity structure* defines the scope of action for social movements such as women's movements (Beckwith 2013; Knappe and Lang 2014). Usually, political institutions define the policymaking agenda, not women's organisations, and only a 'window of opportunity' allows for considerable change. Until then, organisations' activities consist mainly of lobbying for policy change and less in contentious mass mobilisation, a result of trade-offs between access to policymaking and protest (Sanchez Salgado 2014). As an effect, women's organisations react instead of act in policy processes, not least when they receive funding from the institutions involved (Sanchez Salgado 2014; Stubbergaard 2015). Undeniably, resources play a role in how organisations (can) operate. Organisations receiving limited resources can find it hard to cover intersectionality to a greater extent. In addition, limited resources can lead to competition and conflict between organisations working on different grounds of discrimination (Hancock 2007; Verloo 2006) with the effect that none of them adopt intersectionality. Nevertheless, insufficient resources do not necessarily lead to competition and conflict, and satisfactory resources do not automatically lead to the adoption of intersectionality (Ahrens 2019).

With a view to the specific political opportunity structure defining women's organisations' scope of influence, we would expect a better intersectional representation in Belgium because of the national tradition of creating consensus among different interests and the multilingual setting which led the different communities to dispose of far-reaching autonomy so as to be able to reconcile the particular needs of each community. We could expect that a context in which much attention is paid to diverse needs and interests makes accepting intersectionality more likely as a means to accommodate diverse needs.

Cases, methods, and data

The Belgian and German cases both originate in first-wave feminism and are nowadays organised in overarching umbrella organisations, bringing together many different groups and initiatives in countries with an increasingly diverse population. Nevertheless, the two countries look back on different trajectories regarding women's rights. The German women's movement was successful in gaining universal suffrage after WWI, while universal suffrage has never been a core claim of the Belgian women's movement (Meier 2012) and was only adopted after WWII. While the German gender equality regime, with its strong male breadwinner model, only recently has been weakened (Henninger and von Wahl 2018), Belgium surpassed this model already in the previous century with half of the female population in the age group 25 to 54 working by the mid-1980s (IGVM 2011). Belgium was from the start a multi-ethnic state with religious cleavages and a colonial heritage impacting its society after WWII, which makes it a likely case for intersectional aspects to be adopted in women's councils. Germany, on the other hand, is a less likely case for intersectionality given that societal cleavages occurred mainly along class with gender aspects subordinated or ignored (Marx Ferree 2012) and the idea of being an immigrant country integrating new citizens was strongly rejected until recently.

Because of the language divide, Belgium comprises two women's councils, respectively the Conseil de Femmes Francophones de Belgique (CFFB) and the Vrouwenraad (VR).[1] The VR has about 40 member organisations and the CFFB about 60, which difference is mainly because the CFFB counts more local sections of member organisations. But in both cases, members range from political parties' women's groups, trade union sections, professional organisations, and organisations targeting specific groups of women, but also broader organisations such as certain public administrations or international organisations such as Amnesty International. Both have close ties with the EWL (Lafon 2017a) and run its Belgian coordination, and both are members of the International Women's Council. Both umbrella organisations also have a similar structure, in which the everyday functioning is ensured by a director and a small staff. The director works together with the executive committee to prepare all major decisions. A specific feature of the CFFB and of the VR is that the executive committee is chaired by a president who is selected from alternating different ideological branches of the Belgian political spectrum, non-democratic parties excluded. This method means that the women's councils are always chaired by a woman with a particular tie to one of the political parties. Finally, there is the general meeting of members, which is the supreme decision-making body. Members have to adhere to the goals and values of the women's council as expressed in their statutes, the bottom line being the promotion of gender equality. Both the CFFB and the VR receive structural funding (as opposed to project funding), not from the federal government, but from the sub-state government of the same language group in charge of community-related matters, respectively the Federation of Wallonia – Brussels and the Flemish Community. Given the stronger financial situation of the latter, the VR disposes of more means than the CFFB. Both women's councils also obtain project funding from their government and sometimes also from other governments of the same language group (Celis and Meier 2017). Therefore, the CFFB and the VR are both well embedded within their own language group and also have international ties. They have a less strong and visible position at the federal level, unless they work together. But both are members of the federal Advisory Council of Equal Opportunities for Men and Women.

The DFR[2] comprises 60 member organisations ranging from trade union sections, church-affiliated women's groups, and lesbian groups to migrant women groups. Prerequisites for DFR membership are at least 90 percent female membership share or independent decision-making and representative bodies for female members in an organisation, more than 300 individual members in at least five Bundesländer, and two years of experience on the federal level. Applicants cannot simultaneously be members of other DFR member organisations. The general assembly decides on applications with a two-thirds majority required for approval. Leadership is organised into a board of volunteers and a central office with an executive director and currently 12 employees.

The DFR is a member of a variety of civil society organisations, public administration expert groups, prize committees, and organisation boards. It is the official German representative to the EWL, a member of the European Academy for Women in Politics and Economy, and a founding member of the national Forum for Equal Pay Day. It sits on the advisory board of the Federal Antidiscrimination Agency as well as in expert groups or advisory boards of several ministries, including the monitoring committee for implementing the European Social Fund in Germany. The DFR is the only German women's organisation receiving structural funding from the federal government (Icken 2002). Hence, the DFR is nationally and internationally well embedded in networks, interest groups, and civil society, and – compared to other German women's organisations – privileged as regards access to policymaking and funding. According to its website, the DFR completely reorganised in 2016 with the goal of being better able to respond to today's societal challenges. Since then, the member meetings adopt an annual work programme with core topics; in 2016–2017, for instance, topics selected were refugees and integration, women's health, and federal elections.

Towards our goal of analysing what role intersectionality plays in these women's umbrella organisations, we relied on secondary literature to understand the history of these organisations and publicly accessible primary data, mainly from the organisation's own websites, on the current situation. Data analysed comprises statutes, information on member organisations, the organisations' team and leadership, annual reports, website content, newsletters, press releases, conference proceedings, and policy briefs.

We looked for signs of intersectionality in organising the women's councils (descriptive representation for the offices and also in member organisations) and in doing intersectionality (substantive representation for policy issues like employment, migration, and family), and we tried to detect whether the organisations challenge their own power and privileges. In the following sections we present, first, the historical account of intersectional engagement – as this history, in our view, determines profoundly whether, how, and why the three organisations become more inclusive in the present. Next, we provide snapshots of how the women's councils deal with intersectionality descriptively and substantively.

Institutionalising national women's councils

Belgium: from one to two councils – gaining and losing intersectional dimensions

The Belgian Women's Council was founded during the heyday of the first wave of feminism, in 1905, by Marie Popelin, a Belgian lawyer, well known for the fact that she had not been accepted to the bar for being a woman because she was 'too weak' to exercise such a function (the so-called Popelin Affair of 1892). She was also very active in the international women's movement and organised an international congress in Belgium in 1897. The Belgian delegates at that gathering decided to join in one national organisation, but it took them some years to put their idea into operation. The Belgian Women's Council brought together the League of Women's Rights (founded in the wake of the Popelin Affair), the Belgian Society for the Improvement of the Position of Women, and the Union of Belgian Women Against Alcoholism. These organisations – and by extension the Belgian Women's Council – were pluralistic, but many of the members were middle-class, liberal, anticlerical, and secular. It thus had a narrow ideological scope and agenda, limiting the range of gendered needs and interests and the solutions meant to tackle them. This situation did not facilitate the pursuit of an intersectional praxis (which was actually the case for all Belgian women's movement organisations). This particular composition has to be understood in the light of Belgian politics of that time, which were very much characterised by an ongoing struggle between liberal, vehemently secular anticlerical forces, the Catholic establishment, and the socialists on the rise since the late 1880s. Feminists with a socialist profile were mainly active within the Belgian Workers' Party, founded in 1885, and more particularly the National Federation of Socialist Women. Catholic and often clerical circles also founded initiatives to promote the position of women, most of which were mainly anti-socialist initiatives. Each major ideological tendency tried to tie citizens, and thus also women, to a broad network of organisations. This strong pillarisation of Belgian society explains the particular character of the Belgian Women's Council at its foundation. Actually, both Catholic and socialist feminists took their distance from the Belgian Women's Council and only joined decades later. In the beginning, the Belgian Women's Council grouped together mainly autonomous women's organisations, groups not part of one of the pillars characterising Belgian political and social life (Celis and Meier 2007).

Organisations such as the League of Women's Rights and the Belgian Society for the Improvement of the Position of Women strived for formal de jure and economic equality of the sexes, including the equality of men and women within marriage and women's full access to the labour market (including liberal professions and the public sector). These rights were considered more important than political rights. The Union of Belgian Women Against Alcoholism was the only founding organisation of the Belgian Women's Council striving for female suffrage, as such a gain would allow women to make politicians tackle the problem of alcoholism. Many liberals and socialists feared that mainly the Catholics would benefit from female suffrage and maintained a low profile on this topic, which led to an atypical situation in which mainly the Catholics defended female suffrage in Belgium (Meier 2012).

After some early political victories, the Belgian Women's Council suspended its activities during WWI and remained low profile until the mid-1930s, when the liberal Marthe Boël was elected president. She chaired the Belgian Women's Council until 1952 (in combination with the presidency of the International Women's Council from 1936 to 1947). During WWII, activities again were kept to a low profile. After WWII, education, women's access to all segments of the labour market, equal pay, and the subordinate position of married women remained high on the agenda. The National Women's Council was by then also fighting for their full political rights. The Council broadened its number of permanent committees and working groups and started organising conferences from 1950 onwards. The number of member organisations rose, and the women's organisations of the major pillars, mainly Catholic and socialist, joined.

The second feminist wave led to the foundation of many new women's groups, broadening the horizon of topics to include abortion, but also drugs and health issues, the position of lesbian women, and more recently, prostitution, rape, and gender-based violence, many of which were also picked up by the Belgian Women's Council. Many of these topics led to tensions within all segments of the Belgian women's movement (the issue of abortion even led to an institutional crisis and a 24-hour abdication of the king in 1990), especially for organisations with a Catholic foundation or Catholic members. A less controversial issue was the descriptive representation of women – the struggle for gender quotas and parity democracy – notwithstanding the fact that many liberal feminists were not in favour of legislating for representation (De Weerd 1980).

However, in organisational terms, it is the rising language cleavage that has most marked the Belgian Women's Council. From the 1960s onwards, the struggle between Flemish and French actors dominated the political scene. It led to a linguistic split of (nearly) the entire political spectrum – parties, civil society organisations, the media, public administrations, and services – and finally a federalisation of Belgium in the early 1990s (Deschouwer 2012). This evolution also marked the Belgian Women's Council. In 1974, during the heyday of the second wave, the Flemish and French wings of the Belgian Women's Council developed their own self-contained structure, and in 1979, they split into the CFFB and the VR. Over the years, the two monolingual umbrella organisations have followed different routes. The VR developed into a stronger and more professional organisation than the CFFB, supported by extensive public funding from the Flemish Community, especially from the mid-1990s onwards when the sub-state level was fully operational. Another factor facilitating the professionalisation of the VR was the adoption of the open method of coordination (OMC)[3] by the Flemish government from 2005 onwards (Celis and Meier 2011). Inspired by this EU *modus operandi*, and in order to give shape to its gender mainstreaming policies, the Flemish government adopted an OMC cycle, which made the VR a structural consulting partner for the Flemish government, providing it with stability and permanent access to the government. The CFFB is less structurally connected to the government and has maintained more of a civil society organisation character.

While the Belgian Women's Council initially hosted mainly middle-class, liberal, secular, and anticlerical women's organisations, it evolved into a pluralist and more intersectional umbrella organisation once the large Catholic and socialist women's organisations joined. Taking into consideration a broader diversity of women, it was also more open to a broader range of intersections and their political and social consequences. This trend was reinforced as the political parties saw their own women's groups emerge, most of which joined the umbrella organisation of their language group. The CFFB and VR lost part of their intersectional dimension when splitting into monolingual umbrella organisations, thereby subordinating the concept of women to that of language groups. But both umbrella organisations further broadened their scope at the same time, to women with a non-Belgian background and to lesbian women. This shift did not go without major tensions, as will be explained later.

Germany[4]: the DFR and closed doors to intersectional aspects

Over time, all German women's movements have become institutionalised and part of policymaking, yet, the processes differed widely in the different waves (Marx Ferree 2012). The origin of the German women's movements is simultaneously characterised by a joint struggle for universal suffrage and social and citizenship rights as well as strong divisions and mobilisations along class lines; class was the dominating intersectional aspect in Germany and other categories were almost (made) invisible until the 1980s (Marx Ferree 2012; Weber 2015). While the Weimar Republic brought universal suffrage, abortion as an element of women's rights found no broad support in parliament and, in conjunction with the German male breadwinner model, excluded women and their movements from the public sphere. The situation deteriorated during the fascist period (1933–1945), when women's movements either dissolved themselves or were replaced by fascist women's organisations (Marx Ferree 2012, pp. 38–43). Immediately after WWII, multiple local women's movements and organisations emerged facing broader organisational problems due to legal restrictions on associations in the three sectors governed by France, the United Kingdom, and the United States, and also due to cleavages about movement issues (Icken 2002, pp. 52–54). The 1950s brought the foundation of the 'Informationsdienst für Frauenfragen' (Information Service for Women) in the American sector, and the 'Deutscher Frauenring' (German Women's Circle) in the British Sector, which merged as DFR in 1969 (Icken 2002). Many of the member organisations at this point were the successors of pre-war conservative or church-based organisations, focused on family issues and civic education rather than interfering with (party) politics, and opposed to the socialist women's movements that were prevalent in the sector governed by the Soviet Union (Icken 2002, pp. 52–76; Marx Ferree 2012, pp. 44–46). Hence, the DFR was a quite old-fashioned and conservative organisation, satisfied with the formal principle of equality between men and women included in the new German constitution.

The second-wave movement organisations clashed with the DFR not only on the concept of motherhood but also about institutionalised involvement in politics (Marx Ferree 2012). They rejected the DFR as a bourgeois women's movement, and instead linked up with Marxist traditions and the proletarian women's movement; the latter not well represented by the DFR (Gerhard 1982). According to Sabine Lang (2007), the NGO-isation that took place in the German feminist movement from the 1980s onwards changed little in this regard. Lang (2007, p. 138f) identifies three distinct organisational clusters: (1) the DFR as the accepted centralised representative of German women's civil society in politics; (2) smaller and decentralised grassroots organising projects, like women's shelters and other services, dependent on the will of local politics to provide public funding; and (3) 'femocrats' and feminist or women's advocates that work within state institutions, parties, and universities.

The positions of the DFR regarding engagement in politics changed over time, as did the preference for the male breadwinner model, making the DFR a little more 'liberal-leaning . . . in protests for gender equality in pay and employment' (Marx Ferree 2012, p. 210). The change was partly related to the new supranational EWL in 1990 and its – from a DFR perspective – progressive stance on gender equality (ibid., p. 211). The DFR strongly lobbied for the establishment of the EWL and became the primary German representative to it (Icken 2002, p. 139). Simultaneously, the DFR became more 'permeable' (Icken 2002, pp. 165, 190f); its members became more numerous and diverse, for instance with lesbian as well as single parents organisations joining, and through engagement during reunification. Nonetheless, becoming a member of the DFR was not always easy given the regulations (limited to organisations meeting a certain level of individual membership) and membership fees that make it difficult for (local) organisations operating with limited funding (Icken 2002).

Of Lang's (2007) three clusters promoting women's rights, the German public administration and the DFR were less receptive to certain intersectional aspects. The Aktionsbündnis muslimischer Frauen Deutschland (AmF; Action Coalition of Muslim Women), for instance, had to fight hard to be acknowledged as a representative organisation and was still not invited to core expert groups. Weber (2015, p. 29) traces this development to the way in which religious difference, specifically Islam, is racialised in Germany. She highlights that ideas of intersectionality were already present in German feminist thought in the 1980s and women of colour and migrant heritage carried out the majority of such research; a contribution often simply neglected by white German feminists (Weber 2015, p. 27f; see also Marx Ferree 2012). As for the DFR, female migrant organisations were still not listed as members by 2002 (Stoehr and Pawlowski 2002). The AmF, for instance, registered formally as an association to prove DFR eligibility (minimum 300 individual members in five Bundesländer, 90 percent female members, and two years of federal activities). Likewise, intersectional queer and/or feminist activism in Germany increased considerably with foci on different intersections clearly outside the institutionalised women's organisations, while a (neo)liberal feminism appeared simultaneously (Degele and Winker 2010).

The development of the internet also impacted mobilisation and communication activities of the DFR. Knappe and Lang (2014), examining differences in the British and German women's movements, found that networks among German women's movements are highly centralised and institutionalised as well as stratified along certain issues; the DFR was the second most important actor next to the Federal Ministry for Family, Seniors, Women and Youth, with all other actors having much fewer network links (ibid., p. 366f). The overall set-up of the German network affects its strategies, with more one-way information-providing interactions than interactions among members, leading even to almost total silence in recent online mobilisations around sexual harassment. Knappe and Lang (2014, p. 375) point out that a 'few powerful actors dominate and possibly block participation by diverse actors' and that the DFR, with its institutional funding, 'adds to the prevalence of institutional advocacy.'

Intersectionality?

Against these different trajectories of women's umbrella organisations in Belgium and Germany, we explore how far intersectionality is picked up as an approach to inclusivity and a method of organising in the two countries. As a start, we found that explicit mentions of intersectionality as a term were close to non-existent on the organisations' extensive websites.[5] Yet, when looking at descriptive and substantive representation, the judgment is not so clear.

The CFFB and VR – struggling to truly engage with intersectionality

In terms of descriptive representation, both umbrella organisations cover the traditional ideological and philosophical divides characterising Belgian society and go beyond them. They both include Jewish women's organisations, those focusing on migrants and ethnic minorities (meaning, having a Muslim background), and the African Great Lakes Region (mainly Congo). Contrary to the CFFB, the VR also counts a LGBTQI umbrella organisation among its members. However, this apparent diversity loses scope when one considers which civil society organisations and other actors operating in the broad feminist field are not members of the CFFB or VR. For instance, Ella, a major expertise centre on gender and ethnicity, focusing initially on Muslim women but broadening its scope over time and explicitly adopting an intersectional approach, has chosen not to be a member of the VR. The same goes for other organisations focusing on women with a Muslim background, with respect to both the CFFB and the VR, and for LGBTQI organisations, especially when it comes to the CFFB. While the umbrella organisations cover the diversity of the traditional Belgian ideological and philosophical landscape, they are less successful when it comes to the diversity and intersections characterising Belgian society today.

The CFFB counts a more diverse range of profiles among its board and staff members than the VR. While the latter looks very Flemish, the CFFB counts more people from different national backgrounds characterising the Belgian population. This diversity might be explained by the fact that the VR tends to focus on the Flemish level, while the CFFB is traditionally strongly embedded in Brussels and represents its diversity. That said, there are limits to this diversity, and numerous intersections are missing. The CFFB actually still carries part of the heritage of the National Women's Council: many of its leading figures are liberal or socialist, but especially strictly secular. While their geographic roots may vary, including in the religious or philosophical backgrounds that come with that difference, the group is still very homogenous and not much different from the profiles of board and staff members of the VR. While both umbrella organisations show openings to diversity in their descriptive representation, intersectionality is by no means mainstreamed at that level. This limited descriptive representation is not an issue of conscious tokenism on behalf of the umbrella organisations. It rather is a mixture of their incapacity to truly broaden their scope and a number of organisations therefore not wanting to join, as will be explained later.

The same issue can be found when looking at the substantive dimension of representation, to an extent that it explains part of the lack of intersections in the descriptive dimension. Lafon (2017b) points, for instance, at the strictly secular character of the CFFB, rooted in a strong adherence to the French tradition of universalism, and the way in which this principle led to a vehement opposition to the headscarf. This position led to a major conflict within the CFFB, in the wake of which a number of member organisations left the CFFB. Amongst them were also women's and feminist organisations not (primarily) representing Muslim women, such as the Belgian network for gender studies, because they no longer recognised themselves in an umbrella organisation standing only for a segment of Belgian women and not representing their diversity – and actually reflecting and reproducing white privilege. The debate on the headscarf led to similar, though less vehement, discussions within the VR. Similarly, both the CFFB and the VR take a strict abolitionist position when it comes to prostitution, relating it to human trafficking, defining it essentially as a form of violence, and seeing it as an ultimate expression of a patriarchal system. Again, this makes a number of women's or feminist organisations, working on prostitution or not, feel out of sync with the position taken by the umbrella organisation, and therefore they prefer not to be part of it. Another example are LGBTQI actors. Only one such organisation is a member of the VR; the CFFB counts none of them in its ranks, only some individual lesbian women who do not represent an organisation. Many LGBTQI actors consider the umbrella organisations to be too institutionalised and not radical enough in their theoretical and political approach (Lafon 2017b). They ignore or neglect many issues of concern to LGBTQI people, again a reason not to be a member.

Indeed, if we look at the main topics dealt with by both women's councils, we find a predominant focus on schooling and education; women's participation in the labour market, the pay gap, and the career gap; maternity rights, parental leave, father's leave, child care, and care work; the gender bias in social security and fiscal rights discriminating towards couples; the precarious position of mainly women after divorce, an insufficient protection of alimony rights, and the female face of poverty in general; the prevalence of, insufficient legal and other protection against and assistance in case of sexism, rape, and gender-based violence in general; the gendered nature of human rights, war, and the recognition of the importance of women in peace processes, women migrants, refugees, and their limited asylum rights. While the range of topics addressed is broad, issues of importance to migrant women, especially from different ethnic or religious backgrounds, LGBTQI people, as well as problems related to ageism and disability, are close to if not completely absent. The closest either come is the CFFB's inclusion of interculturality; by which it refers to cultural differences and minorities, but exclusively framing their issues in terms of precarious positions in education, the labour market, housing, and other related areas. While relevant, this focus reduces the topic of interculturality to one of social position and class, without addressing interculturality as such. It therefore is not only a good showcase of epistemic privilege, but also explains why many groups do not feel represented by the CFFB.

What Lafon (2018) calls the 'Belgian consensual spirit' indeed seems to characterise the two women's councils. While having broadened their scope, they did not adopt all intersections characterising Belgian society, let alone mainstream them in the descriptive and substantive dimension of their representative work. They do not speak for all women, and therefore lose some women's and feminist organisations. While it might be difficult for umbrella organisations to come up with sharp positions and still defend all intersections, they do not seem to problematise the fact that they therefore do not take into account particular intersections.

The DFR – opening up to intersectional approaches

The DFR's 60 member organisations come from a multitude of backgrounds: church/faith-based organisations (Protestant, Catholic, Jewish, Muslim), women's caucuses of all major political parties (plus the feminist party), professional women's associations (doctors, academics, midwives, craftswomen, domestic workers, business and management, social workers, engineers, science and technology, arts, equal opportunity officers of public administration, civil servants, etc.), migrant women's organisations, trade unions, feminist and lesbian groups (webgrrrls, Weibernetz, Lesbenring, etc.), disabilities associations, women's shelter associations, family and mother associations (single parents, binational parents, working mothers), and social, cultural, and sports associations. The original members by now form a small minority, and this broadening over time demonstrates the ability of the DFR to include intersectional groups in the mainstream movement.

While the member organisations cover a broad range, this diversity does not translate equally well into who represents the DFR in public. The board consists of five white, older, middle-class women from a sports association, a Protestant and Catholic organisational background, the Christian Democratic Party (CDU), and a business association; quite similar to the founding members. The DFR office team of 12 women seems more diverse as it includes women of colour and/ or with surnames not typically considered originating from Germany.

By definition of membership rules and highlighted by its descriptive representation, the DFR sticks to its roots and clearly puts gender first: associations not dominated by women are prohibited as members, but every organisation putting gender first can apply to join the DFR umbrella. Despite its broad membership, we found no indication in DFR documents that making the board more diverse is an issue; who represents 'all women' is not problematised.

With a view to substantive representation and intersectionality, we find more variation in the DFR repertoires. In 2015, the DFR initiated the Convention on the Elimination of all Forms of Discrimination Against Women (CEDAW) shadow report, which was then compiled by 38 organisations consisting of DFR members and other volunteering organisations recruited through an open call. Reporting has become quite an institutionalised process in which the DFR holds a privileged position and receives government funding for its organising work. Nevertheless, the CEDAW process shows the DFR's ability to use intersectionality as a coalition strategy and to include representatives of different intersectional groups beyond their members and on an equal level. Moreover, the final text allowed for expressing specific issues in the context of a mainstream agenda.[6] The DFR accentuated the horizontal – read: intersectional – application of issues like employment, age, poverty, health, disabilities, LGBTQI, migration and refugees, East and West German differences, racism, and social class; all working groups had to reflect on all issues and also their intersections.

When we look more into how the DFR deals with intersectionality in policy fields, we see that challenging their (epistemic) privilege (Evans and Lépinard, this volume) occurs unevenly and selectively. Migration and asylum have dominated the policy debate in Germany since 2015, and the DFR also has selected it as a priority topic from 2016 to 2018. In 2018, the DFR, women migrant groups, and refugee support groups co-organised the conference 'Integration gemeinsam gestalten' (Shaping integration together) on supporting the societal integration of migrants and refugees. The DFR position paper resulting from its engagement with this topic highlighted the voice and input from women migrants and refugee organisations, but it was solely transmitted by the DFR to decision makers, not by all participants. Scrutinising the content of the position paper further shows that topics like social background, single parents and women minors, marriage and divorce, and gender-based violence were addressed, while other aspects like disabilities or LGBTQI rights did not appear or appeared only in other documents related to the topic.

The selective treatment of different intersectional aspects can also be found for family policy, which has changed considerably over the last decade in Germany (Henninger and von Wahl 2018). Here, marriage equality had been another hot topic until it was legislated in 2017. DFR documents are somewhat contradictory: whether LGBTQI issues appear or not varies greatly between different subject working groups. For instance, the DFR officially promotes trans rights and recently announced an internal debate about how to change in the light of overcoming gender binary concepts. Also, homosexual couples are simply mentioned alongside with heterosexual ones when demanding changes in health policy related to giving birth. Yet, the growing harassment and violence towards trans people is not mentioned in documents on gender-based violence, despite a major 2016 DFR campaign 'No means No' that resulted in Germany signing the Istanbul Convention and a considerable tightening of criminal law. Thus, LGBTQI rights are not consistently attended to in the DFR's work.

The DFR sometimes reflects on its limitations in treating intersectionality. In 2017, the W20 summit[7] brought together a broad range of international and national organisations and finished with the presentation of the W20 communiqué to German chancellor Angela Merkel. While the DFR highlighted the importance of W20 addressing gender equality, it also noticed and welcomed the criticism raised on the W20 as 'one-per-cent-feminism' or 'business feminism.' Overall, economic, social, and employment policy has become one of the most important areas of DFR engagement; quite a change compared to the DFR position after WWII (Marx Ferree 2012). Nevertheless, it is here that intersectional aspects are treated only marginally. The specific challenges of women migrants, older women, and disabled women are not visibly addressed. The focus is clearly on (working) class and motherhood, connected with discussions on minimum wage, return from parental leave to part-time to full-time work, and equal pay.

Conclusion

In this chapter we examined the Belgian and German women's umbrella organisations regarding their claims to represent all women. We used their official positions and publications to exemplarily investigate if intersectionality has become visible in their organisational structure and output. We were interested in whether and how old and institutionalised women's movement organisations change from within, regarding membership and topics addressed, and how these relate to intersectionality. What can we learn from our cases?

These three first-wave movement organisations were quite successful in surviving. Today, all three are institutionally privileged in accessing policymaking due to the firm institutionalisation in their national contexts over the course of time. Institutionalisation occurred despite (or alongside) critical junctures. WWII put their work on hold and led to post-war reorganisation. Moreover, the Belgian Women's Council had to adjust to federalisation and the German DFR to a new landscape after the reunification of the 1990s. However, external pressure cannot fully explain engagement with (or rather lack of) intersectional aspects, and explanations tend to differ for the three umbrella organisations. As for the DFR, the growing variety of members seemingly unfolds bottom-up pressure and results in slowly but steadily growing attention for intersectional aspects in political issues. The impact of increasingly diverse member organisations is not so clearly detectable for the CFFB or VR and needs more investigation in the future. For all three umbrella organisations, top-down pressure is an important factor in extending the political agenda (without necessarily engaging with intersectional aspects). That the EWL secretary general has originated from CFFB and from DFR reflects close ties. For CFFB and VR this also coincides with geographical closeness. Despite these connections, the national context strongly shapes which topics are picked up and whether intersectionality plays a role.

Indeed, the political opportunity structure is an important factor influencing intersectional engagement in these women's umbrella organisations. In Belgium, the consensus-building policy tradition, both within the organisations and overall, as well as their institutionalisation within the political system, limits (new) radical positions. The only exceptions are principles going back to their roots, such as patriarchy (in the case of prostitution) or secularism (in the CFFB position on the headscarf), but these rather contribute to blocking off intersectionality. The situation is different for the DFR, which can – with reference to its members – take a more pronounced or even conflictual position towards politics. The DFR can use its privileged position in German policy networks for promoting more progressive (although certainly not radical) positions.

From a more methodological point of view, a longitudinal thick description seems to be a fruitful approach to grasp current praxis of old movement organisations and the limited intersectional praxis they showcase. Still, a major challenge remains for all three umbrella organisations: how can they reconcile potentially contradictory intersectional positions? By becoming more diverse and broadening their scope, they also run the risk of intersectional interests conflicting. How can they solve this balancing act, what should they prioritise, and which theoretical principles might guide the umbrella organisations in this exercise? All of these questions bring us back to the root issue of how feminist principles are bound not only by place and time but also by intersections.

Notes

1 *Conseil de Femmes Francophones de Belgique.* www.cffb.be/; *Vrouwenraad beslist feminist* www.vrouwenraad.be/ [accessed 27 June 2019].
2 *Der Deutsche Frauenrat.* www.frauenrat.de/ [accessed 27 June 2019].
3 The OMC is a soft law mechanism typically using guidelines, indicators, and best practice sharing.

4   This chapter focuses on the developments of the DFR in former West Germany, the Federal Republic of Germany. For an overview of the history of former East Germany, the German Democratic Republic, and changes after reunification please see Marx Ferree (2012).
5   Two hits for the DFR; none for the CFFB and VR.
6   This information relies on data from the DFR as well as information provided by Petra Ahrens, who participated in the reporting process on behalf of one's organisation.
7   *W20 Argentina.* https://w20argentina.com/en/ [accessed 25 May 2019].

References

Ahrens, Petra. 2019. "Gender Equality and Intersectionality in Supranational 'Equality CSOs': A Mountain Skyline?" In *Gendered Mobilization and Intersectional Challenges: Contemporary Social Movements in Europe and North America*, edited by Jill Irvine, Sabine Lang, and Celeste Montoya, 244–261. London: Rowman & Littlefield.

Bassel, Leah, and Akwugo Emejulu. 2014. "Solidarity Under Austerity: Intersectionality in France and the United Kingdom." *Politics & Gender* 10 (1): 130–136.

Beckwith, Karen. 2013. "The Comparative Study of Women's Movements." In *The Oxford Handbook of Gender and Politics*, edited by Georgina Waylen, Karen Celis, Johanna Kantola, and S. Laurel Weldon, 411–436. Oxford: Oxford University Press.

Celis, Karen, and Petra Meier. 2007. "State Feminism and Women's Movements in Belgium: Complex Patters in a Multi-Level Setting." In *Changing State Feminism: Women's Policy Agencies Confront Shifting Institutional Terrain*, edited by Johanna Kantola and Joyce Outshoorn, 62–81. New York, NY: Palgrave Macmillan.

Celis, Karen, and Petra Meier. 2011. "Convergence and Divergence: The Federalization of Belgian Equality Politics." *Regional and Federal Studies* 21 (1): 55–71.

Celis, Karen, and Petra Meier. 2017. "Other Identities in Ethnofederations: Women's and Sexual Minorities' Advocacy in Belgium." *National Identities* 19 (4): 415–432.

Crenshaw, Kimberlé. 1991. "Mapping the Margins: Intersectionality, Identity Politics and Violence Against Women of Color." *Stanford Law Review* 43 (6): 1241–1299.

Degele, Nina, and Gabriele Winker. 2010. "Feminismen im Mainstream, in Auflösung – oder auf intersektionalen Pfaden." *Freiburger Frauenstudien* 24: 79–93.

Deschouwer, Kris. 2012. *The Politics of Belgium: Governing a Divided Society.* New York, NY: Palgrave Macmillan.

De Weerd, Denise. 1980. *En de vrouwen? Vrouw, vrouwenbeweging en feminisme in België: 1830–1960.* Ghent: Masereelfonds.

Gerhard, Ute. 1982. "A Hidden and Complex Heritage: Reflections on the History of Germany's Women's Movement." *Women's Studies International Forum* 5 (6): 561–567.

Hancock, Ange-Marie. 2007. "When Multiplication Doesn't Equal Quick Addition: Examining Intersectionality as a Research Paradigm." *Perspectives on Politics* 5 (1): 63–79.

Henninger, Annette, and Angelika von Wahl. 2018. "This Train Has Left the Station: The German Gender Equality Regime on Course Towards a Social Democratic Model (2013–17)." *German Politics*. doi:10.1080/09644008.2018.1551484

Icken, Angela. 2002. *Der Deutsche Frauenrat.* Berlin: VS Verlag für Sozialwissenschaften.

IGVM. 2011. *Vrouwen en mannen in België. Genderstatistieken en -indicatoren. Editie 2011.* Brussels: IGVM.

Irvine, Jill, Sabine Lang, and Celeste Montoya, eds. 2019. *Gendered Mobilization and Intersectional Challenges: Contemporary Social Movements in Europe and North America*. London: Rowman & Littlefield.

Knappe, Henrike, and Sabine Lang. 2014. "Between Whisper and Voice: Online Women's Movement Outreach in the UK and Germany." *European Journal of Women's Studies* 21 (4): 361–381.

Lafon, Claire. 2017a. "La professionnalisation des militantes féministes au sein du Lobby Européen des Femmes: le cas des salariées spécialisées et des bénévoles nationales déléguées au LEF." In *La professionnalisation des luttes pour l'égalité: genre et féminisme*, edited by Petra Meier and David Paternotte, 67–86. Louvain-La-Neuve: Academia L'Harmattan.

Lafon, Claire. 2017b. "Research Notes Field Work Brussels 20/04/2017." Unpublished paper. Brussels: Université Saint Louis.

Lafon, Claire. 2018. "Europeanization Through the European Women's Lobby: A Sociological Comparison of the French and Belgian National Coordinations." *Journal of Contemporary European Research* 14 (2): 154–168.

Lang, Sabine. 2007. "Gender Governance in Post-Unification Germany: Between Institutionalization, Deregulation, and Privatisation." In *Changing State Feminism*, edited by Joyce Outshoorn and Johanna Kantola, 124–143. Houndmills, Basingstoke: Palgrave Macmillan.

Lépinard, Eléonore. 2014. "Doing Intersectionality: Repertoires of Feminist Practices in France and Canada." *Gender & Society* 28 (6): 877–903.

Marx Ferree, Myra. 2012. *Varieties of Feminism: German Gender Politics in Global Perspective*. Stanford, CA: Stanford University Press.

McBride, Dorothy, and Amy Mazur. 2013. "Women's Policy Agencies and State Feminism." In *The Oxford Handbook of Gender and Politics*, edited by Georgina Waylen, Karen Celis, Johanna Kantola, and S. Laurel Weldon, 654–678. Oxford: Oxford University Press.

Meier, Petra. 2012. "Caught Between Strategic Positions and Principles of Equality: Female Suffrage in Belgium." In *The Struggle for Female Suffrage in Europe: Voting to Become Citizens*, edited by Blanca Rodriguez-Ruiz and Ruth Rubio-Marin, 407–420. Leiden: Brill.

Mohanty, Chandra Talpade. 2003. *Feminism Without Borders: Decolonizing Theory, Practicing Solidarity*. Durham, NC: Duke University Press.

Nyhagen Predelli, Line, and Beatrice Halsaa. 2012. *Majority-Minority Relations in Contemporary Women's Movements: Strategic Sisterhood*. Houndmills, Basingstoke: Palgrave Macmillan.

Sanchez Salgado, Rosa. 2014. *Europeanizing Civil Society: How the EU Shapes Civil Society Organizations*. Houndmills, Basingstoke: Palgrave Macmillan.

Stoehr, Irene, and Rita Pawlowski. 2002. *Die unfertige Demokratie: 50 Jahre "Informationen für die Frau"*. Berlin: Deutscher Frauenrat.

Strid, Sofia. 2014. *Gendered Interests in the EU: The European Women's Lobby and the Organization and Representation of Women's Interests*. Saarbrücken: GlobeEdit.

Strolovitch, Dara Z. 2007. *Affirmative Advocacy: Race, Class, and Gender in Interest Group Politics*. Chicago, IL: Chicago University Press.

Stubbergaard, Ylva. 2015. "Conflict and Cooperation: Interactions Among EU-Level Civil Society Organisations in the Field of Gender Equality." In *EU Civil Society: Patterns of Cooperation, Competition and Conflict*, edited by Hakan Johansson and Sara Kalm, 119–136. Houndmills, Basingstoke: Palgrave Macmillan.

Verloo, Mieke. 2006. "Multiple Inequalities, Intersectionality and the European Union." *European Journal of Women's Studies* 13 (3): 211–228.

Weber, Beverly M. 2015. "Gender, Race, Religion, Faith? Rethinking Intersectionality in German Feminisms." *European Journal of Women's Studies* 22 (1): 22–36.

Wiercx, Joke. 2011. *Democratic Legitimacy of European Social Movement Organizations: All for One and One for All?* Baden-Baden: Nomos.

Yuval-Davis, Nira. 2012. "Dialogical Epistemology – An Intersectional Resistance to the 'Oppression Olympics'." *Gender and Society* 26 (1): 46–54.

Chapter 4

Intersectional complexities in gender-based violence politics

Sofia Strid and Mieke Verloo

Introduction

Violence is a crucial domain for better understanding intersectionality: the field of gender-based violence is at the heart of reflections on intersectionality and its exclusionary effects. The seminal article by K. Crenshaw (1991) (who coined the term but not the concept) indeed developed the framework of intersectionality based on an empirical investigation of gender-based violence politics in the US. But neither intersectionality, nor its relation to violence, started with Crenshaw; there has been a long running interest in how to conceptualise, theorise, and empirically analyse multiple simultaneously existing inequalities and the relationship between social groups, social justice projects, and feminist movements (Hartmann 1976; Brownmiller 1976; Verloo 2006; Walby, Armstrong, and Strid 2012). Because violence is shaped by social positions and gender orders, and multiple inequalities are cause and consequence of gender-based violence, violence is a crucial domain for better understanding intersectionality. Consequently, there cannot be a sound understanding of gender-based violence and its mechanisms without including intersectional components of gender inequality in its definition and practice.

This chapter explores feminist politics against violence as a social justice project, referring not only to feminist movements organised against gender-based violence, or what might be called the violence against women movement, but invoking a broader social justice project that involves a mixture of activism, political work, policy development, and research. For this 'feminist project', the chapter shows how intersectional gender relations regarding race, class, nationality, sexuality, age, and disability have been addressed in their politics against violence. The chapter provides a critical analysis of the ways in which these feminist politics integrate, or not, intersectionality in their processes.

The chapter assesses if the crux of intersectionality politics has indeed been applied in the domain of gender-based violence: how is gender-based violence politics inclusionary or exclusionary of other equality projects? The chapter asks, do the considered forms of gender-based violence have an impact on the inclusion/exclusion of inequalities? Second, does the framing of gender-based violence policy, including whether this framing is explicitly gendered, have an impact on the inclusion/exclusion of inequalities? It shows that the ways in which gender-based violence is focused, framed, and de/gendered enable and/or prevent the inclusion of multiple inequalities and intersectionality in specific ways, thereby privileging some inequalities over others.

To explore and untangle the intersectional complexities involved in gender-based violence politics, we first address the articulation and the conceptual links between intersectionality and violence. To truly incorporate intersectionality as part of analysing gender-based violence is challenging for a range of reasons; two important, and related, ones are conceptual: the multiple meanings of inter-sectionality and of violence (see e.g. Cho, Crenshaw, and McCall 2013; Lutz, Herrera Vivar, and Supik 2011; Van der Haar and Verloo 2013; Hearn 2013; Walby et al. 2017). For researchers, activists, policymakers, and service provid-ers alike, it is imperative to make progress on this; there is a need to clarify these conceptual matters so that research, activism, policies, and services can be bet-ter, more focused, and more inclusive. If gender is always already intersected by other inequalities, there is a need to ensure that gender-based violence politics integrates intersectionality. This chapter therefore aims first to untangle some of the complexities involved by clarifying a perspective on intersectionality and a perspective on violence.

Second, the chapter draws on illustrative examples from gender-based vio-lence policy in Sweden, the Netherlands, and the UK. We illustrate how the forms of violence studied or politicised, as well as the framing of these policies (included their genderedness), impact the potential for addressing intersectional violence. In our analysis of the three countries, we argue that the dominant form of gender-based violence addressed is domestic violence. This form of violence is traditionally and continually associated with the private sphere and is not conducive to bringing attention to intersectionality, undermining the inclusion of multiple inequalities. Further, we argue, the fragmentation and degender-ing of gender-based violence politics negatively affect the possibilities for inclusivity. We find that the relative invisibility of intersecting inequalities in policy debates is, in part, caused by the process of degendering. Degendering may lead to exclusionary policy, and we argue that degendering should there-fore be done cautiously as it seems that, in our material, it prevents an overall framing of gender-based violence as inequality. Not only is power lost when policy is degendered, but it is harder to bring attention to how other dimen-sions of power – centring on race, class, sexuality, age, and ability – produce violence, by themselves or in their intersections. Simultaneously, minoritised women remain invisible in policy whether it is degendered or not. In focusing on the relations between different political domains, we show how (sensitiv-ity to) intersectionality in the domain of violence needs to include attention to developments in other domains, such as economy or the polity.

The chapter concludes by showing how our approaches contribute to a more comprehensive understanding of intersectionality and of gender-based violence.

Conceptual and theoretical frameworks: social complexity theory, intersectionality, and violence

On intersectionality

To clarify the concept of intersectionality, Crenshaw's classic distinction between structural and political intersectionality is a good starting point (Crenshaw 1991).[1] Structural intersectionality occurs when inequalities and their intersections are directly relevant to the experiences of people in society. Political intersectionality indicates how inequalities and their intersections are relevant to political strategies, and how strategies on one axis of inequality are seldom neutral toward other axes. By simultaneously paying attention to strategies for coalition building *between* social justice projects and between inequalities *within* a social justice project, political intersectionality combines 'coalitional intersectionality' and 'intersectionality as a repertoire for inclusivity' (Evans and Lépinard, introduction, this volume).

When studying violence, thinking in terms of *structural intersectionality* means asking questions about how different social categories are affected by (different forms of) violence, and how different social categories might be involved in doing violence. The structural intersectionality question is about how other inequality regimes intersect with the gender regime, creating incentives and opportunities for violence, and about differentiating which persons socially located at the intersections of these inequality regimes are most at risk from violence.[2] Research has shown that who is affected by violence and who is performing[3] violence is strongly linked to social positioning on inequality dimensions such as gender, race/ethnicity, class, ability, and sexuality (McLennen 2005; Armstrong, Strid, and Walby 2007; Armstrong, Walby, and Strid 2009; Hearn et al. 2016). The direction observed when multiple inequalities are considered is that violence occurs from the relatively privileged or dominant to the subordinated or relatively disadvantaged. This observation is contrary to conventional, non-intersectional studies within, for example, sociology, psychology, or criminology, which contend that violence is the acting out, protest, or reaction of the socially and economically disadvantaged or otherwise dysfunctional individuals or families. At the intersections of inequality regimes, specific patterns or forms of violence can occur. Taking structural intersectionality seriously in policy on gender-based violence requires making all forms of violence and the intersections between inequalities and domains and framings visible, and doing so within a framework of a gender regime/patriarchy (Armstrong et al. 2009; Strid, Walby, and Armstrong 2013).

To understand gender-based violence in its intersectional dimensions also requires a broader framework of not just the intersecting inequality regimes impacting it, but also potentially competing or solidarising social justice projects, or projects working against social justice (Verloo 2018). *Political intersectionality* shifts the focus from societal violence to actions; to what is being done in reaction to violence. Given the political nature of such actions, in this chapter we distinguish between what is being done to address the causes and the consequences of violence. An important part of understanding political intersectionality in gender-based violence thus implies analysing how the feminist project manages (or not) to work against intersectional gender-based violence[4] in coalition with other social justice projects. Drawing on Weldon (2006) and what Evans and Lépinard (introduction, this volume) call intersectionality as the basis for coalition, this task means exploring how intersectionality can be used as a strategy for coalition building, through policy and politics.

In this perspective, we must scrutinise how both movements and the state define what violence is, what forms of violence are legitimate or not, and what is offered in terms of prevention, protection, and sanctioning (Krizsán, Skjeie, and Squires 2012). The feminist movements, the civil rights movements, and the LGBTQI movements all have a long history of questioning forms of violence that were deemed legitimate or accidental and exposing them as pervasive structures of oppression. What might be called the violence against women movement, involving a mixture of activism, political work, policy development, and research, has addressed intersectional gender relations regarding race, class, nationality, sexuality, age, and disability for many years (Brownmiller 1976; Crenshaw 1989; Kelly 1988). In this body of work, the intersections of gender with class, ethnicity, and racialisation are often stressed (Sokoloff and Dupont 2005; Sosa 2017). Indeed, working-class women and minority ethnic and racialised women tend to be subject to more interpersonal violence, or at least more direct physical violence, whether from men in their own social stratum or from men from other, usually superordinate, social strata. Relative disadvantage on one social dimension is likely to increase vulnerability to interpersonal violence, for example, through lack of resources as affected by class, ethnic, and racialised subordination.

On violence

Research has shown that the ways in which actors propose or enact ways of addressing gender-based violence come with a large set of problems. One set is linked to the *framing of gender*: the link between gender inequality and violence can be ignored, denied, or strategically hidden through framing gender-based violence in various degendered ways, such as by using 'domestic violence' in legal texts, 'perpetrators of sexual assault' in policy texts, and 'family violence' in media texts. But the opposite can also happen, in that gender-based violence can be framed in essentialising ways, where all men are violent and all women are vulnerable.

Another set is linked to the *framing of gender-based violence*. There are many different ways of naming gender-based violence, including gender-based violence against women, violence against women, gender-based violence, family violence, intimate partner violence, gendered violence, and intersectional gender violence. Naming is not an innocent practice: each way of naming violence excludes or includes particular forms of violence, particular patterns, particular actors – and problem definitions and solutions. In our thinking about intersectional violence, we start from gender-based violence, both because of the extensive activism and scholarship about it and because we want to keep the attention on gender when addressing intersectionality. We chose the concept of gender-based violence because (a) it includes violence that is directed towards women because they are women (Watts and Zimmermann 2002), but (b) denotes gender rather than sex, and thereby expands to other categories than women only, and (c) underlines the gendered relationship between victims and perpetrators. The development of this naming and framing recognises the *structural* elements of violence; that is, that violence is shaped by social positions and gender orders and serves to maintain inequality (Lorber 2000; Russo 2006; Russo and Pirlott 2006; Watts and Zimmermann 2002). Gender-based violence is violence that is directed against a woman because of her gender, gender identity, or gender expression, or violence that affects persons of a particular gender disproportionately. The focus on the structural dimension opens the possibility to integrate attention to intersections with gender inequality. In our understanding, the definition allows for the inclusion of gender-based violence against cis women, transwomen, and transpersons and partly also violence targeting people outside of the heteronormative scheme.

Yet another part of understanding political intersectionality in the context of gender-based violence activism and policymaking is to analyse if and how different forms of violence are connected. Violence is not limited to physical injury; it includes forms of violence that may result in physical, sexual, emotional, psychological, or economic harm (Walby et al. 2017). It includes, but is not necessarily limited to, what is called domestic violence (e.g. violence by a current or former partner, spouse, or family member), sexual violence (e.g. rape, sexual assault, and sexual harassment), stalking, trafficking, harmful practices (e.g. forced marriage, female genital mutilation), so-called honour-related violence (e.g. threats, blackmail, retaliation for perceived crimes in accordance with family/clan laws) (see Baianstovu and Strid 2018), and cyber violence, including social media–amplified intimidations, threats, extortions of physical and sexual violence, stalking, shaming, and revenge pornography (Strid 2018; Hall and Hearn 2017).

The framing of gender and of gender-based violence, and the varying focus on different forms of violence, all impact the potential for intersectionality: minoritised women are often excluded, as they remain invisible in policy (Crenshaw 1991; Burman and Chantler 2005; Hankivsky and Cormier 2011); attention can be directed to some inequalities but exclude others, which produces analyses that are politically problematic, less policy-relevant, and less analytically sound (Bredström 2006); and intersectionality can be reduced to diversity, cultural difference, subjective experience, identity, and the uniqueness of the struggles of minoritised groups, resulting in structures of risk being left out of focus (Prins 2006; Verrlo 2006; Prins and Saharso 2008). Here again, the link between existing violence and specific inequalities can be ignored, denied, strategically hidden, or – in an opposite form – it can be highlighted, essentialised, and used to construct some human beings as always violent and others as eternal victims.

In the following section we present the empirical material used to illustrate the main arguments and the methods used to gather and analyse it. Then we introduce, briefly, how policy on gender-based violence has developed in our three countries, with a focus on what forms of violence have been named, which inequalities have been given visibility/been regarded as important – and how they intersect, and provide a section on the production of violence politics, including the framing of violence, the fragmentation of violence, and degendering strategies. Throughout this discussion we focus on how intersectionality is included. We then draw some tentative conclusions.

Studying intersectionality in gender-based violence politics in the Netherlands, Sweden, and the UK

The data used here to illustrate the conceptual arguments is based on and developed from the results of the EU Framework 6 funded project *Quality in Gender+ Equality Polices in Europe* (QUING) (2006–2011). QUING involved some 50 researchers from across Europe and analysed gender-based violence policy in all EU member states, Turkey, and the EU itself by exploring questions about differences, similarities, and inconsistencies in gender+ equality policies around Europe, the conceptualisation of gender and gender equality, and how gender relates to other grounds of inequality in policy. For this chapter, we draw on the data reports on intersectionality (activity STRIQ) and issue histories (activity LARG) originally produced for each EU member state, the EU, Croatia, and Turkey, and the sections on policy on gender+-based violence. In the QUING project, STRIQ studied how intersectionality and intersectional bias were dealt with in policies across the EU and its member states, and LARG was a frame analysis.[5] We base this chapter on the results of the analysis of intersectionality and framings of gender-based violence in laws, policy plans, parliamentary debates, and civil society texts. The material, some 2,000 policy documents, out of which some 500 are on gender-based violence, was gathered and analysed by national-level experts and researchers, with the instructions to sample policy documents based on the experts' assessments of the most prominent issues in their country of expertise. *Domestic violence* was the only form of violence that was sampled and analysed in all of the 31 cases/countries. This points towards at least two issues: domestic violence is the form of gender-based violence most prevalent in policy, and domestic violence is the form of gender-based violence believed by experts to be the most important to study in relation to gender in/equality.

We take here examples from three countries: the Netherlands, Sweden, and the UK, which are very different in terms of gender history and politics and relations of gender, feminism, and the state. The Netherlands, originally classified as a mixed welfare state regime (Esping-Andersen 1990), has a policy history marked by a shift from gendered to degendered and a fragmented policy field. Its history stands out with a specific gender focus in early policy plans, but a gradual degendering in later policies by turning attention to boys and men as (potential) victims and de-emphasising the gendered distribution of both victimisation and abuse (Lauwers and van der Wal 2010). Sweden, classified as a social democratic welfare state regime, has a history of hyper-gendering its state-centred gender-based violence policy field, and also has a history of state feminism. For example, Sweden is among the European countries with the most proactive policies on gender-based violence and where the state has long been seen as the ally of feminist projects. Finally, the UK, classified as a liberal welfare state regime, has a long history of feminist activism and mobilisation outside of – and to a large extent against – the state in the field of gender-based violence. This activism includes feminist pressure on the state and, sometimes, feminist involvement in local and central policy development (particularly with the women's refuge/shelter movement) even with a strong separatist tradition, increasingly in complex relations with state institutions that have been themselves subject to state cutbacks.[6] The differences between the three countries from which we draw our examples underline how our cases are used as strategic and selective illustrations rather than in the sense of 'comparative politics.' They do, however, make an excellent starting point for asking questions about the inclusion and exclusion of multiple inequalities.

A last note on methods: policy and legislation can be inclusive without explicitly mentioning multiple inequalities or intersectionality. There is a range of concepts and terms used in our policy documents to denote intersectionality and include disadvantaged women without indicating which intersections are meant specifically, and using only the formal categories of race, class, and sexuality: vulnerable women, women in the communities, homeless women, economically disadvantaged women, lone mothers, lower-skilled women, to name a few. For our analysis of gender-based violence and intersectionality, several groups are identified at the point of intersection within the policy field of violence against women, but one group especially stands out: ethnic minority women.[7]

Forms and degendering dynamics in gender-based violence politics

In this section, we examine the inclusion and exclusion of inequalities in gender-based violence policy in two ways. First, do the forms of gender-based violence that are considered have an impact on the inclusion/exclusion of inequalities? In other words, why does the focus on violence remain in the private sphere, and what are the consequences for intersectionality? Second, does the framing of gender-based violence policy, including whether this framing is explicitly gendered, have an impact on the inclusion/exclusion of inequalities?

Forms of violence and the inclusion/exclusion of inequalities

Not all violence is equal in the eyes of researchers, activists, policymakers, and service providers. Some forms of violence seem to matter more for certain actors. The choice of which form of violence to study is linked to the distinction between the public and the private sphere, because the various domains in which violence occurs have different links to inequality regimes and to equality projects, and because these domains should be analysed as each other's environment. The question then of course is, what violence is seen to matter, what violence is deprived of attention or gets skewed attention, and what are the consequences of these decisions, in particular for the inclusion and exclusion of multiple inequalities?

In the Netherlands, gender-based violence was first addressed comprehensively after the government invited feminist activists and policymakers to set goals and principles for state policy. In 1984 (after a nine-month window of opportunity with a feminist State Secretary for Social Affairs and Employment, responsible for the portfolios of equality and emancipation) a first policy plan was issued to fight violence against women. The plan adopted a feminist analysis of the problem and framed violence against women as a problem rooted in the unequal power relations between men and women and as a central mechanism for maintaining inequality. The comprehensive approach was followed by a focus on sexual violence with the *Progress Note on Policy to Combat Sexual Violence Against Women and Girls* (1990). In Sweden, the first naming of any form of gender-based violence was marital violence in 1764, but the actual politicisation of violence took place 200 years later and started, policy-wise, with the criminalisation of marital rape in 1965 (Kvist 2010; Wendt Höjer 2002).[8] In the UK, it was domestic violence that was first politicised (1976) as a result of civil society advocacy, involving NGOs such as Chiswick Women's Aid, which set up the first refuge for women and children who had experienced domestic violence in 1971 (Strid, Armstrong, and Walby 2010).

Hence, in both Sweden and the UK, policy on gender-based violence has developed from the domestic sphere, based on notions of heterosexual relationships/ marriage. In both countries, the policy field has focused on the private relationship between victim and perpetrator, based on the gendered categories of wife and husband. In the Netherlands, however, the field developed out of the concept of violence against women.[9] This choice for a particular domain is made to the detriment of other domains. If intimate partner violence and/or domestic violence are prioritised, then the main spotlight is on the private sphere, on kinship and relationships (what Verloo would call *cathexis* 2018). This domain comprises a specific intersection of inequality regimes: to a large extent, intimate partner relations are homogeneous in terms of age, class, race/ethnicity, and sexuality. If we interpret violence as a means of the powerful or privileged to enact their power or privilege, then the relative homogeneity of this domain impacts what violence will occur there. Intimate partner relations in a predominantly heteronormative society will mostly differ along sex/gender, and violence against women would be the expected form of violence. In contrast, racist violence might occur, but it will be less frequent given the scarcity of interracial marriages alone. Homophobic violence can occur, surely, but will be rare for similar reasons. In conclusion, a focus on intimacy tends to reduce the possibility to address intersectionality in gender-based violence politics.

Framing and fragmentation of violence and the inclusion/exclusion of inequalities

The locus of gender-based violence – public or private – is one part of the framing of the issue as a whole, which in turn influences the different framings of gender-based violence policies (Bacchi 1999; Verloo 2007; Lombardo and Rolandsen Augustin 2012). Different framings lead to, or make possible, more or less inclusionary policies for multiple inequalities and marginalised groups, as well as different social justice projects. To fully grasp intersectionality in the production of violence policy, one has to engage with how the problem of gender-based violence is framed: what is the 'problem' of gender-based violence and how does it address intersectionality? Gender-based violence can be framed as a crime and justice issue, leading to specific policy responses, or as a broader gender equality issue. We develop here how these diverging frames, as well as processes of fragmentation of the policy field, actually impact the inclusion and exclusion of multiply-marginalised women in the policy responses developed.

The Netherlands offers an example of how a crime and justice framing combined with the fragmentation of gender-based violence into multiple subfields enables exclusionary – i.e. non-intersectional – policy, which individualises the problem of violence and risks producing less relevant and sound policy solutions. First, in the Netherlands, where specific policies to combat gender-based violence developed in the 1980s, gender-based violence was initially framed as a problem of the unequal power relations between men and women, which structurally maintained the existence of inequality between men and women (Ministerie van Sociale Zaken en Werkgelegenheid en Ministerie van Justitie 1984). These early policies focused on different forms of sexual violence and included the inequality axes of gender, age, and ethnicity. The literal translation of violence framing from these early years is 'sexual violence against women,' a framing which focused on the form of violence rather than on perpetrators or victims. The contemporary period has seen a shift, from violence as a problem of gender equality to violence as a problem of crime and justice (Lauwers and van der Wal 2010, p. 26), indicating a focus on individual sanctioning rather than on empowerment or support for victims. Moreover, gender-based violence policy is fragmented into subfields of violence and linked to the specific labelling of certain types of violence as culturally specific, as in so-called honour crimes, female genital mutilation, forced marriage etcetera. Ethnicity has become a hypervisible intersectional inequality in these Dutch politics.

The crime and justice framing and fragmentation allows for a compartmentalisation and individualisation of the problem of violence: specific intersectional groups are singled out and included, whereas most of the privileged groups are excluded from the problem formulation. The 'majority' group or 'privileged' group is never seen as part of the problem. Ethnicised-gendered actors are a separate group that causes or is suffering from 'specific' problems. This means that groups at the intersection of gender and ethnicity are very visible – one could say that they are hypervisible – but this hypervisibility is not contributing to a better understanding of the social mechanisms of intersectional gender-based violence. While there is indeed attention to the problems of these groups, this attention is often exclusive of their interests, and at the same time, they are singled out as belonging to a culture that is problematic as such, in a context that is already stigmatising their culture and 'othering' them (see also Roggeband and Verloo 2007; Van der Haar and Verloo 2013; Emejulu and Bassel 2017).

In the UK, the same combination of ethnic hypervisibility, a crime and justice framing, and fragmentation of violence in policy are dominant. Framings of violence vary across the fragmented subfields. Nonetheless, the British Home Office portal paragraph on violence states:

> Violence against women and girls (VAWG) are *serious crimes*. These *crimes* have a huge impact on our *economy*, *health* services, and the *criminal* justice system. Protecting women and girls from violence, and supporting victims and survivors of sexual violence, remains a priority of this government.
>
> (Home Office 2018, emphasis added)

The same crime framing dominated the Conservative government's *Violence Against Women and Girls Strategy* (Home Office 2016) and the *Call to End Violence Against Women and Girls: Action Plan* (Home Office 2014). Two contemporary legal initiatives, the criminalisation of forced marriage (2014) and the coming into force of the coercive or controlling behaviour offence (2015), continue this crime framing. Further, policy on gender-based violence remains fragmented and divided into subfields: there is no single comprehensive legislation covering all forms of gender-based violence or violence against women. Instead, there is a range of legislation and policies against violence and abuse in general, which provide sanctions and remedies for various forms of violence against women.

The narrow focus on crime, perpetrators, and punishment coexists with few visible intersections between gender and other inequalities. The most frequently named inequalities are ethnicity (ethnic minorities) and age (children). Other intersections include, to a lesser extent, religion and national and migrant status. Overall, class, sexual orientation, marital/family status, and disability are rarely addressed in policy documents. Class as such is not named at all, but there is reference to class inequality by the designation of lower-skilled, unemployed, or economically disadvantaged groups, and there is reference to forms of violence that can specifically affect lone mothers, which, in the British context, is a reference to the intersection of gender and social class. Some minority groups are named, again, primarily based on ethnicity and religion: e.g. minority ethnic or racialised groups and minority or non-dominant religious groups. Majority groups are not named and never constructed as part of the problem of violence – the problem is minorities and victims. Here, we suggest that if policy is written such that minorities and victims are seen as the problem, they will be the ones that policy aims to change, rather than the majority groups and perpetrators. This focus means losing sight of the privileged and relatively powerful. It bears similarity to the debate on visions of gender equality in which the liberal vision of sameness 'demands' that women, to be treated equally, need to become the same as men. The relatively powerless and 'vulnerable,' in this view, are to become less vulnerable, empowered, and relatively powerful. Instead, we would argue that vulnerability – be it based on gender or ethnicity or sexuality – needs not to be 'overcome,' but rather that societies need to be organised so that all people can be as vulnerable as they are.

In Sweden, the gender-based violence policy field was framed more broadly as a political concern throughout the 1970s; through successive phases of poli-cymaking, it was framed as an issue of unequal gendered power relations. By 1991, gender-based violence was framed as a gender equality issue and con-ceived as an expression of the unbalanced power relations between women and men: '[r]ape, assault and other abuse against women are serious expressions of a lack of equality and hence also for the current unbalanced power relations between the sexes' (Governmental Bill 1991) (see Wendt Höjer 2002 for the politicisation of violence against women). In the 2010s, the dominant fram-ing of gender-based violence in the Swedish policy context was still violence as a problem of gender equality, power, and oppression (see the *Action Plan for Combating Men's Violence Against Women, Violence and Oppression in the Name of Honour* (SOU 2015, p. 55) and *Violence in Same-Sex Relationships* (2007)). It was characterised as a major social problem that affects the whole of society. The crime framing was only prevalent within policy addressing rape and sexual violence. In the Swedish case, the analysed policy documents address gender, ethnicity, religion and beliefs, and sexuality with reference to violence in same-sex relationships. The Criminal Code requires a more severe punishment of a crime if the crime is motivated by hatred of a person due to that person's race, skin colour, nationality, ethnicity, religion/faith, sexual orienta-tion, or 'other similar circumstance' (Criminal Code, 29 §2).

In further contrast to the Dutch and British cases, and since 1997, in Sweden a comprehensive body of legislation on violence against women was collected under the Women's Peace Legislation (1997). It includes violence in an honour context, leading to a different form of visibility of 'the problem' of culturalised communities: minority men's (perceived or real) gender unequal attitudes and minority masculinities. Here, in contrast to the UK case, the relatively powerful (minority men) remain visible, rather than the relatively powerless (minority women). The equality framing of gender-based violence enables a comprehen-sive rather than a fragmented approach to gender-based violence, which also makes multiple inequalities and their intersections more visible in gender-based violence policy.

Degendering and intersectionality: ambivalent outcomes

This section uses the three countries to illustrate how gender-based violence is framed with different levels of gendering of policy, in turn impacting the visibility of multiple inequalities and their intersections. Our argument is that the relative invisibility of intersecting inequalities in policy debates is, in part, caused by the process of degendering. Degendering is not the same as gender blind or gender neutral: gender blind means the denial of gender inequality and its consequences for gendered people; gender neutral is the pretence that gender inequality does not reach certain parts of life; while degendering can range from attempts to formulate problematic gendered social positions in ways that do not contribute to further stereotyping (such as the phrasing 'persons who combine paid and unpaid labour') to ways of strategically hiding gender to enable alliances or results that are deemed good for feminist progress (see Lorber 2000; Strid et al. 2013).

British policy and debates show variations in the extent to which they are degendered, but the last 15 years have seen a rapid mobilisation of men's groups and their degendering of violence against women in arguing that the use of violence is gender balanced (Armstrong et al. 2007). Previously gendered categories have become degendered in policy on violence against women or are in the process of degendering. Examples include references to a 'victim of domestic violence' and a 'perpetrator of sexual assault.' When policy is degendered, there are no immediately visible intersections of gender and other inequalities. Degendering may lead to exclusionary policy, and we argue that degendering should be done cautiously, as it seems that it prevents an overall framing of gender-based violence as inequality. Not only is power lost when policy is degendered, but it is harder to include attention to how other dimensions of power, those centring on race, class, sexuality, age, and ability, produce violence, by themselves or in their intersections.

In the Netherlands, anti-violence policy on sexual harassment and domestic violence is often degendered, while policies against what is labelled honour-related violence and female genital mutilation are not (Lauwers and van der Wal 2010). Looking at the absences, class is a very clear absence in Dutch policies on violence. Lauwers and van der Wal (2010, p. 47) see the absence of class in the issue of gender-based violence as related to the degendering (especially in relation to domestic violence and sexual harassment) and to the uncoupling of the gender-based violence documents from the notion of structural gender inequality in the Dutch multi-year emancipation plans (2008–2011) – where class *is* mentioned in the chapter on violence against women. This plan states that the social-economic dependence of women on men is a cause of the unequal power between the genders and that violence against women in turn is a consequence of this power difference. In this generic gender equality plan the issue is gendered and linked to structural (power) inequalities between men and women in society, while in documents specifically dedicated to violence issues, this is not the case. The framing of violence as also linked to unequal resources between men and women opens a wider perspective that can include other social groups that are materially disadvantaged.

Swedish policy on gender-based violence was, in the examined period, not degendered to the same extent as British policy, nor does it show the 'hyper-visibility' of the intersection of gender and ethnicity as in the Dutch policy. 'Women' is the most common group referred to as victims of violence. Girls and young women are often mentioned in relation to honour-related crimes, but also boys, bisexuals, homosexuals, transgendered persons, and men. Honour-related crimes are described as different from other forms of violence due to its 'collective nature' with multiple perpetrators and victims (SOU 2015, p. 55). Perpetrators are predominantly named as men, with the exception for policy on same-sex violence, in which case perpetrators are non-gendered (Kvist 2010). Women are, therefore, not named as perpetrators. Overall, there is privileging of gender through a strong emphasis on women and on men, leading to other forms of exclusions. The categories 'women' and 'men' are referred to as two internally unified groups with mutually exclusive interests and living conditions. The lack of degendering of Swedish policy may be a consequence of the underlying understanding of a pervasive sex/gender power system. Instead of degendering, we see a marginalisation of minoritised and 'othered' groups in Swedish gender equality policy in general and in policy on violence against women. The sex/gender power framing and the strong focus on a unified and cohesive voice of 'women' may risk excluding voices of women who for one reason or other do not fit the norm description (see de los Reyes and Mulinari 2005; Hellgren and Hobson 2008). It should be noted that the field of sexual violence marks an exception: this policy field was recently made gender neutral.

Our empirical examples illustrate a lack of gender intersecting with other inequalities, but caution is needed because of what can be identified as the process of degendering. We see a tendency that previously gendered categories have become degendered in policy on violence against women. When policy is degendered, there are no (can be no) immediately visible intersections of gender and any other inequality. When policy is degendered, and gender is downplayed or absent, former research has shown that a focus on intersectionality may paradoxically weaken the gender equality project, especially if it reduces the visibility of gender itself (Strid et al. 2013). This 'degendered intersectionality,' or alternatively making one major single exception to such degendering (as in the case of ethnicity/gender in the Netherlands), can obscure the absences of other intersectional groups, such as lesbian women and women living in poverty. In contrast to such degendered policy, the visibility of a more comprehensive range of *interrelations and intersections* of multiple, and indeed gendered, inequalities increase the quality of gender-based violence policy.

Conclusions

The chapter asked how gender-based violence politics is inclusionary or exclusionary of other inequality projects, by presenting arguments and empirical illustrations that untangle some of the intersectional complexities involved in violence politics. Relative disadvantage on one social dimension is likely to increase vulnerability to interpersonal violence, for example, through lack of resources as affected by class and ethnic and racialised subordination. Policy framings of gender-based violence that are not attentive to intersectionality are problematic in that they, firstly, cannot correctly diagnose the underlying problem, and secondly, they exclude policy solutions that encompass the full range of inequalities and vulnerable groups positioned at the intersections.

Moreover, certain forms of violence against intersectional categories are completely excluded. An example of such absence in the texts looked at for the three countries is violence against trans* people, which is not mentioned at all, and therefore also is invisible and excluded in gender-based violence politics.

The analysis shows how framings, namings, and definitions of gender-based violence are still predominantly focused on domestic violence, thereby producing forms of *epistemic privilege* – the primacy of gender in the analysis (see Evans and Lépinard, introduction, this volume); there is limited capacity for policy and politics to take multiple forms of inequalities and their intersections into account, in turn reproducing privilege. Intersectionality is negotiated, deliberated, and struggled over in gender-based violence politics, but not within its main framings. This produces constraints for intersectional politics, inbuilt in policy, institutions, and knowledge production. On the other hand, different framings and degrees of fragmentation of different forms of gender-based violence fields enable some forms of coalitions and disable others. By singling out, for example, forced marriage as a specific from of gender-based violence, with its internal power dimensions, power axes, and inequalities where ethnicity is *hypervisible*, it becomes 'an ethnic minority' issue, which no longer needs to be negotiated with majority movements or the overall equality project. Hence, certain forms of violence are 'ascribed' to specific intersectional constellation groups, which in turn means that if the form of violence is not specifically named in policy, the group becomes invisible.

The constraint in framing and fragmentation is to some extent a re-articulation of the classic Crenshaw dilemma: how do we name and make marginalised groups visible in policy, practice, and as social justice projects, without simultaneously stigmatising that group? One tentative solution to the dilemma is to refocus attention to the relatively powerful: instead of addressing minority groups as the problem in need of a solution, policy should address majority groups' privileges. The relatively marginalised and powerless need not, as in the liberal vision of equality through sameness, become the same as majority groups through integration or assimilation. The relatively powerless and vulnerable need not become less vulnerable. Instead, we conclude, vulnerability, be it based on gender or ethnicity or sexuality, does not need to be 'overcome': societies need to be organised so that all people can be as vulnerable as they are.

Notes

1 Intersectional perspectives, and the complex social phenomena to which they refer, go under many different names and labels, including interrelations of oppressions, multiple oppressions, multiple social divisions, mutual constitution, multiple differences, hybridities, simultaneity, multiculturalisms, multiplicities, postcolonialities, and indeed 'diversity,' amongst many more (see Hearn et al. 2016).
2 In this chapter we follow Walby's (2009) use of gender regime.
3 Performing here includes, but is not restricted to, doing. An alternative conceptualisation, currently under development, is that of 'producing violence' and 'the production of violence' (see Strid et al. 2019).
4 As the authors both always use gender to mean gender+, that is, gender as unavoidably intersected by other inequality axes, it might seem strange that here we talk about intersectional gender-based violence. We do it here precisely to flag the fact that this is how gender-based violence *should* be addressed, and to explore the difficulties that might come with it.
5 All data reports and documents are available via www.quing.eu. For a complete list of the national policy documents included in the analysis here, see QUING. 2007. www. iwm.at/projects/quing/www.quing.eu/files/results/sampling_documents.pdf [accessed 15 June 2019].
6 The situation in the UK is also complicated by some differences between England, Northern Ireland, Wales, and especially Scotland, which has its own legal system. The focus of this policy analysis was mainly England and Wales.
7 This point resonates with Van Der Haar and Verloo's (2013) conclusion when analysing the full QUING database of 2088 texts: minoritised women were most mentioned in texts on domestic violence.
8 There was legislation even earlier in Sweden, namely the 13th-century Birger Jarl's Law on Women's Peace (Hearn et al. 2016). Birger Jarl (1210–1266) was a Swedish statesman – the Duke of Sweden – who played a crucial role in the consolidation of the country.
9 These results are in line with what we see in European policymaking: the Council of Europe Convention on preventing and combating violence against women and domestic violence (2011) (the Istanbul Convention) mostly pays attention to intimate partner violence.

References

Armstrong, Jo, Sofia Strid, and Sylvia Walby. 2007. *Issue Histories: Series of Timelines of Policy Debates in Selected Topics*. Deliverable No. 19 to the European Commission. QUING.

Armstrong, Jo, Sylvia Walby, and Sofia Strid. 2009. "The Gendered Division of Labour." *Benefits* 17 (3): 263–275.

Bacchi, Carol. 1999. *Women, Policy and Politics: The Construction of Policy Problems*. London: Sage.

Baianstovu, Rúna, and Sofia Strid. 2018. *Det hedersrelaterade våldets och förtryckets uttryck och samhällets utmaningar*. Stockholm: Göteborg and Malmö städer.

Bredström, Anna. 2006. "Intersectionality: A Challenge for Feminist HIV/AIDS Research?" *European Journal of Women's Studies* 13 (3): 211–228.

Brownmiller, Susan. 1976. *Against Our Will: Men, Women and Rape*. New York, NY: Simon and Schuster.

Burman, Erica, and Khatidja Chantler. 2005. "Domestic Violence and Minoritisation: Legal and Policy Barriers Facing Minoritised Women Leaving Violent Relationships." *International Journal of Law and Psychiatry* 28 (1): 59–74.

Cho, Sumi, Kimberlé Williams Crenshaw, and Leslie McCall. 2013. "Toward a Field of Intersectionality Studies: Theory, Applications, and Praxis." *Signs: Journal of Women in Culture and Society* 38 (4): 785–810.

Council of Europe. 2011. *Convention on Preventing and Combating Violence Against Women and Domestic Violence*. Council of Europe Treaty Series – No. 210.

Crenshaw, Kimberlé Williams. 1989. "Demarginalizing the Intersection of Race and Sex: A Black Feminist Critique of Antidiscrimination Doctrine, Feminist Theory and Antiracist Politics." *University of Chicago Legal Forum* 139: 139–168.

Crenshaw, Kimberlé Williams. 1991. "Mapping the Margins: Intersectionality, Identity Politics, and Violence Against Women of Color." *Stanford Law Review* 43 (6): 1241–1299.

de los Reyes, Paulina, and Diana Mulinari. 2005. *Intersektionalitet: Kritiska reflektioner over (o)jämlikhetens landskap*. Stockholm: Liber.

Emejulu, Akwugo, and Leah Bassel. 2017. "Whose Crisis Counts? Minority Women, Austerity and Activism in France and Britain." In *Gender and the Economic Crisis in Europe*, edited by Johanna Kantola and Emanuela Lombardo, 185–208. Cham: Palgrave Macmillan.

Esping-Andersen, Gösta. 1990. *The Three Worlds of Welfare Capitalism*. Princeton, NJ: Princeton University Press.

Governmental Bill. 1991. *Regeringens Proposition 1990/1991:113 om en ny jämställdhetslag*. Stockholm: Regeringen.

Hall, Matthew, and Jeff Hearn. 2017. *Revenge Pornography: Gender, Sexualities and Motivations*. London: Routledge.

Hankivsky, Olena, and Renee Cormier. 2011. "Intersectionality and Public Policy: Some Lessons from Existing Models." *Political Research Quarterly* 64 (1): 217–229.

Hartmann, Heidi. 1976. "Capitalism, Patriarchy and Job Segregation by Sex." *Signs* 1: 137–170.

Hearn, Jeff. 2013. "The Sociological Significance of Domestic Violence: Tensions, Paradoxes, and Implications." *Current Sociology* 16 (2): 152–170.

Hearn, Jeff, Sofia Strid, Liisa Husu, and Mieke Verloo. 2016. "Interrogating Violence Against Women and State Violence Policy: Gendered Intersectionalities and the Quality of Policy in The Netherlands, Sweden and the UK." *Current Sociology* 64 (4): 551–567.

Hellgren, Zenia, and Barbara Hobson. 2008. "Cultural Dialogues in the Good Society: The Case of Honour Killings in Sweden." *Ethnicities* 8 (2): 385–404.

Home Office. 2014. *A Call to End Violence Against Women and Girls: Action Plan*. London: Home Office.

Home Office. 2016. *Violence Against Women and Girls Strategy*. London: Home Office.

Home Office. 2018. *Violence Against Women and Girls*. London: Home Office.

Kelly, Liz. 1988. *Surviving Sexual Violence*. Minneapolis, MN: University of Minnesota Press.

Krizsán, Andrea, Hege Skjeie, and Judith Squires, eds. 2012. *Institutionalizing Intersectionality: The Changing Nature of European Equality*. Houndmills, Basingstoke: Palgrave MacMillan.

Kvist, Elin. 2010. *Report Analysing Intersectionality in Gender Equality Policies for Sweden and the EU*. QUING. Vienna: Institute for Human Sciences.

Lauwers, Sophie, and Femke van der Wal. 2010. *Report Analysing Intersectionality in Gender Equality Policies for the Netherlands and the EU*. QUING. Vienna: Institute for Human Sciences.

Lombardo, Emanuela, and Lise Rolandsen Augustin. 2012. "Framing Gender Intersections in the European Union: What Implications for the Quality of Intersectionality in Policies?" *Social Politics* 9 (4): 446–481.

Lorber, Judith. 2000. "Using Gender to Undo Gender: A Feminist Degendering Movement." *Feminist Theory* 1 (1): 79–95.

Lutz, Helma, M. T. Herrera Vivar, and Linda Supik, eds. 2011. *Framing Intersectionality: Debates on a Multi-Faceted Concept*. Farnham, UK: Ashgate.

McLennen, Joan C. 2005. "Domestic Violence Between Same-Gender Partners: Recent Findings and Future Research." *Journal of Interpersonal Violence* 20 (2): 149–154.

Ministerie van Sociale Zaken en Werkgelegenheid en Ministerie van Justitie. 1984. *Nota Bestrijding van sexueel geweld tegen vrouwen en meisjes* (policy plan on Combatting Sexual Violence Against Women and Girls). The Hague: Ministerie van Sociale Zaken en Werkgelegenheid.

Prins, Baukje. 2006. "Narrative Accounts of Origins: A Blind Spot in the Intersectional Approach." *European Journal of Women's Studies* 13 (3): 277–290.

Prins, Baukje, and Sawitri Saharso. 2008. "In the Spotlight: A Blessing and a Curse for Immigrant Women in the Netherlands." *Ethnicities* 8 (3): 365–384.

QUING (Quality in Gender+ Equality Polices). 2007. *List of Documents for Frame Analysis: 29 Countries and the EU*. Vienna: Institute for Human Sciences.

Roggeband, Conny, and Mieke Verloo. 2007. "Dutch Women Are Liberated, Migrant Women Are a Problem: The Evolution of Policy Frames on Gender and Migration in the Netherlands, 1995–2005." *Social Policy & Administration* 41 (3): 271–288.

Russo, Nancy. 2006. "Violence Against Women: A Global Health Issue." In *Proceedings of the 28th International Congress of Psychology Beijing, 2004*. New York, NY: Psychology Press.

Russo, Nancy, and Angela Pirlott. 2006. "Gender-based Violence: Concepts, Methods, and Findings." *Annals of the New York Academy of Science* 1087 (1): 178–205.

Sokoloff, Natalie, and Ida Dupont. 2005. "Domestic Violence at the Intersections of Race, Class, and Gender: Challenges and Contributions to Understanding Violence Against Marginalized Women in Diverse Communities." *Violence Against Women* 11 (1): 38–64.

Sosa, Lorena. 2017. *Intersectionality in the Human Rights Legal Framework on Violence Against Women: At the Centre or the Margins?* Cambridge, UK: Cambridge University Press.

SOU. 2015. *Nationell strategi mot mäns våld mot kvinnor och hedersrelaterat våld och förtyck* [Action Plan for Combating Men's Violence Against Women, Violence and Oppression in the Name of Honour]. Stockholm: Fritzes.

Strid, Sofia. 2018. "Patriarchy Fights Back: Violent Opposition to Gender Equality in Online Contexts." In *Varieties of Opposition to Gender Equality in Europe*, edited by Mieke Verloo, 57–77. London; New York, NY: Routledge.

Strid, Sofia, Jo Armstrong, and Sylvia Walby. 2010. *Report Analysing Intersectionality in Gender Equality Policies for the United Kingdom and the EU*. QUING. Vienna: Institute for Human Sciences.

Strid, Sofia, Anne Laure Humbert, Jeff Hearn, and Dag Balkmar. 2019. "States of Violence: From Welfare State Regimes to Violence Regimes." Paper presented at the *European Conference of Gender and Politics*, July 4–7, University of Amsterdam.
Strid, Sofia, Sylvia Walby, and Jo Armstrong. 2013. "Intersectionality and Multiple Inequalities: Visibility in British Policy on Violence Against Women." *Social Politics* 20 (4): 558–581.
Van der Haar, Marleen, and Mieke Verloo. 2013. "Unpacking the Russian Doll: Gendered and Intersectionalized Categories in European Gender Equality Policies." *Politics, Groups, and Identities* 1 (3): 417–432.
Verloo, Mieke. 2006. "Multiple Inequalities, Intersectionality and the European Union." *European Journal of Women's Studies* 13 (3): 211–228.
Verloo, Mieke, ed. 2007. *Multiple Meanings of Gender Equality: A Critical Frame Analysis of Gender Policies in Europe*. Budapest: CPS Books.
Verloo, Mieke. 2013. "Intersectional Cross-Movement Politics and Policies: Reflections on Current Practices and Debates." *Signs* 38 (4): 893–915.
Verloo, Mieke, ed. 2018. *Varieties of Opposition to Gender Equality in Europe*. London; New York, NY: Routledge.
Walby, Sylvia. 2009. *Globalization and Inequalities: Complexity and Contested Modernities*. London: Sage.
Walby, Sylvia, Jo Armstrong, and Sofia Strid. 2012. "Intersectionality: Multiple Inequalities in Social Theory." *Sociology* 46 (2): 224–240.
Walby, Sylvia, Jude Towers, Susie Balderston, Consuelo Corradi, Brian Francis, Markku Heiskanen, Karin Helweg-Larsen, Lut Mergaert, Philippa Olive, Emma Palmer, Heidi Stöckl, and Sofia Strid. 2017. *The Concept and Measurement of Violence Against Women and Men*. Bristol, UK: Policy Press.
Watts, Charlotte, and Cathy Zimmermann. 2002. "Violence Against Women: Global Scope and Magnitude." *The Lancet* 359 (9313): 1232–1237.
Wendt Höjer, Maria. 2002. *Rädslans politik: Våld och sexualitet i den svenska demokratin*. Stockholm: Stockholm University.
Weldon, S. Laurel. 2006. "Inclusion, Solidarity, and Social Movements: The Global Movement Against Gender Violence." *Perspectives on Politics* 4 (1): 55–74.

Chapter 5

Organising as intersectional feminists in the Global South

Birth and mode of action of post-2011 feminist groups in Morocco

Emmanuelle David

Introduction

In 2011, popular uprisings revealed and fostered the emergence of a new generation of feminists in Morocco (Salime 2012). Women were heavily involved in the
February 20 Movement, the nation-wide protest movement in favour of social
justice. The February 20 Movement gathered diverse actors whose configuration
varied from one locality to another (Bennani-Chraïbi and Jeghllaly 2012). Nonetheless, scholars identify four main groups, namely the socio-economic struggle
networks, the leftish and far-left partisan youths, the former opponents of King
Hassan II, and Islamists of the organisation Al Adl wa Al Ihsane (Smaoui and Wazif
2013). While the activists who took to the streets called for a profound change of
social order, institutional feminist organisations quickly withdrew because they
refused to march alongside Islamists.[1] Instead, they took part in the drafting of
the new constitution, announced in the king's speech on 9 March 2011, in order
to defuse the situation. Meanwhile, female February 20 activists created women's
commissions to defend their rights in several cities (Abounaï 2012; Barkaoui and
Bouasria 2013) and led coordinating committees (Salime 2016), talks, and demonstrations (Salime 2012; Barkaoui and Bouasria 2013; Salime 2016). Since then,
a network of young feminists who do not identify with institutional feminism has
developed. They have launched spontaneous initiatives that are often online and
informal and have been described by scholars as a 'new feminism' designed to be
'plural, antiestablishment, and anticonformist' (Salime 2014, p. 18). For the first
time, feminists who identified with intersectional feminism started to organise.

Intersectional theory is well established amongst Western feminists (Knapp
2005). Studies about Western countries show that there is an important difference between how intersectional theory is discursively used by feminist groups
and how it is implemented as a feminist praxis (Lépinard 2016; Evans 2016) and
a collective identity (Roth 2004). Yet, few studies have empirically considered
the reception of intersectional theory in feminist groups from the Global South[2];
indeed, there are questions regarding how and in what ways it travels as a concept
(Salem 2018). Drawing upon original qualitative data and analysis of a Moroccan independent feminist group, I argue that intersectional praxis (1) raises the

question of race in a non-whiteness context, (2) confronts male privilege inside social justice movements, (3) addresses elitism within second-generation feminist groups, and (4) fosters an activist 'repertoire' (Tilly 1984) which is based on creativity and self-transformation. This case study shows that Moroccan intersectional feminists partially and critically appropriate intersectional vocabulary and charge it with new meanings. These findings lead to a better understanding of the multiple meanings of self-identification as an intersectional feminist. The chapter begins with a literature review, and then provides an overview of the methods before providing analysis of the data. The following literature review discusses the questions of privilege in feminist groups and social movements and feminist organisation in networks, and then gives a brief overview of feminism in Morocco.

Peggy McIntosh defined male privilege as 'an invisible package of unearned assets' (McIntosh 1988, p. 1) which 'takes institutionalised and embedded forms' (McIntosh 1988, p. 2). Going further, the founding texts on intersectional theory emerging from Black feminists of the United States underlined the intersection between race and gender (Crenshaw 1989; Hill Collins 1990). They argue that in the experience of discrimination, members of a discriminated group can be otherwise privileged. Focusing on the most privileged group member marginalises those who are multiply burdened (Crenshaw 1989, p. 140). Thus, Twine and Gardener recognise five characteristics of privilege: it is always a relation of power; it can be invisible; it is multifaceted; it is a relation; and it is flexible (Twine and Gardener 2013). It is essential to take into consideration 'multiple levels of privilege' (Pease 2010, p. 23) to understand that privilege, especially under the form of class and race hierarchy, has always been present within feminist groups (Lutz, Herrera Vivar, and Supik 2011). However, depending on the context, some privileges have been more addressed than others (Evans 2016). Aida Hurtado stated that privilege is *relational* as it is considered in relation to white male privilege (Hurtado 1996, p. 6) and that it is *contextual* as it varies according to social context. White privilege in Western contexts is well documented (McIntosh 1988; Feagin and O'Brien 2004) and includes privilege directly linked to whiteness, as well as 'Western privilege,' the benefit from the exploitation of countries of the Global South (Goudge 2003; Pease 2010). Furthermore, additional research has revealed the various forms of male privilege in social movements (Taylor 1999; Van Dyke, McAdam, and Wilhelm 2000; Fillieule and Roux 2009). Not only are social movements organised along gender lines (Taylor 1999), but gender relations are re-enacted inside and *by* activism (Van Dyke et al. 2000; Dunezat 2008). Class privilege is also a concern within feminist movements. Since the 1995 Beijing Conference on Women, feminist movements from several countries of the Global South have followed the same path towards NGO-isation and institutionalisation (Cisne, Gurgel, and Prévost 2017). In response to this institutionalisation, autonomous feminist groups have emerged and reproached these institutional groups for working in collaboration with the state. According to the autonomous feminists, when they become 'femocrats' (Lovenduski and Baudino

2005), institutional feminists move away from the interests of women from the lower class. Through the question of elitism, autonomous feminists address the question of class privilege.

Replacing the more restrictive concept of 'social movement organisation' (McCarthy and Zald 1977), the concept of 'social movement community,' coined by Buechler (Buechler 1990) and defined by Taylor and Whittier as 'a network of individuals and groups loosely linked through an institutional base, multiple goals and actions, and a collective identity that affirms members' common interests in opposition to dominant groups' (Taylor and Whittier 1992, p. 107), seems much more heuristic to understand the fluidity of post-2011 feminist groups. This definition puts the emphasis on the continuity of social movements and particularly fits the Moroccan context, where founders of new feminist groups reinvest militant skills previously acquired in other structures. They are not novice activists; in fact they are part of a history of struggle. When I use the term 'feminist generation' in this chapter, I refer more to a shift than to a clear rupture. The term 'generation' raises several issues, but the discussion of this concept exceeds the scope of this chapter. Thus, I will use the term 'generation' because it is the term used by the activists themselves, and because the alternative vocabulary of 'waves of feminism' refers broadly to a Western historical context (Evans and Chamberlain 2015).

Feminism in Morocco

Three generations of feminists are usually identified in Morocco. Historically, the first feminist generation was born in the 1940s and was embedded in the nationalist and independence movements. It was structured as a women's section within political parties and paved the way for the emergence of a women's rights movement based on a human rights' defence (Roussillon and Zryouil 2017). A second generation emerged in the early 1980s under the reign of Hassan II, in the form of independent feminist organisations. Originally, groups of women started to organise as feminist sections inside political parties. Some of these groups, influenced by Marxist and socialist ideas, ran feminist newspapers. Shortly after, they organised as associations[3] pursuing two directions: advocating for legal change and offering assistance to women in situations of vulnerability (e.g. illiterate women, victims of domestic violence, child mothers). Since the 1995 Beijing Conference on Women, they started to work with funded projects and financial resources provided by international NGOs. The loosening of state authoritarianism and the pro-women's rights international context[4] favoured what some have called an international 'UN' feminism (Barkaoui and Bouasria 2013). At the same time, the main organisations participated in the broader reforms of the regime (Ouali 2008). These feminist associations of the second generation are still the most prevalent on the feminist scene. Meanwhile, in the 2000s, Islamic feminism – the stream that concentrated on the feminist interpretation of the Quran – developed in Morocco with Asma Lamrabet as a leading figure (Borrillo 2016b).

The late 1990s and the reign of Mohammed VI saw the rise of 'state feminism' in Morocco (Mouaqit 2008; Alami M'Chichi 2010) under the form of both
the 'activities of femocrats in government and administration' and 'the capacity
of the state to contribute to the fulfilment of a feminist agenda' (Lovenduski
and Baudino 2005, p. 4). The monarchy also carried out a policy to increase
female representation in religious institutions (Dirèche 2010). In 2004, the king
pushed for a new reading of the Quran to introduce legislative modification of
the Family Code (also called Mudawana).[5] This policy was implemented not
only in response to feminist demands for equality, but also because the monarchy wanted to appear as a pioneer in moderate Islam. Consequently, some scholars coined the term 'Islamic state feminism' (Eddouada and Pepicelli 2010) to
describe these actions. Although the Moroccan state is regularly depicted as
experiencing democratisation, the liveliness of authoritarianism is clearly not
hampered (Vairel 2014). Scholars have shown that transitology is a language of
power in Morocco (Vairel 2007) and that state feminism has become part of this
language (Ouali 2008).

Some authors identify a third generation of feminists, close to 2011 social
movements (M'Chichi 2014). This third generation was born in the 2010s, under
the reign of Mohammed VI, in a context of large social contestation (February 20
Movement). Feminist individuals organised as self-managed collectives (informal
groups) without legal status, and thus no possibility of opening a bank account
and receiving grants. They are critical towards foreign funding and see it as a
constraint that would imply accountability and thus reduce their scope of action,
their impact, and their creativity. Lastly, these groups have discarded advocacy
and given an important place to politics of self-transformation, to diversity of
their means of expression, and to their access to public space. Moreover, in recent
years, feminist activism in Morocco has been characterised by the development of
numerous online initiatives (Borrillo 2016a) as well as a vitality of feminist topics
in the cultural sector.

Aïcha Barkaoui and Leïla Bouasria state that the criticism of Western feminism
in Morocco emerged in the 1980s (Barkaoui and Bouasria 2013). Yet, feminist
associations from the second generation do not articulate this criticism around
intersectional theory. Unlike Western countries, where there has been a normalisation of an intersectional framework (Evans 2016), self-identification as an intersectional feminist remains marginal amongst feminists in Morocco.

This chapter speaks to debates around the reception of intersectional theory
in feminist movements, addresses the issue of activist appropriation of privilege
theory, and questions the use of intersectional vocabulary out of its context of
emergence. The case study reveals that the activists appropriate some intersectional terms but refuse part of the intersectional vocabulary that was developed
in Western countries. They develop strategies to bring to light male privilege
through challenging narratives within social justice movements. They refuse class
privilege, which they associate with institutional feminism, and they prefer flexible organisation. Lastly, they develop their own repertoire of contention that is

creative and that prioritises self-transformation. The following section exposes the methods of investigation and the different stages of the research.

Methods

Aiming to explore what it means to organise as an intersectional feminist in Morocco, I pursued the angle of privilege as a guideline. I began from the question: how do activists perceive privilege and what are the consequences of this perception? Excluding institutional groups, I focused on bringing to light the process of appropriation of intersectionality among a newer feminist group born after 2011 and highlighting 'the conditions under which processes may occur' (Hamidi 2012, p. 93). This empirical case accurately displays the mechanisms that link intersectional views with the questioning of race, class, and male privileges.

The first stage of the research process consisted of mapping those groups which, unlike groups from the second generation, operate as informal collectives and thus are difficult to identify. By following social media, I made a list of active collectives and their members. One of them recommended I meet with a woman whom I shall call Ayda, who was involved in the February 20 Movement. I interviewed Ayda in Rabat in 2016 and I found out that she is the founder of a feminist group that I shall call 'MF.'[6] Ayda then added me to the closed MF Facebook group, composed of an online network launched in 2015 and gathering 4,300 individuals. Members are mostly Moroccan young women, who typically share content in Moroccan Arabic, with some posts in French, English, and literary Arabic. MF also takes collective offline actions and has no legal status. This group is particularly relevant as a case in this study because it (1) integrates intersectional views, which is specific to the third generation; (2) is active, unlike some of the groups that were born right after the February 20 Movement but later ceased to exist; and (3) gave me the opportunity to access this group through the contacts established during my fieldwork.

The second step of the research consisted of trying to join meetings and talk to the activists. Many times, my requests to join meetings were rejected. My presence as a French woman was not always welcomed because of the group's critique of White feminism. The explanation given was that the group had not gathered for a while, and the activists would rather keep among themselves a safe space for Moroccan women. I managed to attend one meeting in Rabat, which was held in Moroccan Arabic, after which I held discussions with 15 of the participants. I observed some distrust amongst participants, who, realising my nationality, quickly decried French anti-headscarf feminists. In contrast, the fact that I was the same age as the activists and also a student and a feminist facilitated the interactions. Indeed, the most active members were students in the public higher education system in Rabat. In terms of socio-economic background, most of the women could be categorised as middle class. On the one hand, few came from francophone families, which are typically the most dominant class, nor did they attend private universities. Yet they live in an urban context and are educated women who are far from the poorest strata in Morocco. Plus, in Rabat, which is a university town that gathers students from other regions, young women often share flats – a useful resource for the feminist groups that have been created after the February 20 Movement because they do not have permanent premises and they regularly hold meetings at the activists' houses. Many group members had participated in the February 20 Movement and in other organisations: the Moroccan Association for Human Rights,[7] the student collective UECSE,[8] or a left-wing political party.[9]

Then, I decided to focus on the women who were most active in the group, because as leaders who convey the discourse on Facebook and initiate the collective action, they are at the heart of the appropriation process of intersectional theory. My main interlocutors were the founder of the group, Ayda, and three other activists (Imane, Meriem, and Rim). Between 2016 and 2019 we met in Rabat, Casablanca, and Marrakech in several set-ups: in-depth interviews, attending conferences on feminism and cultural events together, or even meeting for coffee.

The following analysis explores the circulation and appropriation of intersectional theory by looking at the multiple ways through which activists address privilege. The chapter first explores the question of race privilege in a context of non-whiteness and then the confrontation of male privilege by challenging narratives, before moving to the criticism of elitism inside feminist organisations and finally to the use of creativity in the repertoire of contention.

Questioning race as an intersectional feminist in a context of non-whiteness

'The content, meaning, and relevance' of the category "race" are organised by different modalities that vary with the context (Patil 2013, p. 857). This section raises the question of how activists address race privilege in a context of non-whiteness. The case study reveals how Moroccan feminists reinterpret the intersectional vocabulary.

The reinterpretation starts with the very translation of the term. I noticed that Ayda, the founder of the group, alternates between the term 'intersectionality' in English, in Arabic (*taqāta'a*), and in French (*intersectionnalité*). She also defines herself as a radical (in Arabic '*rādīcālī*') which, for her, means attacking the root of the problem. The activists use the term intersectionality in a fluidity of language that coincides with the fluidity of language in the Moroccan context. In the groups I observed, Arabic (Moroccan and literary) is the first language, but English appears more often than French – which is usually the dominant second language in Morocco.

More generally, the language of systemic racism does not express the experiences of these activists. As women of the Global South, they see privilege rather in the light of Western hegemony. The founder of the MF group, who had read Angela Davis' texts, is critical towards what she calls 'feminists from imperialist and colonialist countries,' as she found their analysis limited to their contexts. She finds that the Moroccan context 'has little in common with the United States, in terms of culture and ethnicity.' During a conference given in Rabat by a French racialised and decolonial feminist, Ayda recounts:

> Sometimes people come to me saying that I am a racialised woman [in French, '*femme racisée*']. And I am like . . . 'no.' It does not fit my context. For me, it has no meaning.

Thus, Ayda does not perceive herself as a racialised woman. According to her, a mechanical application of intersectional theory does not make sense. Concerning MF reflexive practice, the founder claims that the group 'did not succeed in connecting with "*women of Colour*," in particular sub Saharan African women and Amazigh women who could not speak literary Arabic and Moroccan Arabic.' In this way, she excludes herself from what would be a racialised subject in the Moroccan context.

Because Morocco is a context of non-whiteness does not mean that 'race' disappears. On the contrary, Black feminists have shown that 'race is a structure that organises people globally' (Salem 2018, p. 5). It means that the history of colonialism and the international organisation of labour influence the fact that 'applications of intersectionality also continue to be shaped by the geographies of colonial modernity' (Patil 2013, p. 853). In that case, along which lines might race privilege be organised for MF activists? Race privilege is addressed by MF intersectional feminists as a Western privilege that comprises economic advantage, mobility, and cultural representation. First, it is seen as an economic privilege because Western expatriates in Morocco earn higher salaries than locals do. They have a buying power that might influence rising prices. Next, it is a privilege of mobility. White people enjoy international mobility with passports that give them easy access to numerous countries. They can also access certain touristic spaces (restaurant and hotels) inside Morocco, from which Moroccan people are denied access, as has happened several times in Marrakech over the past few years. Ayda analysed this phenomenon as a neo-colonial dynamic in the construction of tourism. Finally, it is a privilege of positive representation. It can take the form of White hegemonic beauty, as Ayda pointed out during an interview: 'Look, we are now sitting in a café in Rabat, and what do we see? A White woman in an advertisement here, another White woman in an advertisement there.' It can also take the form of the positive representation of the term 'expatriate' in contrast to the word 'immigrant.'

Salem has shown that intersectionality has been considered along with other terminology by Third World Liberation women who put forth the 'triple oppression' (Salem 2018, p. 5). In the Facebook group, the members refer to feminists from the Middle East and North Africa region who have articulated an overlapping of power relationships without explicitly using 'intersectionality,' like Nawal Saadawi,[10] Asma Lamrabet,[11] and Fatema Mernissi.[12] These references might play a role in the appropriation of a local understanding of intersectionality.

This case study shows that in a context of non-whiteness, intersectional feminists might distance themselves from the intersectional vocabulary which makes them 'racialised subjects' and adapt the definition of White privilege in order to fit the specific context of the Global South. The chapter now explores how MF activists tackle the question of male privilege by imposing the presence of women in the narratives of social justice movements.

Bringing to light male privilege: gendering collective frames within struggles for social justice

Acknowledging that men enjoy a relational privilege in social movement organisations which advocate for social justice reveals the invisibility of women inside their narratives. It leads to the challenge of male privilege by creating a discursive space for the experience of women inside the movement.

Counter narratives in the February 20 Movement

Regarding the framing processes of social movements, feminist narratives operate as 'counter narratives' (Contamin 2010) generating 'frame disputes' (Benford 1993). Research on the feminist cohorts inside a broader social movement is an insightful contribution on how frames can be questioned from inside the social movement. In addition, the obliteration of the feminist struggle for the benefit of a larger cause is topical and has been documented in other contexts.[13] Thus, challenging narratives is often a strategy used by feminists. During the February 20 Movement, women challenged the discursive space by chanting slogans that put the emphasis on a female 'martyr,' such as 'We all are Fadoua Laroui'[14] (*koulouna Fadoua Laroui*) and 'We are all Amina Filali'[15] (*koulouna Amina Filali*) (Barkaoui and Bouasria 2013, p. 137). This strategy is represented again in the experience of MF activists during the 2016 Hirak Movement.

Existing as a feminist collective during the Hirak Movement

The Hirak Movement in 2016 rose up as a national wave of protests against the 'ḥogra' – an Arabic term referring to the strong feeling of social injustice and disrespect experienced by the people as emanating from state authorities. In October 2016, the death of Mohcine Fikri, a fishmonger who was ground to death by a rubbish truck operated by authorities, was the spark that set fire to the Rif region and set off this social movement. MF activists had not participated as a group in the February 20 Movement because the group was only created in 2015. However, during the Hirak Movement in 2016, MF activists joined the demonstrations not only to rally for the cause but also to restate the 'ḥogra' experienced by women. Their intention was to draw attention to the fact that, in recent years, a large number of women had set themselves on fire or killed themselves because of a run-in with authorities. Primarily, they aimed to underline that the deaths of these women did not generate a wide protest movement, precisely because of their gender. During a demonstration in November 2016, about 15 MF activists in Rabat protested as a collective for the first time, in a watershed moment. Among the protest signs we could read are 'Welcome to COP22, we grind people here,' which showed pictures of the deceased, and slogans like '*koulna Mohcine Fikri*' meaning 'We are all Mohcine Fikri.' While embracing the cause, feminists also showed their discontent: 'We had the feeling that everyone was focusing on Mohcine Fikri while before him there were other victims that were women, but women never brought out the crowd,' claimed Ayda. In an attempt to challenge the narrative, the MF activists waved signs on which they wrote the names of some of these women, such as Mmi Fatiha,[16] Khadija Souidi,[17] Amina Filali, and Fadoua Laroui, to make women's experiences visible. The watchword for MF activists was, 'The system ground a man, but it burned several women.' Asking the question, 'Why were there no demonstrations for female victims?' the MF activists also waved placards in which they wrote in Arabic and English: '*al-ʾism: al-karāma*/Name: Dignity.' However, during the demonstration, they faced unpleasant reactions like mockery and harassment.

In response, MF activists challenged gendered slogans to make a space for their expression as a female collective. Ayda recounts her perception of the event:

> When they were chanting 'freedom, dignity and social justice' we were chanting right after them as an echo, 'and real equity!' And when they were shouting, for example, '*monāḍilīn*,' which means 'activists' but male activists, because Arabic is a gendered language, we were always echoing '*ou monāḍilāt*' which means 'and female activists' and we were moving along the crowd, shouting.

Yet, both the limited number of MF members in the demonstration and the decibel level of the crowd's slogans limited the effect of their alternative chants. Therefore, the group did not chant all the slogans they had come up with. They recount that they received a lukewarm reception, with some positive gazes, notably from women, and other comments implying that their placards were incongruous, as if 'dignity did not concern women' as Ayda construed, or as if the other protesters considered it was the wrong place and time for their message. Most of the activists of the group experienced the same feeling of being seen as 'separatists,' 'of someone not there in entirety,' while observing that 'the entirety is masculine.' Here, the attempts of MF activists to impose female figures in gendered collective frames evidence that gender hierarchy is persistent and leads to inferiority and invisibility processes. The MF members acknowledged that even inside social justice struggles, women occupy a subordinate place and suffer violence in the activist scene. To describe the invisibility of women inside the narratives, Ayda coined the expression, 'it's a *hogra* inside the *hogra*, it's an imbrication of *hogra*.' Their strategy highlights that male privilege can take the form of being visible inside the protest narratives.

Counter narratives are part of MF activists' strategy to bring to light male privilege within the struggle for social justice, thereby putting forward the argument that women are multiply burdened in the experience of domination (Crenshaw 1989). This type of protest is one manifestation of the way in which these young feminist individuals struggle to open up new spaces more adapted to their radical ideology, in opposition to the elitism of the second-generation feminist organisations, as explored in the next section.

Criticism towards second-generation feminist organisations: a sensibility to class privilege

The intersectional lens adopted by MF members revealed the relational class privilege held by institutional feminists. Because of their critics, they decided to create their own new space in which they can express their radicality and push for inclusivity.

Addressing elitism

The elitism and co-optation of institutional feminists is at the heart of MF activists' criticisms. It is the main criticism articulated by Meriem, who denounces the elitist discourse and nature of second-generation feminist associations. According to Meriem:

> Women who are targeted by the actions [of feminist associations] are considered alienated and submissive women who cannot have an opinion, and who need to be liberated by women who are considered already free.

Meriem adds, 'I see there an orientalist conception of liberation.' According to her, second-generation feminist organisations' repertoires of contention are not effective because they fail to give the people access to the major social issues. She argues:

> When you work on a project that is funded by another international NGO, your scope of action is reduced, and so is your impact. If projects are your principal activity, then you curb your creativity and you limit the access for other people.

Furthermore, Ayda regrets that economic and social justice issues are generally overlooked inside feminist struggles. In her perception, feminism around the world is becoming more and more neoliberal.

In brief, second-generation groups 'are perceived as representing the interests of an urban elite' (Gray 2013, p. 136). Ayda affirms that she does not want to lay blame on these feminists and that she respects the Marxist and socialist positions that they took in their context of emergence. She adds, 'But I believe that now, a large part of this left is an ambitious, careerist left. These activists aspired to positions of power.' Without fully discrediting the second generation's work, most of the young activists position themselves in terms of what they call a 'critical continuity.' Even though MF members do not come from precarious conditions, criticising class privilege and economic domination is important to them, as their presence in the Hirak Movement has shown. They often prefer the expression '*ḥogra*' than 'poverty' to outline 'class privilege,' as Ayda explains: 'We do not use the term "poor." It is not poverty, it is *ḥogra*. It means that you come from a social class which has been deprived of its economic rights.' This expression resonates with the local history of struggle.

Creating their own space

In addition to elitism, MF activists address other criticisms to their predecessors: the lack of radicality and of inclusivity. Rim questions the long-term efficiency of the second-generation feminist organisations' methods to fight against the patriarchal culture. She also expresses her discontent in terms of a difficulty to find her place: 'Because, yes, I am a woman who promotes women's rights, but also . . . I am not a Muslim. Also, I identify myself as an ecologist, I identify myself as pro-minorities, I identify myself as pro-LGBTQ.' According to her, second-generation feminist organisations do not provide a space that facilitates discussions regarding different types of feminism. Taking these challenges into account, the young female activists decided to launch self-organised groups. Imane clarifies:

> After February 20th, some other girls and myself, we noticed that there are no large spaces that are free and that can help us. Even when you find free spaces, you won't find the same vision, the same way of seeing things, the same tools of activism, the same tools of involvement, and even the understanding is not the same . . . and so we found ourselves far from these organisations' views and we said: why not? Why not have our own experience in which we will reflect upon new approaches, upon new tools.

MF activists chose to organise as an informal collective and not as an association. Although creating an association would facilitate the organisation of their activities, Rim explained to me that the matter is partly ideological, 'Most of us consider this option as traditional, and we want to invent other means of expression within society, which are not political parties, trade unions, associations, organisations.' Because of their mode of organisation, they have to renounce fundraising, because as a collective, they do not legally exist and thus they cannot open a bank account. If we look at the materials used by groups of the second generation and the new generation, the difference is clear: while second-generation organisations have physical headquarters, use megaphones, plasticised banners, flyers, leaflets, bound reports, and large posters, and can organise large-scale events, new groups frequently host their meetings in cafés, public spaces, or at an activist's home and use homemade placards. The founders of the collectives insist on their will to remain nonpartisan, unstructured, and non-institutionalised. They assume that this position will bring them closer to more women and feminists.

In addition, Imane points out that the long protocol to become a member of a second-generation feminist group can be a hindrance to involvement. On the contrary, young people can easily reach out to informal groups, as they are accessible through social media. However, the immateriality of informal groups is also a disadvantage as the commitment might be weaker. The lack of commitment is reflected in the volatility of the activists who attend the events. Unlike second-generation feminist groups, where the activists feel bound by a rigid structure, MF faces defections and lacks a militant base.

MF is closer to being a network of individuals than a formal association, converging with Taylor and Whittier's definition of a 'social movement community' (Taylor and Whittier 1992). The benefit of this form of organisation is to escape institutionalisation. But fluidity is also a disadvantage, as few activists are fully involved in all events. The chapter now explores other benefits of fluidity, such as how creativity and innovation of form constitute a repertoire of self-transformation for MF activists.

Creative tools and the politics of self-transformation

In their process to appropriate intersectionality, MF members discard advocacy to the benefit of creative repertoires which are orientated towards self-transformation. As seen in other contexts, conventional forms of action (demonstration) coexist with new forms (Chaponnière, Roux, and Ruault 2017), like the use of the body as a repertoire (Cisne et al. 2017) and the building of an online safe space.

Self-transformation

I argue that one important difference between the second and third generations of feminists in Morocco is the ability of the latter to set action not only in public settings but also, and mainly, in private settings. This distinction echoes Taylor and Whittier's analysis of the overlapping between 'doing' and 'being' in social movements. They draw a line between 'the politics of the public sphere, or world transformation directed primarily at the traditional political arena of the state' and 'the politics of identity, or self-transformation aimed primarily at the individual' (Taylor and Whittier 1992). MF provides several striking examples of innovative forms of action that strive for self-transformation.[18] With the objective of 'working towards their intellectual, cultural, and expressional liberation,' as Ayda says, they set up different kinds of events. First, the so-called F for F, standing for 'Feminist for Feminist' (originally in English), in which a woman or a group comes together to share their skills. The group staged four 'F for F' events during the period of research. The first one consisted in organising a football match in Casablanca with young women from the disadvantaged neighbourhood of Ain Diab. For the second one, the instruction was, 'Bring your make-up for feminist artistic use,' and they sought out a young artist from Agadir who draws rugged women's bodies with make-up. In July 2016 they planned a meeting with the theme 'let's discuss feminist economics.' The last one, in December 2016, was an evening on the beach of Rabat and consisted of writing new feminist songs. These events did not all turn out as successful as expected due to the small number of people that showed up. However, they reflect the ambition to initiate innovative forms of mobilisation.

Body as a repertoire

MF activists also rolled out a cycle of events called 'clitoral mass' (originally in English) in which young women gathered and drew clitorises in an anatomical way, giving imaginary names to the different parts in Moroccan Arabic. One of the founders of the collective explains:

> I really believe that it is a problem of language. A problem of breaking away from this language which denies women their sexuality. The aim was to try to reinvent another language that would have liberating effects on women's sexuality.

She continues:

> So we gathered the first time, it was in a café. It was a very popular café where there were only men, and we did our clitoral invasion (she laughs) and then we started to draw clitorises in a café . . . full of men.

During these sessions, which occurred five times with different participants, they acknowledged the belated discovery of the clitoris' anatomy and the medical lack of interest in it, and more broadly for women's illnesses. The drawings were carried out with ballpoint pens, whether in the participants' notebooks or on a separate sheet of paper. The lines are thick, dark blue or black and the arrows indicate imaginary names: the main issue is not to achieve aesthetic goals. These practices of women-only meetings aiming to discuss women's sexuality have occurred in other contexts. In the 1970s in the United States, networks of non-specialist women assumed a critical position towards medical institutions (Ruault 2016) and articulated revindications relative to reproductive rights and gynaecological health under the name of 'self-help.' As these practices have appeared in several countries, we can assume that they are part of a transnational circulation of practices. Nevertheless, the self-help movements' practices of group gynaecological examination differ considerably from the MF activities. Here, dissimilarly, the practice is not gynaecologic but artistic and discursive. Yet, in the Moroccan context, feminist groups are traditionally less likely to bring up issues of sexuality.

The purpose of these meetings is to empower women by encouraging them to talk about their sexuality. In the same vein, MF occasionally organised what they called 'special days' like 'period day' or 'clitoris day' during which they painted clitorises on their faces and took to the streets to show the existence of their sexuality (in Morocco sex outside marriage is punishable by law[19]). These small-scale initiatives did not lead to any reaction from authorities. Passers-by merely glanced at the activists, and there were no altercations.

An online safe space

The form of the Facebook group allows discussions on sensitive topics, such as contraceptive methods, sexual harassment and abuse, physical prejudice, and abortion. For example, the members share information about doctors who practice abortions. They can also provide guidance and support to the members who are facing the procedure. Abortion is extremely restricted in Morocco and can carry a penalty of one to five years of imprisonment.[20] Repeatedly, members of the group created private conversations in which they invited a selected number of people to contribute a certain amount towards the operation. Each time, I observed that the fundraising was achieved within a few hours. Although the group has a limited militant base, the development of solidarity is based on shared experiences. In accordance with Sreberny's conclusions, I construe online activism as an opening of new spaces that lead to new modes of engagement (Sreberny 2015), easily accessible for young women that have never experienced traditional forms of activism. In addition, it is clear that social media platforms give access to a solidarity network beyond the control of parents and transcending physical distance.

Taking into account intersectional claims and the possibilities that online activities present, Moroccan female activists are thus extending the content and reach of their feminist struggles. Exploring the repertoire of contention of MF (women-only meetings, creative tools, online activism) highlights that mobilising intersectionality is far from mechanical and consistent. Here, the politics of self-transformation is very central to intersectional praxis, at the expense of a repertoire directly targeting the state.

Conclusion

While intersectionality has circulated broadly within feminist groups in Western countries to the point where it is now part of the discourse, it has remained barely used by feminists from the Global South. Considering privilege as something *contextual* and *relational* has paved the way for a reflection on how intersectionality travels south and is appropriated as a collective identity. This case study points out that the reception of intersectional theory amongst Moroccan feminists give important insights about its appropriation in Southern countries.

Historically, feminists from Southern countries have described an 'overlapping matrix of oppressions' (Hill Collins 1990) that they articulated with colonial history and global economic domination. However, the origin context of intersectional theory makes it difficult to adapt to a context which is totally different on the question of race. This chapter has argued that against all odds, in a context of non-whiteness, young feminists have decided to appropriate intersectional theory and, further, that they have adapted its vocabulary in order to make it relevant in their context. In their conception, White privilege acquires a contextual meaning that comprises advantages of economic status, mobility, and cultural representation. Feminist activists also draw on local feminist references to restate the specificity of their experience.

Here, intersectionality is appropriated as a collective identity according to which multiply-marginalised women should organise on their own in order to challenge, by creating a new space, their exclusion from the broader social movement in favour of social justice. They develop a strategy of visibility that challenges the production and reproduction of male privilege in the discursive space of social mobilisation. They also assert that the expression 'ḥogra' is linked to the notion of 'class privilege' – without completely corresponding to it, as it restates more precisely the experience of social injustice.

The February 20 Movement revealed that not all feminists found satisfaction in the very structured activism that was proposed by the second-generation feminist associations. These activists strive for a more radical, spontaneous, and fluid activism. Addressing the relational privilege of class that institutional feminists enjoy, they propose a shift from a politics of the public scene to a politics of identity. Institutional feminists are still the major feminist force in Morocco, and feminist individuals who identify as intersectional still represent a minority. Yet, we assume that the reinterpretation of intersectional theory in Morocco is still in its beginning.

Self-transformation takes a key place as a repertoire as these activists share their skills, appropriate their bodies through creative tools, and build an online safe space to tackle sensitive topics such as abortion. The examination of their repertoire points out that, despite differences in the conception of privilege, intersectional praxis in Morocco has a lot in common with other feminist praxis around the world. Feminist scholars have stated that intersectionality is a theory 'constantly under construction' (Hill Collins and Bilge 2016, p. 31); by using it in their practice and by modelling intersectional vocabulary, feminists from the Global South make an insightful contribution to the theory.

Notes

1 I refer here to Ismail's definition: 'The term "Islamist politics" is used here to refer to the activities of organisations and movements that mobilise and agitate in the political sphere while deploying signs and symbols from Islamic traditions. It is also used to refer to political activism involving informal groupings that (re)construct repertoires and frames of reference from Islamic traditions. The term "Islamism" is used to

encompass both Islamist politics as well as re-Islamisation, the process whereby various domains of social life are invested with signs and symbols associated with Islamic cultural traditions' (Ismail 2006).

2 Few studies concentrate on activist groups which define themselves as 'intersectional' in the Global South, but more analyse how social movement organisations use intersectionality as an analytic tool, for example in Hill Collins and Bilge (2016).

3 Such as the Association Démocratique des Femmes du Maroc (1985), Union de l'Action Féminine (1987), and Fédération de La Ligue pour les Droits des Femmes (1993).

4 The years 1976 to 1985 were declared the International Decade of Women by the UN.

5 About the reform of the family code, see (N'Diaye 2012).

6 With the aim of protecting my respondents from damaging consequences, I have anonymised the group as well as the individuals involved.

7 The Moroccan Association for Human Rights (in French AMDH, which stands for 'Association Marocaine des Droits Humains') is a human rights association that was an initiator of the February 20 Movement.

8 In French 'Union des Étudiants pour le Changement du Système Éducatif,' meaning 'Student union for the change of the education system.'

9 Annahj Addimocrati, in French 'La Voie Démocratique' (Democratic Way), which is a Marxist political party constituted in 1995 and legalised by the Moroccan state in 2004.

10 Nawal Saadawi is an Egyptian feminist writer who addressed the topics of women in Islam and of violence against women's bodies.

11 The Moroccan theologian Asma Lamrabet is an international leader in *ijtihad*, the revision of sacred Islamic texts, and a third-way feminist. From 2011 to 2018, she was the Director of Feminine Studies within the Mohammedian Council of Scholars in Morocco, a body created by King Mohammed VI. In March 2018 she was forced to resign because she was advocating gender equality in inheritance. The term 'third-way feminism' was coined by scholar Doris H. Gray to describe 'conceptual approaches to gender justice that are in essence the same as gender equality, and are developed by Moroccan thinkers and activists who insist on references to Islam.' See "The Many Paths to Gender Equality in Morocco." *Oxford Islamic Studies Online.* www.oxfordislamicstudies.com/Public/focus/essay1009_gender_equality_in_morocco.html [accessed 8 July 2019].

12 Fatema Mernissi (1940–2015) is a sociologist and essayist who documented the way that Western orientalist arts participated in the subjection of women in the Arab world.

13 For example, Dina Beblawi has pointed out how the feminist struggle was required to yield to the revolutionary struggle during the Egyptian revolution (Beblawi 2016).

14 Fadoua Laroui, 25 years old, was the first Moroccan woman to set herself on fire on 21 February 2011 after being kicked out of her small shack where she lived with her two children. She had been denied social housing with the argument that, as a single mother, she could not be head of a family.

15 Amina Filali was forced to marry her rapist at the age of 16 in accordance with article 475 of the penal code (repealed in 2014), which gave the rapist the opportunity to not be punished for his crime by marrying the victim. She committed suicide by oral ingestion of rat poison.

16 Mmi Fatiha was a street crepe vendor of the city of Kenitra who was beaten by a caïd (as a representative of the Ministry of the Interior, the caïd is a local administrator who exerts power in his administrative area) who ripped off her veil and mishandled her in a public place. He also confiscated her goods. After going to the administrative district to ask for restitution, she came out and sprinkled her body with flammable liquid before setting herself on fire, on 9 April 2016.

17 Khadija Souidi, from the city of Ben Guerir, was raped in 2015 by eight men and sub-jected to other forms of torture. The suspects were quickly arrested but were released after what was described by the local press as an unfair trial. Shortly after, they came back to Khadija and started to blackmail her, threatening to upload the images of the collective rape that they videotaped with their smartphones on the Internet if she went on telling her story. Khadija, aged 16, set herself on fire in the street and quickly suc-cumbed to her injuries the following day.

18 On the contrary, the main feminist organisations tended to fall back on capacity devel-opment of rural and poor women, but they do not use empowerment as a means to give power to the activists themselves. They give priority to what Taylor and Whittier call 'world transformation directed primarily at the traditional political arena of the state'(Taylor and Whittier 1992, p. 183).

19 Article 490 of the Penal Code punishes persons of different sexes who are not married and have sexual relations with one month to one year in prison.

20 Until 2015, abortion in Morocco was only permitted if the health of the mother was in danger, according to article 453 of the penal code. Since then, King Mohamed VI announced that it could be legalised in a few cases, namely when the pregnancy results from rape or incest. According to the Moroccan Association for the Fight Against Clan-destine Abortion (AMLAC), between 600 and 800 clandestine abortions are carried out each day in the country. "Abortion in Morocco: A Delicate Debate." *Middle East Eye.* www.middleeasteye.net/news/abortion-morocco-delicate-debate [accessed 8 July 2019].

References

Abounaï, Aïcha. 2012. "Les femmes marocaines et ' le printemps arabe '." *Tumultes* 38–39 (1): 115–132.

Alami M'Chichi, Houria. 2010. *Le Féminisme d'État au Maroc: jeux et enjeux politiques.* Paris: Harmattan.

Barkaoui, Aicha, and Leila Bouasria. 2013. "Les Paradoxes de l'indigène: La voix d'une femme est une révolution." *Revue Des Femmes Philosophes* 2–3: 123–147.

Beblawi, Dina. 2016. "L'invisibilisation du féminisme dans la lutte révolutionnaire de la gauche radicale égyptienne." *Nouvelles Questions Feministes* 35 (2): 35–50.

Benford, Robert D. 1993. "Frame Disputes Within the Nuclear Disarmament Movement." *Social Forces* 71 (3): 677–701.

Bennani-Chraïbi, Mounia, and Mohamed Jeghllaly. 2012. "La dynamique protestataire du Mouvement du 20 février à Casablanca." *Revue française de science politique* 62 (5): 867–894.

Borrillo, Sara. 2016a. "Égalité de Genre Au Maroc Après 2011? Les Droits Sexuels et Reproductifs Au Centre Des Récentes Luttes de Reconnaissance." *Studi Maghrebini* 14: 393–418.

Borrillo, Sara. 2016b. "Islamic Feminism in Morocco: The Discourse and the Experi-ence of Asma Lamrabet." In *Moroccan Feminisms: New Perspectives*, edited by Moha Ennaji, Fatima Sadiqi, and Karen Vintges, 111–127. Trenton: Africa World Press.

Buechler, Steven M. 1990. *Women's Movements in the United States: Woman Suffrage, Equal Rights, and Beyond.* New Brunswick, NJ: Rutgers University Press.

Chaponnière, Martine, Patricia Roux, and Lucile Ruault, eds. 2017. "Nouvelles formes de militantisme féministe." *Nouvelles Questions Féministes* 36 (1).

Cisne, Mirla, Telma Gurgel, and Héloïse Prévost. 2017. "Les nouvelles formes de féminisme autonome au Brésil." *Nouvelles Questions Féministes* 36 (2): 34–49.

Contamin, Jean-Gabriel. 2010. "Cadrages et luttes de sens." In *Penser les mouvements sociaux: Conflits sociaux et contestations dans les sociétés contemporaines*, edited by Éric Agrikoliansky, 55–75. Paris: La Découverte.

Crenshaw, Kimberle. 1989. "Demarginalizing the Intersection of Race and Sex: A Black Feminist Critique of Antidiscrimination Doctrine, Feminist Theory and Antiracist Politics." *University of Chicago Legal Forum* 1989 (140): 138–167.

Dirèche, Karima. 2010. "Les Murchidât au Maroc: Entre islam d'État et islam au féminin." *Revue des mondes musulmans et de la Méditerranée* 128: 99–111.

Dunezat, Xavier. 2008. "La division sexuelle du travail militant dans les assemblées générales: le cas des mouvements de 'sans'." *Amnis* 8.

Eddouada, Souad, and Renata Pepicelli. 2010. "Maroc: vers un 'féminisme islamique d'État'." *Critique internationale* 46: 87–100.

Evans, Elizabeth. 2016. "Intersectionality as Feminist Praxis in the UK." *Women's Studies International Forum* 59: 67–75.

Evans, Elizabeth, and Prudence Chamberlain. 2015. "Critical Waves: Exploring Feminist Identity, Discourse and Praxis in Western Feminism." *Social Movement Studies* 14 (4): 396–409.

Feagin, Joe R., and Eileen O'Brien. 2004. *White Men on Race: Power, Privilege, and the Shaping of Cultural Consciousness*. Mississauga; Boston, MA: Beacon Press Random House of Canada, Limited.

Fillieule, Olivier, and Patricia Roux, eds. 2009. *Le Sexe du militantisme*. Paris: Presses de la Fondation nationale des sciences politiques.

Goudge, Paulette. 2003. *The Power of Whiteness: Racism in Third World Development and Aid*. London: Lawrence & Wishart.

Gray, Doris H. 2013. "Feminism, Islamism and a Third Way." In *Contemporary Morocco: State, Politics and Society Under Mohammed VI*, edited by Bruce Maddy-Weitzman and Daniel Zisenwine, 136–146. Abingdon: Routledge.

Hamidi, Camille. 2012. "De quoi un cas est-il le cas?" *Politix* 100 (4): 85–98.

Hill Collins, Patricia. 1990. *Black Feminist Thought: Knowledge, Consciousness, and the Politics of Empowerment: Perspectives on Gender* (Vol. 2). Boston, MA: Unwin Hyman.

Hill Collins, Patricia, and Sirma Bilge. 2016. *Intersectionality: Key Concepts Series*. Cambridge, UK ; Malden, MA: Polity Press.

Hurtado, Aída. 1996. *The Color of Privilege: Three Blasphemies on Race and Feminism: Critical Perspectives on Women and Gender*. Ann Arbor, MI: University of Michigan Press.

Ismail, Salwa. 2006. *Rethinking Islamist Politics: Culture, the State and Islamism*. London: Tauris.

Knapp, Gudrun-Axeli. 2005. "Race, Class, Gender: Reclaiming Baggage in Fast Travelling Theories." *European Journal of Women's Studies* 12 (3): 249–265.

Lépinard, Éléonore. 2016. "Praxis de l'intersectionnalité: répertoires des pratiques féministes en France et au Canada." *L'Homme et la société* 198: 149–170.

Lovenduski, Joni, and Claudie Baudino, eds. 2005. *State Feminism and Political Representation*. Cambridge, UK; New York, NY: Cambridge University Press.

Lutz, Helma, Maria Teresa Herrera Vivar, and Linda Supik, eds. 2011. *Framing Intersectionality: Debates on a Multi-Faceted Concept in Gender Studies: The Feminist Imagination: Europe and Beyond*. Farnham, UK; Burlington, VT: Ashgate.

McCarthy, John D., and Mayer N. Zald. 1977. "Resource Mobilization and Social Movements: A Partial Theory." *American Journal of Sociology* 82 (6): 1212–1241.

M'Chichi, Houria Alami. 2014. "Les féminismes marocains contemporains: Pluralité et nouveaux défis." *Nouvelles Questions Féministes* 33 (2): 65–79.

McIntosh, Peggy. 1988. *White Privilege and Male Privilege: A Personal Account of Coming to See Correspondences Through Work in Women's Studies*. Wellesley, MA: Wellesley College, Center for Research on Women.

Mouaqit, Mohammed. 2008. *L'idéal égalitaire féminin à l'œuvre au Maroc: féminisme, islam(isme), sécularisme: Histoire et Perspectives Méditerranéennes*. Paris: Harmattan.

N'Diaye, Marième. 2012. "La politique constitutive au Sud: refonder le droit de la famille au Sénégal et au Maroc." In *Science Politique*. Bordeaux: Université Montesquieu – Bordeaux IV.

Ouali, Nouria. 2008. "Les réformes au Maroc: enjeux et stratégies du mouvement des femmes." *Nouvelles Questions Féministes* 27 (3): 28–41.

Patil, Vrushali. 2013. "From Patriarchy to Intersectionality: A Transnational Feminist Assessment of How Far We've Really Come." *Signs: Journal of Women in Culture and Society* 38 (4): 847–867.

Pease, Bob. 2010. *Undoing Privilege: Unearned Advantage in a Divided World*. London; New York, NY: Zed Books.

Roth, Benita. 2004. *Separate Roads to Feminism: Black, Chicana, and White Feminist Movements in America's Second Wave*. Cambridge, UK ; New York, NY: Cambridge University Press.

Roussillon, Alain, and Fatima-Zahra Zryouil. 2017. *Être femme en Égypte, au Maroc et en Jordanie*. Le Caire: CEDEJ – Égypte/Soudan.

Ruault, Lucile. 2016. "La circulation transnationale du self-help féministe: acte 2 des luttes pour l'avortement libre?" *Critique internationale* 70 (1): 37–54.

Salem, Sara. 2018. "Intersectionality and Its Discontents: Intersectionality as Traveling Theory." *European Journal of Women's Studies* 25 (4): 403–418.

Salime, Zakia. 2012. "A New Feminism? Gender Dynamics in Morocco's February 20th Movement." *Journal of International Women's Studies* 13 (5): 101–114.

Salime, Zakia. 2014. "New Feminism as Personal Revolutions: Microrebellious Bodies." *Signs: Journal of Women in Culture and Society* 40 (1): 14–20.

Salime, Zakia. 2016. "'The Women Are Coming': Gender, Space, and the Politics of Inauguration." In *Freedom Without Permission*, edited by Frances S. Hasso and Zakia Salime, 138–165. Durham, NC: Duke University Press.

Smaoui, Sélim, and Mohamed Wazif. 2013. "Etendard de lutte ou pavillon de complaisance? S'engager sous la bannière du 'Mouvement du 20 Février' à Casablanca." In *Au Cœur Des Révoltes Arabes: Devenir Révolutionnaires*, edited by Amin Allal and Thomas Pierret, 55–85. Paris: Armand Colin.

Sreberny, Annabelle. 2015. "Women's Digital Activism in a Changing Middle East." *International Journal of Middle East Studies* 47 (2): 357–361.

Taylor, Verta. 1999. "Gender and Social Movements: Gender Processes in Women's Self-Help Movements." *Gender & Society* 13 (1): 8–33.

Taylor, Verta, and Nancy Whittier. 1992. "Collective Identity in Social Movement Communities: Lesbian Feminist Mobilization." In *Frontiers in Social Movement Theory*, edited by Aldon D. Morris and Carol McClurg Mueller, 104–129. New Haven, CT: Yale University Press.

Tilly, Charles. 1984. "Les origines du répertoire d'action collective contemporaine en France et en Grande-Bretagne." *Vingtième Siècle: Revue d'histoire* 4 (1): 89–108.

Twine, France Winddance, and Bradley Gardener, eds. 2013. *Geographies of Privilege* (1st ed.). New York, NY: Routledge.

Vairel, Frédéric. 2007. "La transitologie, langage du pouvoir au Maroc." *Politix* 80 (4): 109.

Vairel, Frédéric. 2014. *Politique et mouvements sociaux au Maroc: la révolution désamorcée? Sociétés en mouvement*. Paris: Presses de Sciences Po.

Van Dyke, Nella, Doug McAdam, and Brenda Wilhelm. 2000. "Gendered Outcomes: Gender Differences in the Biographical Consequences of Activism." *Mobilization: An International Quarterly* 5 (2): 161–177.

Chapter 6

Intersectionality or unity? Attempts to address privilege in the gynecological self-help movement

Lucile Quéré

Introduction

Since the mid-2010s, France has seen the emergence of a critical and feminist analysis of health. In particular, women have been uniting their voices to challenge the permanence of doctors' and gynaecologists' power over their bodies, emphasising how this power continues to shape their oppressive experiences. They fight for their right to have control over their own bodies, particularly in medical consultations. This claim for bodily autonomy in health is linked to the denunciation of 'obstetric and gynaecological violence' and to the resurgence of a repertoire of action based on the strategies of the feminist self-help movement. Feminist self-help activism was born at the end of the 1960s in the United States, and its activists founded some of the feminist health centres (see Morgen 2002; Kline 2010). It was part of a large women's health movement which travelled to Europe in the mid-1970s and took different shapes according to national and local contexts. In the current French sense of the term, 'self-help' has three overlapping meanings. The first one designates the American self-help movement. The second refers to a set of practices through which women aim to take back control of their body, health, and sexuality, which include, among other things, support groups, collecting and sharing of information on specific bodily issues and alternative therapies, and self-observation of the genitals (Haraway 1997; Murphy 2004; Davis 2007). Finally, it also refers to one particular practice: gynaecological self-examination. Vulva, vaginal, and/or cervical self-observation is emblematic of the self-help movement because of its highly symbolic value.

This chapter draws on the recent resurgence of body and health appropriation practices in France, in particular through the iconic practice of collective vaginal self-examination, which has a central place in the resurgence of self-help collective sessions. In so doing, the research fills a gap in the literature since studies on self-help practices are still very scarce in Europe – perhaps as a result of their perception as being a historic form of activism associated with feminist politics of the 1970s and 1980s (Dardel 2007; Ruault 2016; D'Hooghe 2013). Contemporary self-help activities in Europe are usually organised as follows: they begin with the transmission and collective production of anatomical knowledge, as well as the sharing of experiences pertaining to the body, health, and sexuality. They then move on to the practical investigation of the genitals with a mirror and a flashlight, and possibly a speculum. Thus, the resurgence of vaginal self-exam is based, as in the 1970s, on a do-it-yourself ethos, a politicisation of health, and a strategy of taking back one's body from medicine. It carries both a radical critique of the ways in which clinical exams are led by health professionals, and an attempt to do healthcare another way – a feminist way, that is, a way in which women experience control over their own bodies, self-sovereignty, and collective care.

Consequently, this chapter argues that self-help practices are in line with prefigurative forms of politics, the aims and means of which are to bring about the desired society (Leach 2013). This particular prefigurative strategy relies upon the crafting of new ways of relating to each other to construct 'imagined egalitarian communities' (Srivastava 2005, p. 34) not based on domination and authority and the shaping of feminist selves. Indeed, vaginal self-exam is portrayed today, as in the 1970s (see Murphy 2012, pp. 47–48), as having a 'consciousness-raising effect,' producing new ways of seeing the world, new subjectivities, and radical change in women's lives. Because of its supposed politicising effect, the experience of self-exam should lead to an awareness of the mechanisms of oppression and to identification with feminism. Hence, self-help practices are supposed to create feminists and to shape a certain kind of feminist, whose subjectivities are not shaped by power relations. The women's body is thus framed as a tool for politicisation and the creation of feminist subjects. Since prefiguration takes place in a society structured by relations of power and domination, I argue that the literature on intersectionality is a particularly heuristic tool to critically seize possible renewals of power relations within prefiguration, and thus to question prefigurative politics' conditions of possibility.

This chapter also reveals how intersectionality shapes the feminist identity and practices of self-help activists. It shows that self-help activists are mostly concerned with inclusion. Indeed, they frame intersectionality as a set of practices for inclusion. Their approach to intersectionality is thus in line with the third way of practicing intersectionality identified in the introduction to this book: they see it as a 'repertoire for inclusivity.' This chapter argues that the activists' intersectional expectations (Schuster 2016) are not always sufficient to prevent processes of marginalisation and informal exclusion. The analysis of the emotional dimensions of contemporary self-help practices is central to understanding both the claim for and the non-performativity of intersectionality. It especially shows that self-help's empowering politics also rely on the social homogeneity of the self-help spaces. While it could be expected that the historic claim of diversification of feminisms through the self-help movement (Davis 2007) and the pervasiveness of an intersectional vocabulary would be signs of the enforcement of an intersectional praxis, this chapter explores the difficulties that activists face in performing intersectionality. It especially shows that a discursive commitment to intersectionality does not prevent the exclusion of minority women from feminist spaces.

This chapter unfolds by first discussing the prefigurative dimensions of contemporary self-help activism and the contributions of the literature on intersectionality to the study of prefigurative forms of politics. It then introduces the empirical study and discusses the main findings. This discussion explores first the ways in which the self-help activists of the case study frame intersectionality as a repertoire for inclusivity and use it as a lens to shape a feminist praxis based on the acknowledgement of privileges. Second, it focuses on a particular conflict which shows that emotional dimensions underlie the prefigurative politics of self-help and shape processes of informal exclusion.

Prefiguration and intersectionality in contemporary self-help practices

Prefigurative spaces of feminist becoming

The concept of 'prefigurative politics' is part of a field of research that focuses on the political practices of social movements. Aiming to seize the attempts to create utopian configurations in the present, it was first developed by Carl Boggs to designate 'the embodiment, within the ongoing political practice of a movement, of those forms of social relations, decision-making, culture, and human experience that are the ultimate goal' (Boggs 1977, p. 100). The term seeks to give meaning to the attempts to experiment with transformative political possibilities and imaginaries. According to Darcy K. Leach, the notion refers to

> a political orientation based on the premise that the ends a social movement achieves are fundamentally shaped by the means it employs, and that movements should therefore do their best to choose means that embody or 'prefigure' the kind of society they want to bring about.
>
> (Leach 2013, p. 1004)

The concept of prefiguration is thus particularly useful to analyse the questioning of dominant norms and the attempts to transform society 'in practice.'

The configurations in which the practices of self-help occur, whether in the form of workshops or regular group sessions, are in line with the prefiguring imaginary of the consciousness-raising groups of the so-called second wave (Polletta 1999; Fantasia and Hirsch 1995). They are based on a consciousness-raising strategy as well, through the collective crafting of knowledges and the acknowledgement of the political nature of private and intimate relationships (Evans 1979). The spaces of feminist becoming being studied can be understood as temporary zones of prefiguration that are built through the modelling of alternative modes of relationality. In this way, they seek to implant in the here-and-now the modes of relationality that would shape the society that is prefigured. Self-help spaces thus attempt to constitute 'free spaces,' defined by Francesca Polletta and Kelsy Kretschmer as 'small-scale settings within a community or movement that are removed from the direct control of dominant groups, are voluntarily participated in, and generate the cultural challenge that precedes or accompanies political mobilization' (Polletta and Kretschmer 2013, pp. 478–479).

Three dimensions are central to the implementation of the prefigurative imaginary of self-help practices: the crafting of a radically alternative care politics, the promotion of alternative modes of relationality, and the shaping of the political subjects of the society that is prefigured. The experimentation of a care politics defined by norms other than the ones of the existing biomedical system is based on the blurring of the frontier between experts and laywomen. Contemporary self-help spaces attempt to achieve the horizontality of the caring relationship, the collective appropriation of expert tools and knowledges, and the recognition of the knowledge of laywomen, based on their own experiences. In this way they are in continuity with the self-help politics of the women's health movement analysed by Michelle Murphy (2012).

In the face of institutions whose organisational modes are seen as producing medical and gynaecological violence, contemporary self-help activists try to build 'safe' and 'benevolent' spaces. They thus promote alternative modes of organisation of the work of care. For instance, the practice of self-examination has been framed as a way of resisting the medical structure regulating the gynaecological exam (Murphy 2004), based on the objectification of women's bodies and the invalidation of their subjective experience. In this respect, self-examination can be defined as a counter-practice (De Lauretis 2007, p. 72), a practice carried out in opposition to an already existing practice, fashioning another way. Self-help activists also experiment with other modes of relationality. The group form is perceived as emancipatory, contrary to the individuation of the care relationship within Western medicine. Not only do they insist on the collective dimension of care, but they also try to embody other forms of being as a group, charting new kinds of relationships. In this respect, activists attempt to implement some practices that are intended to reduce the authority they embody because of their status as organisers or because of their medical profession. In line with the attempts to implement radical democratic politics, they, for instance, try to implement egalitarian deliberative interactions, through the allocation of speaking slots. The prefigurative politics of self-help also involve the arrangement of space in a horizontal way, as the practice of sitting on the floor in a circle exemplifies. Objects are part of the process too: the speculum is made of plastic in order to avoid the coldness of metal, cushions and beds replace the gynaecological chair, the sharing of a meal symbolises a conviviality that cannot be found in medical settings. In the face of what they understand as the structural violence of health institutions, they attempt to create a benevolent space, providing 'a vision of how reproductive service *can* be' (Dayi 2011, p. 204).

The experimental dimension of self-help politics is also embodied by the collective appropriation of the experts' tools and knowledges. The use of the speculum by laywomen, a tool which symbolises the work instrument of women's health professionals, becomes a subversive political act. The story of the origins of the speculum, wrought by a white male doctor on enslaved women (McGregor 1998), is regularly told during self-help sessions, which also testifies to the political importance of narratives in mobilising and creating political solidarity (Polletta 2006, 2013). The circulation of knowledges forged in anatomical science embodies the critical appropriation of expert knowledge within self-help spaces. Finally, the prefigurative politics of care of the contemporary configurations of self-help requires the recognition of lay and experiential knowledge. Self-help activists affirm the legitimacy of the knowledge derived from experience, assigning an 'epistemic privilege' to experience (Murphy 2004). Self-help activism is an epistemological project (Tuana 2006; Murphy 2012) involving the construction of a knowledge based on 'the evidence of experience' (Scott 1991). Those three dimensions of self-help rest on the blurring of the boundaries between patients and caregivers. They subvert the (gendered) division and hierarchy between lay-women and experts resulting from the historical male appropriation of women's knowledge of their bodies (Ehrenreich and English 1973).

Intersectional critiques of prefiguration

This chapter argues that an intersectional reading can deepen our understanding of prefigurative politics. Feminist and women's movements constitute a privileged site for the renewal of studies on prefigurative politics. This literature has seldom questioned the reproduction of the complexity of power relations in prefigurative settings which intend to identify, name, neutralise, or subvert them. The affective and relational dimensions of collective action are particularly strong within those movements (Taylor and Rupp 1993; Achin and Naudier 2013), which invite a renewal of the focus on friendship, conflicts, tensions, and the diverse ways in which interpersonal relationships shape collective action. The study of the contemporary feminist self-help movement enables further questioning of the scope of sociability and affects for the materialisation of utopian settings (Lin et al. 2016). In that regard, the literature on intersectionality is a useful tool to understand how power relations are contested and can sometimes be reproduced in prefigurative settings, especially since the lexical field of intersectionality is successful in self-help spaces. Intersectionality is part of the vocabulary of a number of participants, and many of them clearly state their consciousness of intersectional oppressions. Those elements invite the researcher to question the overlapping of multiple axes of oppression and the complex formation of identities within prefigurative spaces.

The literature on prefiguration often ignores the fact that power relations and their enmeshment are reproduced in prefigurative spaces (Young and Schwartz 2012). Francesca Polletta identified the difficulty of maintaining prefigurative groups 'in societies characterized by taken-for-granted assumptions about class, race, gender, expertise and authority' (1999, p. 12). Her analysis derives from Nancy Fraser's outlook that 'social inequalities can infect deliberations, even in the absence of any formal exclusion' (1994, p. 81). Thus, the adoption of an intersectional lens enables us to question the understanding of prefiguration as necessarily empowering and emanci-patory (Cooper 2008). Those elements invite the development of a critical understanding of prefiguration as a space that can both produce emancipatory dynamics and reproduce power relations. This chapter argues that the con-flicts sometimes dividing feminist prefigurative spaces and the attempts for coalitional politics are worth studying in order to deepen our understanding of both prefigurative and feminist politics.

Methods and data

The self-help movement is characterised by the circulation of activists, discourses, knowledges, objects, and practices. Thus, it constitutes a semi-autonomous field efficiently captured by a multi-sited ethnography. Ethnography has been iden-tified by social movements anthropology as the most accurate methodology to grasp the diversity of lived experiences and the ways in which participants make sense of their practices (Edelman 2001; Whittier 1995). Feminist research has more particularly called for more reflexive forms of ethnography (Shepard 2011; Taylor and Rupp 1993) that consider social movements participants' emotions in the analysis. Multi-sited ethnography is more accurate to understand contempo-rary self-help practices than comparison, mostly because the movement's political project is not influenced only by the state in which it develops. Multi-sited eth-nography pays attention to the circulation of discourses and the configuration of practices in diverse places, and to their relationships (Marcus 1995), thus enabling a study of marginal forms of politics. My data was gathered over a three-year period (2015–2018) and is composed of diverse sources. I conducted 12 sessions of participant observation during self-help activities, lasting from two hours to two days. I always introduced myself as a researcher to all participants, posi-tioning myself as both an observer and a participant, and in line with the ethical norms of presentation of oneself and of confidentiality of each activity. Feminist zines – 'independent, not-for-profit publications that are circulated via subcultural networks' (Kempson 2015, p. 459) – and written productions were collected dur-ing those sessions. I also observed online self-help activities through local femi-nist mailing lists, social networks, and websites. Finally, I conducted 65 in-depth interviews. I recruited interviewees through the activities I attended and through referrals from other interviewees. The interviews were conducted with (1) organ-isers of self-help workshops, (2) occasional participants to self-help practices, (3) members of self-help groups, and (4) health professionals who integrate a self-help approach in their activity.

In this chapter, I use a case study based on an ethnographic observation of a self-help encounter that took place in France. The event was attended by 15 participants, including the three organisers, for two days. It was organised by three health professionals whose aims were to 'take up self-help as a practice of professional care' and to foster an 'inclusive and horizontal professional practice.' Most of the participants were midwives, but a medical intern and a sex worker attended as well. I took some notes in a notebook during the days, as did some of the participants, and wrote up more precise and consistent field notes during the evenings. I sometimes use these notes in the following text. The case study is also based on nine interviews. One was conducted before the event with one of the organisers, and eight interviews were conducted afterwards, with the two other organisers and six participants. The interviewees all identify as cisgender women and their ages range from 29 to 59. All of the event participants apart from one – Laure[1] – identify as white. Laure did not respond to my interview requests. She was directly involved in the conflict described below and extensively politicised daily practices and discourses employed by the organisers, which may account for this refusal. In the conflict that is described below, silences were framed as political and ideological 'complicity' with the status quo. The moral division of this framing leads to a political condemnation of the researcher's position and can explain her unwillingness to answer me. I use pseudonyms when I refer to the interviewees, and they were all guaranteed anonymity. The interviews ranged in length from one-and-a-half hours to three hours, and were fully transcribed. They were coded using Atlas.ti, a qualitative data analysis software, through the identification of major themes in subjective experiences of self-help and activism, as well as professional, procreative, and bodily trajectories. I translated the interview extracts, choosing to stay as close as possible to the interviewees' original words and idiomatic expressions.

The desire for intersectionality

The case study focuses on a two-day activity entitled 'self-help' by the three organisers, who described it as a meeting around gynaecological self-help practices. Emilie and Lisa are midwives, and Cha identifies as a 'witch,' an 'artist,' and a 'support person.' The three of them are white, educated, and come from middle-class backgrounds. They organised the activity in order to spread 'support in self-help' amongst health professionals and midwives. Several activities took place during the weekend: an 'introduction to self-help'; a time dedicated to the 'needs and expectations of sex workers regarding their medical follow-up' through the intervention of a sex worker by videoconference; a self-examination practice; a simulation of self-examination 'guidance' as in an individual medical consultation; and collective times for feedback. The activities took place in the office of one of the organising midwives, a large room furnished with mattresses and cushions. Mealtimes were shared in a space set up as a kitchen, where books and zines could be consulted or bought. The aim was to build a space of sharing for health professionals to discard the hierarchy of knowledge between experts and lay participants. In that regard, the event was based on a prefigurative strategy aiming to bring about a radically alternative care politics which would not be based on the hierarchy of knowledges and the frontier between experts and laywomen. Intersectionality was given a major role within the project, through the acknowledgement of privileges and the development of practices of inclusion.

Intersectionality was framed, as will be shown, as the way to bring about a really free space and a truly feminist prefiguration.

Acknowledging privileges

The organisers of this self-help event acknowledge their position as privileged people in society. Their awareness shapes their political and professional practices. They construct their own privileges as a problem, and therefore try to develop a set of practices based on the aim of inclusivity. Inclusivity is thus thought of as the concrete implementation of intersectionality. Practices of inclusion are framed as the feminist praxis of intersectionality, and the acknowledgement of privileges as a first step toward it.

The organisers of the self-help activity studied acknowledge the structural dimension of inequalities and exclusions, and question their own complicity in the perpetuation of the system. In so doing, they are in line with the 'race cognizance' discursive repertoire that Ruth Frankenberg defines as based on the acknowledgement of difference, 'understood in historical, political, social and cultural terms rather than essentialist ones' (Frankenberg 1993, p. 157). This is particularly true when they refer to their feminist identity. Lisa, a 29-year-old midwife, for instance, explains her attention to 'check her privileges.' She insists on her awareness of the structural dimension of oppressions. She affirms her willingness not to reproduce at an individual level a problem she frames as collective.

The organisers also pay attention to the ways in which oppressive structures shape their own experiences as privileged. Emilie tells me how the privileges linked to her whiteness influence her social experiences:

> I'm sure everyone has tried saying exactly the same thing as a black person in the room, and that it has been heard only because you, you are white. Anyway, I have already experienced that. *Emilie, organising midwife, 37 years old.*

Emilie recognises her white privilege when it comes to the legitimacy of her own words and the ways in which race organises the forms of relationality she develops. She thus names and highlights the privileges linked to the social construction of whiteness, which is characteristically thought of as invisible (Frankenberg 1993) and concealing the oppressive dimension of its normativity (Phoenix 1997; Garner 2006). The organisers resist a framing of racism as something with no link to their lives, experiences, and subjectivities.

While acknowledging the privileges organising their lives, the organisers of this self-help activity are attentive to the privileges linked to their profession. The criticism of professional privileges rests on the analysis of health professionals' social status and of the subsequent authority they derive from it. Self-help activists denounce violence against women linked to this social status. This criticism can sometimes lead them to refuse to exercise their jobs as midwives, as Lisa's trajectory shows:

> When I finished my studies and got my diploma, I wanted to cry so hard that day, because I was so ashamed of what I did, and I felt like my hands were full of blood, because of all the times I collaborated with the oppressor, in order to make things easier for the women who were assaulted [by health professionals] during labour. . . . So I decided to stop and I left for several years. . . . Then, I discovered self-help and I thought about a way of practicing in line with my political ideas, my values, what I wanted to be useful for. *Lisa, organising midwife.*

Lisa sees self-help as a tool able to deactivate power relations between professionals and laywomen. She hopes that self-help can subvert the ways midwifery is practiced, by overturning the caring power relationship based on the social hierarchy of knowledge between experts and laywomen. Lisa thus stands against the monopolisation by health professionals of knowledge about health and the body. Organisers of self-help activities try to suggest collective answers to the issue of professional privilege via the diffusion of self-help-inspired ways of doing, based on experimentation.

Their declarations of awareness of their embodied privileges lead these activists to see and name the self-help activities' social homogeneity. The acknowledgement of the lack of diversity is followed by its criticism. Cha argues that the white and cis composition of the group obscures some topics within the movement, such as the racial history of plants and medicine, and the inclusion of trans, intersex, and non-binary people. She develops a critical analysis of her activism. Consequently, the organisers aim at widening what they define as the traditional repertoire of self-help, by developing practices of inclusion in order to diversify participation and to represent the diversity of women's interests.

Desire for intersectionality and practices of inclusion

Intersectionality is a desirable goal for the organisers of this self-help activity. They consider it as an answer to counter the reproduction of power relations and exclusions within the self-help spaces. Intersectionality is seen as the solution to truly realise the prefigurative politics of feminist self-help based on the hope for a space free from power relations. Therefore, the organisers seek to implement intersectionality through the development of practices of inclusion.

During the weekend and in the interviews, the organisers used the vocabulary of intersectionality. Intersectionality is a discursive resource from which they draw to give meaning to their practices and activism. While it is common for some self-help practice participants to use a lexical field referring to the multiplicity and interweaving of power relations, organisers directly and frequently used the terms 'intersectional' and 'intersectionality.' Their awareness of intersectional oppressions is the cornerstone of their feminist activism, as Emilie declares:

> The feminism I defend . . . is being aware that you live in different degrees of oppression, that some people find themselves at the intersection of many of them, but that still, they are a person. *Emilie, organising midwife.*

They particularly bring up intersectionality when they mention the beginning of their feminist activism. Intersectionality gives meaning to their feminist identity, and this identification contrasts with other ideological trends that they name as 'white' or 'essentialist.' In that way, they also consider that intersectionality should become part of the participants' feminist identity. They acknowledge the major role it played in their own feminist subjectification, and believe that it should similarly influence the participants' subjectivities, bringing them to adhere to intersectional ideas if they do not already. Intersectionality is thus a 'normative goal' for them (Weldon 2008). Self-help practices are supposed to create feminists and to shape a certain kind of feminist.

Consequently, intersectionality principles underlie a set of practices that the organisers implement as tools for the achievement of intersectionality in self-help spaces. Inclusion is central to those practices (Evans 2015). First, the activists routinely begin the self-help activities they organise with time dedicated to explaining why certain social norms led them to experiment with other ways of caring and listing a number of rules to make this experiment possible.

> At the beginning of the weekend . . . I set the scene, explaining the . . . oppressive norms that can be [reproduced], such as heterosexual, penetrative, gender norms. . . . I asked the participants to say 'I' rather than 'we,' so that everybody can freely exist without complying with standards. . . . I asked that they care about the speaking time, about confidentiality . . . like a space to experiment being truly free to own your body. *Lisa, organising midwife.*

The prefigurative dimension of the self-help space requires the development of a number of practices aimed at deactivating social norms and power relations. Organisers are particularly aware of the exclusionary effects that a discourse based on the negation of differences between women can have. As a result, they tried to invite community-based health organisations, a way to blur the frontiers between lay experiences and expert knowledges.

Furthermore, the organisers resist the primacy of gender-sameness and are careful not to impose the category 'women,' which has associated feminism with essentialism. Hence, they develop a discursive apprehension to inclusion and formulate an alternative vocabulary by substituting other terms to designate the subjects of self-help activities. Self-help activists acknowledge diversity of experience and criticise the exclusion of transgender and non-binary identities from discourses. They give discourse a major role in the implementation and effectiveness of inclusion by emphasising that it can actively exclude some people from feminist practices of autonomy. Their strong invitation to refer to 'person assigned woman at birth' or 'menstruator' shows their attempt to set up a transgender and non-binary inclusive politics by building an alternative way of naming. The request to participants to use those terms is a way to build and ensure a space that would not be exclusionary to transgender people, along with making participants sensitive to power relations within the feminist movement. It thus has a 'pedagogical function' (Bobel 2010, p. 156), but it also intends to shape the feminist subjects that will embody new ways of relating to each other.

Finally, the organisers usually suggest that vulva parts should no longer be named after white male practitioners. They frame this choice as a means to counter the appropriation of women's bodies by men and experts and as a way of decolonising medical history and women's bodies. They attempt to counter the invisibility of black women in history by highlighting the history of gynaecology's racial dimensions. Thus, they suggest that genital glands should be renamed after Lucy, Anarcha, and Betsy, three enslaved women who underwent surgical gynaecological experiments without anaesthesia (Kapsalis 1997; McGregor 1998). The hope for intersectionality thus is expressed through the development of a decolonising discourse on the racial dimensions of the history of health, medicine, and gynaecology within a very white-dominated movement. It works as a decolonising strategy of rhetorical inclusion (Vats 2016).

Declarations of privileges and practices of inclusion indicate a commitment to intersectionality as both a theory and praxis. They are aimed at transforming self-help activism and at prefiguring an alternative care politics with political subjects free from power relations.

The non-performativity of intersectionality

In this case study, intersectionality is framed by self-help activists as a set of knowledges and practices enabling the realisation of feminist utopia. However, acknowledgement of privileges and practices of inclusion can 'function as claims to performativity rather than as performatives' (Ahmed 2004, p. 10). The prefigurative experimentation observed in this case study was the subject of internal criticism within the group, which led to conflict and informal exclusion. I argue that the analysis of the failures of this power-relations-free space reveals the ways in which affects underlie processes of marginalisation. The study highlights that the self-help prefigurative politics rests on a desire for feminist unification, which can downplay power relations and their reproduction. In the end, the realisation of the self-help empowering politics seems to depend on the social homogeneity of the self-help spaces.

A practical criticism of prefigurative politics

The second day of the activity was marked by a conflict resulting from two different framings of an event that happened in the morning. It reveals the tensions around both the definition of prefigurative politics and what a prefigurative politics should be.

> On the second-day morning, some participants who arrived early met in the kitchen. The informal discussion gradually focused on Julie, a sex worker participating in a community-based health organisation for and by sex workers. The participants asked her questions about her work and the sex workers' needs for care. Cha and her friend Laure came into the room several times. They rolled their eyes and seemed irritated by the conversation. *Field note extract, 2017.*
>
> Then Emilie came to tell me: 'it's so nice, the conversation continues on how to be inclusive with sex workers.' And then Cha arrived. She looked really moved and was about to cry, saying that what she had wanted to avoid was happening. She felt that it was very violent that a sex worker had to educate everybody. . . . When we officially started the day, Cha and Laure wanted to talk about that. I was not OK with that because I could feel that they were really angry. *Lisa, organising midwife.*

This event marked the beginning of a day-long conflict. The issue of the value placed on knowledge, especially on lay knowledges, was at the core of this conflict. Cha and Laure denounced the use of a layperson's knowledge of her own body by health professionals. They particularly feared that health professionals could then take advantage of this knowledge by merchandising it in a medical consultation, while Julie did not make any profit from sharing it. They exposed the exploitation of Julie in the process, whose work for the elaboration and diffusion of this knowledge was not recognised as such and was unpaid – a process named by one of the participants as 'resource plundering.' They thus pointed to the economic dimension of the hierarchy between lay and expert knowledges.

The issue of privileges was central to the conflict that followed. The theme was present in all the discussions over the weekend, as these notes show:

> On Saturday morning, during a discussion on neutrality, Laure, who identifies as 'lesbian and a bit black,' considered that 'it is because some midwives are middle class, white, and heterosexual' that they believe in neutrality. Another participant, Sybille, answered, 'I am middle class, white, and heterosexual.' Laure specified, 'it is not an insult.' After a silence, she added, 'well, yes, it is an insult.' *Field note extract, 2017.*

The attempt to problematise privileges highlighted both the privileges of health professionals in the consultation and their privileges within the space of the self-help activity. Cha and Laure developed a criticism of the experimental space of self-help, delimited by a framework aimed at deactivating power relations and creating a 'free space.' The following scene highlights this criticism:

> While Sybille said she did not feel safe anymore once her questions to Julie were considered 'absurd' by Laure, the latter answered that she had not felt

safe once since the beginning of the weekend, referring among other things to a racialising term Sybille had used the day before. *Field note extract, 2017.*

Sybille blamed Laure for breaking the framework based on 'benevolence' and on the absence of 'value judgements.' On the contrary, Laure denounced the nature of the framework and its contours. She highlighted that this framework was made only for those who had the privilege to not question its limits, and especially insisted on the racial privilege linked to Sybille's whiteness. This episode can be framed as an attempt by Laure and some other participants, like Cha, to put into practice an intersectional criticism of the feminist self-help prefigurative politics.

The prefigurative project of the weekend was based on the creation of an inclusive space that gave major discursive and practical importance to intersectionality. Inclusion was conceived as the cornerstone for the implementation of intersectionality within an activism based on the attempt to fulfil other ways of being in the world and building relationships. But this desire for intersectionality does not prevent the reproduction of power relations within prefigurative spaces. The attempt to politicise power dynamics led to a backlash, the development of a discourse based on universalist principles, and a sanction. The latter could be seen in Laure's ostracisation, as Sophie, a 33-year-old midwife committed to intersectional analysis, recounts:

> During lunchtime, I was struck by the fact that we put Laure aside. I felt like we ostracised her. . . . It was terrible to see that we were all carefully avoiding talking to her. Apart from Laure, in the end everyone tried to calm things down and comfort each other. But we could only manage to do so at the cost of excluding someone from the group, and that was not satisfactory. I didn't feel like I was doing something right then. *Sophie, midwife.*

Laure's exclusion from the group is the sign of the organisers' unsuccessful attempt to realise intersectionality through inclusion. Minority groups can thus be excluded from self-help spaces despite practices of inclusion. The realisation of the self-help empowering politics depends on the social homogeneity of the self-help spaces and leads to the informal exclusion of minority groups.

The emotional dimensions of exclusion

Laure's exclusion is paradigmatic of the reproduction of racial social relations within contemporary self-help spaces. I argue that dynamics of exclusion rest on emotional dimensions. Self-help is formed by a set of practices which produce and frame emotions. They build a hierarchy between emotions, and this division is underpinned by power relations, particularly racial ones.

Discourses and practices on self-examination constitute a privileged site for the study of the affective dimension of self-help practices. Self-examination is what Hochschild has labelled emotion work, which refers 'to the act of evoking or shaping, as well as suppressing, feeling in oneself' (Hochschild 1979, p. 561).

This work of raising and shaping participants' emotions is done by the organisers of the self-help activity. The act of evoking emotions is particularly significant in the self-examination activity, which is framed as having emotion-raising effects. Emilie explains that she has 'never met anybody who feels nothing during a self-exam.' In this respect, self-examination is an emotional imperative. She adds, 'I'm not saying everybody has to start crying when looking at their own pussy, but you cannot not feel anything. It's just not possible.' The shaping of emotions also involves the emotions' degree. Not only do the organisers expect emotions to emerge, but they also expect strong emotions. Emilie states that her first self-examination experience was 'almost a revolution,' and she hopes to offer the same feelings to participants. Finally, the nature of emotions is also framed by the organisers. Some emotions are highly expected, such as joy and a sense of power. Thus, there are strong emotional expectations toward the self-examination practice. The participants' emotions constitute a material to work on, and self-help activities are regulated by feeling rules (Hochschild 1979) framing the ways emotions are shaped and expressed.

Those emotional expectations can enable the transformation of deviant emotions into political agency (Taylor 1996), but they also participate in the reproduction of power relations and exclusions. They rest on the stigmatisation and condemnation of some emotions whose expression is not in accordance with what is expected. The case of Laure's anger is a concrete example of the reproduction of racial power relations underlying the emotional dimensions of self-help. Anger was an unexpected emotion in the event, as Emilie's words show:

> I hadn't expected anger. I had expected all kinds of emotions, but not anger. There was a participant [Laure] who was very, very, very angry. *Emilie, organising midwife.*

Laure's anger was unexpected, and its political dimensions are downplayed, although the importance of anger in political mobilisation has been widely documented (Lyman 1981; Collins 1990; Broqua and Fillieule 2012; Johsua 2013). The role of anger in raising feminist identity has been particularly underlined (Taylor 1996; Hercus 1999; Holmes 2004; Cardoso 2017), especially since it can have subversive dimensions in relation to gender norms. But Laure's anger is downplayed as a deviant feeling in the self-help prefigurative space and condemned for that reason as 'extremely violent' by some organisers and participants. Yet anger is accepted when it is directed at health professionals outside of the prefigurative space. The expression of anger is thus condemned when the prefiguration project is at stake. It reveals the repetition of racial dynamics within prefiguration, especially since the denunciation of privileges and anger were accepted when they came from Cha, who identified as white. Sybille's comments evidence that process:

> I appreciated that Cha told us she did not feel at ease with what happened. . . . However, Cha's friend [Laure], I could feel she is an extremely angry woman,

in a state of great aggressiveness, and it didn't fit with the group because it wasn't the approach. In a setting in which the rules are made to ensure benevolence, so that everybody feels comfortable, she looked really aggressive. *Sybille, midwife, 37 years old.*

These elements confirm Mary Holmes' analysis on anger in feminist writings from the 'second wave' (Holmes 2004). She argues that feminists had difficulties in dealing with anger, particularly because of the political ideal of sisterhood and 'the realities of dealing with other women in often new and experimental political processes' (Holmes 2004, p. 209). As a consequence, feminists promoted the idea that 'good feminists' did not get angry with each other, as Magali, a 38-year-old white midwife, does:

Maybe she was a feminist and had a lot of beautiful ideas, but as a woman I found it very harsh. I thought she was not very respectful. I need roundness, I like a little cup of tea, I like humour, I like things that make you feel comfortable, I like connections and so on. *Magali, midwife, 38 years old.*

As she attempts to politicise power relations based on race and authority within the prefigurative space of feminist self-help, Laure expresses a criticism which the group finds disturbing. Her anger, directed at people within the same space of political sisterhood, is thus condemned and leads to her informal exclusion from the group. This exclusion rests on emotional dimensions that reproduce racial power relations.

Conclusion

This chapter has revealed that the contemporary spaces of self-help activism are based on a prefigurative strategy that aims to realise the kind of society and political subjects they want to bring about. In these spaces, activists attempt to implement a radically different type of care politics, to fashion other modes of relating to each other, and to shape the political subjects accordingly. By focusing on one particular ethnographic observation from my fieldwork that took place during a self-help encounter by and for health professionals, this chapter highlights the importance given to intersectionality in this prefigurative strategy and the difficulty of realising an intersectional praxis when intersectionality is seen as a repertoire for inclusivity. Self-help activity organisers are committed to intersectionality, and they use it as a discursive tool to give sense to their feminist activism. In doing so, they acknowledge both their racial and professional privileges and the way it shapes their subjectivity. More particularly, they rely heavily on intersectionality in their attempt to create a self-help space free from power relations. They develop practices of inclusion by setting a clear set of rules, based on benevolence and care to the self and others. In their attempt to deactivate axes of oppression, they particularly pay attention to the reproduction of power dynamics along the lines of gender, sexuality, and authority and try to challenge the privileges linked to them.

However, the particular conflict presented in this chapter shows that activists' acknowledgement of privileges and practices of inclusion are not always sufficient to ensure a free space. The analysis of the use of intersectionality in the self-help movement has shown that activists identify their individual privileges without assuming their collective dimension. Thus, they do not succeed in challenging relational and epistemic privilege. As explained, some participants had a dissenting understanding of what political intersectionality should be in practice. They developed and voiced a criticism of the rules set up by the organisers, thus emphasising that these rules did not, in fact, prevent the reproduction of some power relations. The development of such a criticism can be partly explained by the dominated social status of these dissidents, in particular in terms of race and expertise.

Then, focusing on the dynamics that led to the marginalisation of one of these dissidents within the group, this chapter demonstrates that this particular prefigurative space reproduced racial power relations in spite of the activists' intersectional expectations. In doing so, it has identified how prefigurative spaces rely on a strong social and political homogeneity. In addition, it has also revealed the affective dimensions of self-help activism. Indeed, self-help settings, and more particularly self-examination practices, rest on an emotional imperative. The discourses underlying these practices frame how and what practitioners should feel. Hence, some emotions are expected, while the expression of others is sanctioned. The analysis shows more particularly that anger was unwelcome, in particular when it tried to politicise power relations within the group. The denial of the political dimensions of anger led the group to downplay the reproduction of oppressive dynamics – particularly of race – within a space seeking to undermine them.

Note

1 This name is a pseudonym.

References

Achin, Catherine, and Delphine Naudier. 2013. "L'agency en contexte: réflexions sur les processus d'émancipation des femmes dans la décennie 1970 en France." *Cahiers du Genre* 55: 109–130.
Ahmed, Sara. 2004. "Declarations of Whiteness: The Non-Performativity of Anti-Racism." *Borderlands* 3 (2).
Bobel, Chris. 2010. *New Blood: Third-Wave Feminism and the Politics of Menstruation*. New Brunswick, NJ: Rutgers University Press.
Boggs, Carl. 1977. "Marxism, Prefigurative Communism and the Problem of Workers' Control." *Radical America* 6 (1): 99–122.
Broqua, Christophe, and Olivier Fillieule. 2012. "Chapitre 6: Act Up ou les raisons de la colère." In *Emotions . . . Mobilisations!* Paris: Presses de Sciences Po.

Cardoso, Auréline. 2017. "C'est comme si on avait de la colère pour elles ." *Terrains travaux* 30 (1): 31–53.

Collins, Randall. 1990. "Stratification, Emotional Energy, and the Transient Emotions." In *Research Agendas in the Sociology of Emotions*, edited by T. D. Kemper. Albany, NY: State University of New York Press.

Cooper, Davina. 2008. "Intersectional Travel Through Everyday Utopias. The Difference Sexual and Economic Dynamics Make." In *Intersectionality and Beyond: Law, Power and the Politics of Location*, edited by Emily Grabham, Davina Cooper, Jane Krishnadas, and Didi Herman. Lodon: Routledge.

Dardel, Julie de. 2007. *Révolution Sexuelle et Mouvement de Libération Des Femmes à Genève (1970–1977): Histoire*. Lausanne: Ed. Antipodes.

Davis, Kathy. 2007. *The Making of Our Bodies, Ourselves: How Feminism Travels Across Borders: Next Wave: New Directions in Women's Studies*. Durham, NC: Duke University Press Books.

Dayi, Ayse. 2011. "Feminist Centers Negotiating Medical Authority in the 21st Century: Implications for Feminist Care and the U.S. Women's Health Movement." In *Access to Care and Factors That Impact Access, Patients as Partners in Care and Changing Roles of Health Providers*, 197–228. Research in the Sociology of Health Care 29. Bingley: Emerald Group Publishing Limited.

De Lauretis, Teresa. 2007. *Théorie queer et cultures populaires: de Foucault à Cronenberg*. Paris: La Dispute.

D'Hooghe, Vanessa. 2013. *Spéculum, miroir et identités: le self help gynécologique à Bruxelles dans les années soixante-dix*. Bruxelles: Éditions de l'Université de Bruxelles.

Edelman, Marc. 2001. "Social Movements: Changing Paradigms and Forms of Politics." *Annual Review of Anthropology* 30 (1): 285–317.

Ehrenreich, Barbara, and Deirdre English. 1973. *Witches, Midwives, and Nurses: A History of Women Healers*. New York, NY: The Feminist Press.

Evans, Elizabeth. 2015. *The Politics of Third Wave Feminisms: Neoliberalism, Intersectionality, and the State in Britain and the US*. Basingstoke: Springer.

Evans, Sara M. 1979. *Personal Politics: The Roots of Women's Liberation in the Civil Rights Movement and the New Left*. New York, NY: Knopf.

Fantasia, Rick, and Eric L. Hirsch. 1995. "Culture in Rebellion: The Appropriation and Transformation of the Veil in the Algerian Revolution." In *Social Movements and Culture*, edited by Hank Johnston and Bert Klandermans, 4: 144–160. London: Routledge.

Frankenberg, Ruth. 1993. *White Women, Race Matters: The Social Construction of Whiteness*. Minneapolis, MN: University of Minnesota Press.

Fraser, Nancy. 1994. "Rethinking the Public Sphere: A Contribution to the Critique of Actually." In *Between Borders: Pedagogy and the Politics of Cultural Studies*, edited by Henry A. Giroux and Peter McLaren. New York, NY: Psychology Press.

Garner, Steve. 2006. "The Uses of Whiteness: What Sociologists Working on Europe Can Draw from US Research on Whiteness." *Sociology* 40 (2): 257–275.

Haraway, Donna J. 1997. "The Virtual Speculum in the New World Order." *Feminist Review* 55: 22–72.

Hercus, Cheryl. 1999. "Identity, Emotion, and Feminist Collective Action." *Gender and Society* 13 (1): 34–55.

Hochschild, Arlie Russell. 1979. "Emotion Work, Feeling Rules, and Social Structure." *American Journal of Sociology* 85 (3): 551–575.

Holmes, Mary. 2004. "Feeling Beyond Rules: Politicizing the Sociology of Emotion and Anger in Feminist Politics." *European Journal of Social Theory* 7 (2): 209–227.

Johsua, Florence. 2013. "Nous vengerons nos pères. . . ." *Politix* 104 (4): 203–233.

Kapsalis, Terri. 1997. *Public Privates: Performing Gynecology from Both Ends of the Speculum*. Durham, NC: Duke University Press Books.

Kempson, Michelle. 2015. "'My Version of Feminism': Subjectivity, DIY and the Feminist Zine." *Social Movement Studies* 14 (4): 459–472.

Kline, Wendy. 2010. *Bodies of Knowledge: Sexuality, Reproduction, and Women's Health in the Second Wave*. Chicago, IL: University of Chicago Press.

Leach, Darcy K. 2013. "Prefigurative Politics." In *The Wiley-Blackwell Encyclopedia of Social and Political Movements*, edited by Donatella Della Porta, David Snow, Doug McAdam, and Bert Klandermans. Chichester: Blackwell Publishing Ltd.

Lin, Cynthia S., Alisa A. Pykett, Constance Flanagan, and Karma R. Chávez. 2016. "Engendering the Prefigurative: Feminist Praxes That Bridge a Politics of Prefigurement and Survival." *Journal of Social and Political Psychology* 4 (1): 302–317.

Lyman, Peter. 1981. "The Politics of Anger." *Socialist Review* 11: 55–74.

Marcus, George E. 1995. "Ethnography in/of the World System: The Emergence of Multi-Sited Ethnography." *Annual Review of Anthropology* 24 (1): 95–117.

McGregor, Deborah K. 1998. *From Midwives to Medicine: The Birth of American Gynecology*. New Brunswick, NJ: Rutgers University Press.

Morgen, Sandra. 2002. *Into Our Own Hands: The Women's Health Movement in the United States, 1969–1990*. New Brunswick, NJ: Rutgers University Press.

Murphy, Michelle. 2004. "Immodest Witnessing: The Epistemology of Vaginal Self-Examination in the U.S. Feminist Self-Help Movement." *Feminist Studies* 30 (1): 115–147.

Murphy, Michelle. 2012. *Seizing the Means of Reproduction: Entanglements of Feminism, Health, and Technoscience*. Durham and London: Duke University Press.

Phoenix, Ann. 1997. "'I'm White, So What?' The Construction of Whiteness for Young Londoners." In *Off White*, edited by M. Fine, L. Powell, L. Weiss, and M. Wong, 187–197. New York, NY: Routledge.

Polletta, Francesca. 1999. "'Free Spaces' in Collective Action." *Theory and Society* 28 (1): 1–38.

Polletta, Francesca. 2006. *It Was Like a Fever: Storytelling in Protest and Politics* (New ed.). Chicago, IL: University of Chicago Press.

Polletta, Francesca. 2013. "Narratives." In *The Wiley-Blackwell Encyclopedia of Social and Political Movements*, edited by Darcy K. Leach, Donatella Della Porta, David A. Snow, Doug McAdam, and Bert Klandermans. Chichester: Blackwell Publishing Ltd.

Polletta, Francesca, and Kelsy Kretschmer. 2013. "Free Spaces." In *The Wiley-Blackwell Encyclopedia of Social and Political Movements*, edited by Donatella Della Porta, David Snow, Bert Klandermans, and Doug McAdam. Chichester: Blackwell Publishing Ltd.

Ruault, Lucile. 2016. "La circulation transnationale du self-help féministe: acte 2 des luttes pour l'avortement libre?" *Critique internationale* 70: 37–54.

Schuster, Julia. 2016. "Intersectional Expectations: Young Feminists' Perceived Failure at Dealing With Differences and Their Retreat to Individualism." *Women's Studies International Forum* 58: 1–8.

Scott, Joan W. 1991. "The Evidence of Experience." *Critical Inquiry* 17 (4): 773–797.

Shepard, Benjamin. 2011. *Queer Political Performance and Protest* (Reissue ed.). London: Routledge.

Srivastava, Sarita. 2005. "'You're Calling Me a Racist?' The Moral and Emotional Regulation of Antiracism and Feminism." *Signs* 31 (1): 29–62.

Taylor, Verta. 1996. *Rock-a-by Baby: Feminism, Self-Help, and Post-Partum Depression: Perspectives on Gender*. New York, NY: Routledge.

Taylor, Verta, and Leila J. Rupp. 1993. "Women's Culture and Lesbian Feminist Activism: A Reconsideration of Cultural Feminism." *Signs: Journal of Women in Culture and Society* 19 (1): 32–61.

Tuana, Nancy. 2006. "The Speculum of Ignorance: The Women's Health Movement and Epistemologies of Ignorance." *Hypatia* 21 (3): 1–19.

Vats, Anjali. 2016. "(Dis)Owning Bikram: Decolonizing Vernacular and Dewesternizing Restructuring in the Yoga Wars." *Communication and Critical/Cultural Studies* 13 (4): 325–345.

Weldon, Laurel S. 2008. "Intersectionality." In *Politics, Gender, and Concepts: Theory and Methodology*, edited by Amy Mazur and Gary Goertz, 193–218. New York, NY: Cambridge University Press.

Whittier, Nancy. 1995. *Feminist Generations: The Persistence of the Radical Women's Movement*. Philadelphia, PA: Temple University Press.

Young, Kevin, and Michael Schwartz. 2012. "Can Prefigurative Politics Prevail? The Implications for Movement Strategy in John Holloway's Crack Capitalism." *Journal of Classical Sociology* 12 (2): 220–239.

Thinking through differences in feminist and queer movements

Chapter 7

Disability and intersectionality

Patterns of ableism in the women's movement[1]

Elizabeth Evans

Introduction

Intersectionality provides a critical tool for understanding how difference affects women's lives (Crenshaw 1991; Combahee River Collective 1982). Offering a framework for theorising oppression and marginalisation, intersectionality enables us to identify structural intersections within power dynamics, whilst acknowledging individual experiences of difference (Collins and Bilge 2016). Intersectionality can also be considered a social movement strategy (Verloo 2013), albeit one that raises various challenges for activists (Laperrière and Lépinard 2016). Exploring how, when, and where social movement actors choose to engage with intersectionality and the politics of privilege can reveal patterns of marginalisation, conflict, and/or cooperation (Evans and Lépinard, this volume). Whilst women's movement actors have increasingly sought to engage with intersectional politics, the emphasis has remained focused upon the three 'original' signifiers: gender, race, and class (Erevelles 2011).

It has been over 20 years since scholars such as Nasa Begum (1992) and Jenny Morris (1996) explored the intersections between disability, race, gender, and feminism in the UK, revealing the numerous ways in which disabled women[2] were marginalised and excluded from political debate and participation – both within the disability rights movement but also from within the women's movement. Morris observed that a women's movement which included the issues and interests of disabled women would require a radical rethink of feminist 'terms of analysis' (1996, p. 7); arguing that including the experiences and perspectives of disabled women would result in a more explicit feminist resistance to oppression. Incorporating disabled women's varied epistemologies would provide a more meaningful engagement with the politics of difference and would necessitate a critical engagement with able-bodied and able-minded privilege.

Despite being a well-known social and political category of difference, disability receives little attention from scholars, or activists, looking to explore inter or intra-movement intersectional politics (Garland-Thomson 2005; Erevelles 2011). Drawing on feminist disability scholarship, and in particular theoretical work on ableism, this chapter explores how, when and where disability features within the UK women's movement. Based upon original empirical research undertaken with disabled women activists and two high-profile women's organisations, the chapter reveals that whilst the women's movement is in some respects attempting to adopt an intersectional framework in order to become more *inclusive* of disabled women (Evans and Lépinard, this volume), in particular through attempts to adopt a pedagogical approach to intersectionality, which incorporates disability, disabled women feel that the movement is inherently ableist.

The research raises wider questions for social movement scholars regarding the ways in which we analyse, understand, and classify intersectional praxis. By comparing different types of feminist organisation, the study reveals that discursive commitments to intersectionality are not always sufficient to address ableist politics or able-bodied/able-minded privilege. The research identifies three key critiques that disabled women activists make with regards the wider women's movement: (1) it is *ignorant* with regards disability; (2) that where disabled women are included this is simply *tokenistic*; and (3) that there is a *failure to engage reflexively* on organising strategies and accessibility. The chapter begins by reviewing some of the key ideas within critical and feminist disability scholarship, paying particular attention to the concept of ableism; the chapter then briefly sets out the methodology employed, before presenting and analysing the empirical data.

Disability, feminist disability, and ableism

It is difficult (and arguably undesirable) to offer a precise definition of disability, given its discursive, juridical, and political fluidity. Although all identity markers are open to contestation (Marx Ferree 2009), approaches to disability in particular have been characterised by conflicting, contradictory, and overlapping definitions and models (Davis 2013). Historic and contemporary medical-scientific approaches have established discursive frameworks and classificatory systems, which in turn have exerted social control over the minds and bodies of disabled people (Tremain 2015). In these analyses, disability is posited as an individual problem to which a solution must be found. In UK law, a disability is considered a 'physical or mental impairment' that 'has a substantial and long-term adverse effect on [a person's] ability to carry out normal day-to-day activities' (Equality Act 2010). Such an individualist account of impairment negates the role of society in creating and sustaining disabilities and in particular the historical and material context within which disability/ies are produced.

Disability

The social model of disability rejects an individualist or medical-based approach to disability (Oliver 1983) and has had a profound impact on the UK disability rights movement. The social model describes how society disables people. Instead of focusing on ways to treat, cure, or manage an individual's disability/ies, the emphasis is on changing society so as not to disable people. The most obvious example is that of wheelchair users, who might be impaired but not disabled in a world in which everyone used a wheelchair and no one built stairs (Siebers 2006, p. 12). Proponents of the social model argue that it facilitates activism because it calls for a unified community of disabled people (Shakespeare 1993). The social model analyses the obstacles that prevent equality and perpetuate cultural discrimination (Morris 2001), whilst emphasising the fluid nature of disability; as Tobin Siebers observes, 'the nature of disability is such that every human being may be considered temporarily able-bodied' (2006, p. 11).

Feminist disability

Whilst feminist disability scholars have had sympathy with the social model, they have also critiqued its failure to adequately incorporate gender into its analysis (Wendell 1989; Lloyd 1992). Creating a unified disability rights movement is at the core of the social model approach, rendering attempts to adopt an intersectional approach contentious (Vernon 1999). Accordingly, feminist disability scholars have played an important role in revealing the intersections between gender and disability (see Fawcett 2018 for an overview). Drawing on Foucault, writers have identified the historic links between the treatment of women and disabled people in paternalist capitalist systems (Miles 1988), in which medical professionals have sought to eliminate or discipline women's bodies (Sherwin 1992). Disabled women, especially migrant women, deemed biologically inferior to non-disabled women, have had their reproductive rights curtailed, for instance through enforced sterilisation, and they are at increased risk of having their children removed from their care (Silvers 2007). Whilst feminist disability scholars have brought a gendered lens to disability, they have also raised contentious questions for the wider feminist movement, particularly regarding care[3] and reproductive rights.[4] Observing that these 'difficult' issues are too often overlooked by feminist activists, Lloyd argues that disabled women struggling to 'locate themselves within organizations whose theoretical and ideological base is for them inadequate or partial' (1992, p. 218).

For those interested in pursuing an intersectional analysis, a materialist feminist account of disability offers a useful analytical framework. Such an approach delineates the ways in which bodies and minds not only matter to understanding disability politics, but are constituted along gendered, racialised and classed lines, called into being by capitalist systems (Inckle 2015; Erevelles 2011). Building on this, Price develops the concept of the 'bodymind,' which she defines as 'sociopolitically constituted and material entity that emerges through both structural (power- and violence-laden) contexts and also individual (specific) experience' (2015, p. 271). The theoretical links to intersectionality are clear: the interconnectedness between body and mind and the subsequent effects of impairment on the lived experiences of gendered, racialised, classed, nationalised disabled people have material consequences that require political attention and action. Indeed,

'disabling attitudes, stereotypes and policies' all but guarantee that disabled people remain amongst the most economically disadvantaged in society (Vernon
1999, p. 388). In order to theorise such a material context, scholars and activists
have developed the concept of 'ableism' to refer to a set of beliefs and attitudes
that privilege the able-bodied/able-minded.

Ableism

Ableist ideology infuses our institutions and social relations (Chouinard 1997),
revealing itself in the belief that a disabled person is not only defined by their disability but that they are essentially inferior to non-disabled people (Ho 2008); as
such, disabled people occupy an abject or 'diminished' position in society (Campbell 2001, p. 44). The drive for 'compulsory able-bodiedness' (McRuer 2013)
has led to both the pathologisation of disability, and conterminously, to a practice
wherein disability is 'unthought,' a process by which disabled people constitute
spectral visions at the peripheries of society (Campbell 2009). Despite the pervasive nature of ableism, Linton suggests that there is little consensus regarding
the specific behaviours or discourse that might be deemed ableist, because 'the
nature of the oppression of disabled people is not yet as widely understood' (2006,
p. 161). Thus, ableism is underpinned by a pervasive able-bodied/able-minded
privilege.

For disability rights activists, ableism is analogous to other systemic structural
forms of oppression, such as sexism, racism, or homophobia. Whilst ableism has
been a particularly useful means by which to name the oppression of disabled
people, it is also true that unlike other structural forms of oppression it has not had
a significant purchase within wider society (Goodley 2014). The material effects
of ableism are such that there is an effective 'removal and/or erasure of disability'
in spaces that claim an inclusive agenda, requiring disabled people to assimilate in
order to be included (Erevelles 2011, p. 33). For social movements, able-bodied/
able-minded privilege can therefore be identified where little thought has been
given to issues of accessibility either with respect to discourse, campaigns, or the
range of tactical repertoires adopted.

Such privilege also manifests itself in the default assumption that the object,
and subject, of analysis is based upon the experiences and abilities of non-disabled
people (Goodley 2014). Even when non-disabled people are the subject of political inquiry, there is typically a failure to recognise the varied forms of ableism, for
instance biological-based ableism or cognitive-based ableism (Wolbring 2008),
which results in a stereotypical idea of what constitutes a disabled person. For
social movement activists, a failure to address either the exclusion or the homogenisation of disabled people will reinforce ableist logic (Inckle 2015). Drawing
upon ideas of ableism, this research explores these themes with regards to the
inclusion of disabled women and disability-related issues in the UK women's
movement; in so doing the research reveals the wider need for social movement
actors to challenge privilege framed by ableism.

Methods

Analysis of intersectionality within social movement activism typically involves close study of specific groups and campaigns, in order to identify the extent to which different types of organisation, and organising, are more conducive or resistant to intersectional frameworks (see Bonane, this volume; David, this volume; Labelle, this volume). This research evaluates how disabled women and their issues and interests are included within the UK movement, specifically through analysis of three key groups: Fawcett Society, Sisters Uncut, and disabled women's collective Sisters of Frida.

Fawcett Society, the largest women's civil society organisation in the UK, was established in the mid-19th century to campaign for women's rights. Fawcett is a membership organisation which undertakes national high-profile campaigns as well as organising around the country in local groups. Fawcett can broadly be defined as a liberal feminist organisation, seeking to work through official political channels to effect change. Whilst critics have identified a lack of radicalism, it has at times sought to strike a more defiant tone; for example, it sued the government for failing to take account of gender in its austerity measures. The organisation is viewed by some (especially younger) feminists as part of the establishment (Evans 2015), which at times seems at odds with an increasingly radical and queer (Chamberlain 2017) UK women's movement. The research draws upon analysis of the organisation's policy documents and briefs, campaigns, and qualitative data gathered from those involved with policymaking and events organisation.

Sisters Uncut are a grassroots direct-action group established in 2014 as an offshoot of anti-austerity group UK Uncut; they were formed by, amongst others, domestic violence survivors in order to defend women's services from austerity (Guest 2016). Since then they have expanded and now include a number of groups across the UK. Their high-profile tactics have attracted attention for the causes that they champion; for example, they have reclaimed highly visible public spaces, such as Holloway Prison (the former women's prison) and poured red dye into the fountains at Trafalgar Square (to symbolise blood), in order to call attention to the violence against women wrought by cuts to women's services. Sisters Uncut were formed in a feminist landscape that was increasingly seeking to address intersectionality. Whilst the context within which they were formed does not make it automatic that they would choose to adopt an intersectional approach, their lack of historical baggage, in comparison to Fawcett, has made it easier for them to pursue an intersectional praxis. Exploring how they address disability within their work is based on analysis of their organising principles, actions, and campaigns.

Neither Fawcett nor Sisters Uncut identify themselves as an organisation run specifically in the interests of disabled women; whilst there are undoubtedly disabled women active in both organisations, it is important to ensure that the views of those who are active on issues surrounding disabled women are central. As such, the last strand of the research focuses on Sisters of Frida, a disabled women's collective, and includes a qualitative survey undertaken with 24 of its activists (they do not have a membership list). Sisters of Frida, named after disabled feminist artist Frida Kahlo, is, according to its website, an 'experimental collective of disabled women' who share experiences and challenge oppression.

Established in 2014 to fight for disabled women's voices to be heard in 'diverse places of influence,' the group seek to highlight the interconnectedness of structural forms of oppression. Activists were asked about their experiences of the UK women's movement – how inclusive they considered the movement to be and how the movement could improve. Accessibility was the primary concern, so an online form was used with the questions written in plain English. Follow-up questions were conducted via email correspondence. The responses of the activists are not intended to provide a representative sample but rather serve to highlight the views of disabled women activists. Informed by intersectional theory, this research recognises the diverse experiences of disabled women, not just in terms of the impact of cross-impairments but also how their experiences are refracted through their race, ethnicity, class, sexuality, language, immigration status, and age; in short, it seeks to avoid creating a 'typical disabled woman' (Silver 2007, p. 132). Finally, it is important to note that I am not a disabled woman. Whilst I have sought to prioritise the voices of disabled women within this chapter, I recognise that there might be instances of ableism that have not been apparent to me as a non-disabled woman.

Contrasting approaches to disability

Fawcett Society (FS) and Sisters Uncut (SU) differ with respect to their emergence, organisation, ideology, and tactical repertoires: FS is an historic organisation with roots in the women's suffrage movement, whereas SU are a relatively new group that emerged out of the anti-austerity movement; FS is a membership organisation with paid staff based in London, conversely SU is a grassroots collective; FS is widely viewed as championing a liberal feminist agenda, whilst SU adopt a more radical and socialist feminist politics; and finally, FS engages with politicians and policymakers, whilst SU undertake direct-action protests. The two groups also differ in their approach to and incorporation of intersectionality. Intersectionality came rather late to FS – there are no references to it on their website prior to 2017; however, interviews with FS revealed that a 'commitment to intersectionality' is now central to their strategy. Meanwhile, the intersectional commitment of SU is explicit in their 'Feministo' which sets out their ideology, campaign priorities, and key demands. Despite these differences, comparing the ways in which disabled women and disability-related issues feature within their politics is a useful exercise, not least because they are two high-profile feminist organisations in the UK which receive regular media attention in mainstream as well as social media. The exploration of the two groups' approaches to intersectionality and disability is considered through analysis of three key areas: their discursive commitments to intersectionality; the role of intersectionality in their campaigns; and how they practice intersectionality.

Discursive commitments to intersectionality

SU claim that they are 'committed to centring disabled women'; such a commitment is unusual for activist groups who don't have disability as their central focus. On their website, SU highlight interconnected systems of oppression, including 'sexism, racism, anti-blackness, classism, disableism, ageism, homophobia, transphobia, transmisogyny, whorephobia, fat-phobia, islamophobia, and antisemitism.' SU use the term 'disableism' rather than 'ableism,' a common elision though the terms are analytically distinct,[5] it is clear that they view the structural oppression of disabled women as a part of their agenda. However, it is worth reflecting on the shortfalls of this type of list-based approach to intersectionality which, whilst demonstrating a discursive commitment, can be difficult to translate into practice; not least when the list is long.

The approach to disability adopted by SU reveals itself to be one that is also mindful of the complexities of cognitive disabilities, an area typically marginalised in discussions surrounding disability. SU adopt a nuanced analysis of disability, one informed by debates within disability rights activism and by the social model approach, but also grounded in a materialist feminist account of disability. This perhaps suggests that a materialist feminist approach can be considered particularly well suited for discursive commitments to intersectionality and disability. Indeed, SU's analytical framework seeks to prioritise disability, by focusing on disabled women as amongst those most affected by austerity, emphasising that government cuts disproportionately affect disabled women.

Conversely, disability does not feature in FS's analytical approach to gender equality. Indeed, when asked, a representative from FS acknowledged that they had not done any work that 'specifically/solely focuses on some of the challenges that disabled women face.' There are 51 briefings on their website, used to inform and influence political debate concerning women's equality, dating back to 2010: there are no briefings that specifically address disability, nor is disability included in briefings covering analysis of austerity and government budgets, despite cuts to benefits and the introduction of work capability assessments rendering disabled women particularly vulnerable. Furthermore, a search of the FS website for the term 'disability' reveals few references, although there is a blog written by disability rights activist Nicky Clark who argues that the government needs to do more to meet the needs of unpaid carers (this is accompanied by a gendered photo of feminine hands pushing a man in a wheelchair).[6]

Exploring whether disability is included within an organisation's discursive approach toward women's equality is an important means by which to gauge the presence of ableism. Research on the two groups reveals that whilst disability is a central element of SU's analysis, it was virtually absent from FS's. Given that FS are the largest women's civil society organisation in the UK, the absence of disabled women from their analytical framework is particularly problematic. In order to explore this in greater depth, the chapter now considers the extent to which disability is included within campaigning.

Intersectionality in feminist campaigns

SU's campaigns revolve around issues connected to violence against women (broadly conceived to include physical, psychological, economic, and political forms of violence); analysis reveals that they frequently seek to incorporate disability as a core part of this agenda. For instance, they marked the International Day of People with Disabilities by drawing attention to the fact that disabled women are more likely to face domestic violence, highlighting the 'additional layers of power and control' that perpetrators can wield and noting that disabled women are not always believed by those from whom they are seeking help. Relatedly, SU have campaigned on specific issues facing disabled women, ranging from perpetrators who withhold medicine to those who refuse to hand over benefits.

SU have also campaigned for the need to improve accessibility in refuges. Disabled women face a dilemma when leaving a home which may have been specially adapted for their needs, because many refuges are simply not accessible. SU note that when domestic violence service budgets are cut, this disproportionately affects disabled women and migrant women, who have specific needs not offered in many refuges. As noted in the previous section, SU do not rely upon a 'stereotypical' disabled women, and they have drawn attention to the woeful provision of domestic violence refuges for women with cognitive disabilities; just one specialist refuge exists in the country. More broadly, SU have emphasised the interconnectedness between state/police violence, sexual violence, and those with mental health needs in order to campaign for criminal justice reform alongside greater provision of women's services and improved accessibility for disabled women with multiple disabilities.

FS recently conducted a sex discrimination law review to examine the gaps in sex discrimination legislation, to establish whether equality law is 'fit for purpose.' The final report, published in January 2018, runs to some 96 pages, covering Brexit, women in the workplace, violence against women and girls, promoting equality, multiple discrimination, and sex equality in Northern Ireland.[7] In total there are just four references to disability in the report. It is discussed twice in relation to equal pay: first it includes a call for a breakdown of the gender pay gap reporting by 'age, disability, ethnicity, LGBT and part-time status' (p. 5) and second to note that disabled women earn on average '6.1% less than non-disabled women.' A section on dress codes notes that they should not be discriminatory 'in the case of disability employees have the right to have reasonable adjustments made where it is necessary' (p. 46). Finally, there is a call for the law to account for multiple discrimination (p. 83). It is only in relation to employment legislation that disability is considered. There is no recognition of the fact that disabled women are more likely to be victims of abuse or of the disproportionately high levels of economic inactivity amongst disabled women.

Conversely, FS's Local Government Commission, exploring aspects related to the political representation of women, did include the experiences of disabled women and included a campaign for job-sharing for Members of Parliament (MPs) which, according to one representative from FS, 'had a strong disability focus.' FS believe that in promoting job-sharing for MPs, that this will increase the potential number of disabled women who feel able to run for office; it is certainly true that the current system of political recruitment leaves much room for improvement with regards issues of access. FS's engagement with issues of disability tend to revolve around the political representation of disabled women, rather than providing any deeper structural analysis of how disability and gender intersect to reproduce inequalities. This is perhaps unsurprising given the liberal nature of Fawcett's ideology and its focus on institutional politics.

Of course, whilst SU are engaging in grassroots activism and FS are engaged in the production of policy briefs, they are both driven by a desire to campaign for change. Hence, whilst they approach their goals in different manners, the extent to which they include disability in their campaigns is important. Analysis reveals that SU have sought to incorporate disability into the full range of their campaigns regarding women's equality, whilst FS's inclusion of disability was limited to discussions of employment or political representation. We now turn to the issue of accessibility and the extent to which disabled women are enabled to participate.

Practicing intersectionality

SU differ from FS in a number of ways, but perhaps one of the most significant is in their choice of tactical repertoires. Whilst FS work closely with political parties, politicians, and prominent journalists, SU employ direct-action tactics, principally through staging high-profile protests and reclaiming spaces. Their tactics have garnered significant media attention; for instance, they recently protested on the red carpet at the 2018 BAFTAs, regarding the lack of support for survivors of domestic violence contained within the proposed Domestic Violence and Abuse Bill, and at the London premier of the film *Suffragette*.[8] SU aims to highlight the issues facing some of the most marginalised and vulnerable women in society, explaining that 'we use direct action because it demands acknowledgement and answers on a large scale'[9] and 'direct action is disruptive, and we want to disrupt both the cuts to domestic violence services as well as the silence surrounding domestic violence. It forces people to pay attention to you and it gets your message across clearly.'[10]

It would be incorrect to suggest that direct-action repertoires exclude disabled people *per se*. Direct-action tactics have a long history within the disability rights movement where it has helped reinforce a sense of autonomy, independence, and power (Shakespeare 1993). Indeed, disability rights activists traditionally engage in direct action as a means by which to challenge stereotypical perceptions of capability. However, recognising the ways in which physical and mental pain affects some disabled people also means acknowledging that some forms of political protest are difficult if not impossible for them to engage with. SU deals with this tension by adopting a reflexive approach to organising, stating that they will 'continually revisit the ways in which we practically implement intersectionality in our organising spaces, our actions and our relationships with each other.'[11] The group further expand upon this need for active engagement with their organising principles, including a request for Sisters to be 'aware of your privileges, including less obvious or invisible hierarchies'; activists are called upon to learn about things they don't understand and are reminded that if an activist has 'acted or spoken harmfully, even if unintentionally,' then this will be discussed with them.

FS do not have a current accessibility policy for their events, nor are there formalised 'rules' regarding the organising principles for activists at the national or local level. Their website does, however, contain information regarding their use of technology to provide accessible web content; moreover, it provides further guidance for how to adapt it to suit particular needs. Discussing their approach to accessibility, a representative used the example of D/deaf attendees to illustrate their consultative approach:[12]

> for all three of the cases where I've run events with a D/deaf woman attendee or speaker, they've wanted a palantypist (essentially a live stenographer) rather than a BSL interpreter because the former enables a greater depth of engagement with the detail of what's said and the 'feel' of the room, especially where a discussion is happening at speed.

In the case of D/deaf attendees, FS's approach meant that they avoided providing a 'default' approach to specific impairments but actively sought to ensure that individuals were able to actively participate in a manner which best suited them. Rather than adopting a blanket accessibility policy, Fawcett's consultative approach empowers disabled women whilst also recognising that accessibility is about more than wheelchair access. In short, their approach acknowledges that non-disabled people should not presume to understand the needs of disabled people, whilst also avoiding homogenising D/deaf women.

Both SU and FS have tried to include disabled women in their activism: whilst the former have addressed this in their organising principles, the latter have recognised the heterogeneity amongst disabled women by opting for a consultative approach. SU recognises the challenges of intersectional activism, and in particular the need for activists to reflect upon their own privilege and conscious and unconscious biases. Their willingness to 'learn' about issues indicates a feminist praxis which fully understands the implications of 'doing' intersectionality; that it requires work on the part of activists and a desire to engage in issues that are new or challenging. Meanwhile, FS have not really engaged with the politics of intersectionality and in particular issues of disability, to the extent that it influences either their analytic framework or their campaign focus. Indeed, patterns of ableism, especially with regards the absence or erasure of disabled women or their homogenisation, are readily identified within this analysis of FS. Having considered the differing approaches to disability on the part of two high-profile groups, the chapter now turns to the views of disabled women and the extent to which they feel included within the wider women's movement.

Disabled women's activism

The mission statement of Sisters of Frida (SoF) includes specific references to intersectional praxis, which in part they demonstrate through 'seeking out' disabled women from diverse backgrounds.[13] Their commitment to intersectionality is reinforced through their stated values and ethical principles, which describe how oppression is mediated via difference. The group also state that they 'believe in the self-definition of identity and commit to not policing our identities,' a perspective in keeping with the social model of disability. SoF pay particular attention to three areas: disabled women's unpaid labour, sexual violence, and domestic abuse. They are active on social media and have also produced a number of important online resources, including a list of academic reports and articles and a statistical factsheet which explores disabled women and employment, health, and public life.[14] In order to explore the extent to which disabled women felt included by the wider women's movement, activists within SoF were asked about their experiences; their views are analysed below.

Calls for the women's movement to look more diverse has resulted in questioning whose voices dominate and whose voices are marginalised (Poster 1995; Marx Ferree and Tripp 2006). However, this has not, for the most part, focused on disabled women.[15] Indeed, the overwhelming majority of disabled women surveyed did not believe that the UK movement was inclusive of disabled women; only a handful of respondents suggested that it was 'a little' or 'somewhat' inclusive. A number of explanations for the failure of the movement to be inclusive of disabled women were offered by the respondents; these can be broadly grouped as follows: (1) that the movement is *ignorant* with regards disability; (2) that where disabled women are included this is simply *tokenistic*; and (3) that there is a *failure to engage reflexively* on organising strategies and accessibility. All of these explanations reflect a perception of the women's movement as inherently ableist.

Ignorance

Those who are not disabled or have significant experience of engaging with disabled people do not always recognise their own able-bodied/able-minded privilege, which can translate into ignorance when it comes to recognising disability and disabled identity (Kafer 2003; Polombi 2013). Epistemological and ontological privileges thus obscure or erase disability, making it harder for disabled women to engage with, and operate within, spaces which are not specifically created for disabled women. Many of the respondents argued that the movement was neglectful vis-à-vis the inclusion of disabled women. Activists observed that despite a rhetorical commitment to inclusivity, groups often ignored or overlooked disabled women. One woman noted, 'Intersectional feminists often neglect to include disability in their rhetoric,' whilst another observed that 'the movement just doesn't care about disabled women.' Respondents highlighted the 'thoughtlessness' of the women's movement, reflecting on the irony of 'so-called intersectional feminists' who failed to consider disability or disabled women.

One activist reported that non-disabled feminists repeatedly use 'offensive language about disability,' whilst another identified that some in the wider movement used 'non-social model language which is preferred in the UK by most disabled activists.' Several respondents felt that the movement did not value the 'experiences' or 'lived realities' of disabled women, and that until it did so disabled women would continue to be 'marginalised' and 'excluded.' This impression of a movement ignorant of disability is strongly associated with a pervasive ableist culture, one that assumes able-bodied/able-mindedness as the default subjectivity.

Explaining why they felt that the wider movement failed to include disabled women, many respondents reported that there was a lack of understanding or awareness regarding disability, as one activist stated, 'we don't enter into their thoughts at all because they simply don't understand our lives.' Whilst for some, this lack of awareness was a result of a more deliberate sense of neglect, others felt that it was due to a broader lack of visibility regarding issues that affect disabled people, 'feminist groups, like the rest of society, don't talk about disability because they don't hear much about it in the media . . . it just doesn't register with them because they're never exposed to the issues.' Activists decried the failure to offer a platform to disabled women; one respondent noting that there was an 'urgent need to read disabled women, listen to disabled women, meet with disabled women, hire disabled women.' Without disabled women 'at the table,' feminist groups would not be able to move forward in this area, nor would they be able to defend their self-described intersectional activism. These responses illustrate how ableist logic absents or erases disability; in other words, privilege can ignore what it does not want to see. The responses of the activists cited above chimes with the experiences of other marginalised groups within the women's movement, in particular the desire for autonomous organising in response to ongoing patterns of privilege (Thomlinson 2012).

Tokenism

Attempts to engage in intersectional praxis can sometimes run the risk of appearing tokenistic, especially when a marginalised group, or an issue that particularly affects a marginalised group, is added as an afterthought to pre-existing campaigns or agendas (Gökarıksel and Smith 2017). For disabled women, who can sometimes be highly visible, their presence at an event is used to symbolise or demonstrate that the organisers or event is intersectional. The decision to invite a visibly disabled woman to participate in an event recalls Audre Lorde's frustration with the way in which white women activists issued her with a last-minute invitation to speak at event in order that they might be considered inclusive or diverse (1984).

Some activists noted that the inclusion of disabled women tended to be tokenistic, and consequently there was only a superficial engagement with the issues and with disabled women. One activist argued, 'they [feminist groups] would like to be able to say they are inclusive of disabled women . . . but we never see their support. They invite us – but it can be tokenistic,' whilst another respondent stated that the movement 'tries occasionally but it often feels tokenistic.' Others felt as though disability was included as part of a 'checklist' approach to intersectionality, and there was a strong feeling that the movement did little beyond adopt a rhetorical approach to inclusivity. One respondent explained how disability was only included by groups 'as a way in which to prove they were diverse' or to 'secure funding by including disability.'

For some, the tokenistic approach was connected to a sense of instrumentalism amongst the wider movement that ensured disability was mentioned and included but not centred, and certainly not understood. Tokenism is incompatible with an intersectional politics that includes a rigorous analysis of ableism; in fact, it suggests a superficial approach to intersectionality – an approach that does not (and indeed cannot) provide sufficient analysis of the structural intersections that perpetuate the marginalisation and exclusion of disability and disabled women.

Accessibility

Issues of accessibility have been foundational to intersectional analysis; Crenshaw's original exploration of the marginalisation of women of colour explicitly included analysis of the ways in which migrant women were denied access to domestic violence refuges in New York (1981). The focus on accessibility is not, however, always explicitly addressed either in scholarly work on by social movement actors, yet it is a basic prerequisite for enabling some disabled women to actually participate in the movement. Accessibility is of course itself varied and covers a range of issues from buildings, to transportation, to the formatting of accessible materials.

The lack of any meaningful attempts to organise in an accessible way was considered to be a serious issue, as one respondent noted,

> well, you know they make a big deal about the venues being accessible, although usually only for a wheelchair as if that's the only type of disability, so then they feel like they'd better have someone in a wheelchair to show how thoughtful they've been.

Another respondent argued that feminist groups 'don't prioritize accessibility' whilst another noted that inclusion depended on the type of activity,

> in online spaces we're seeing an upswing in sharing our message, but in practical ways not at all. Demos are often inaccessible, and in the drive for intersectionality we're usually the last group thought of – if we're thought of at all.

If meetings, debates, demos, assemblies, and other forms of activism aren't accessible, any subsequent discussion of disability is rendered inherently problematic because disabled activists can't participate.

Taking the issues of ignorance, tokenism, and accessibility together, a picture is revealed of a movement which assumes that participants are non-disabled. Such an assumption not only reflects a widespread perception of an ableist culture within the movement but also a set of privileges related to able-bodied/able-mindedness.

Improving intersectional praxis

Of course, disabled women are not the only group to have experienced marginalisation within the women's movement (Zack 2005). Indeed, whilst there are barriers to participation and inclusion that are specific to disability and particular types of impairment, the frustration on the part of disabled activists resonates with those criticisms levelled by other groups, including women of colour (hooks 1981; Bassel and Emejulu 2014), migrant women (Anthias and Yuval-Davis 1983), and transwomen (Serano 2007). Similarly, the idea that the women's movement is engaged in a superficial approach to intersectionality, expressed by the disabled activists, speaks to wider concerns regarding its usage (Carastathis 2014). However, moving beyond the politics of exclusion and marginalisation, which come about because of the privilege embodied by those whose voices have tended to dominate the movement, it is clear that disabled women have a specific set of concerns regarding the ability of the wider movement to be truly intersectional. When asked for their views on how the wider movement could improve, the responses largely coalesced around three key changes: (1) practical steps to inclusion; (2) improving the representation of disabled women; and (3) developing a greater sense of the issues and discourse surrounding disability.

Practical steps to inclusion

Improving accessibility was cited as a critical area for improvement, and one that needed to go beyond simply ensuring wheelchair access. One respondent noted that at a large event it had to be pointed out to the organisers that the venue was inaccessible, 'they just hadn't thought about it.' Several respondents argued that there needed to be a more nuanced approach to accessibility, as one activist noted, 'being more aware of invisible barriers to participation. Staging a conference networking meeting in a bar, for instance, is often bad for people suffering from vestibular disorders, migraines, and neurological issues with sensory overload,' whilst another observed that resources should be available to help 'fund Personal Assistants or travel.' Respondents repeatedly stressed the importance of engaging with disabled women to help ensure accessible events, hence 'centering the experiences of disabled women and their accessibility needs is the only way to ensure full inclusion.' The responses of the activists emphasised the need for organisers to be proactive with regards inclusion strategies not only by thinking carefully about venues but also by educating themselves about disability.

Representing disabled women

Activists were also concerned that disabled women simply weren't invited to events or given a platform to speak. For one disabled woman this was especially ironic given that 'feminists have fought for so long for women to be included, by challenging all-male line ups and now they themselves fail to provide a platform for disabled women.' The lack of visibility for disabled women within the movement, and in the media, was seen to be a real issue and further entrenched a sense of marginalisation and exclusion. There was a recognition that not all disabled people actually identify as disabled, and that there were some who are unwilling to 'talk openly about their disability'; hence, providing a platform for activists who are engaged in disability rights activism is a critical way in which to increase and improve the visibility of disabled women. The absence of high-profile disabled women amongst the feminists who frequently appeared in the media was noted, as one activist suggested, 'they should give up some of their privilege and opportunity in order to promote disabled women's voices.'

Knowledge

Increasing the presence of disabled women was seen as a key step towards ensuring that the movement addressed disability-related issues and interests, in part because 'non-disabled women can't understand or even comprehend the various things we have to negotiate so we have to be present to tell them about it.' Similarly, there was a strong belief that non-disabled activists needed to hear from disabled women in order to develop their own knowledge of disability. Several respondents observed that some people find it 'difficult' or 'challenging' to discuss disability, and so including disabled women would help bring disability into mainstream feminist discourse. One activist noted that there was a reluctance to talk about disability because of a fear of saying the wrong thing,

> I think that there is a fear of disability, not only in terms of what it might mean at an individual level, but also for some feminists there is a worry about using the wrong language; the only way to resolve this is to make sure that disabled women are present.

Others noted that feminists should seek to educate themselves about disability as part of their commitment to social justice, because disabled women should not have to serve as 'educators' to the wider movement. Finally, some respondents observed that despite disability being in the news more regularly, particularly with regards to cuts to welfare provision, women's groups were 'absent' from the debate and 'seemingly have nothing to say about the devastating cuts effecting women's lives.'

Conclusions

Challenging ableism is not only a normative good and in the interests of all of those interested in equality and social justice, but, as Jenny Morris identified more than 20 years ago, would result in a more radical form of feminist politics. This research has explored the inclusion of disabled women and disability-related issues, analysed how and why disability remains marginalised, and sought to argue that challenging ableism within the women's movement is an important task. Of course, this research only tells part of the story concerning the intersection between gender and disability, and future research should explore how, when, and where gender features within disability rights activism.

The analysis presented here reveals a complicated picture with regards ableism in the UK women's movement. It would be fair to argue that disability is largely absent from Fawcett's approach to gender inequality, although they have adopted a consultative approach to organising events; meanwhile, Sisters Uncut have included disability within their campaigning and through their calls for a pedagogy of intersectionality. However, disabled women are very clear that there is pervasive ableism within the women's movement. Despite the fact that disability rights activism is relatively high profile, this has not proven to be a sufficiently favourable context within which ableist logic is challenged within parts of the women's movement. If we understand intersectionality to be concerned with addressing multiple intersecting points of oppression, then challenging able-bodied and able-minded privilege is a critical and urgent task.

Notes

1 I use the term women's movement rather than feminist movement in recognition of the fact that Sisters of Frida, a disabled women's collective, does not define itself specifically as a feminist organisation.
2 In line with UK feminist disability scholarship, this chapter uses the term disabled women/disabled feminists rather than women with disabilities; this foregrounds the disabling role that society plays (Morris 2001) and is also more reflective of the discourse used by disabled feminists in the UK.
3 For instance, many feminists argue for the removal of the informal burden of care undertaken by women, whilst disability rights activists reject approaches that could see disabled people institutionalised instead of enabling their freedom (Erevelles 1996, p. 552).

4 Debates around selective abortion can raise divisions between disabled women and feminist pro-choice activists, where the former have expressed concerns about eugenics and the attempt to erase disabled people through genetic screening for foetal impairment (Kallianes and Rubenfeld 1997).

5 Whilst ableism refers to the cultural norms which promote the idealisation of able-bodied/able-mindedness, disablism refers to the practice of explicitly excluding or marginalising people based upon their impairments (see Campbell 2009).

6 For further details see www.fawcettsociety.org.uk/Blog/time-new-deal-care-carers [accessed 2 March 2018].

7 For the full report see www.fawcettsociety.org.uk/sex-discrimination-law-review-final-report [accessed 2 March 2018].

8 Mumford, Gwilym. 2018. "Domestic Violence Activists Sisters Uncut Invade Baftas Red Carpet." *The Guardian*, February 18. www.theguardian.com/film/2018/feb/18/sisters-uncut-baftas-red-carpet-protest-theresa-may [accessed 24 April 2019].

9 Sisters Uncut. "Comment." https://inews.co.uk/opinion/comment/theresa-may-acknowledges-demands-will-continue-use-direct-disruptive-action/ [accessed 3 March 2018].

10 For full details of the interview see www.thefword.org.uk/2016/01/sisters-uncut/ [accessed 27 March 2018]; www.thefword.org.uk/2016/01/sisters-uncut/ [accessed 27 March 2018].

11 Ibid.

12 D/deaf refers to those who are Deaf (sign language users) and those who are deaf (hard of hearing people with English as their first language who may lip-read and/or use hearing aids).

13 Their mission statement and values and principles are available on their website www.sisofrida.org/about/sisters-of-frida-vision-and-values/ [accessed 30 January 2018].

14 Factsheets are available online www.sisofrida.org/resources/disabled-women-facts-and-stats-2/ [accessed 5 February 2018].

15 For example, a 6 February 2018 Channel 4 News Report covering the 100-year anniversary since (some) women got the vote spent much of the discussion analysing how the movement could and should be more diverse; see www.channel4.com/news/joan-bakewell-on-feminism-the-ball-is-rolling-and-it-is-not-going-to-stop [accessed 27 March 2018].

References

Anthias, Floya, and Nira Yuval-Davis. 1983. "Contextualizing Feminism – Gender, Ethnic and Class Divisions." *Feminist Review* 15 (1): 62–75.

Bassel, Leah, and A. Akwugo Emejulu. 2014. "Solidarity Under Austerity: Intersectionality in France and the United Kingdom." *Politics & Gender* 10 (1): 130–136.

Begum, Nasa. 1992. *Something to be Proud of: The Lives of Asian Disabled People and Carers in Waltham Forest*. Race Relations Unit and Disability Unit, London Borough of Waltham Forest, London.

Campbell, F. Kumari. 2001. "Inciting Legal Fictions: Disability's Date With Ontology and the Ableist Body of the Law." *Griffith Law Review* 10: 42–62.

Campbell, F. Kumari. 2009. *Contours of Ableism*. Houndmills, Basingstoke: Palgrave Macmillan.

Carastathis, Anna. 2014. "The Concept of Intersectionality in Feminist Theory." *Philosophy Compass* 9 (5): 304–314.

Chamberlain, Prudence. 2017. *The Feminist Fourth Wave: Affective Temporality*. Basingstoke: Palgrave.

Chouinard, Vera. 1997. "Making Space for Disabling Difference: Challenges Ableist Geographies." *Environment and Planning D: Society and Space* 15: 379–387.

Combahee River Collective. 1982. "A Black Feminist Statement." In *But Some of Us are Brave*, edited by Gloria T. Hull, Patricia Bell Scott and Barbara Smith, 13–22. New York, NY: Feminist Press.

Crenshaw, Kimberlé. 1991. "Mapping the Margins: Intersectionality, Identity Politics and Violence Against Women of Color." *Stanford Law Review* 43 (6): 1241–1299.

Davis, Leonard, ed. 2013. *The Disability Studies Reader*. New York, NY: Routledge.

Equality Act. 2010. Available online http://www.legislation.gov.uk/ukpga/2010/15/contents

Erevelles, Nirmala. 1996. "Disability and the Dialectics of Difference." *Disability and Society* 11 (4): 519–538.

Erevelles, Nirmala. 2011. *Disability and Difference in Global Contexts: Enabling a Transformative Body Politics*. New York, NY: Palgrave Macmillan.

Evans, Elizabeth. 2015. *The Politics of Third Wave Feminisms*. Houndmills, Basingstoke: Palgrave Macmillan.

Fawcett, Barbara. 2018. *Feminist Perspectives on Disability*. London: Routledge.

Garland-Thomson, Rosemarie. 2005. "Feminist Disability Studies." *Signs: Journal of Women in Culture and Society* 30 (2): 1557–1587.

Gökarıksel, Banu, and Sara Smith. 2017. "Intersectional Feminism Beyond US Flag Hijab and Pussy Hats in Trump's America." *Gender, Place & Culture* 24 (5): 628–644.

Goodley, Dan. 2014. *Dis/ability Studies: Theorizing Disablism and Ableism*. New York, NY: Routledge.

Guest, Carly. 2016. *Becoming Feminist*. Houndmills, Basingstoke: Palgrave Macmillan.

Hill Collins, Patricia, and Sirma Bilge. 2016. *Intersectionality*. Cambridge, UK: Polity Press.

Ho, A. 2008. "The Individualist's Model of Autonomy and the Challenge of Disability." *Journal of Bioethic Inquiry* 5: 193–207.

hooks, bell. 1981. *Ain't I a Woman*. London: Pluto Press.

Inckle, Kay. 2015. "Debilitating Times: Compulsory Ablebodiedness and White Privilege in Theory and Practice." *Feminist Review* 111 (1): 42–58.

Kafer, Alison. 2003. "Compulsory Bodies: Reflections on Heterosexuality and Able-Bodiedness." *Journal of Women's History* 15 (3): 77–89.

Kallianes, Virginia, and Phyllis Rubenfeld. 1997. "Disabled Women and Reproductive Rights." *Disability and Society* 12 (2): 203–221.

Laperrière, Marie, and Eléonore Lépinard. 2016. "Intersectionality as a Tool for Social Movements: Strategies of Inclusion and Representation in the Québécois Women's Movement." *Politics* 36 (4): 374–382.

Linton, Simi. 2006. "Reassigning Meaning." In *The Disability Studies Reader*, edited by Leonard Davis, 161–172. New York, NY: Routledge.

Lloyd, Margaret. 1992. "Does She Boil Eggs? Towards a Feminist Model of Disability." *Disability, Handicap and Society* 7 (3): 207–221.

Lorde, Audre. 1984. *Sister Outsider: Essays and Speeches*. New York, NY: The Crossing Press.

Marx Ferree, Myra. 2009. "Inequality, Intersectionality and the Politics of Discourse: Framing Feminist Alliance." In *The Discursive Politics of Gender Equality*, edited by Emanuela Lombardo, Petra Meier, and Mieke Verloo, 86–104. London: Routledge.

Ferree, Myra Marx, and Aili Mari Tripp. eds. 2006. *Global Feminism: Transnational Women's Activism, Organizing, and Human Rights*. New York: NYU Press.

McRuer, Robert. 2013. "Compulsory Able-Bodiedness and Queer/Disabled Existence." In *The Disability Studies Reader*, edited by Leonard Davis. New York, NY: Routledge.

Miles, Agnes. 1988. *Women and Mental Illness: The Social Context of Female Neurosis*. London: Harvester Wheatsheaf.

Morris, Jenny, ed. 1996. *Encounters With Strangers: Feminism and Disability*. London: The Women's Press.

Morris, Jenny. 2001. "Impairment and Disability: Constructing and Ethics of Care That Promotes Human Rights." *Hypatia* 16 (4): 1–16.

Oliver, Mike. 1983. *Social Work With Disabled People*. Basingstoke: Macmillan.

Palombi, Barbara. 2013. "Women With Disabilities: The Cultural Context of Disability, Feminism, Able-bodied Privilege, and Microaggressions." In *The Oxford Handbook of Feminist Multicultural Counseling Psychology*, edited by Elizabeth Nutt Williams and Carolyn Zerbe Enns, 199–220. Oxford: Oxford University Press.

Poster, Winifred R. 1995. "The Challenges and Promises of Class and Racial Diversity in the Women's Movement: A Study of Two Women's Organizations." *Gender & Society* 9 (6): 659–679.

Price, Margaret. 2015. "The Bodymind Problem and the Possibilities of Pain." *Hypatia* 30 (1): 268–284.

Serano, Julia. 2007. *Whipping Girl*. Berkeley, CA: Seal Press.

Shakespeare, Tom. 1993. "Disabled People's Self-Organisation: A New Social Movement?" *Disability, Handicap & Society* 8 (3): 249–264.

Sherwin, Susan. 1992. *No Longer Patient: Feminist Ethics and Health Care*. Chicago: Temple University Press.

Siebers, Tobin. 2006. "Disability Studies and the Future of Identity Politics." In *Identity Politics Reconsidered*, edited by Linda Alcoff, Michael Hames-García, Satya Mohanty, Paula M. L. Moya, 10–30. New York, NY: Palgrave Macmillan.

Silvers, Anita. 2007. "Feminism and Disability." In *The Blackwell Guide to Feminist Philosophy*, edited by Linda Martin Alcoff and Eva Feder Kittay, 131–142. Oxford: Blackwell.

Thomlinson, Natalie. 2012. "The Colour of Feminism: White Feminists and Race in the Women's Liberation Movement." *History* 97 (327): 453–475.

Tremain, Shelly. 2015. *Foucault and the Government of Disability*. Ann Arbor, MI: University of Michigan Press.

Verloo, Mieke. 2013. "Intersectional and Cross-Movement Politics and Policies: Reflections on Current Practices and Debates." *Signs: Journal of Women in Culture & Society* 38 (41): 893–915.

Vernon, Ayesha. 1999. "The Dialectics of Multiple Identities and the Disabled People's Movement." *Disability and Society* 14 (3): 385–398.

Wendell, Susan. 1989. "Toward A Feminist Theory of Disability." *Hypatia: A Journal of Feminist Philosophy* 4 (2): 104–124.

Wolbring, Gregor. 2008. "The Politics of Ableism." *Development* 51 (2): 252–258.

Zack, Naomi. 2005. *Inclusive Feminism*. New York, NY: Rowman & Littlefield.

Chapter 8

Difficult intersections
Nation(ALISM) and the LGBTIQ movement in Cyprus

Nayia Kamenou

Nationalism is in and of itself a discourse of gender and sexuality, since nationalist discourses become authoritative of what normal and abnormal gender and sexual behaviour is, while the borders of national belonging and exclusion correspond to legitimised and delegitimised gender and sexual identities (Kumari 2018; Mole 2016; Mosse 1985). Nationalist discourses on nationhood and ethnicity, sexuality, and gender have historically served to create and maintain boundaries of belonging in, and exclusion from, national collectivities based on the construction and privileging of rigid and essentialist gender and sexual identities (e.g. Beatty 2016; Hoegaerts 2014; Romano 2019; Scott 1996; Timm and Sanborn 2007). They have also underpinned legal, political, social, economic, and cultural mechanisms of regulation and hierarchisation of lives within and across national communities (e.g. Anthias 2013, 2018; Mosse 1985; Parker et al. 1992; Pryke 1998; Yuval-Davis 1997, 2013; Yuval-Davis and Anthias 1989). This is particularly the case in troubled contexts marked by ethnic animosity, conflict, occupation, colonialism, and postcolonialism (Bryant 2004; Cockburn 2004; Hadjipavlou 2010; Kamenou 2011, 2012, 2016, 2019; Karayanni 2004, 2006, 2017). This tight relationship between nationalism and gender and sexuality identities may nonetheless be troubled in some contexts by processes such as European Union (EU) admission and Europeanisation/transnationalisation that trigger dynamics of reconfiguration of conceptions of nationhood and open up spaces for transnational activism based on gender- and sexuality-nonconforming identities.

In this chapter, 'Europeanisation' is broadly defined as a transnationalisation process that includes the emergence and development of European-level structures of governance and institutions and of collective ideas, norms, and values (e.g. Ayoub 2013; Featherstone and Radaelli 2003; Green Cowles, Caporaso, and Risse 2001; Richardson 2006). It is employed to denote 'a set of regional economic, institutional, and ideational forces of change also affecting national policies, practices, and politics' (Schmidt 2002, p. 41). Therefore, and as the discussion of the case of Cyprus will corroborate, Europeanisation is often bolstered by EU accession processes, as well as by the prospect of these processes. However, the outcomes of such processes are nonfixed, contingent, and complex. EU admission and its prospect, and Europeanisation processes initiated from above and below, may both emasculate and reinforce notions of privilege and exclusion based on gender and sexual identities, both within and across national communities (e.g. Ayoub 2015, 2016; Ayoub and Paternotte 2014; Belavusau and Kochenov 2016; Bilić 2016; Kamenou 2011, 2012, 2016, 2019; Kristoffersson, van Roozendaal, and Poghosyan 2016; Slootmaeckers and Touquet 2016).

This chapter examines these problems by focusing on the case of Cyprus, a postcolonial EU member country divided along ethnic lines that has been marked by conflict, occupation, and tensions about what an 'authentic' national identity entails – including in relation to modalities of gender and sexuality. It studies Cypriot lesbian, gay, bisexual, trans*, intersex, and queer (LGBTIQ) intersectional politics amidst the socio-political environment within which these are articulated, marked by strong nationalistic discourses as well as tensions with European identity and belonging. Specifically, it examines the ways in which local and transnational EU discourses about nationhood and ethnicity, gender, and sexuality shape dynamics of intersectionality. It does so by analysing how gender and sexual identities are formed at the intersection of nationalist/European discourses and by questioning how these formations inform LGBTIQ movement politics in contentious contexts.

Using an 'intersectionality-sensitive' empirical analysis (Bilić and Kajinić 2016, p. 13), the chapter draws from the insights of gender and sexuality, feminist intersectionality, Europeanisation, and movements literature. It employs a qualitative research design and thematically analyses empirical ethnographic data that includes interviews with Greek-Cypriot and Turkish-Cypriot LGBTIQ participants. It studies intra-ethnic and inter-ethnic dynamics of in-group exclusions that are reinforced by local notions about 'Europe,' expressed through the 'Europe/West-versus-the-Rest' dichotomy. It shows that, based on this dichotomy, some LGBTIQs reproduce ideas about nationhood and ethnicity that render other gender- and sexuality-nonconforming Cypriots as inferior. Nonetheless, it also finds that the successes of the Cypriot LGBTIQ movement have been based on opportunities afforded by 'Europe' and Europeanisation. Namely, the chapter finds that, due to the predominance of nationalism and the ensuing partitocracy, the LGBTIQ movement is often forced to resort to strategic non-intersectional activism that exacerbates in-group exclusions. However, through the employment of discourses and practices promoted by EU institutions, which find their way into local ideological and practical repertoires due to the country's EU admission and to Europeanisation processes, the LGBTIQ movement has managed to shift to intersectional politics that challenge gender and sexuality privilege, as well as power imbalances within and beyond the movement.

Therefore, the chapter argues that, in troubled contexts, intersectional political action becomes possible when marginalised groups critically employ transnational EU norms and discourses while strategically balancing them with predominant local ones. In doing so, it helps develop our thinking about the workings and implications of understandings of nationhood and ethnicity, gender, and sexuality on LGBTIQ politics when the 'Rest' meets the 'West/Europe' and adds to the body of gender and sexuality, feminist intersectionality, Europeanisation, and movements scholarship.

Nationalism, Europeanisation, and intersectionality

The literature on nation-building, national identities, and nationalism has convincingly made the argument that nationalism is in and of itself a discourse of compulsory ('nature-based' sexual) uniformity, privilege, and exclusion (e.g. Anderson 1983; Breuilly 1982; Brubaker et al. 2006; Gellner 1983; Hobsbawm 1992; Mosse 1985; Skey and Antonsich 2017). In nationalistic discourses, belonging is defined in juxtaposition to exclusion, and nationalisms privilege and reward specific practices, experiences, and identities via sanctioning others. For example, the privileging of heterosexuality and cisgenderism has been premised on their rendering as the *sine qua non* of the protection of the nation's unity against internal and external enemies (e.g. Kamenou 2011, 2012, 2016, 2019; Karayanni 2004, 2006, 2017; Kumari 2018; Mole 2016; Mosse 1985; Parker et al. 1992; Pryke 1998). Another example in the opposite direction – i.e. in the direction of (sexual) diversity – is the portrayal of others by nationalist political forces as carriers of monocultures that are incompatible with the 'European/Western' value of sexual and gender diversity, in order to keep 'non-Western/European,' 'backward' others outside the borders of 'civilised' 'Europe/the West' (Bracke 2012; Colpani and Habed 2014; Paternotte 2018; Puar 2007, 2013; Rao 2015; Rexhepi 2016; Sadurní, Montenegro, and Pujol 2017).

The concept of homonationalism has been forged to specifically address the issue of the intersection and interplay between sexuality and nationalism and to describe the modes of inscription of tolerance towards sexual diversity/sexual minorities in conceptions of nationhood and national identity that, nonetheless, do not necessarily challenge the heteronormative underpinning of nationalist projects (Kahlina 2015; Puar 2007, 2013; Sadurní et al. 2017). Namely, homonationalism is a type of ethnonationally endorsed non-heterosexuality/non-cisgenderism that functions 'as a regulatory script' of normative LGBTIQ-ness based on, and via reinforcing, the nation's norms and boundaries in relation to national, gender, and sexual identities (Puar 2007, p. 2). Nationalistic discourses that are premised on the 'us' versus 'them' distinction – no matter how the 'us' and 'them' are defined in terms of gender and sexual identity – tend to enjoy more appeal in postcolonial, ethnically divided, and conflict-ridden contexts, where the stakes of a widely shared national identity are perhaps particularly higher. Cyprus is such a place, whose historic turns have caused a profound crisis in Cypriot identity (Bryant 2004; Hadjipavlou 2010; Kamenou 2011, 2012, 2016, 2019; Karayanni 2006).

It has been argued that EU admission and its prospect have played an important role in enabling mobilisation and in addressing the exclusion of gender and sexual minorities, both at the national and the transnational level. Legal and policy measures resulting from EU conditionality and EU membership have contributed to the amelioration of the lives of sexuality- and gender-nonconforming people in a number of EU candidate and member states (Ayoub 2015, 2016; Belavusau and Kochenov 2016; Kristoffersson et al. 2016; Mole 2016; Slootmaeckers and Touquet 2016). As a transnationalisation process that involves the development of transnational norms and discourses regarding citizenship, Europeanisation may enable the building of commonalities and the promotion of equality based on difference. For example, in relation to Cyprus, EU admission and Europeanisation have facilitated the creation of civil society organisations (CSOs) and have afforded opportunities for political mobilisation around issues which, due to the predominance of nationalism, were previously considered to lie outside the remits of the political. The availability and easier accessibility of EU funding and of moral, knowledge, and practical support by transnational umbrella non-governmental organisations (NGOs) to national CSOs have enabled the creation of LGBTIQ organisations on both parts of the island and have assured their survival amidst a hostile legal and socio-political environment (Kamenou 2011, 2012, 2016, 2019).

However, Europeanisation has had varied and mixed effects both at the national and the transnational level, not least in relation to LGBTIQ politics. Even if aimed to be egalitarian and cooperative, based on their appropriation on the ground, Europeanisation and its accompanying discourses and activism paradigms may become elitist and exclusionary (Bilić 2016; Bilić and Stubbs 2016; Colpani and Habed 2014; D'Agostino 2018; Héritier 2005; Kamenou 2011, 2012, 2019; Paternotte 2018; Rao 2015; Rexhepi 2016). In the context of Europeanisation, through the interaction and collaboration of different national and supranational actors, transnational discourses and activism paradigms disperse in national contexts where they merge, cross, or collude with local ones. Particularly in national contexts in the periphery of 'Europe,' due to historical legacies – e.g. colonialism, communism, and ethnonational conflicts – and current challenges – e.g. Euroscepticism, nationalism, and populism – the multilevel and cross-level interplay between discourses and practices might lead to results other than those anticipated.[1] However, as this chapter will argue, informed by intersectionality as theory and praxis that aims to challenge power structures, privilege, and exclusion, LGBTIQ activists employ Europeanisation and transnational discourses and paradigms of action made available by the EU in ways that erode nationalism and exclusions.

As a complex of social practices and as an organising strategy, intersectionality is employed by numerous movements in a variety of national contexts while, as an analytical framework and tool, it has global application (Collins and Bilge 2016; Greenwood 2008; Hancock 2016; Laperrière and Lépinard 2016; May 2015; Yuval-Davis 2006). Numerous scholars of intersectionality have convincingly made the argument that intersectionality has the potential to bring about structural change and sustainable social justice (e.g. Hancock 2016; Lombardo and Forest 2012; Lombardo and Verloo 2009; May 2015; Verloo 2006, 2013, 2018; Yuval-Davis 2006). Nonetheless, research has shown that, as a movement strategy, intersectionality can entail different practices with potentially conflicting goals, which do not always lead to the recognition of the socio-political marginalisation of minority groups within movements. When it is not the product or source of reflexivity, intersectionality may reinforce, rather than attenuate, intra-movement divisiveness (Bilge 2013; D'Agostino 2018; Dhamoon 2011; Evans 2015, 2016; Knapp 2005; Laperrière and Lépinard 2016; Lombardo and Verloo 2009; Luft and Ward 2009; Santos 2013).

Despite intersectionality's global reach, historical contingencies and context and time specificities matter. Research on whether and how the intersectional politics of sexuality- and gender-nonconforming groups in contentious contexts challenge privilege and power imbalances remains limited. This results in the dearth of context-specific understandings of the different processes through which power differentials and relations form and operate within and across the national and the transnational level, and of how different LGBTIQ groups are affected by, and affect, these processes. Moreover, while some scholars have highlighted the potential problems and opportunities of intersectionality in relation to movements, little empirical research has been done that incorporates LGBTIQs' understandings of, and responses to, these problems and opportunities (e.g. Ayoub 2016; Ayoub and Paternotte 2014; Bilić and Kajinić 2016; D'Agostino 2018).

Methods

To address these gaps in research, in this chapter I focus on LGBTIQ politics in Cyprus where complex, overlapping, and conflicting currents of local and transnational discourses and activism paradigms unfold. The data for this chapter comes from ethnographic study in Cyprus on gender, sexuality, Europeanisation, and ethnonational politics. Field research was conducted during numerous trips to, and long stays on, the island from 2007 to 2018, to identify changes in participants' opinions about the impact of nationalism and Europeanisation from the initial stages of the LGBTIQ movement formation until today. The current analysis is based on data derived from in-depth one-to-one and group interviews with Greek-Cypriot and Turkish-Cypriot LGBTIQ participants, which addressed their experiences as LGBTIQ individuals and activists living in Cyprus.

The interviews were structured as conversations, and broad open-ended questions were asked to enable detailed accounts (Orbuch 1997; Riessman 2008). The employed participant-centred research approach enabled me to situate participants within multiple complex, overlapping, and conflicting currents of local and transnational EU discourses and practices and, thus, to investigate the various aspects and mechanisms of inclusion, exclusion, privilege, political agency, and politics formation (Levy and Hollan 2015).

Group interviews were not initially one of my chosen methods since I was concerned with maintaining anonymity and confidentiality. However, they were the only available option when, in some instances, I would go meet an individual participant and found a group of people who wanted to talk to me. Group interviews turned out to be very useful. As they closely resemble participant observation and naturally occurring talk, they afforded me the opportunity to get an insight into participants' conflicting and crossing discourses, as well as into the ways through which they negotiate their different positions on common interests (Kitzinger 1994).

To recruit interviewees, I used a snowball sampling method that began with personal networks. I conducted the interviews in person and interviewed participants in Greek or English. Interviews with Greek Cypriots were conducted in Greek and interviews with Turkish Cypriots were conducted in English. The interviews lasted from one to three hours. I audio-recorded them upon participants' agreement and later transcribed them verbatim. The interviews conducted in Greek were translated into English after being transcribed.

Two major themes emerged from the data analysis: (1) nationalism and non-intersectional activism and (2) transnational discourses/practices and intersectional politics. They are discussed in this order in the analysis sections. I selected interview excerpts as exemplars of each of these themes. Quotes have been edited for clarity, but not content. All participants are quoted only by fake initials to maintain anonymity and confidentiality and to ensure their nonidentification.

The case of Cyprus

A detailed discussion of the troubled history of the island is beyond the scope of this chapter. However, a brief – and, admittedly, oversimplified – overview will allow readers unfamiliar with the case of Cyprus to understand the context in which this chapter is written.

Cyprus came under British colonial rule in 1878. Some Greek Cypriots' demand for union with Greece took the form of armed struggle against the British from 1955 to 1959. In 1956, some Turkish Cypriots called for the partition of the island along ethnic lines and formed their own fighters' organisation in 1957. Despite the aspirations of the two ethnic communities, in 1960, the Republic of Cyprus (RoC) was formed as an independent state. From 1963 to 1964 and in 1967 Cyprus witnessed intense inter-ethnic conflict. In an attempt to fulfil the aspiration for union with Greece, some Greek Cypriots formed a militant group and launched a campaign of killings, violence, and intimidation, which culminated in a coup in 1974. Ostensibly to provide humanitarian assistance to Turkish Cypriots, in the same year, Turkey invaded Cyprus, and it is still occupying the north part of the island. Many Greek and Turkish Cypriots endured forced displacement, the former to the south and the latter to the north part of the island. In 1983, the occupied north was self-declared as an independent state under the name 'Turkish Republic of Northern Cyprus' (TRNC). The two ethnic communities remained separated until April 2003 with the partial opening of the checkpoints on the 'Green Line' that divides the island by the TRNC. The recurrent rounds of UN-assisted peace negotiations have failed to bring about a solution to the Cyprus imbroglio. Nonetheless, the RoC became a member of the European Union (EU) in 2004 (Borowiec 2000; Bose 2007, pp. 55–104; Diez 2002; Hitchens 1997).

In Cyprus, the legacies of colonialism and ethnonational conflict have led to a narrow conceptualisation of the political and to nationalism becoming a central element of the country's socio-political life, leaving little space for discussions about the privileges and exclusions it produces and perpetuates. Within this context, civil society politics around issues of gender and sexuality is a relatively recent phenomenon. The Greek-Cypriot LGBTIQ movement has its roots in the Cypriot Gay Liberation Movement that was created in 1987 by Alecos Modinos, an architect with ties to the Greek-Cypriot political elite. Due to the hostile political, institutional, and social environment that impeded collective mobilisation, using his ties to the political elite, Modinos engaged in lobbying for the decriminalisation of same-sex sexual conduct. Since no political party was willing to support his cause, using the right of individual petition afforded by Article 25 of the pre-1998 version of the European Convention on Human Rights that the RoC had ratified in 1962, Modinos turned to the European Court of Human Rights (ECHR), which decided in favour of the applicant in 1993 (Kamenou 2011, 2012, 2016).

Ecclesiastical mobilisation, fragile governing coalitions that necessitate cohesive behaviours, familialism, and a general culture that favours the safeguarding of the 'traditional' family and morals have stalled LGBTIQ-friendly legal amendments also elsewhere in Europe (Albaek 2003; Lombardo and Del Giorgio 2013). Nevertheless, the decriminalisation of same-sex sexual contact could not be avoided, as the Council of Europe had warned the RoC that non-abidance with the ECHR ruling could mean expulsion. Consequently, in 1998, the Cypriot parliament was forced to decriminalise same-sex sexual contact amidst fierce opposition by the Orthodox Church of Cyprus (Kamenou 2011, 2012, 2016).

After the late 1990s, LGBTIQ issues were again pushed into invisibility and were almost completely banished from public dialogue. Like elsewhere, EU admission – formal negotiations for which began in March 1998 – and Europeanisation – certain processes of which began as early as 1990, when the RoC applied for full EU membership (Featherstone 2000; Sepos 2008) – affected changes in political opportunity structures (Helfferich and Kolb 2001; Marks and McAdam 1999). These changes facilitated the formation on a new LGBTIQ organisation in 2009 and enabled its attempts towards pushing for LGBTIQ rights.

The vision of Accept-LGBTI Cyprus is 'the formation of a society based on respect for each individual and their diversity, free from discrimination and prejudice in particular as regards to their sexual orientation.'[2] Its mission includes 'the implementation of policies, laws, programs and jurisprudence of the European Union and the Council of Europe with regards to combating discrimination and promoting the principle of equality, especially regarding sexual orientation and social gender' and 'the recognition of equal marriage, adoption, inheritance rights, insurance, health and other needs, for all citizens of Cypriot society without discrimination.'[3] Since its creation, it has been working on building contacts with officials from all political parties. This has been premised on the rationale that since no political party is more pro-LGBTIQ than the others due to the predominance of nationalism and partitocracy, the objective should be to create alliances with officials from as many political parties as possible, by strategically using Europeanisation and the wish on the part of some politicians to appear to be 'EU-friendly' (Kamenou 2016).

Whether individuals, groups, or parties, influential allies are extremely important since they may moderate the degree of repression and exclusion and advocate in favour, and on behalf of, marginalised groups (Tarrow 1994, pp. 160–169). Furthermore, the framing of LGBTIQ activism in the language of 'Europe,' as well as the idea of 'European socialization' – i.e. 'the process of inducting actors to the norms of the EU community' (Ayoub 2013, p. 22) – resonate among most politicians. For example, like Accept-LGBTI Cyprus, in their attempts to get same-sex sexual conduct decriminalised, Turkish-Cypriot LGBTIQ groups have strategically used the desire of some Turkish-Cypriot politicians to show that, even though not an EU member, the TRNC is more 'European' than the RoC (Kamenou 2011, 2012, 2016).

Through its politics, Accept-LGBTI has been successful at pushing for the recognition of same-sex civil partnerships and the adoption of hate speech and crime legislation in 2015. Nevertheless, achieving substantive equality is still a work in progress. As the next sections of this chapter will demonstrate, this elite-targeting and 'incremental politics' approach (Holzhacker 2007, 2012) – i.e. a mode of interaction between CSOs and their political environment, in which CSOs attempt to build upon previous successes through elite-level lobbying and by adjusting their claim-making based on elite and predominant values – has been limiting the movement's ability to engage in intersectional politics, thus resulting into both intra-ethnic and inter-ethnic in-group exclusions. This is evidenced in two types of discourse/practice, which are discussed in the following two sections: nationalism and non-intersectional activism, and EU-appropriated transnational discourses/practices and intersectional politics.

Nationalism and non-intersectional activism

To paraphrase Puar (2007, p. XXIV), in 'European' nationalist Cyprus, an opportunity for forms of LGBTIQ inclusion in the national imaginary and body politic rests upon specific performances of 'European' LGBTIQ-ness vis-à-vis 'backward,' 'non-European' nonconforming modalities of gender and sexuality. 'Europe' and the 'West' become sites of LGBTIQ identity struggle, in which the 'non-European/non-Western' gender- and sexuality-nonconforming other is articulated as a threat to the nation and to its 'Europeanness' (Colpani and Habed 2014; Puar 2007, 2013; Rexhepi 2016; Sadurní et al. 2017). The following excerpt from an interview with a gay male couple is illustrative of how homonationalism operates and manifests in Cyprus:

AK: A guy I know liked this Turkish-Cypriot man and everyone would tell him: 'With a Turkish Cypriot? Why?' . . . [W]e left aside the fact that he is gay and

> now the issue is: 'With a Turkish Cypriot?' . . . whereas with a British [man] or a German [man] or whatever, there is no problem.
>
> XM: I wouldn't do it. . . . He is Turkish Cypriot! . . . He is Turkish!
>
> AK: Why not?
>
> . . .
>
> XM: Would you have sex with a Turkish Cypriot?
>
> AK: Would you have sex with a British?
>
> XM: Yes! Why not?
>
> AK: Why not with a Turkish Cypriot?
>
> XM: The British is European!
>
> AK: So, what? A Turkish Cypriot is European too! He lives on the other half of Cyprus that is [part of] Europe!
>
> XM: If there is a solution [to the Cyprus problem] and the rest of Cyprus becomes part of Europe, I'll think about it!

Like some other interviewees, in this interview, one of the participants employed nationalist discourses and the 'Europe/West-versus-the-Rest' dichotomy to define themselves, both as Greek Cypriot and as non-heterosexual, against the Turkish-Cypriot non-heterosexual ethnic other, whom they described as 'non-European' and 'backward.' Such homonormative discourses replicate and reinforce nationalist and essentialist conceptions of gender and sexuality and exclusionary and imperialist conceptions of 'Europeanness' – in this interview, British and German but not, for example, Latvian or Polish men are rendered as the paragons of 'Europeanness' – and impact the ways in which LGBTIQ politics may be articulated.

Describing the difficulties in fostering inter-ethnic intersectional LGBTIQ politics, an LGBTIQ activist explained:

> The idea of working with other groups . . . has been put on the table. However, it does not resonate with the majority of the members [of the LGBTIQ movement]. . . . Some argue we cannot afford alienating some of our hard-won political allies by being involved in [such] politics. . . . Personally, I believe that everything is linked to everything. Social justice is and should be about everyone. But we need to be realistic and take into consideration the Cypriot particularities (KN).

Non-intersectional activism that remains embedded in nationalism and partitocracy inhibits inter-ethnic and intergroup collaboration. In a context of limited resources and political opportunities where non-intersectional activism seems to be the only promising tactic – at least short-term – movements hesitate to share hard-won resources, whether these are financial or network, as each movement tries to actualise its own particular goals instead of prioritising the finding of commonalities and intersectional praxis (Evans 2015, 2016; Santos 2013).

Nationalism is inherently built upon imposed coherence, systematic exclusions, and 'nature-based' gender-specific conceptions of identity and, thus, bolsters non-intersectional discourses, including in relation to gender nonconformity. Rules about propriety and gender performances and identities are inextricably linked to the belonging and exclusion boundaries that the national community prescribes (e.g. Anthias 2013, 2018; Mosse 1985; Parker et al. 1992; Pryke 1998; Yuval-Davis 1997, 2013; Yuval-Davis and Anthias 1989). Moreover, power resides in the ability to name both the self and the other (Binnie 2015; Epstein 1987). Namely, identity formation is situated within a matrix of power, where players seek to position themselves and secure their position by distancing themselves from abject others. In the case of non-heterosexual Cypriots, nonconforming sexual identities are often constructed through the alienation of other others – i.e. of gender-nonconforming people. For example, a gay man stated:

> I am probably negating myself by telling you this, but I feel annoyed, I don't feel comfortable, I don't feel nice. . . . I am annoyed by 'trans*'; I mean 'trans*' as an image . . . There is something about it I consider to be repulsive (EV).

In order to render their sexual identities as 'proper,' some Cypriot non-heterosexuals pathologise gender fluidity, non-binary gender identifications, and non-cisgender individuals (Sedgwick 1991, 1993, 2008).

What we call ourselves and others has immense implications for political practice (Binnie 2015; Epstein 1987). Therefore, beyond reinforcing gender binarism and promoting cisgenderism as normative, such views create in-group distinctions and hierarchies, thus limiting the possibility for intersectional LGBTIQ politics. For example, a trans* participant explained:

> They [i.e., LGBs] look down on us. . . . A lesbian . . . once told me that I'm not really a trans* man but a lesbian in confusion. . . . Another time, a gay guy told me that we keep them back from achieving their goals, as if their goals matter and ours don't. . . . I'm going to leave the group if they don't let us be autonomous (BQ).

Many trans* participants who are active in the LGBTIQ movement stated that they remain marginalised within it, as gender fluidity and transgression of binary gender identities is perceived by some LGB activists as a threat to the movement's successes, which were based on the employment of binary gender identities.

Rejecting gender transgression and fluidity as grounds of political identity, rendering cisgenderism as a type of privilege, the lack of intersectionality, and the marginalisation of trans* people within the LGBTIQ movement has not been particular to the case of Cyprus (e.g. DeFilippis, Yarbrough, and Jones 2018; George 2018; Mananzala and Spade 2008; Minter 2000; Spade 2015). When gender nonconformity is detached from the generic 'LGBTIQ' acronym and examined in its own right, the limitations and perils of neoliberal notions of identity rights become evident. In relation to the employment of the concepts 'sexual orientation' and 'gender identity' in transnational human rights discourses, it has been argued that they instil a distinctive gender and sexuality matrix that could potentially function as a reconfiguration of what Judith Butler (1990, p. 151) calls the 'heterosexual matrix.' As the argument goes, these concepts continue to be subject to dominant interpretations that privilege the gender binarism status quo, naturalise bodies, genders, and desires, and ignore the ways in which gender and sexuality are intertwined with social structures (McGill 2014; Waites 2009). The sources of exclusion are overshadowed under the notion of rights, while intersectional aspects of lived realities are obscured under reductive notions of identity (Manan-zala and Spade 2008; Spade 2015).

However, despite their imperfections and limitations, the European legal and human rights system and Europeanisation as a process of transnationalisation of norms and discourses regarding citizenship have been important driving forces behind intersectional LGBTIQ politics at the national and the transnational level (Ayoub 2013; Ayoub and Paternotte 2014; Sudbery 2010). It has already been mentioned how Europeanisation and the appeal of 'Europe' has been used by Cypriot LGBTIQ groups to circumvent the negative effects of the pervasiveness of nationalism and partitocracy, and to premise an elite-targeting and 'incremental politics' approach (Holzhacker 2007, 2012) as a viable strategy. As the next section will demonstrate, by critically employing transnational LGBTIQ discourses and practices made available by the EU while strategically balancing them with predominant local ones, Cypriot LGBTIQs have also managed to initiate a shift from strategic non-intersectional to intersectional politics, and to challenge intra-ethnic and inter-ethnic in-group divisions.

Transnational discourses/practices and intersectional politics

In Cyprus, as elsewhere, the predominance of nationalism and of partitocracy have forced movements with radical orientations to assume a strategic essentialist approach to political mobilisation and to aim at inclusion in the status quo (Kamenou 2011, 2012, 2016). In this vein, during the first years of its creation and mobilisation, the Greek-Cypriot LGBTIQ movement did not raise issues of intersectional exclusion and postponed forming (official) coalitions with the Turkish-Cypriot LGBTIQ movement (ibid.). Nonetheless, the view that justice does not end in the recognition of rights and that the time is ripe for a shift towards LGBTIQ intersectional politics is progressively gaining ground. For example, an LGBTIQ activist stated:

> We suck up to parties and politicians to give us what they will give us anyways because of Europe, like same-sex civil partnerships, and we think we have achieved something. . . . We allow them to gain votes on our backs. We are their alibi so that they can pretend to be progressive, while most of them continue to talk about 'the foreigner,' 'the economic migrant' as the

abomination. . . . They sweep under the carpet their xenophobia, their nationalism, their power games, and we are the carpet! . . . They say 'give them some rights, the minimum ones, and it's a win-win situation.' As if superficial rights, like same-sex civil partnerships, do away with injustice and all those things we, the privileged ones, pretend do not exist (RF).

This interview excerpt highlights two issues. The first one is the strategic use of homonationalism by some Cypriot parties and politicians. Namely, they support minimal thresholds of LGBTIQ legal recognition – since this is an unavoidable obligation that stems from the RoC's EU membership – and instrumentalise LGBTIQ rights so that they simultaneously gain LGBTIQs' electoral support – by appearing to be LGBTIQ-friendly – and maintain structural inequalities and notions of privilege and exclusion based on ethnicity, religion, race, class, immigration status, and other realities of experience (Kamenou 2011, 2012, 2016, 2019). The second issue is the approach towards, and use of, the EU as a strategic resource by Cypriot LGBTIQ activists. As this excerpt shows, while recognising that transnational LGBTIQ rights discourses made available by the EU do not suffice to dismantle locally predominant nationalist, homonationalist, and other exclusionary discourses and practices, because they resonate among most politicians, they strategically employ them in the transition from legal single-issue-based to substantive intersectional equality (ibid.).

Social movements' ethnographic particulars, political opportunity structures, institutional and cultural factors, and the competing and overlapping discourses and practices within which they are situated in specific locales at specific times are important for evaluating their ability to politicise issues and serve as vehicles for modifying relationships of power (Fisher 1997; Gamson 1997; Giugni and Passy 2004). Nevertheless, critical-reflexive exercise of political agency by local actors is important in order for a movement's aims and objectives to remain meaningful to those it is supposed to be representing. In Cyprus, an occasion for the development of intersectional politics across ethnic and other divides is created by the crossing of local and transnational discourses and paradigms. Another LGBTIQ activist explained:

It took a while for some [LGBTIQ] movement members to come to terms with the fact that one cannot be advocating against LGBTI exclusions and simultaneously be saying that they have nothing in common with other groups, like with other ethnic groups or with immigrants and asylum seekers. . . . People think this way because this is how we were brought up and taught in schools and brainwashed by the church. But I think that after the first [LGBTIQ] Pride [March], things have started to change. . . . ILGA-Europe [i.e., the European Region of the International Lesbian, Gay, Bisexual, Trans and Intersex Association] has played an important role in this [change]. . . . I know many LGBTI people who have changed their views completely and got to realise that it's 'one for all and all for one' (SP).

This excerpt substantiates the argument that, like elsewhere (Ayoub 2013, 2015, 2016; Ayoub and Paternotte 2014; Holzhacker 2007, 2012; Sudbery 2010), based on assistance of transnational umbrella LGBTIQ NGOs, like ILGA-Europe, and through trans-European networks, the LGBTIQ movement in Cyprus has managed to bring to the political forefront pro-LGBTIQ EU norms and discourses and to communicate to its constituency and the political elite that issues of LGBTIQ marginalisation cannot be described or tackled independently of realities of experience other than gender and sexuality (Kamenou 2012, 2016). Thus, it has set the premises for the formation of transnational intersectional coalitions that transcend divisions created and nurtured by nationalism.

It has been argued that the cultural production, circulation, and reception of a presumably transnational LGBTIQ movement is problematic, since the subordination of local particularities by transnational structures and the hierarchical relations between 'metropolises' and 'peripheries' are concealed under reductive notions of identity, which ignore intersectional aspects of lived realities (Mananzala and Spade 2008; Spade 2011, 2015). However, transnational LGBTIQ discourses and paradigms of activism are not monolithic or inflexible. They are adopted in multiple and constantly negotiated ways in different settings, as part of the process of formulating intersectional, counter-hegemonic responses to privilege and exclusions. For example, with the help of ILGA-Europe, Accept-LGBTI Cyprus and the Turkish-Cypriot NGO Queer Cyprus collaborated over the organisation of the first Cyprus LGBTIQ Pride March in 2014, thus striking a blow against nationalism and partitocracy that are premised on, and nurture, the island's ethnic division (Kamenou 2016, 2019).

Events such as this, which often become possible due to the support of 'European' organisations, constitute examples of successful attempts at intersectional political praxis that challenges not only inter-ethnic, but also intra-ethnic, ingroup divisions. Describing the struggle of some LGBTIQ activists to balance exclusionary discourses and practices in relation to gender nonconformity, which were prevalent within and beyond Accept-LGBTI Cyprus, with intersectional politics, an LGBTIQ activist explained:

> At its initial stages, the organisation didn't want to bring to the surface the gender identity issue. . . . Although our name contained the acronym 'LGBTI,' there were no trans* members. I wanted to invite some trans* friends to join the group, but I knew others wouldn't agree. They'd say that they [i.e., trans* members] . . . would endanger the organisation's image and objectives. . . . We needed to show we are good gays and lesbians, proper men and women, like the straights . . . if we were to bring members on board and have a chance of not getting destroyed by nationalists and by the Church and win the support of some politicians. . . . The 2016 Pride theme was trans* rights, and trans* legislation will pass soon. But it took a lot of work to get to this point. The role of TGEU [i.e., Transgender Europe] has been essential (PL).

Similarly, talking about the struggles of Turkish-Cypriot LGBTIQs, a Turkish-Cypriot activist said:

> Thanks to the support of ILGA-Europe, TGEU and other [LGBTIQ] groups in other countries, we have learned how to talk to society and to politicians about these [i.e., LGBTIQ] issues as human rights and as European issues. . . . In the north [of Cyprus], 'Europe' has a lot of currency, because of the need to prove to ourselves and to others that we belong to the 'West' and to 'Europe' and the EU (DH).

Despite limitations and arguments about their inherent hierarchies, the European human rights discourse and the multilevel system of the protection of fundamental rights in Europe have enhanced political opportunities for national and transnational mobilisation around gender and sexuality, under the umbrella of transnational NGOs that are assisting national activists in advancing their cause at the national level (Ayoub 2016; Ayoub and Paternotte 2014). When transnational discourses and paradigms of action find their way into local ideological and practical repertoires through an uncritical transplantation process, they may reinforce already existing hierarchical dichotomies of superiority-inferiority, privilege-abjection, and belonging-exclusion. Nonetheless, when these are critically and reflexively appropriated and used by taking into account contextual particularities, not only are their potentially oppressive and divisive effects evaded, but they also become the pillars of intersectional, transversal, and counter-hegemonic politics (Lombardo and Forest 2012).

Conclusion

This chapter examined the processes through which Cypriot LGBTIQ politics are shaped within a socio-political environment marked by the dynamics of the multilevel and cross-level interplay between local and EU norms and discourses regarding nationhood, gender, and sexuality. It discussed how gender and sexual identities are formed and mobilised amidst nationalistic discourses and alternative discourses and paradigms of political action, which gain impetus through Europeanisation.

Analysing data from in-depth interviews with Cypriot LGBTIQ participants it found that, within the Cypriot context – where nationalism and partitocracy prevail due to the legacies of colonialism, ethnonational conflict, and occupation – gender- and sexuality-nonconforming identities have been formed and have been strategically mobilised in ways that do not challenge – and often reinforce – existing hierarchical dichotomies of superiority-inferiority, privilege-abjection, and belonging-exclusion. In turn, this creates and reinforces intra-ethnic and inter-ethnic in-group exclusions. However, the research also found that by strategically using Europeanisation and the wish of some politicians and LGBTIQs to appear to be 'EU-friendly' and 'European,' the Cypriot

LGBTIQ movement has managed to initiate a shift from strategic non-intersectional to intersectional politics. This politics is progressively gaining ground and emasculates intra-ethnic and inter-ethnic in-group divisions, the privileging of heterosexuality and cisgenderism, and essentialist notions of nationhood, ethnic identity, and collective self.

In doing so, this analysis addressed the dearth of literature on whether and how the politics of LGBTIQ groups in contentious contexts challenge privilege and power and contributed to the research in this area with empirical data that develop our thinking about the workings and implications of understandings of nationhood and ethnicity, gender, and sexuality on LGBTIQ politics when the 'Rest' meets the 'West/Europe.' By revealing that the multilevel and cross-level interplay between discourses and practices is context-contingent, and that Europeanisation and the intersectionalisation of gender and sexuality politics are not one-way – i.e. from 'Europe/the West' to the 'Rest' – straightforward, or uncontested processes, it enabled the unearthing of alternative political action that becomes possible by the space that opens up when national and transnational discourses, paradigms, and practices merge, cross, or collude. Thus, it offered a nuanced, contextualised, and elucidating account of the intersectionality approach, and added to the body of gender and sexuality, feminist intersectionality, Europeanisation, and movements scholarship.

To borrow from Rawson (2010, p. 46), intersectionality is not only an identity theory 'but a strategy, a politic, an outlook on the world.' In order for the Cypriot LGBTIQ movement to remain meaningful to those it is supposed to be representing, local grassroots actors need to engage with, and bring to the political forefront, issues of intersectional marginalisation, and to move all the way from compartmentalised, strategic non-intersectional activism to intersectional politics. Through their theoretical and research endeavours, scholars working in the fields of intersectionality, gender, and sexuality have an important role to play in this process, by assisting in the opening up of the concept of activism as one that consists of multiple voices and perspectives beyond rigid identities, privilege, and markers of hierarchical differentiation.

Notes

1 Challenging the homogenisation of varied regions and historical experiences and the division and hierarchisation of the world, in this chapter, 'Europe' and 'the West' are understood not as geographic regions or unique civilisations, but as symbolic counters of identity. Therefore, by 'periphery of the 'West/Europe,'' I refer to contexts characterised by identity formation tensions that arise from attempts to balance local historical experiences and traditions with contemporary standards of 'progress,' according to which progress means the marginalisation of traditional ways of thinking and living (Burton and Kennedy 2016; Palmer 1977; Pouillion and Vatin 2014).
2 See Accept-LGBTI Cyprus website: www.acceptcy.org/en/node/241
3 See Accept-LGBTI Cyprus website: www.acceptcy.org/en/node/242

References

Albaek, Erik. 2003. "Political Ethics and Public Policy: Homosexuals Between Moral Dilemmas and Political Considerations in Danish Parliament Debates." *Scandinavian Political Studies* 26 (3): 245–267.

Anderson, Benedict. 1983. *Imagined Communities: Reflections on the Origins and Spread of Nationalism*. London; New York, NY: Verso.

Anthias, Floya. 2013. "Identity and Belonging: Conceptualisations and Political Framings." *Nordic Journal of Migration Research* 2 (2): 102–110.

Anthias, Floya. 2018. "Identity and Belonging: Conceptualizations and Reframings Through a Translocational Lens." In *Contested Belonging: Spaces, Practices, Biographies*, edited by Kathy Davis, Haleeh Ghorashi, and Peer Smets, 137–159. Bingley, UK: Emerald.

Ayoub, Phillip M. 2013. "Cooperative Transnationalism in Contemporary Europe: Europeanization and Political Opportunities for LGBT Mobilization in the European Union." *European Political Science Review* 5 (2): 1–32.

Ayoub, Phillip M. 2015. "Contested Norms in New-Adopter States: International Determinants of LGBT Rights Legislation." *European Journal of International Relations* 21 (2): 293–322.

Ayoub, Phillip M. 2016. *When States Come out: Europe's Sexual Minorities and the Politics of Visibility*. New York, NY: Cambridge University Press.

Ayoub, Phillip M., and David Paternotte. 2014. "Introduction." In *LGBT Activism and the Making of Europe: A Rainbow Europe?*, edited by Phillip M. Ayoub and David Paternotte, 1–25. Houndmills, Basingstoke: Palgrave Macmillan.

Beatty, Aidan. 2016. *Masculinity and Power in Irish Nationalism, 1884–1938*. London: Palgrave Macmillan.

Belavusau, Uladzislau, and Dimitry Kochenov. 2016. "Federalizing Legal Opportunities for LGBT Movements in the Growing EU." In *The EU Enlargement and Gay Politics: The Impact of Eastern Enlargement on Rights, Activism and Prejudice*, edited by Koen Slootmaeckers, Heleen Touquet, and Peter Vermeersch, 69–96. London: Palgrave Macmillan.

Bilge, Sirma. 2013. "Intersectionality Undone: Saving Intersectionality from Feminist Intersectionality Studies." *Du Bois Review: Social Science Research on Race* 10 (2): 405–424.

Bilić, Bojan. 2016. "Europeanisation, LGBT Activism, and Non-Heteronormativity in the Post-Yugoslav Space: An Introduction." In *LGBT Activism and Europeanisation in the Post-Yugoslav Space: On the Rainbow Way to Europe*, edited by Bojan Bilić, 1–22. London: Palgrave Macmillan.

Bilić, Bojan, and Sanja Kajinić, eds. 2016. *Intersectionality and LGBT Activist Politics: Multiple Others in Croatia and Serbia*. London: Palgrave Macmillan.

Bilić, Bojan, and Paul Stubbs. 2016. "Beyond EUtopian Promises and Disillusions: A Conclusion." In *LGBT Activism and Europeanisation in the Post-Yugoslav Space: On the Rainbow Way to Europe*, edited by Bojan Bilić, 231–248. London: Palgrave Macmillan.

Binnie, Jon. 2015. "Classing Desire." In *Global Justice and Desire: Queering Economy*, edited by Nikita Dhawan, Antke Engel, Christoph F. E. Holzhey, and Volker Woltersdorff, 147–160. Abingdon; New York, NY: Routledge.

Borowiec, Andrew. 2000. *Cyprus: A Troubled Island*. Westport, CT: Praeger.

Bose, Sumantra. 2007. *Contested Lands*. London; Cambridge, MA: Harvard University Press.

Bracke, Sarah. 2012. "From 'Saving Women' to Saving Gays': Rescue Narratives and Their Dis/Continuities." *European Journal of Women's Studies* 19 (2): 237–252.

Breuilly, John. 1982. *Nationalism and the State*. Manchester: Manchester University Press.

Brubaker, Rogers, Margit Feischmidt, Jon Fox, and Liana Grancea. 2006. *Nationalist Politics and Everyday Ethnicity in a Transylvanian Town*. Princeton, NJ: Princeton University Press.

Bryant, Rebecca. 2004. *Imagining the Modern: The Cultures of Nationalism in Cyprus*. London: I. B. Tauris.

Burton, Antoinette, and Dane Kennedy, eds. 2016. *How Empire Shaped Us*. New York, NY: Bloomsbury.

Butler, Judith. 1990. *Gender Trouble: Feminism and the Subversion of Identity*. London: Routledge.

Cockburn, Cynthia. 2004. *The Line: Women, Partition, and the Gender Order in Cyprus*. London: Zed Books.

Collins, Patricia H., and Sirma Bilge. 2016. *Intersectionality*. Cambridge, UK: Polity Press.

Colpani, Gianmaria, and Adriano J. Habed. 2014. "'In Europe It's Different': Homonationalism and Peripheral Desires for Europe." In *LGBT Activism and the Making of Europe: A Rainbow Europe?* edited by Phillip M. Ayoub and David Paternotte, 79–93. Houndmills, Basingstoke: Palgrave Macmillan.

D'Agostino, Serena. 2018. "Intersectional Mobilization and the EU: Which Political Opportunities Are There for Romani Women's Activism?" *European Yearbook of Minority Issues Online* 15 (1): 23–49.

DeFilippis, Joseph N., Michael W. Yarbrough, and Angela Jones, eds. 2018. *Queer Activism After Marriage Equality*. Abingdon; New York, NY: Routledge.

Dhamoon, Rita K. 2011. "Considerations on Mainstreaming Intersectionality." *Political Research Quarterly* 64 (1): 230–243.

Diez, Thomas, ed. 2002. *The European Union and the Cyprus Conflict: Modern Conflict, Postmodern Union*. Manchester; New York, NY: Manchester University Press.

Epstein, Steven G. 1987. "Gay Politics, Ethnic Identity: The Limits of Social Constructionism." *Socialist Review* 93: 9–54.

Evans, Elizabeth. 2015. *The Politics of Third Wave Feminism: Neoliberalism, Intersectionality and the State in Britain and the US*. Houndmills, Basingstoke: Palgrave Macmillan.

Evans, Elizabeth. 2016. "Intersectionality as Feminist Praxis in the UK." *Women's Studies International Forum* 59: 67–75.

Featherstone, Kevin. 2000. "Cyprus and the Onset of Europeanization: Strategic Usage, Structural Transformation and Institutional Adaptation." *South European Society and Politics* 5 (2): 141–164.

Featherstone, Kevin, and Claudio M. Radaelli, eds. 2003. *The Politics of Europeanization*. Oxford: Oxford University Press.

Fisher, William F. 1997. "Doing Good? The Politics and Antipolitics of NGO Practices." *Annual Review of Anthropology* 26 (1): 439–464.

Gamson, Joshua. 1997. "Messages of Exclusion: Gender, Movements, and Symbolic Boundaries." *Gender & Society* 11 (2): 178–199.

Gellner, Ernest. 1983. *Nations and Nationalism*. Oxford: Blackwell.

George, Marie-Amélie. 2018. "The LGBT Disconnect: Politics and Perils of Legal Movement Formation." *Wisconsin Law Review* 3: 503–591.

Giugni, Marco, and Florence Passy. 2004. "Migrant Mobilization Between Political Institutions and Citizenship Regimes: A Comparison of France and Switzerland." *European Journal of Political Research* 43 (1): 51–82.

Green Cowles, Maria, James Caporaso, and Thomas Risse, eds. 2001. *Transforming Europe: Europeanization and Domestic Change.* Ithaca, NY: Cornell University Press.

Greenwood, Ronni Michelle. 2008. "Intersectional Political Consciousness: Appreciation for Intragroup Differences and Solidarity in Diverse Groups." *Psychology of Women Quarterly* 32 (1): 36–47.

Hadjipavlou, Maria. 2010. *Women and Change in Cyprus: Feminisms and Gender in Conflict.* London: I. B. Tauris.

Hancock, Ange-Marie. 2016. *Intersectionality: An Intellectual History.* New York, NY: Oxford University Press.

Helfferich, Barbara, and Felix Kolb. 2001. "Multilevel Action Coordination in European Contentious Politics: The Case of the European Women's Lobby." In *Contentious Europeans: Protest and Politics in an Emerging Polity,* edited by Doug Imig and Sidney Tarrow, 143–162. Lanham, MD: Rowman & Littlefield.

Héritier, Adrienne. 2005. "Europeanization Research East and West: A Comparative Assessment." In *The Europeanization of Central and Eastern Europe,* edited by Frank Schimmelfenning and Ulrich Sedelmeier, 199–209. Ithaca, NY: Cornell University Press.

Hitchens, Christopher. 1997. *Hostage to History: Cyprus from the Ottomans to Kissinger.* London; New York, NY: Verso.

Hobsbawm, Eric. 1992. *Nations and Nationalism Since 1780: Programme, Myth, Reality* (2nd ed.). Cambridge, UK: Cambridge University Press.

Hoegaerts, Josephine. 2014. *Masculinity and Nationhood, 1830–1910: Constructions of Identity and Citizenship in Belgium.* London: Palgrave Macmillan.

Holzhacker, Ronald. 2007. "The Europeanization and Transnationalization of Civil Society Organizations Striving for Equality: Goals and Strategies of Gay and Lesbian Groups in Italy and the Netherlands." European University Institute Working Paper RSCAS 2007/36.

Holzhacker, Ronald. 2012. "National and Transnational Strategies of LGBT Civil Society Organizations in Different Political Environments: Modes of Interaction in Western and Eastern Europe for Equality." *Comparative European Politics* 10 (1): 23–47.

Kahlina, Katja. 2015. "Local Histories, European LGBT Designs: Sexual Citizenship, Nationalism, and 'Europeanisation' in Post-Yugoslav Croatia and Serbia." *Women's Studies International Forum* 49: 73–83.

Kamenou, Nayia. 2011. "Queer in Cyprus: National Identity and the Construction of Gender and Sexuality." In *Queer in Europe,* edited by Lisa Downing and Robert Gillet, 25–40. Surrey; Burlington, VT: Ashgate.

Kamenou, Nayia. 2012. *"Cyprus Is the Country of Heroes, Not of Homosexuals": Sexuality, Gender and Nationhood in Cyprus.* PhD dissertation, King's College, London.

Kamenou, Nayia. 2016. "Sexual Politics – Party Politics: The Rules of Engagement in the Case of Cyprus." In *Party – Society Relations in the Republic of Cyprus: Political and Societal Strategies,* edited by Giorgos Charalambous and Christophoros Christophorou, 129–148. London; New York, NY: Routledge.

Kamenou, Nayia. 2019. "Sexuality, Gender and the (Re)making of Modernity and Nation-hood in Cyprus." *Women's Studies International Forum* 74: 59–67.

Karayanni, Stavros S. 2004. *Dancing Fear and Desire: Race, Sexuality, and Imperial Politics in Middle Eastern Dance.* Ontario: Wilfrid Laurier University Press.

Karayanni, Stavros S. 2006. "Moving Identity: Dance in the Negotiation of Sexuality and Ethnicity in Cyprus." *Postcolonial Studies* 9 (3): 251–266.

Karayanni, Stavros S. 2017. "Zone of Passions: A Queer Re-imagining of Cyprus's 'No Man's Land'." *Synthesis: An Anglophone Journal of Comparative Literary Studies* 10: 63–81.

Kitzinger, Jenny. 1994. "The Methodology of Focus Groups: The Importance of Interaction Between Research Participants." *Sociology of Health & Illness* 16 (1): 103–121.

Knapp, Gudrun-Axeli. 2005. "Race, Class, Gender: Reclaiming Baggage in Fast Travelling Theories." *European Journal of Women's Studies* 12 (3): 249–265.

Kristoffersson, Mattias, Björn van Roozendaal, and Lilit Poghosyan. 2016. "European Integration and LGBTI Activism: Partners in Realising Change?" In *The EU Enlargement and Gay Politics: The Impact of Eastern Enlargement on Rights, Activism and Prejudice*, edited by Koen Slootmaeckers, Heleen Touquet, and Peter Vermeersch, 45–67. London: Palgrave Macmillan.

Kumari, Kanchan. 2018. "Heterosexual Nationalism: Discourses on Masculinity and Femininity." *International Journal of Social Science Studies* 6 (11): 34–39.

Laperrière, Marie, and Eléonore Lépinard. 2016. "Intersectionality as a Tool for Social Movements: Strategies of Inclusion and Representation in the Québécois Women's Movement." *Politics* 36 (4): 374–382.

Levy, Robert I., and Douglas W. Hollan. 2015. "Person-Centered Interviewing and Observation." In *Handbook of Methods in Cultural Anthropology*, edited by Harvey Russell Bernard and Clarence C. Gravlee, 2nd ed., 313–342. London: Rowman & Littlefield.

Lombardo, Emanuela, and Elena Del Giorgio. 2013. "EU Antidiscrimination Policy and Its Unintended Domestic Consequences: The Institutionalization of Multiple Equalities in Italy." *Women's Studies International Forum* 39: 12–21.

Lombardo, Emanuela, and Maxime Forest, eds. 2012. *The Europeanization of Gender Equality Policies: A Discursive-Sociological Approach.* London: Palgrave Macmillan.

Lombardo, Emanuela, and Mieke Verloo. 2009. "Institutionalizing Intersectionality in the European Union? Policy Developments and Contestations." *International Feminist Journal of Politics* 11 (4): 478–495.

Luft, Rachel E., and Jane Ward. 2009. "Toward an Intersectionality Just out of Reach: Confronting Challenges to Intersectional Practice." In *Perceiving Gender Locally, Globally, and Intersectionally*, edited by Vasilikie Demos and Marcia Texler Segal, 9–37. Bingley, UK: Emerald.

Mananzala, Rickke, and Dean Spade. 2008. "The Nonprofit Industrial Complex and Trans Resistance." *Sexuality Research & Social Policy* 5 (1): 53–71.

Marks, Gary, and Doug McAdam. 1999. "On the Relationship of Political Opportunities to the Form of Collective Action: The Case of the European Union." In *Social Movements in a Globalizing World*, edited by Donatella della Porta, Hanspeter Kriesi, and Dieter Rucht, 97–111. New York, NY: St. Martin's Press.

May, Vivian M. 2015. *Pursuing Intersectionality, Unsettling Dominant Imaginaries.* New York, NY: Routledge.

McGill, Jena. 2014. "SOGI . . . So What? Sexual Orientation, Gender Identity and Human Rights Discourse at the United Nations." *Canadian Journal of Human Rights* 3 (1): 1–38.

Minter, Shannon. 2000. "Do Transsexuals Dream of Gay Rights? Getting Real About Transgender Inclusion in the Gay Rights Movement." *New York Law School Journal of Human Rights* 17: 589–622.

Mole, Richard C. 2016. "Nationalism and Homophobia in Central and Eastern Europe." In *The EU Enlargement and Gay Politics: The Impact of Eastern Enlargement on Rights, Activism and Prejudice*, edited by Koen Slootmaeckers, Heleen Touquet, and Peter Vermeersch, 99–121. London: Palgrave Macmillan.

Mosse, George L. 1985. *Nationalism and Sexuality: Respectability and Abnormal Sexuality in Modern Europe*. New York, NY: H. Fertig.

Orbuch, Terri L. 1997. "People's Accounts Count: The Sociology of Accounts." *Annual Review of Sociology* 23 (1): 455–478.

Palmer, Richard E. 1977. "Postmodernity and Hermeneutics." *boundary 2* 5 (2): 363–394.

Parker, Andrew, Mary Russo, Doris Sommer, and Patricia Yaeger, eds. 1992. *Nationalisms and Sexualities*. New York, NY: Routledge.

Paternotte, David. 2018. "Coming out of the Political Science Closet: The Study of LGBT Politics in Europe." *European Journal of Politics and Gender* 1 (1–2): 55–74.

Pouillion, François, and Jean-Claude Vatin, eds. 2014. *After Orientalism: Critical Perspectives on Western Agency and Eastern Re-Appropriations*. Leiden; Boston, MA: Brill.

Pryke, Sam. 1998. "Nationalism and Sexuality: What Are the Issues?" *Nations and Nationalism* 4 (4): 529–546.

Puar, Jasbir K. 2007. *Terrorist Assemblages: Homonationalism in Queer Times*. London; Durham, NC: Duke University Press.

Puar, Jasbir K. 2013. "Rethinking Homonationalism." *International Journal of Middle East Studies* 45 (2): 336–339.

Rao, Rahul. 2015. "Echoes of Imperialism in LGBT Activism." In *Echoes of Empire: Memory, Identity and Colonial Legacies*, edited by Kalypso Nicolaïdis, Berny Sèbe, and Gabrielle Maas, 355–372. London: I. B. Tauris.

Rawson, Kelly J. 2010. "Queering Feminist Rhetorical Canonization." In *Rhetorica in Motion: Feminist Rhetorical Methods & Methodologies*, edited by Eileen E. Schell and Kelly J. Rawson, 39–52. Pittsburgh, PA: University of Pittsburgh Press.

Rexhepi, Piro. 2016. "From Orientalism to Homonationalism: Queer Politics, Islamophobia and Europeanization in Kosovo." *Southeastern Europe* 40 (1): 32–53.

Richardson, Jeremy, ed. 2006. *European Union: Power and Policy-Making*. Abingdon: Routledge.

Riessman, Catherine K. 2008. *Narrative Methods for the Human Sciences*. Thousand Oaks, CA: Sage Publications.

Romano, Gabriella. 2019. *The Pathologisation of Homosexuality in Fascist Italy: The Case of 'G'*. Cham: Palgrave Pivot.

Sadurní, Núria, Marisela Montenegro, and Joan Pujol. 2017. "National Construction and LGBTI Rights: Exploring Catalan Homonationalism." *Sexualities*. Online first. doi:10.1177/1363460717716399

Santos, Ana Christina. 2013. *Social Movements and Sexual Citizenship in Southern Europe*. Houndmills, Houndmills, Basingstoke: Palgrave Macmillan.

Schmidt, Vivien A. 2002. *The Futures of European Capitalism*. Oxford: Oxford University Press.

Scott, Joan W. 1996. *Only Paradoxes to Offer: French Feminists and the Rights of Man*. Cambridge, MA: Harvard University Press.

Sedgwick, Eve K. 1991. "How to Bring Your Kids up Gay." *Social Text* 29: 18–27.

Sedgwick, Eve K. 1993. *Tendencies*. Durham, NC: Duke University Press.

Sedgwick, Eve K. 2008. *Epistemology of the Closet*. Berkeley and Los Angeles, CA: University of California Press.

Sepos, Angelos. 2008. *The Europeanization of Cyprus: Polity, Policies and Politics*. Houndmills, Basingstoke: Palgrave Macmillan.

Skey, Michael, and Marco Antonsich, eds. 2017. *Everyday Nationhood: Theorizing Culture, Identity and Belonging After Banal Nationalism*. London: Palgrave Macmillan.

Slootmaeckers, Koen, and Heleen Touquet. 2016. "The Co-Evolution of EU's Eastern Enlargement and LGBT Politics: An Ever Gayer Union?" In *The EU Enlargement and Gay Politics: The Impact of Eastern Enlargement on Rights, Activism and Prejudice*, edited by Koen Slootmaeckers, Heleen Touquet, and Peter Vermeersch, 19–44. London: Palgrave Macmillan.

Spade, Dean. 2011. "Laws as Tactics." *Columbia Journal of Gender & Law* 21 (2): 40–71.

Spade, Dean. 2015. *Normal Life: Administrative Violence, Critical Trans Politics, and the Limits of Law*. London; Durham, NC: Duke University Press.

Sudbery, Imogen. 2010. "The European Union as Political Resource: NGOs as Change Agents?" *Acta Politica* 45 (1–2): 136–157.

Tarrow, Sidney G. 1994. *Power in Movement: Social Movements, Collective Action and Politics*. Cambridge, UK: Cambridge University Press.

Timm, Annette F., and Joshua A. Sanborn. 2007. *Gender, Sex and the Shaping of Modern Europe: A History from the French Revolution to the Present Day*. New York, NY: Berg.

Verloo, Mieke. 2006. "Multiple Inequalities, Intersectionality and the European Union." *European Journal of Women's Studies* 13 (3): 211–228.

Verloo, Mieke. 2013. "Intersectional and Cross-Movement Politics and Policies: Reflections on Current Practices and Debates." *Signs* 38 (4): 893–915.

Verloo, Mieke, ed. 2018. *Varieties of Opposition to Gender Equality in Europe: Theory, Evidence and Practice*. Abingdon; New York, NY: Routledge.

Waites, Matthew. 2009. "Critique of 'Sexual Orientation' and 'Gender Identity' in Human Rights Discourse: Global Queer Politics Beyond the Yogyakarta Principles." *Contemporary Politics* 15 (1): 137–156.

Yuval-Davis, Nira. 1997. *Gender and Nation*. London: Sage.

Yuval-Davis, Nira. 2006. "Intersectionality and Feminist Politics." *European Journal of Women's Studies* 13 (3): 193–209.

Yuval-Davis, Nira. 2013. "Religion and Gender in Contemporary Political Projects of Belonging." In *Religion, Gender, and the Public Sphere*, edited by Niamh Reilly and Stacey Scriver, 31–44. London; New York, NY: Routledge.

Yuval-Davis, Nira, and Floya Anthias, eds. 1989. *Woman-Nation-State*. London: Palgrave Macmillan.

Chapter 9

Feminist whiteness

Resisting intersectionality in France

Éléonore Lépinard

Introduction

Despite the proliferation of intersectionality in feminist discourses in many contexts, research documents how hegemonic feminist practices continue to reproduce various hierarchies of power and privilege, and how the 'desire' for intersectionality rarely translates into practice, even when it is openly embraced by younger generations of white feminists (Evans 2015, 2016; Reger 2012; Schuster 2016; Strolovitch 2007). Gaps in the implementation of intersectionality, in its conversion from discourses to practice (Bacchetta 2015; Bassel and Emejulu 2017), are however maybe not surprising. Indeed, if, as the introduction to this volume suggests, a main goal of intersectionality as a political and conceptual tool is to challenge privileges, this goal is bound to meet resistance. While privilege manifests itself through entitlement to various social positions and is secured institutionally, 'it can also be defined as permission to escape or avoid any challenges to this entitlement' (Vodde 2000, p. 3, cited in DiAngelo 2011, p. 65). Given that intersectionality centrally challenges racial privilege, among others, we can expect that there will be white resistance, through avoidance, denial, indifference, emotional anger, or 'white women's tears' to the attempt to dismantle privilege within feminist organisations (McIntosh 1988; DiAngelo 2011, 2019). However, this resistance is often silent: intersectionality is rarely openly resisted, rather, it fails to become, and remains what Sara Ahmed describes as non-performative.

Indeed, exploring institutional commitments to anti-racism, Sara Ahmed notes the persistence of non-performativity (Ahmed 2004, 2006): despite declared intentions and acknowledgement that racism exists and should be combatted, these speech acts remain utterly non-performative, never encountering the social conditions of their realisation – which is not, Ahmed argues, a failure of the speech act but, ironically in this case, the revelation of its true meaning. Indeed, Ahmed contends that these declarations of commitment to anti-racism were never meant to be realised. On the contrary, 'they "work" by not bringing about the effects that they name' (Ahmed 2006, p. 105) Such a non-performativity is certainly at work in the repeated admissions of a 'lack of intersectionality' that white feminist activists and organisations regularly issue. However, Ahmed also suggests that this non-performativity reflects the institutional politics of safeguarding the centrality of whiteness (Ahmed 2004). In the context of feminist mobilisations, the non-performativity of intersectionality may thus also be understood as deriving from the attempt to secure the centrality of whiteness both as an *institutional* privilege and as an *epistemic* privilege within the feminist project. Indeed, feminist theorists of colour have long emphasised how white feminists universalise their experiences to parade as the preferred and 'natural' feminist subject, thereby orienting and appropriating feminism's priorities and discourses (hooks 1984; Frye 1983; Anzaldúa and Moraga 1983; Lorde 1984). How can calls for more intersectionality be performative if the centrality of whiteness within feminism is not dislodged?

Hence, in order to understand the non-performativity of intersectionality, we must focus our attention on the various ways in which white feminists secure their privileged positions as the preferred subject of feminism, and thereby *resist* intersectionality in practice. Concepts such as privilege and whiteness thus must be central to the analysis. Recent scholarship on whiteness in third-wave feminist movements describes a new set of repertoires of whiteness, which express a desire for 'diversity' and the rhetorical inclusion of feminists of colour's works in feminist narratives (Rowe 2000; Mane 2012; Jonsson 2016). These repertoires often reproduce whiteness as privilege instead of displacing its centrality in feminism, for example through an understanding of diversity as a proliferation of differences.[1]

I pick up this line of inquiry in this chapter, investigating how whiteness entrenches forms of resistance to intersectionality within feminist movements. Indeed, in order to account for the slowness of adoption of intersectional *practices*, we must understand where resistance to intersectionality is located and how it is sustained. I argue in this chapter that what I call *feminist whiteness* is a prime location of resistance to intersectionality. Feminist whiteness designates the ways in which feminism is *made white* by white feminists. It allows us to document the discursive and epistemological repertoires that white feminists use to make feminism white, securing their privileged position, and it is particularly useful to identify and analyse resistances to intersectionality.

In the following section I define further the concept of feminist whiteness, explicating its analytical purchase to study exclusions and inclusions in feminist movements. I then turn to my case study, documenting the variegated forms of feminist whiteness in contemporary French feminist organisations. I first identify the various repertoires that French white feminists use to maintain the centrality of whiteness to the feminist project, bypassing or downplaying, in particular, the importance of racism and Islamophobia. Second, I explore the feminist repertoires which discursively produce non-white women as 'others.' A first way in which white feminists make non-white women into 'others' is by defining them as vulnerable subjects in need of help. Feminist whiteness is then displayed through a form of *patronising solicitude*. Another way in which white feminists perform othering is by framing non-white women, in particular veiled Muslim women, as improper feminist subjects. Here, feminist whiteness is expressed through *indignant anger*. Finally, I reflect in the conclusion on how documenting the forms and expressions of feminist whiteness can orient the reflection to describe, examine, and maybe dislodge white privilege within feminist movements and make calls for intersectionality to be actually performative.

Feminist whiteness and intersectionality

Whiteness as a critical concept must be understood as a process of subjectivation that results from racism and racialisation, rather than as a given identity (Frankenberg 1993a, 1993b; McWhorter 2005). Whiteness is a material, cultural, and subjective location and 'is also a relational category, one that is co-constructed with a range of other racial and cultural categories, with class and with gender' (Frankenberg 1993b, p. 236). Furthermore, and importantly, studies of whiteness also explore the moral and emotional dimensions of this social position of privilege. Whiteness is saturated by affects and moral dispositions, such as entitlement, denial, guilt, postcolonial melancholia, anger, and violence (Frankenberg 1993b; Fellows and Razack 1998; Srivastava 2006; Gillman 2007; DiAngelo 2011; Wekker 2016). Hence, whiteness, as a social location of privilege, is also sustained and expressed by specific moral and emotional dispositions.

The literature on whiteness provides two important insights to understand how whiteness shapes feminism and entrenches resistance to intersectionality. A first claim documented by whiteness studies is the privilege of ignorance, and the epistemology of ignorance that is sustained by whiteness: whiteness presents itself as an invisible and unmarked category – for those who inhabit it, not for those marked as non-white – and as a position of ignorance (Lorde 1984; Frankenberg 1993a; C. W. Mills 1997; C. Mills 2007; Mueller 2017). A second claim, developed in particular by Sara Ahmed, is that an effect of racialisation processes is to mark some bodies as others (Ahmed 2007). For Ahmed, whiteness is the quality of what has been made white, thanks in part to a process of making others as others, by marking and othering their bodies. The concept of whiteness thus reveals how racial privilege assigns race to others and impacts those bodies recognised as non-white (Ahmed 2004). This process is the necessary complement to the process of whiteness as seeing oneself as 'unmarked' by race when one is white.

These processes are evidenced in feminist movements. The pervasive whiteness of many feminist movements and organisations has been the object of critical scrutiny by feminists of colour for many decades (hooks 1984; Frye 1983; Anzaldúa and Moraga 1983; Lorde 1984; Mohanty and Martin 2003; Mohanty 2003). However, the turn to the concept of intersectionality in feminist research (Davis 2008; Mügge et al. 2018) – and activism – has so far focused attention on the dynamics of under/mis/representation of identities and interests within movements, rather than more precisely on the perpetuation of privilege. Along with, or complementing, these analyses of intersectionality within feminist movements, a smaller body of scholarship analyses more specifically the resistance of white feminists in acknowledging racism and racial privilege, and how this denial shapes race relations among feminists and the dynamics of feminist coalitions and exclusions. While white feminists may acknowledge the pervasiveness of racism in society, they are often unwilling to apply this analysis to their own organisation and their own behaviour. Some studies thus show the ways in which privileged positions within feminist movements are perpetuated thanks to a universalisation of white feminists' interests and a denial of racism in women's movements in locations as diverse as the US (Smith 1995; Zajicek 2002), Uruguay (Townsend-Bell 2013), the UK (Bassel and Emejulu 2017), Norway, Spain, and the UK (Predelli and Halsaa 2012), Australia (Wilson 1996), Belgium (Ouali 2015), and France (Guénif-Souilamas 2006).

These findings encourage us to conceptualise more precisely the role played by *whiteness* in feminist activism and to focus research on intersectionality in feminist movements on an analysis of privilege, in particular white privilege. To do so, I propose the concept of *feminist whiteness* to designate the discourses and practices by white feminists which make feminism white, secure privileges attached to whiteness, and mark non-white feminists as feminist others. Tracing the construction of *feminist whiteness* thus means documenting how feminism is made white, how white feminists' desire to ignore realities of racism preserves their 'innocence' (Ortega 2006; Wekker 2016), and how they contribute to mark non-white feminist subjects as others, racialised and improper subjects to be excluded from the feminist collective project. In the vein of whiteness studies, the concept of feminist whiteness aims to direct our analytical attention both to the discursive operations that maintain white privilege – and its ignorance – and to the operations which mark non-white feminists as others. To do so, an approach focused on whiteness must explore the articulation between political identity and moral dispositions and emotions, moving beyond an understanding of intersectionality politics that is too often limited to the vocabulary of social movements studies focused on identities and interests. Indeed, I argue that to understand resistances to intersectionality we must pay attention not only to inequalities and power dynamics within movements, but also to how they are embedded in racialised attachments to the feminist project, and to racialised definitions of what it is to be a 'good' feminist subject (Srivastava 2005). The concept of feminist whiteness thus demands that we document how white privilege is discursively maintained, and how it is attached to emotions and moral dispositions which contribute to produce feminist 'others.' I turn to this task in the following sections.

Methods

In the following sections I document feminist whiteness in the context of contemporary French feminist organisations in order to deepen our understanding of resistances to intersectionality. The analysis of feminist whiteness I propose is qualitative and inductive; it is reconstructed from the empirical material collected during a qualitative fieldwork in France (2011–2015). I interviewed feminist activists and officers in 25 French feminist organisations, mainly situated in Paris and its suburbs. Interviews did not explicitly focus on whiteness. Rather, they covered the organisation's history, its activities, its conception of feminism, its engagement with intersectional issues, its coalition work, and the personal history of activism of the interviewee. However, as a white feminist myself, self-identifying as feminist during interviews and interviewing in this case white feminists,[2] I certainly benefited from implicit white solidarity and from the race talk which happens between white people (DiAngelo 2011) in the ways in which the interviewees responded to these questions. The feminist activists that I categorised as white feminists self-identified as members of the ethnic majority group. Or, more precisely, they did not identify racially, thereby adhering to the idea typical of whiteness that they are not marked. They were also officers or volunteers in organisations that did not self-identify as representing a specific ethnic or national group. These organisations – shelters, community centres, and advocacy groups – identified as feminist organisations. This sample of course does not exhaust the variations in feminist whiteness and does not pretend to be representative. However, it does allow for identifying common repertoires and their articulations with broader French narratives about race and colour-blindness, and how they perform resistance to intersectionality.

Research on whiteness has insisted on its contextual and historical nature (Frankenberg 1997), and it is therefore important to underline that the repertoires I analyse in this chapter are embedded in the French historical and social context which must be detailed a little bit here. My empirical exploration of feminist whiteness is set in the context of the 2010s, a period in which Islamic veil debates – starting in 2004 with a law banning conspicuous religious signs in public schools in France – have encouraged the diffusion of Islamophobic discourses in society at large and have shattered the French feminist movement, exposing deep divides and conflicts over secularism, women's agency, Islam, and the definition of emancipation (Scott 2007; Dot-Pouillard 2007; Bouyahia and Sanna 2013; Lettinga and Saharso 2012). In this context, both race and religion – and more specifically Islam, the religion of the formerly colonised – must be taken into account in the production of whiteness, as well as the predominant narrative of colour-blindness and racelessness promoted by French institutions and a large part of its elites.[3] Importantly, white feminists interviewed for this research were also non-Muslim women. Evidently, beyond the focus on Islam, other historical repertoires such as colonialism, immigrant integration, secularism, leftist internationalism, and French republicanism also constitute the discursive field of race and racism and contribute to shape different forms of feminist whiteness.

Starting in the early 2000s, there has been a re-appropriation of Black US feminist writings by Afro-feminist groups in France (Bacchetta 2009, 2015), as well as a (contested) importation of the vocabulary of intersectionality in academia and in new cohorts of feminist organisations.[4] Nevertheless, the institutionalisation of intersectionality in politics and policies remained very weak in the early 2010s (Bassel and Emejulu 2010). While all French women working or volunteering in

white/ethnic majority organisations who were interviewed insisted that the 2004
law banning the veil in public school had raised thorny issues and heated discussions among their members (contrary to the 2010 law banning full veiling in
public spaces, which was presented as quite consensus-based), revealing therefore strong disagreements and political conflicts among them, their discourses
nevertheless reflect common narratives that position white feminists in a specific
location of privilege within society and, as I will focus on here, within feminism. While this specific French context contributes to shape the discourses that
pertain to feminist whiteness, many repertoires used by white French feminists
echo social and cultural discourses that go beyond the French case: how whiteness embodies the norm and parades as universal, how racialised identities are
delegitimised as grounds for group identity and political claims or displaced to
other spaces, outside the nations. Hence, while the repertoires identified here as
defining the contours of feminist whiteness are embedded in a specific context,
they also may be found in other contexts, demonstrating similitudes in the processes which produce and maintain feminist whiteness and privilege within feminist movements.

Feminist whiteness as ignoring race and maintaining privilege

Three main discursive repertoires allow white feminists to ignore, in potent ways,
the reality of the racialisation of non-whites and Muslims and, meanwhile, to
secure the centrality of the white feminist subject: universalism, class vs. race,
and internationalism.

Universalism vs. particularism

A first potent repertoire in the French context is universalism.[5] This ideal irrigates
many aspects of white French feminists' relationship to racial and religious difference (Lépinard 2014). Universalism is expressed both by downplaying differences between women based on race or religion in order to insist on the primacy
of gender as a site of oppression and by critiquing women of colour's autonomous
organising.

For example, Elsa, a young white feminist in her late twenties who volunteers
in an organisation created in 2009 by mostly young women in their twenties and
early thirties, where she is part of the executive as well as in charge of communications, sums up the priorities of her association, listing typical 'universalist'
issues:

> We launched this campaign with a website that aims to show that feminism is
> political, that we can change things, that we can change the lives of millions
> of women. . . . We don't really address different groups of women, although
> of course we are aware that there is a great heterogeneity. . . . We would like

not to forget women living in deprived neighbourhoods; we don't forget that they have daily lives marked by discrimination that are specific to them. But, let's face it . . . we don't come from there. Dare Feminism! is not a group of women from the projects. So it's not that easy. We don't want to mess it up. We try to do some meetings, to understand some things.[6]

Elsa uses the descriptor 'women from the projects' (*femmes des quartiers*) to convey class and racial difference, thereby performing a social distance that she indeed acknowledges a minute later in her interview when she admits that these women are in fact mostly absent from her organisation. However, this absence, even coupled with the admission that racialised women have in fact specific problems and interests, does not lead her to call into question the universalist platform of her organisation. Social distance and social exclusion are acknowledged but never interpreted as the products of power and shaped by institutional racism. Her declaration that her organisation 'would like not to forget women living in deprived neighbourhoods' is typically non-performative in the sense defined by Sara Ahmed, as it is immediately followed by its own – ironic – undoing: the desire 'not to mess it up' legitimises not doing anything. Later in her interview, when asked if her organisation has reflected upon the question of discrimination in employment against veiled Muslim women, she admits that the subject has not been raised. Hence, the universalist approach to the feminist project of her organisation makes invisible and ignores important issues that concern Muslim women. While white feminists such as Elsa denounce racism, and while they identify as anti-racist, they rarely indicate that racism might shape the relationships between white feminists and feminists of colour and may place them in a position of power.

To secure the centrality of whiteness in the feminist project, another discursive repertoire presents racialised women's organising based on ethnic identity as particular, i.e. non-universalist. The idea that organising along ethnic lines goes against the grain of proper feminist politics legitimises the idea that white organisations and feminist whiteness embody a universal feminist subject. Julie, a young Jewish woman who is employed to manage the public relations of a French organisation which identifies as representing marginalised women and girls, in particular those from the 'projects' (i.e. daughters of immigrants), makes it clear in her response:

This logic [to organise on an ethnic or national-origin basis] is not ours. And I think it's not the right way to do it. Today we are the voice of all the women who believe in the feminist conception of equality under the republic, that's our conception, and [the voice of those] who need help at one point or another, whatever their origin, their colour, their sexual orientation. . . . As far as I am concerned [organising along ethnic identities] does not bother me, but me, I like social diversity . . . I find it enriching and it's a shame to lose that. Now if it happens that there is, first, a community organisation because of language, because of community ties, because of a common experience . . .

which helps free the discourse [*libérer la parole*]. Then of course it's necessary. But if it's a discourse that says that nobody other than a Congolese
woman is better placed to talk to another Congolese woman . . . It bothers me.

Julie insisted during her interview that the philosophy of her organisation is in
fact to bring universal women's rights to *all* women, including Muslim girls and
women depicted as particularly vulnerable to patriarchal oppression because
of their economic and social marginality and because of the specificity of religion as a vehicle of women's oppression. She also conveys the idea of a hierarchy between racialised women's organisations, limited to providing a forum
to voice 'specific' and culturalised concerns, and feminist organisations such
as hers, which will truly transform these voices into a universalist and proper
feminist discourse.

Delegitimising race

A second discursive repertoire of feminist whiteness argues that race should not
constitute the basis of political identification because other identities, such as
class, are more important and politically relevant. This repertoire finds its roots
in part of the second-wave French feminist movement – the class struggle trend –
which has had enduring effects on some women's rights organisations. Claudine,
who heads a Women's Rights Collective, a nation-wide coalition of feminist
organisations, was politicised in her teens and youth through her participation in
leftist revolutionary groups and now identities as anti-capitalist feminist. Questioned about whether intersectionality is something her organisation considers
when elaborating its political platform, she answers:

> I don't give up on inequalities. That's it . . . there needs to be a transmission of
> what the class struggle trend did, intersectional, I think we are intersectional,
> but on true issues, true ones, not a veiled woman, a transsexual woman and
> a sex worker!

In her answer, inequalities are primarily linked to class – and supposedly are not
addressed by intersectionality – and there is a clear priority of struggles to be
fought, and others to be marginalised because they are deemed specific, unimpor-
tant, and even improper feminist subjects. In a similar vein, Anick, the founder of
a network of support for immigrant and refugee women, decries the fact that, for
some, race trumps class and condemns the idea that race may structure political
priorities:

> Me, personally, I am against the fact that the social question has been trans-
> formed into an ethnic, or even racial question. And when it comes to the
> legacy of the colonial system, of course it exists, as much in the former colo-
> nies as in the former metropolitan states, but I don't think it is the central

glass through which to see history, be it of the former colonies or the former metropolitan states.

Anick's lament that class has been forgotten and that race is inappropriately used as a ground for political struggle is, like for Claudine, intimately linked with her political subjectivation as a leftist lesbian white feminist in the 1970s in the revolutionary group the Proletarian Left. For white French feminists who came of age in the leftist nebulae of the 1970s and were politicised in revolutionary organisations, the legacy of this political subjectivation has left a profound mark on their vision of feminism. Anick, who volunteers on a daily basis to support undocumented migrant women and was part of support groups for immigrants within the left as early as the 1970s, knows that racism is pervasive and that it is tightly articulated with economic deprivation. However, she firmly rejects the idea that race could provide a positive basis for identification and politicisation. For her, as for Claudine, the politicisation of race runs the risk of fragmenting further an already fragmented feminist movement. Both perceive this oppression, as well as class oppression, as additive to gender. Such an additive conception does not challenge the idea of a possible universal feminist subject, and the position of invisible privilege of the white feminist subject is therefore secured.

Internationalism: locating race outside the nation

A third and last repertoire of feminist whiteness legitimises racial identities and allows for taking them into consideration, but only when they are located *outside* the French nation, and thus places white French feminists in the position of enacting international solidarity. Asked about their positions on the 2004 law banning the veil in public schools, many white feminists mentioned that they had followed the advice of Algerian or Iranian friends and that, in fact, by supporting the ban, they had expressed solidarity with Muslim women . . . abroad and/or exiled in France. This discourse allows white feminists to situate themselves not in the configuration of racial relations in the French contemporary context, which would demand the acknowledgement of their social position of relative privilege vis-à-vis racialised French women, but in racial configurations of international solidarity. For example, Corinne, who heads a network of women's rights community centres, elaborates:

At the beginning [of the debate] we didn't know. Each time we take a position on a law . . . we try to ask: can we have a feminist look at it? Should we position ourselves? We listened, we listened a lot . . . and thanks to the diversity within our ranks, that's our diversity, thanks to these women coming from different countries, different horizons, different social strata . . . we exchanged. We exchanged with Iranians, with Algerians, with women from different countries and continents and we could say: if we retreat on this, if we open the door to this . . . we opened the door to a religious sign in the secular space, a sign of domination . . . at least we consider it as such.

While the law directly impacted French Muslim girls in public schools, the position of the organisation is determined in relation to other Muslim women, not French but Iranian – who fled an oppressive regime in the 1980s – and Algerian – who fled terrorism in the 1990s. In response to further questioning about what will happen to the young French Muslim girls eventually expelled from school as a result of the law, Corinne elaborates further:

That's not true in fact [that they will be expelled]. Our Algerian friends were telling us: don't fall into that trap. It's false. It's not true. . . . Well, there are private schools, which are not secular schools, which are religious schools. So they will go there. So one should not say precisely that we will exclude girls, that they won't go to school. It's false. It's false. And in fact, no more than twenty girls were expelled in the whole national territory . . . In the end, we can tell ourselves that we saved a lot of girls. And what's more, we sent a strong message to our friends who were arriving here in 1994 [from Algeria], saying: if I don't wear the veil well, my life is in danger.

This long quotation interweaves several narratives that intimately shape a particular form of French feminist whiteness, tightly articulated with an embrace of republican secularism. Religion is understood as inherently oppressive to women; feminists must 'save' the Muslim girls who do not want to wear the headscarf, but are much less concerned with those that wish to do so and will admittedly be excluded from public education and confined to a religious school. Corinne identifies with French universalism – with France as 'the country of human rights' as she mentions later in her interview – and its exemplary stance which not only shows solidarity with Muslim women who are victims of state violence in Muslim countries but also pursues the saving of women all over the world. In Corinne's discourse, race is not a local/national issue, and her feminism aims at constructing a diverse collective feminist subject across borders, rather than at home. In a move typical of feminist whiteness, women victims of institutional racism are not seen *here, at home*. White feminists proclaim solidarity with racialised women in other countries, in a place which is always far away from home, while they stay blind and ignorant to racism at home (Vergès 2017). Expulsing race from the borders of the nation (Michel 2015) bolsters their attempt at denying the racist component of the policy they support. Often in interviews, race is defined either as an American import that does not fit the French context or as a side effect of an 'external' event – that is, immigration. It is rarely articulated with colonialism and never acknowledged as a structuring feature of *French* history or a pervasive ground for exclusion from full citizenship. This logic illustrates perfectly what Paola Bacchetta has defined as *internal discourses of colonial feminisms*, which universalise 'feminist analyses and categories' and display 'amnesia about racism and colonialism' (Bacchetta 2015).

By universalising gender oppression, by downplaying the political salience of racism in favour of class inequalities, or by locating race outside the national borders, many French white feminists elaborate discursive repertoires that *actively resist intersectionality* and that make feminism white. Indeed, these discourses contribute to produce and maintain a white feminist subject whose privileges remain untold and invisible, and who is positioned as the preferred subject of feminism.

Feminist whiteness as othering

I documented in the previous section how a position of privileged feminist subject is discursively asserted by French white feminists, using various rhetorical devices which allow them to see themselves as 'unmarked' by race and to understand their interests as universal (Frankenberg 1993a). Now, I turn to the discourses which contribute to mark other women as 'others,' thereby, again, securing the centrality of the white feminist subject. Following a line of inquiry which explores the emotional and moral dimensions of whiteness within feminism (Fellows and Razack 1998; Srivastava 2005, 2006; Wekker 2016), I analyse in this section how white feminists depict 'other' women – the woman migrant, the veiled woman – and mark them as others, using powerful racialised emotional and moral narratives about who can be a 'good' feminist subject and who will be considered a 'bad' one. I document in particular two types of discourse 'othering' non-white women. The first one produces the othering of non-white women by casting them as vulnerable feminist subjects in need of help: they may become 'good' feminist subjects but to do so they need the *patronising solicitude* of white feminists. The second type of narrative casts non-white women, in particular Muslim women wearing the veil, as improper feminist subjects through the legitimate expression of white feminists' *indignant anger*.

Patronising solicitude

A first way in which non-white women are made into others by white feminists is by discursively producing a form of moral relation that introduces both *distance* and *solicitude* for women who are then placed in the position of care receiver rather than active and equal others in the relation. Indeed, this patronising attitude both enacts forms of solicitude – meaning to take care of others – and creates a specific distance because it is based on the assumption that non-white women are in need of a form of help that white feminists can provide. Here, it is important to say that this complex moral relation is not only structured by racial asymmetries but also by the very asymmetry of service providing in feminist organisations (Wilson 1996). Indeed, most white feminists who resort to this repertoire work in service providing organisations and are thus placed, by their professional or activist position, in a situation in which they provide service and guidance. To counter the power relations that infuse this type of service provision, white feminists use professional repertoires delineating a feminist ethos that insists on the fact that women who come to shelters or community centres should find the tools to emancipate themselves, as Martine, a French officer in a network focused on women's health put it: 'we don't give her the tools, she finds them.' Hence, the role of feminists working in these institutions is not to impose their preferred vision of emancipation. However, French white feminists often set aside this ethos, in particular when interacting with veiled Muslim women. The racialised presumption that these women are more oppressed feeds a form of patronising solicitude which very much resembles the Western gaze described decades ago by Chandra Mohanty (1984).

Indeed, in many interviews, racialised/migrant/veiled women are conceived as the object of benevolent feminist care and attention. When talking about their feminist practice, white feminists insist on the fact that migrant women's choices must be respected and that migrant women themselves can make the choices that correspond to their needs, which can differ depending on their culture. However, beyond this benevolence, they also confide that the Islamic veil sometimes raises 'discomfort,' 'tension,' and ambivalence among white feminist volunteers and employees. While all white interviewees declared that they would never turn away a woman in need of help because she wears an Islamic veil, this attitude was not based on the idea of inclusivity of their organisation, but rather on a principle of helping women in need. Martine, an officer at Women's Health, describes what tends to happen when young Muslim women ask for false certificates of virginity in order to assuage their family before their marital engagement:

> For some counsellors, these cases are really difficult ones. There is always this tension, and it's even tenser for certificates of virginity. There's a tension because it's difficult to perceive them as alienated . . . it's not right either. Some counsellors are ok with it; it depends on their individual history if they can help, if they can discuss with the girls, to try to understand why they wear the veil, why they don't, what it means for them. When a girl comes to the centre veiled, it's true it's a real question for us. It questions feminism. This fact that a woman can accept this ideological domination . . . it questions us.

The young Muslim women who come to the centre are here described as if their choice was hard to understand and foreign to Martine's own moral universe and to her feminist values. The question becomes how can 'our' feminism make sense of the agency of Muslim women, bringing an intrusive inquiry into their motivations and their moral dispositions. This narrative, and the us/them binary which structures it, denotes how feminist whiteness produces the otherness of Muslim women. While the same interviewee presented the need to let women make their own choices as the basis of feminist intervention, when it comes to Muslim women this principle is in fact amended with a higher scrutiny for 'proper' motives and moral dispositions, fuelled by a patronising impulse. Yet, this quote also suggests a possible decentring of feminist whiteness, which is left unsaid and unresolved, but rather hovering over the interviewee's consciousness: 'it questions us.'

Furthermore, feminist intervention is also sometimes presented as an effort to enrol non-white women in a predefined feminist collective subject;[7] to do so, their otherness must be made into sameness. Solicitude meets a patronising impulse that mirrors the asymmetry along racial and class lines that characterises the white volunteer/non-white recipient relationship. Chantal, a white feminist in her late forties who runs a shelter in a Parisian suburb, recalls:

> I was discussing with a young woman who arrived veiled for the admission interview in our living centre, but I asked her to take off her veil because here . . . here there is no . . . She explained to me that she chose to wear the veil. She was twelve at the time she chose. It's a little bit young to make a choice. But, it's true she's now a woman who has gone to undergrad, she claims her right to wear the veil, she says it's not compulsory to wear it. So . . . she follows her own path. Maybe with discussions that we will have on women's rights she may evolve or not on this issue of wearing her veil.

> Q: And she accepted your proposal not to wear the veil while she was at the centre?
> Chantal: Oh yes, of course.
> Q: Why did you ask that from her?
> Chantal: Because indeed, I think, as far as I am concerned it is a sign of women's oppression.

While Chantal insisted that not wearing the veil was not a precondition to be received for an admission interview at the shelter, it appears as a precondition to stay and benefit from the protection of the shelter and the services it provides. Interestingly, though she does not deny the agency of her interlocutor, Chantal places herself in the position to actually decide what is a proper age for consent and, what is more, what is the meaning of the Islamic veil. In a move typical of whiteness, she creates a social distance with her interlocutor, making her an 'other' – despite her acknowledged class proximity with her, related to academic achievement.[8] She also omits to reflect on the power she exercises over the woman she interviews, although her position of authority surreptitiously shows in her flat avowal of the result of her demand: 'of course' the woman took off her veil – what other choice did she have in her situation? Here, solicitude and respect for a woman's choice have been replaced by moral judgment, righteousness, and a unilateral definition of what type of practices feminist emancipation should entail. As the 'Muslim veiled woman' changes status, from benevolent object of care to potential feminist subject, since the shelter also aims at transforming its members into feminists, she must be stripped of the otherness that was imposed onto her by removing her veil. In this transaction, and to use Sara Ahmed's terms, feminism is really *made white*.

Indignant anger

While the emotions that surface in relationships characterised by patronising solicitude are enmeshed with self-righteousness, contentment, and sympathy, other more powerful emotions and moral dispositions – such as anger and indignation – are also present and contribute to make racialised women into feminist others definitely excluded from the moral horizon of the feminist project as defined by white feminists.

When racialised, migrant, or Muslim women claim their agency and identity as feminist subjects – that is, when their relationship with white feminists should be defined by reciprocal recognition and equality, rather than by benevolence and asymmetry – then otherness is produced with different moral dispositions and emotions. Several interviewees displayed harsh moral judgments about veiled Muslim women and lamented the loss of a true feminist subject. Their moral dispositions and their emotions efficiently drew the boundary between a good feminist subject and a bad one, making Muslim women in particular into impossible feminist equals. Asked about her analysis of the mobilisation of racialised feminists in an alternate International Women's Day march in Paris, the 'March 8th for all,' Claudine, a white feminist in her sixties who heads an umbrella network for women's rights, declares:

> When I think about the 'March 8th for all' I think that these groups of migrant girls – I don't like the term racialised at all – I think that these groups of migrant girls who go there are completely wrong, it's true it comes from a divergence on the veil issue, certainly, but I don't think that these people will help them . . . They don't even know we exist! . . . They hold a lot of wrong ideas about us.

Moral judgments about the right type of feminism and the right type of feminist subjectivity surface and draw boundaries between 'us' and 'them' in an effective way. On the one hand, Claudine, who speaks from the vantage point of an older and more legitimate generation of feminists, places her conception of feminism, and herself, as a reference point (which should not be ignored or misinterpreted by racialised women, as she thinks it is) – a moral and political standard to be adopted if one wishes to be called and recognised as a feminist. On the other hand, she rejects any responsibility for the deep rift that has emerged between her organisation, which is supposed to be inclusive and representative of the French women's rights movement, and racialised women demonstrating on their own terms and in opposition to the official International Women's Day march. The claims made by racialised women as *feminists* – since the 'March 8th for all' is a self-defined feminist march – are presented as bringing confusion, troubling the boundaries and the identity of the proper feminist collective subject. These discursive repertoires make non-white feminists into others who are never considered as equals, who are dismissed before any interaction can occur, and thus before any resentment or criticism they may utter can be heard and recognised as legitimate.

Conclusion

I have argued that when analysing the dynamics of inclusion and exclusion of feminist subjects from feminist discourses and movements, we must pay attention to whiteness and to how it contributes to draw boundaries and maintain privileges along racial lines. Indeed, what I have termed *feminist whiteness* operates, in the French context under scrutiny here, with two logics: a logic of maintaining privilege through discursive operations such as universalising white women's experience, privileging class over race, or locating race outside of the nation, and a logic of transforming non-white feminists into *others*, thereby making feminism white. I have described how these logics unfold in the French context, underlying how they are also sustained by specific moral dispositions such as patronising solicitude and indignant anger. Studying feminist whiteness helps us understand the extent and depth of resistance to intersectionality in some parts of the feminist movement. In France, these resistances are particularly active in older generations of feminists who came of age as feminists in the seventies and eighties in radical left organisations. However, the prevalence of universalism in French feminists' discursive repertoires, and its ability to secure the privilege of white women within the movement, is not limited to this generation (Lépinard 2014). As both calls for more intersectionality and the self-organisation by women of colour in France have increased in the past half-decade, the privilege of whiteness is made more visible and contested. Hence, feminist whiteness in France is bound to evolve and its discursive repertoires to change. However, its close ties with hegemonic discourses about the nation, secularism, universalism, and colour-blindness must be carefully exposed in order to begin unfastening the co-optation of feminist discourses, through feminist whiteness, in nationalist agendas.

Notes

1 Similarly, Sirma Bilge notes that the institutionalisation of intersectionality in gender studies has produced a form of whitening, i.e. displacing of central concerns of intersectional praxis, see Bilge (2013).
2 Half of the interviewees for this research were white, while the other half of the interviewees self-identified as racialised. I use in this chapter the qualitative interviews with white feminists.
3 On French colour-blindness, see Sabbagh and Peer (2008) and Simon (2008). On the historical formation of the French republican model of integration, see Favell (1998). On the fear of disunity and the need for the invisibility of difference in France, see Lépinard (2015). On racelessness in Europe, see El-Tayeb (2011) and Michel (2015).
4 For an overview of debates on the diffusion of intersectionality to the European context and France in particular, see Fassa, Lépinard, and Roca i Escoda (2016).

5 A wide literature in history and sociology has explored the features of French universalism, e.g. Perreau and Scott (2017). On universalism and race in France, see Larcher
  (2014).
6 All interview transcripts were translated to English by the author.
7 On Québec, see Laperrière and Lépinard (2016).
8 On how school shapes class expectations and relations in France, see Laacher (2005).

References

Ahmed, Sara. 2004. "Declarations of Whiteness: The Non-Performity of Anti-Racism."
  Borderlands 3. www.borderlands.net.au/vol3no2_2004/ahmed_declarations.htm
Ahmed, Sara. 2006. "The Nonperformativity of Antiracism." *Meridians: Feminism, Race,
  Transnationalism* 7 (1): 104–126.
Ahmed, Sara. 2007. "A Phenomenology of Whiteness." *Feminist Theory* 8 (2): 149–168.
Anzaldúa, Gloria, and Cherrie Moraga, eds. 1983. *This Bridge Called My Back: Radical
  Writings by Women of Color* (2nd ed.). New York, NY: Kitchen Table, Women of Color
  Press.
Bacchetta, Paola. 2009. "Co-Formations: Des Spatialités de Résistance Décoloniales Chez
  Les Lesbiennes 'of Color' En France." *Genre, Sexualité & Société* (1).
Bacchetta, Paola. 2015. "Décoloniser le féminisme: intersectionnalité, assemblages, co-
  formations, co-productions." *Les cahiers du CEDREF* (20). https://cedref.revues.
  org/833#quotation
Bassel, Leah, and Akwugo Emejulu. 2010. "Struggles for Institutional Space in France and
  the United Kingdom: Intersectionality and the Politics of Policy." *Politics & Gender* 6
  (4): 517–544. https://doi.org/10.1017/S1743923X10000358
Bassel, Leah, and Akwugo Emejulu. 2017. *Minority Women and Austerity: Survival and
  Resistance in France and Britain*. Bristol, UK: Policy Press.
Bilge, Sirma. 2013. "Intersectionality Undone: Saving Intersectionality from Feminist
  Intersectionality Studies." *Du Bois Review: Social Science Research on Race* 10 (2):
  405–424.
Bouyahia, Malek, and Maria Eleonora Sanna, eds. 2013. *La polysémie du voile: Politiques
  et mobilisations postcoloniales*. Paris: Editions des archives contemporaines.
Davis, Kathy. 2008. "Intersectionality as Buzzword: A Sociology of Science Perspective
  on What Makes a Feminist Theory Successful." *Feminist Theory* 9 (1): 67–85.
DiAngelo, Robin. 2011. "White Fragility." *International Journal of Critical Pedagogy* 3
  (3): 54–70.
DiAngelo, Robin. 2019. *White Fragility: Why it's So Hard for White People to Talk About
  Racism*. London: Penguin UK.
Dot-Pouillard, Nicolas. 2007. "Les Recompositions Politiques Du Mouvement Féministe
  Français Au Regard Du Hijab." *SociologieS [En Ligne]* (October). http://sociologies.
  revues.org/246
El-Tayeb, Fatima. 2011. *European Others: Queering Ethnicity in Postnational Europe*.
  Minneapolis, MN: University of Minnesota Press.
Evans, Elizabeth. 2015. *The Politics of Third Wave Feminisms: Neoliberalism, Intersec-
  tionality, and the State in Britain and the US*. New York, NY: Palgrave Macmillan.
Evans, Elizabeth. 2016. "Intersectionality as Feminist Praxis in the UK." *Women's Studies
  International Forum* 59: 67–75.
Fassa, Farinaz, Éléonore Lépinard, and Marta Roca i Escoda, eds. 2016. *L'intersectionnalité:
  Enjeux Théoriques et Politiques*. Paris: La Dispute.

Favell, Adrian. 1998. *Philosophies of Integration: Immigration and the Idea of Citizenship in France and Britain*. London; New York, NY: Palgrave Macmillan.

Fellows, Mary Louise, and Sherene Razack. 1998. "The Race to Innocence: Confronting Hierarchical Relations Among Women." *Journal of Gender, Race & Justice* 1 (2): 335–352.

Frankenberg, Ruth. 1993a. "Growing up White: Feminism, Racism and the Social Geography of Childhood." *Feminist Review* 45 (1): 51–84.

Frankenberg, Ruth. 1993b. *White Women, Race Matters: The Social Construction of Whiteness*. Minneapolis, MN: University of Minnesota Press.

Frankenberg, Ruth. 1997. "Local Whitenesses, Localizing Whiteness." In *Displacing Whiteness: Essays in Social and Cultural Criticism*, edited by Ruth Frankenberg, 1–33. Durham, NC: Duke University Press.

Frye, Marilyn. 1983. *The Politics of Reality: Essays in Feminist Theory*. New York, NY: Crossing Press.

Gillman, Laura. 2007. "Beyond the Shadow: Re-Scripting Race in Women's Studies." *Meridians* 7 (2): 117–141.

Guénif-Souilamas, Nacira. 2006. *La République Mise à Nu Par Son Immigration*. Paris: Editions La Fabrique.

hooks, bell. 1984. *Feminist Theory: From Margin to Center*. Boston, MA: South End Press.

Jonsson, Terese. 2016. "The Narrative Reproduction of White Feminist Racism." *Feminist Review* 113 (1): 50–67. https://doi.org/10.1057/fr.2016.2

Laacher, Smaïn. 2005. *L'institution Scolaire et Ses Miracles*. Paris: La Dispute.

Laperrière, Marie, and Éléonore Lépinard. 2016. "Intersectionality as a Tool for Social Movements: Strategies of Inclusion and Representation in the Québécois Women's Movement." *Politics* 36 (4): 374–382.

Larcher, Silyane. 2014. *L'autre Citoyen: L'idéal Républicain et Les Antilles Après l'esclavage*. Paris: Armand Colin.

Lépinard, Eléonore. 2014. "Doing Intersectionality: Repertoires of Feminist Practices in France and Canada." *Gender & Society* 28 (6): 877–903.

Lépinard, Eléonore. 2015. "Migrating Concepts: Immigrant Integration and the Regulation of Religious Dress in France and Canada." *Ethnicities* 15 (5): 611–632.

Lettinga, Doutje, and Sawitri Saharso. 2012. "The Political Debates on the Veil in France and the Netherlands: Reflecting National Integration Models?" *Comparative European Politics* 10 (3): 319–336.

Lorde, Audre. 1984. *Sister Outsider: Essays and Speeches*. New York, NY: Crossing Press.

Mane, Rebecca L. 2012. "Transmuting Grammars of Whiteness in Third-Wave Feminism: Interrogating Postrace Histories, Postmodern Abstraction, and the Proliferation of Difference in Third-Wave Texts." *Signs: Journal of Women in Culture and Society* 38 (1): 71–98.

McIntosh, Peggy. 1988. "White Privilege and Male Privilege: A Personal Account of Coming to See Correspondences Through Work in Women's Studies." Working Paper 189. Wellesley, MA: Wellesley Centers for Women.

McWhorter, Ladelle. 2005. "Where Do White People Come from? A Foucaultian Critique of Whiteness Studies." *Philosophy & Social Criticism* 31 (5–6): 533–556.

Michel, Noémi Vanessa. 2015. "Sheepology: The Postcolonial Politics of Raceless Racism in Switzerland." *Postcolonial Studies* 18 (4): 410–426.

Mills, Charles. 2007. "White Ignorance." In *Race and Epistemologies of Ignorance*, edited by Shannon Sullivan and Nancy Tuana, 13–38. Albany, NY: State University of New York Press.

Mills, Charles W. 1997. *The Racial Contract*. Ithaca, NY: Cornell University Press.

Mohanty, Chandra Talpade. 1984. "Under Western Eyes: Feminist Scholarship and Colonial Discourses." *Boundary 2* 12 (2): 333–358.

Mohanty, Chandra Talpade. 2003. *Feminism Without Borders: Decolonizing Theory, Practicing Solidarity*. Durham, NC: Duke University Press.

Mohanty, Chandra Talpade, and Biddy Martin. 2003. "What's Home Got to Do With It." In *Feminism Without Borders: Decolonizing Theory, Practicing Solidarity*, edited by Chandra Talpade Mohanty, 85–105. Durham, NC: Duke University Press.

Mueller, Jennifer C. 2017. "Producing Colorblindness: Everyday Mechanisms of White Ignorance." *Social Problems* 64: 219–238.

Mügge, Liza, Celeste Montoya, Akwugo Emejulu, and S. Laurel Weldon. 2018. "Intersectionality and the Politics of Knowledge Production." *European Journal of Politics and Gender* 1 (1): 17–36. https://doi.org/info:doi/10.1332/251510818X15272520831166

Ortega, Mariana. 2006. "Being Lovingly, Knowingly Ignorant: White Feminism and Women of Color." *Hypatia* 21 (3): 56–74.

Ouali, Nouria. 2015. "Les Rapports de Domination Au Sein Du Mouvement Des Femmes à Bruxelles: Critiques et Résistances Des Féministes Minoritaires." *Nouvelles Questions Féministes* 34 (1): 14–34.

Perreau, Bruno, and Joan Wallach Scott. 2017. *Les défis de la République: Genre, territoires, citoyenneté*. Paris: Sciences Po (Les Presses de). http://journals.openedition.org/lectures/22143

Predelli, Line Nyhagen, and Beatrice Halsaa. 2012. *Majority-Minority Relations in Contemporary Women's Movements: Strategic Sisterhood*. Houndmills, Basingstoke: Palgrave Macmillan.

Reger, Jo. 2012. *Everywhere and Nowhere: Contemporary Feminism in the United States*. New York, NY: Oxford University Press.

Rowe, Aimee Carrillo. 2000. "Locating Feminism's Subject: The Paradox of White Femininity and the Struggle to Forge Feminist Alliances." *Communication Theory* 10 (1): 64–80.

Sabbagh, Daniel, and Shanny Peer. 2008. "French Color Blindness in Perspective: The Controversy over 'Statistiques Ethniques'." *French Politics, Culture & Society* 26 (1): 1–6.

Schuster, Julia. 2016. "Intersectional Expectations: Young Feminists' Perceived Failure at Dealing With Differences and Their Retreat to Individualism." *Women's Studies International Forum* 58 (September): 1–8. https://doi.org/10.1016/j.wsif.2016.04.007

Scott, Joan W. 2007. *The Politics of the Veil*. Princeton, NJ: Princeton University Press.

Simon, Patrick. 2008. "The Choice of Ignorance: The Debate on Ethnic and Racial Statistics in France." *French Politics, Culture & Society* 26 (1): 7–31.

Smith, Barbara Ellen. 1995. "Crossing the Great Divides: Race, Class, and Gender in Southern Women's Organizing, 1979–1991." *Gender & Society* 9 (6): 680–696.

Srivastava, Sarita. 2005. "'You're Calling Me a Racist?' The Moral and Emotional Regulation of Antiracism and Feminism." *Signs: Journal of Women in Culture and Society* 31 (1): 29–62.

Srivastava, Sarita. 2006. "Tears, Fears and Careers: Anti-Racism and Emotion in Social Movement Organizations." *The Canadian Journal of Sociology* 31 (1): 55–90.

Strolovitch, Dara Z. 2007. *Affirmative Advocacy: Race, Class, and Gender in Interest Group Politics*. Chicago, IL: University of Chicago Press.

Townsend-Bell, Erica. 2013. "Intersectional Advances? Inclusionary and Intersectional State Action in Uruguay." In *Situating Intersectionality: Politics, Policy, and Power*, edited by Angelia R. Wilson, 43–61. New York, NY: Palgrave Macmillan.

Vergès, Françoise. 2017. *Le Ventre Des Femmes: Capitalisme, Racialisation, Féminisme*. Paris: Albin Michel.

Vodde, Rich. 2000. "De-centering Privilege in Social Work Education. Whose Job is it Anyway? *Race, Gender & Class* 7 (4): 139–160.

Wekker, Gloria. 2016. *White Innocence: Paradoxes of Colonialism and Race*. Durham, NC: Duke University Press.

Wilson, Tikka Jan. 1996. "Feminism and Institutionalized Racism: Inclusion and Exclusion at an Australian Feminist Refuge." *Feminist Review* 52 (1): 1–26. https://doi.org/10.1057/fr.1996.3

Zajicek, Anna M. 2002. "Race Discourses and Antiracist Practices in a Local Women's Movement." *Gender & Society* 16 (2): 155–174.

Chapter 10

Intersectional praxis from within and without

Challenging whiteness in Québec's LGBTQ movement

Alexie Labelle

Introduction

Social movement scholars have examined the ways in which social movements are marked by multiple activist identities which are fluid and change over time (Reger 2002b; Robnett 1997; Bernstein 2002). There is also a strong consensus around the idea that collective identities are essential and central to social movement organising (Polletta and Jasper 2001; Melucci 1995), be it in sustaining participation (Robnett 2002), interpreting grievances, and formulating demands or in strengthening internal solidarity (Taylor and Whittier 1992). This said, inasmuch as social movements bring together a diversity of activists with diverse trajectories and standpoints, some have pointed to the difficulty of recognising these different identities within social movements, notably because of the potentially fragmenting effect on collective identities that can prevent the elaboration of a common political agenda (Taylor and Whittier 1992; Weldon 2011). Studies conducted on feminist movements have shed light on the ways in which conflicting identities have historically relegated to the margins women of colour, trans and lesbian women, as well as disabled women (Yuval-Davis 2006; Evans 2015; Davis 1981; hooks 1981; Chamberland 1989). While recent work has attended to the ways in which feminist movements use intersectionality – the idea that vectors of oppression intersect, thus (re)producing inequalities and fostering discrimination (Crenshaw 1989) – either as a collective identity, as a tool for building coalitions, or as a repertoire for inclusivity, most argue that feminist movements continue to be dominated by White, middle-class, cisgender, heterosexual, and able-bodied women (Evans 2015; Lépinard 2014; Laperrière and Lépinard 2016; Strolovitch 2006; Weldon 2006). Unfortunately, lesbian, gay, bisexual, trans*,[1] and queer (LGBTQ)[2] movements are no exception and have not been immune to power relations that structure society, notably in terms of gender and race.

Several processes of marginalisation have been observed within LGBTQ movements across Canada, Europe, and the United States (Bilić and Kajinić 2016; Lenon and Dryden 2015; DeFilippis 2016, 2018). For instance, Hodzić, Postić, and Kajtezović's (2016) findings regarding trans activism in Croatia show that the historic invisibilisation of trans activists, and of trans issues thereof, within mainstream LGBTQ organisations, has led trans activists to organise separately within the movement. This echoes Namaste's (2000) work on the invisibilisation of transsexual and transgendered people, artists, and activists in Canada and the United States. Other studies have also underlined lesbians' struggle with sexism in LGBTQ social movement organising (Burgess 2016), as well as the overall invisibilisation of lesbians, be it in LGBTQ spaces or LGBTQ research (Podmore and Chamberland 2015). In addition to cisgenderism and sexism, a growing and more recent body of work has been focusing on race and racialisation within LGBTQ movements (Lenon and Dryden 2015; Bain 2016; DeFilippis 2016; Warner 2002; Trawalé and Poiret 2017; Boston and Duyvendak 2015). For instance, referring to the LGBTQ movement in the United States, DeFilippis (2018) observes an imbalance of organisational power and resources amongst LGBTQ organisations with power resting in the hands of White LGBTQ people, thus leading many LGBTQ communities, particularly trans and people of colour, to feel unrepresented in the political agenda supported by mainstream national organisations.

Québec's LGBTQ movement

The LGBTQ movement in Québec offers an interesting case study on this subject matter wherein processes of racialisation remain overlooked by scholars. In 1977, the government of Québec proceeded to include a protection clause prohibiting discrimination on the basis of sexual orientation in the province's *Charte des droits et libertés*, following massive protests in Montreal sparked by police raids[3] (Podmore 2015; Radio-Canada 2017; Tremblay 2013). Since then, the movement has made several strides, with the *Loi instituant l'union civile et établissant de nouvelles règles de filiation* in 2002, followed by the legalisation of same-sex marriage in 2004 and the recently adopted Law 103 which allows trans* youth of 14 years and older to change their sex mentioned on their birth certificate without undergoing any surgical treatment, to name a few[4] (Radio-Canada 2016). Yet, in spite of these political and judicial breakthroughs, some within the LGBTQ community remain discriminated against and have not benefited from these advances, which is the case for trans* migrants who cannot change their name nor their sex marker on their identity documents before becoming Canadian citizens (Boulianne 2017). In other words, while several claims made by the LGBTQ movement have been recognised and have led to legislative changes, other demands formulated by the movement remain invisibilised and are barely discussed by political leaders.

A plethora of social movement organisations constitutes Québec's LGBTQ movement. Mainstream[5] LGBTQ organisations include *Pride Montreal*, which organises annual Pride celebrations; *Interligne*, which offers continuous telephone support to LGBTQ communities; *Fondation Émergence*, which raises awareness on LGBTQ realities within the broader Québec society; *Groupe de recherche et d'intervention sociale* (GRIS), which trains volunteers in sharing their personal narratives with primary and secondary school students, amongst others; and the *Conseil Québécois LGBT* (CQLGBT), which engages in rights advocacy at a provincial level. These organisations tend to be more profession-alised and have several paid employees. Other, less mainstream, organisations target particular groups within LGBTQ communities. For instance, lesbian groups include the *Réseau des lesbiennes du Québec* (RLQ), which engages in advocacy work, and the *Centre de solidarité lesbienne* (CSL), which offers assistance and services to lesbian communities; trans* groups include the *Aide aux Trans du Québec* (ATQ) and the *Action Santé Travesti(e)s & Transsexuel(le)s du Québec* (ASTTEQ); youth groups include *Project 10* and *Jeunesse Lambda*, which offer support to LGBTQ youth, as well as the *Coalition des groupes jeunesse LGBTQ+* (CGJ-LGBTQ), which also engages in advocacy work.[6]

Various organisations have also been created by and for LGBTQ people of colour (POC). Following the creation of *Gay and Lesbian Asians of Montreal* (GLAM) in the 1990s, other groups, such as *Helem Montréal*, which brings together Leba-nese and other Arab-speaking communities, and *Arc-en-ciel d'Afrique*, intended for LGBTQ communities of Afro-Caribbean descent, were created in the mid-2000s. A range of other initiatives were then launched in early 2010s, such as *Qouleur* festival, which showcased the work of queer, trans*, Black, and Indig-enous artists of colour from 2012 to 2016. Other organisations were created more recently, namely *Black Lives Matter Montreal*, as well as *Jhalak*, a group intended for South Asian LGBTQ communities, formed in 2016 and 2017 respectively.[7] In sum, as in other LGBTQ movements, LGBTQ social movement organising in Québec is diverse and dynamic, with a range of social movement organisations that target different communities within the broader movement.

Racialisation in Québec's LGBTQ movement

There is clear evidence that race and racialisation have shaped, and continue to shape, LGBTQ movements across Canada, thus relegating to the margins people of colour (Warner 2002; Walcott 2006; Bain 2016; Giwa and Greensmith 2012; McCaskell 2018; Crichlow 2004). In their collective work on homonationalisms (Puar 2007), which refers to the ways in which gay rights are integrated into a national discourse set to exclude deviant subjects from the nation, Lenon and Dryden (2015) suggest that ongoing processes of racialisation conform with 'Cana-dian national mythologies that inscribe whiteness as the embodiment of legitimate citizenship and belonging' (p. 5). Smith (2019) argues similarly and demonstrates how Canada has pursued, and continues to pursue, homonationalist policy rhet-oric with regards to the legal recognition of LGBT rights which, according to activists, have been achieved at the expense of racialised others. Lenon's (2011) thorough discursive examination of the struggle for same-sex marriage in Canada further reveals the effects of white normativity, wherein 'pursuit of the "ordinary" in the struggle for same-sex marriage require[d] aligning its discursive representa-tions with a racialised neoliberal citizenship that holds whiteness as its unspoken yet aspirational ideal' (p. 353). This echoes Ward's (2008) ethnographic study of a Los Angeles LGBT organisation which highlighted the enduring presence of white normativity as a cultural norm and practice. Hence, these studies illustrate the racialised nature of mainstream LGBTQ politics in Canada, wherein white activism overshadows other realities, namely those of Aboriginal and POC communities (Smith 2019; McCaskell 2018; Lenon and Dryden 2015).

These dynamics are not foreign to Québec's LGBTQ movement. In his study of LGBTQ people of colour representation in Québec's gay media, Roy (2012) observes a 'constant visual reiteration of *gayness* as *whiteness* [which] constitutes a legitimizing space for an effectively constrained gay subject' (p. 185, emphasis in original). Recent events, such as the interruption of the Montreal Pride March in August 2017 by *Black Lives Matter Montreal* (Eff 2017) and the sudden dismantling of *Arc-en-ciel d'Afrique* in 2018, also point to some of the difficulties faced by LGBTQ-POC activists in a predominantly white movement. This said, how is whiteness defined and conceptualised? Furthermore, how can intersectional praxis challenge whiteness and confront white privilege in Québec's LGBTQ movement?

Whiteness

Whiteness may be defined as a socially constructed category that is invisibilised through privilege (Ahmed 2007; Maillé 2007). In opposition to blackness or brownness, whiteness is never named as it is perceived as a 'non-color,' that is, invisible and unseen (Ahmed 2007). Its invisibilisation thus reflects its privileged social and political position, in the sense that it is normalised as a reference point, as a standard against which other racial groups that are named are held and compared to. Furthermore, Hage (2000) argues that as a historically and culturally constructed category that emerged through colonisation, 'White has become the ideal of being the bearer of "Western colonization." ' (p. 58). In this sense, whiteness does not refer to particular biological attributes *per se*, but rather expresses a category of power characterised by Hage (2000) as the accumulation of various capitals. Hence, in spite of being invisibilised, whiteness holds real implications in that it 'shapes what it is bodies "can do" ' (Ahmed 2007, p. 150).

Building on this concept, scholars have further reflected on the ways in which whiteness shapes social movement organising. For instance, Ward (2008) highlights the notion of white normativity, which she defines as the norms and practices that maintain whiteness in a state of normality and privileged invisibility. This 'implies that even in racially diverse environment in which people of color are extended a degree of institutional power, whiteness may still be a dominant ingredient of the environment's culture and a determinant of prevailing norms for communication and behavior' (Ward 2008, p. 564). Consequently, studying whiteness in feminist organisations, Scott (2005) highlights how racial diversification of social movement organisations necessitates an incorporation of different cultural practices, rather than an assimilation into a white dominant model, that risks perpetuating whiteness. As such, white normativity exposes one of the ways in which white privilege is institutionalised within social movement organisations. This said, recent work on intersectional praxis can provide useful insights on the ways in which white privilege may actually be challenged within social movements.

Intersectional praxis

Since its institutionalisation in the academic field at the end of the 1980s by Kimberlé Crenshaw, the concept of intersectionality has been used in multiple ways (Hill Collins and Bilge 2016; Hancock 2007; Cho, Crenshaw, and McCall 2013), ranging from a theoretical framework to a methodological approach (Dhamoon 2011; Bilge 2009; McCall 2005; Bowleg 2008). Yet, another strand of research has for its part looked more closely at intersectionality as a *praxis*, namely

> the ways in which people, either as individuals or as part of groups, produce, draw upon, or use intersectional frameworks in their daily lives – as everyday citizens with jobs and families, as well as institutional actors within public school, colleges and universities, religious organizations, and similar venues.
> (Hill Collins and Bilge 2016, p. 32)

Drawing from previous work on intersectional praxis, one can identify two ways in which intersectionality is used in the realm of social movements. On the one hand, existing organisations may use intersectionality as a tool to promote individual inclusion within social movement organisations. In this case, 'adopting intersectionality means embracing the diversity of women and making sure that the organizations respond to their needs and include them' (Laperrière and Lépinard 2016, p. 376). On the other hand, activists may also embrace intersectionality to reflect on the movement itself. Laperrière and Lépinard (2016) suggest that this may include using intersectionality 'to reveal [migrant women's] political marginalization within organizations and the broader women's movement and to redress their under-representation' (p. 375). In this case, intersectional praxis can imply organising around separate identities outside mainstream organisations. For instance, in their study of Asian Immigrant Women Advocates (AIWA) in California, Chun, Lipsitz, and Shin (2013) show that 'through AIWA, [activists] redefine their status from members of devalued social groups into grassroots leaders with the experiences, skills, and knowledge to change policy and spearhead innovations in the workplace, industry, and broader society' (p. 920). Furthermore, while intersectionality may be used by groups as a signifier of committed inclusivity, intersectional praxis can also be used to focus on specific and substantive issues, hence shaping groups' activities, as well as their content (Evans 2016).

This chapter thus aims to understand how activists and organisations respond to whiteness within Québec's LGBTQ movement by engaging in intersectional praxis. Drawing on in-depth interviews conducted with LGBTQ-POC and

White-LGBTQ activists, I show that intersectional praxis unfolds in two ways, from within and at the margins. While the former perpetuates white privilege in the LGBTQ movement, the latter does work at challenging whiteness.

Methods and data

I conducted in-depth interviews between January 2018 and January 2019 with 17 LGBTQ activists who identify as people of colour and 10 activists who identify as White, a total of 27 interviews. The content of the interviews was manually analysed inductively and qualitatively on an individual basis, using a coding sheet that was continuously updated. Activists interviewed participated in a range of organisations including institutionalised groups, such as the *GRIS* and the *Fondation Émergence*, and informal collectives such as *Black Lives Matter Montréal* and *Qouleur*. Moreover, interviewees occupied different positions within LGBTQ organisations, for example some were volunteers, others board members, whilst yet others were employees. Some interviewees also participated in more than one organisation over the course of their activist experience. Table 10.1 offers more information pertaining to the gender identity, the sexual orientation, the race, and the age of the interviewees at the time of the interview. This information was collected inductively, for example respondents were asked an open question about their gender identity and were not limited to a particular set of answers. While some interviewees are referenced using a pseudonym, some activists specifically asked to be named as a form of acknowledgement.

Table 10.1 Profile of activists interviewed in terms of gender identity, sexual orientation, race, and age

Gender Identity (n = 27)		Sexual Orientation (n = 27)		Race (n = 27)		Age (n = 27)	
Cisgender Men	8	Gay	8	Caucasian	10	20–29	9
Cisgender Women	10	Lesbian	7	Lebanese	2	30–39	12
Cisgender Non-Binary	2	Bisexual	1	Arab	3	40–49	5
Trans Men	3	Pansexual	6	Black Caribbean	2	50–59	1
Trans Women	1	Queer	3	Haitian	3		
Trans Non-Binary	1	Heterosexual	1	African	1		
Other	2	Other	1	South Asian	1		
				Chinese	1		
				Latinx	1		
				Mixed	2		
				Other	1		

The interviews addressed two main themes. First, interviewees were asked to talk about the trajectory of their engagement and participation within LGBTQ movements. Second, they were asked to talk about how they belonged, or not, to various communities, including LGBTQ communities. In-depth interviews are not only useful in documenting activists' experiences from a first-hand account, but are 'particularly helpful for understanding little-studied aspects of social movement dynamics and for studying social movements that are difficult to locate, generate few documents, or have unclear or changing memberships' (Blee and Taylor 2002, p. 94). This is especially the case for LGBTQ-POC activism, which remains under-studied and under-documented. What is more, the use of this method is in line with feminist epistemologies, which acknowledge that activists – and marginalised groups – are in a better position to know and speak about their own realities and experiences, as well as their own motivations and perceptions pertaining to social movement organising (Davis 2014; Blee and Taylor 2002; Hill Collins 2000). In other words, because of their social positionality, LGBTQ activists have access to certain forms of knowledge.

Intersectional praxis in Québec's LGBTQ movement

Results show that intersectional praxis, as observed within Québec's LGBTQ movement, unfolds in two ways. On the one hand, mainstream-white-dominated LGBTQ organisations build on intersectionality as a way to include people of colour, which I refer to as *intersectional praxis from within*; on the other hand, LGBTQ-POC activists organise around separate identities outside existing organisations, which I refer to as *intersectional praxis at the margins*. While both of these forms perpetuate whiteness as a form of privilege within the LGBTQ movement, the latter form also works at challenging whiteness by rendering visible non-white LGBTQ identities.

Intersectional praxis from within: maintaining whiteness

Mainstream-white-dominated LGBTQ organisations in Québec have been engaging in intersectional praxis in different ways over the last decade. Drawing from interviews conducted with LGBTQ activists who were or are currently involved with these organisations, three specific practices pertaining to the inclusion of people of colour were identified: (1) recruiting LGBTQ-POC activists for awareness campaigns, (2) creating specific 'diversity' committees within organisations, and (3) nominating LGBTQ-POC activists as members of the executive board. While the application of intersectionality through these practices is in most cases normalised and seen as a 'good thing' (Evans 2016) and as a means by which to diversify mainstream-white-dominated organisations, LGBTQ-POC interviewees did not interpret it as such.

The first intersectional practice identified consists of recruiting LGBTQ-POC activists to take part in awareness campaigns launched by mainstream-white-dominated organisations. Several organisations have implemented this type of practice over the years in an attempt to appear more inclusive of LGBTQ-POC and to show the inherent diversity of Québec's LGBTQ community. One interviewee of Haitian descent who participated in one particular campaign reflects on her experience:

> I participated in a photoshoot, they were looking for minorities to make it more colorful, but that's the thing, I don't have any patience for this . . . I often find that they are trying, but I don't have any patience . . . Sometimes there is a good will, but I find that there is sometimes too much thoughtlessness in the ways in which they are trying to include.

While most interviewees acknowledged the importance of rendering visible non-white LGBTQ individuals, they also shared a similar feeling of instrumentalisation when participating in these campaigns.

A second practice observed within various mainstream-white-dominated LGBTQ organisations consists of the creation of 'diversity'[8] committees that are meant to bring together LGBTQ-POC activists involved within an organisation. Their purpose varies from developing outreach strategies to acting as consultative bodies for the organization's executive board. Catherine, a board member of an organisation that put in place a 'diversity' committee, further explains its purpose:

> The diversity committee is responsible for promoting diversity within the [organization], recruiting volunteers from ethnocultural communities, and reaching out to other LGBTQ organizations, such as Arc-en-ciel d'Afrique and Helem. . . . The diversity committee, it's really about doing activities that raise awareness amongst other members about their own realities. For example, this year we created a reading group and we would suggest books to other members that address double, triple, discriminations. And then people read those books, meet up to discuss those books, and we write short articles that we send to all members so that they can be exposed to this.

This practice echoes Reger's (2002a) study of the American National Organization of Women (NOW), wherein specific committees work at accommodating the organization's internal diversity and including minoritised women, such as women of colour. This said, as Jessie, a White LGBTQ activist who presided over an organisation for six years, mentioned, these committees do not always foster a greater sense of inclusivity:

> The way we would do this, and that's what the big issue is with most community organizations, is that we do not do intersectionality. We talk about it, but we cannot put it in place. What we'll do, for instance in [organization X], is

that we'll have one committee for cultural minorities, we'll have a committee for people with disabilities, we'll have one committee for English-speaking women, but that's not what working together is. It's not the [organization] becoming inclusive, it's the [organization] trying to categorize.

This issue is also shared by other White LGBTQ activists who remain critical of such practices. Some of them have indeed raised concerns regarding the possible *tokenisation*[9] of LGBTQ-POC, wherein people of colour are being reduced to their difference as racialised individuals and are only recognised as such rather than being included as LGBTQ individuals regardless of their race. As one interviewee puts it, the creation of such committees may actually limit people of colour's inclusion within LGBTQ organisations by confining LGBTQ-POC within these circumscribed committees rather than rendering the entire organisation more inclusive:

It was too much 'you' versus 'us'. They weren't able to get out of the 'you' versus 'us'. Despite all the good will, the 'us' remained and that was it. And I would tell them that we wouldn't need to have this little group within [the organization]. It needs to be within all of the committees, we shouldn't be one [POC] committee amongst the other committees. That's not the point, that we do our own activities on the side.

This second practice, and its receptivity amongst LGBTQ-POC, resembles the third practice identified, which consists of nominating people of colour on executive boards. Once again, issues of tokenisation were raised by LGBTQ-POC who oftentimes ended up being the only person of colour on an all-white executive board. This was the case for Solange, a trans* activist of African descent, who was invited to become a board member on several mainstream-white-dominated LGBTQ organisations:

Sometimes they would tell me, okay you'll be governor for [organization X], you'll be a board member for [organization Y]. Yes, okay, these are great avenues for sharing what I have to say, but at the same time, I was aware that we were offering me that place because I was Black. And sometimes like, we don't want to be just Black.

Not only did LGBTQ-POC feel tokenised and reduced to their race, but their presence in an all-white executive board also impacted their overall commitment and participation. Louis-Philippe, a Latinx trans* man activist, reflected on his experience in the following way:

The executive board was having difficulty . . . and I was having difficulty to name things because I was the only one that had my skin colour. At some point there was another [POC], but it was still too white for me to say things as they should have been said. I felt all alone.

While intended to foster inclusivity within mainstream-white-dominated LGBTQ organisations, this particular form of intersectional praxis contributes to a shared feeling of tokenisation amongst people of colour that maintains them in a state of marginalisation within mainstream-white-dominated LGBTQ organisations. This contributes to the maintenance of whiteness as a form of institutional privilege within Québec's LGBTQ movement, reflected in a very tokenistic approach to inclusion, in which case LGBTQ-POC are reduced to their racial identity, unlike White activists. This also echoes what Carbado (2013) refers to as *colourblind intersectionality*, wherein 'the racial presence, racial difference, and racial particularity of [W]hite people travel invisibly and undisturbed as race-neutral phenomena over and against the racial presence, racial difference, and racial particularity of people of color' (pp. 823–824). In the end, by maintaining whiteness in a state of privileged invisibility, this form of intersectional praxis remains *non-performative*, as Sara Ahmed (2004) would put it, by not *doing* what it *ought* to do.

Intersectional praxis at the margins: challenging whiteness

In addition to participating in mainstream-white-dominated LGBTQ organisations, people of colour have also been mobilising separately outside of these organisations since the late 1990s and early 2000s. Groups like *Gay and Lesbian Asians of Montreal*, *Arc-en-ciel d'Afrique*, *Helem*, *Jhalak*, and *Black Lives Matter Montreal* attest to that phenomenon, wherein activists organise around particular intersecting identities. This social movement practice, which I refer to as intersectional praxis at the margins, serves two purposes. First, it allows for the emergence of safer spaces dedicated to the well-being of people of colour within the LGBTQ movement, thus facilitating their collective participation in the movement. Second, it renders visible non-white LGBTQ activists and in doing so works at challenging whiteness within Québec's LGBTQ movement.

For most LGBTQ-POC interviewed, the need to organise separately stemmed from their exclusion within mainstream-white-dominated LGBTQ organisations, as well as a lack of acknowledgement of their realities as non-White LGBTQ individuals. In this line of thought, organising separately acted as a way of remaining engaged within the LGBTQ movement while mobilising in safer and non-violent spaces. Lucas Charlie Rose, a trans* masculine activist, referred to the anti-blackness experienced in White LGBTQ collectives as triggering the need for him to organise elsewhere and get involved with *Black Lives Matter Montreal*:

> If I organize, I have to be in an environment where I can focus and I feel good about everything happening, I don't need to be facing violence while I'm organizing for my rights, you know? Obviously, I'm facing violence from people outside of my actions, but that's what I want . . . inside I want to be chill, you know?

While organising separately and creating new organisations promote safer spaces for people of colour, resources do not necessarily follow suit. Activists hereby interviewed all pointed to the lack of funding, the lack of space, the lack of visibility, and the lack of access to decision-making instances of LGBTQ organisations that are by and for people of colour. The recent dismantling of *Arc-en-ciel d'Afrique* in 2018[10] and the previous dismantling of various LGBTQ-POC organisations, namely *Perspectives Ébènes Montréal, GLAM, Ethnoculture,* and *Qouleur,* are testament to an unequal distribution of resources amongst LGBTQ organisations.[11] This unequal distribution of resources between mainstream-white-dominated and LGBTQ-POC organisations unfortunately maintains LGBTQ-POC organisations in an under-privileged position within the movement and perpetuates whiteness as a form of privilege.

Nevertheless, organising separately around intersecting identities also works at challenging whiteness. As explained by Frédérique Duroseau, an activist of Haitian descent, the existence of LGBTQ-POC organisations not only renders visible a particular reality, but also acts as a response to an ongoing invisibilisation of LGBTQ-POC:

> I find it very important what Arc-en-ciel d'Afrique does because when I came out in 2005, people would say that Black gay men don't exist, that homosexuality doesn't exist in Black communities, therefore Arc-en-ciel d'Afrique was a way to render visible our existence, to break the myth and the prejudice that we don't exist. . . .
>
> Arc-en-ciel d'Afrique emerged in a society where most demands for the LGBTQ community had been met. But the Black community was becoming invisible.

In addition to rendering visible non-White LGBTQ realities, activists involved in these organisations also challenge whiteness by claiming their own space. This implies making sure people of colour attend community meetings wherein mainstream-white-dominated LGBTQ organisations are present. For Marc, a Lebanese activist involved with *Helem Montréal,* this was particularly important:

> One thing that was very important for me, even when I wasn't a board member, was to continue representing Helem. Making sure that our community was represented everywhere that was necessary, like on the LGBT Working Committee, on the LGBTQ Youth Coalition, on the CQ-LGBT. . . . I continued to represent the organization and to insist on the importance that someone [from Helem] continues to go to these meetings, with [provincial] ministers, everywhere.

In sum, intersectional praxis at the margins consists of creating separate LGBTQ-POC organisations to provide safer spaces and to ensure representation of people of colour within the LGBTQ movement. As Weldon (2011) states, organising in this way 'increases the ability of marginalized groups to obtain public attention for issues that are important to them' (p. 112). What is more, it allows 'intersection-ally marginalized groups [to] develop and articulate their distinctive perspective, their oppositional consciousness' (Weldon 2011, p. 112). Unlike intersectional praxis from within, this form of intersectional praxis actually works at challeng-ing whiteness by ensuring due representation of non-white identities that can 'lay the groundwork for cooperation across social cleavages' (Weldon 2011, p. 109). This form of intersectional praxis is also in line with the strategy deployed by trans* activists to render visible trans* activism in Croatia (Hodzić et al. 2016).

Yet, as white privilege continues to structure Québec's LGBTQ movement, be it in terms of visibility in the media or in resource distribution, challenging whiteness remains arduous for LGBTQ-POC organisations. This said, the recent dismantling of *Arc-en-ciel d'Afrique*, one of the most visible LGBTQ-POC organi-sation in Québec, has made considerable waves. As the news rapidly disseminated throughout the movement, it rendered visible the struggle faced by LGBTQ-POC organisations, hence triggering instances of internal solidarity amongst groups.

Conclusion

Since social movements are not immune to power relations that structure societies in which they operate, the different identities that compose these movements can sometimes come into conflict. Feminist scholars have thoroughly exposed the ways in which conflicting identities have shaped and continue to shape feminist move-ments, oftentimes resulting in the marginalisation of minoritised women, such as women of colour, lesbian, trans*, disabled women, and so forth. Recent work has also focused on conflicting identities within LGBTQ movements, shedding light on the ways in which people of colour are being relegated to the margins. Québec's LGBTQ movement offers an interesting case study, wherein processes of racialisa-tion remain overlooked by scholars. Drawing from in-depth interviews and building on the concept of intersectional praxis, this chapter sought to understand how activ-ists challenge or maintain whiteness in Québec's LGBTQ movement.

Feminist scholars have previously reflected on the ways in which social movements use intersectionality and engage in intersectional praxis to render feminist movements more inclusive. However, drawing from this case study, I argued that intersectional praxis in Québec's LGBTQ movement unfolds in two ways. Intersectional praxis from within, wherein mainstream-white-dominated LGBTQ organisations imple-ment practices so as to render their organisation more diverse and inclusive, tends to lead to processes of instrumentalisation and tokenisation that perpetuate whiteness and maintain people of colour in a state of invisibility. Such tokenistic uses of inter-sectionality as a repertoire for inclusivity have yet to help challenge white privilege in the movement. Instead, intersectional praxis at the margins, meaning the creation of specific LGBTQ-POC organisations by and for LGBTQ-POC, have worked at resisting and contesting white privilege in the movement by providing safer spaces and rendering visible non-white LGBTQ realities. These results therefore suggest that organising around separate intersecting identities outside existing organisations do not necessarily fragment social movements, but instead help fostering a greater sense of inclusivity within social movements, especially amongst those groups that have historically been relegated to the margins.

Notes

1 The asterisk is used to include all transidentities.
2 Scholars working on LGBTQ movements have evoked the difficulty of naming the movement and the implications it holds (see Altman and Symons 2016; Tremblay 2015). While a variety of terms are being used by scholars, ranging from the gay and lesbian movement, to LGBT, to queer as an umbrella term, I decided to use the LGBTQ acronym as it is currently more prevalent in Quebec's civil society and used by sexual and gender diversity organisations.
3 Two major events sparked massive protests. First, with the advent of the 1976 Olympic Games in Montreal, police repression increased significantly in 1975 and 1976 (Higgins 2011). Raids on gay and lesbian spaces thereby led to the creation of the *Comité homosexuel anti-répression* (CHAR), which later became the *Association pour les droits des gai(e)s du Québec* (ADGQ). Second, the post-Olympic raid on the Truxx bar in October 1977 wherein 146 men were arrested sparked further protests. Two months later, the *Parti Québécois* amended the Quebec Charter of Rights and Freedoms to include sexual orientation as a prohibited ground for discrimination (Podmore 2015).
4 Although the law requires parents' approval to undergo these changes.
5 By mainstream, I mean organisations that are highly visible in the public space, outside of LGBTQ communities, and that have relatively more resources than other LGBTQ organisations.
6 This is an overview of some of the organisations that constitute the movement. Not intended to be exhaustive, this overview rather shows the inherent diversity of LGBTQ social movement organisations in Quebec.
7 This overview of LGBTQ-POC organisations is, once again, not meant to be exhaustive. LGBTQ-POC activism is inherently diverse and is not limited to these organisations.
8 The designation of these committees varies depending on the organisation and has changed over time. I use 'diversity' as an umbrella term.
9 Laws (1975) provides the following definition: 'Tokenism is the means by which the dominant group advertises a promise of mobility between the dominant and excluded classes. . . . The Token is a member of an underrepresented group, who is operating on the turf of the dominant group, under license from it' (p. 51).
10 Arc-en-ciel d'Afrique announced on social media that they were ending all activities. Following their dismantling, the Massimadi Foundation was created to allow for the annual organisation of the Massimadi Festival celebrating Afro-Caribbean LGBTQ+ films and arts.
11 It is worth mentioning that the lack of resources is not the only explanation as to why these groups have dismantled. Other reasons include personal conflict and biographical availability. Nonetheless, the lack of resources played a central part in the dismantling of these organisations.

References

Ahmed, Sara. 2004. "Declarations of Whiteness: The Non-Performativity of Anti-Racism." *Borderlands E-Journal* 3 (2). www.borderlands.net.au/vol3no2_2004/ahmed_declarations.htm

Ahmed, Sara. 2007. "A Phenomenology of Whiteness." *Feminist Theory* 8 (2): 149–168. https://doi.org/10.1177/1464700107078139

Altman, Dennis, and Jonathan Symons. 2016. *Queer Wars.* Cambridge, UK: Polity Press.

Bain, Beverly. 2016. "Fire, Passion, and Politics: The Creation of Blockorama as Black Queer Diasporic Space in the Toronto Pride." In *We Still Demand! Redefining Resistance in Sex and Gender Struggles,* edited by Patrizia Gentile, Gary Kinsman, and Pauline L. Rankin, 81–97. Vancouver: UBC Press.

Bernstein, Mary. 2002. "The Contradictions of Gay Ethnicity." In *Social Movements: Identity, Culture, and the State,* edited by David S. Meyer, Nancy Whittier, and Belinda Robnett, 85–104. Oxford: Oxford University Press.

Bilge, Sirma. 2009. "Théorisations féministes de l'intersectionnalité." *Diogène* 225: 70–88. https://doi.org/10.3917/dio.225.0070

Bilić, Bojan, and Sanja Kajinić. 2016. *Intersectionality and LGBT Activist Politics: Multiple Others in Croatia and Serbia.* London: Palgrave Macmillan.

Blee, Kathleen M., and Verta Taylor. 2002. "Semi-Structured Interviewing in Social Movement Research." *Methods of Social Movement Research* 16: 92–117.

Boston, Nicholas, and Jan Willem Duyvendak. 2015. "People of Color Mobilization in LGBT Movements in the Netherlands and the United States." In *The Ashgate Research Companion to Lesbian and Gay Activism,* edited by David Paternotte and Manon Tremblay, 135–148. New York, NY: Routledge.

Boulianne, Alexis. 2017. "Des modifications législatives réclamées pour les personnes trans migrantes." *Métro* (blog). http://journalmetro.com/actualites/national/1179367/des-modifications-legislatives-reclamees-pour-les-personnes-trans-migrantes/

Bowleg, Lisa. 2008. "When Black + Lesbian + Woman ≠ Black Lesbian Woman: The Methodological Challenges of Qualitative and Quantitative Intersectionality Research." *Sex Roles* 59 (5): 312–325. https://doi.org/10.1007/s11199-008-9400-z

Burgess, Allison. 2016. "The Emergence of the Toronto Dyke March." In *We Still Demand! Redefining Resistance in Sex and Gender Struggle,* edited by Patrizia Gentile, Gary Kinsman, and Pauline L. Rankin, 98–116. Vancouver: UBC Press.

Carbado, Devon W. 2013. "Colorblind Intersectionality." *Signs: Journal of Women in Culture and Society* 38 (4): 811–845. https://doi.org/10.1086/669666

Chamberland, Line. 1989. "Le lesbianisme: continuum féminin ou marronnage? Réfléxions féministes pour une théorisation de l'expérience lesbienne." *Recherches féministes* 2 (2): 135–145. https://doi.org/10.7202/057563ar

Cho, Sumi, Kimberlé Williams Crenshaw, and Leslie McCall. 2013. "Toward a Field of Intersectionality Studies: Theory, Applications, and Praxis." *Signs: Journal of Women in Culture and Society* 38 (4): 785–810. https://doi.org/10.1086/669608

Chun, Jennifer Jihye, George Lipsitz, and Young Shin. 2013. "Intersectionality as a Social Movement Strategy: Asian Immigrant Women Advocates." *Signs: Journal of Women in Culture and Society* 38 (4): 917–940. https://doi.org/10.1086/669575

Crenshaw, Kimberlé W. 1989. "Demarginalizing the Intersection of Race and Sex: A Black Feminist Critique of Antidiscrimination Doctrine, Feminist Theory and Antiracist Politics." *The University of Chicago Legal Forum* 140: 139–167.

Crichlow, Wesley. 2004. *Buller Men and Batty Bwoys: Hidden Men in Toronto and Halifax Black Communities.* Toronto: University of Toronto Press.

Davis, Angela Y. 1981. *Women, Race, & Class* (1st ed.). New York, NY: Random House.

Davis, Kathy. 2014. "Intersectionality as Critical Methodology." In *Writing Academic Texts Differently: Intersectional Feminist Methodologies and the Playful Art of Writing*, edited by Nina Lykee, 17–29. New York, NY: Routledge.

DeFilippis, Joseph Nicholas. 2016. "'What About the Rest of Us?' An Overview of LGBT Poverty Issues and a Call to Action." *Journal of Progressive Human Services* 27 (3): 143–174. https://doi.org/10.1080/10428232.2016.1198673

DeFilippis, Joseph Nicholas. 2018. "Introduction." In *Queer Activism After Marriage Equality*, 1–13. New York, NY: Routledge.

Dhamoon, Rita Kaur. 2011. "Considerations on Mainstreaming Intersectionality." *Political Research Quarterly* 64 (1): 230–243. https://doi.org/10.1177/1065912910379227

Eff, Billy. 2017. "Black Lives Matter Dénonce La Complaisance de Fierté – VICE Québec." www.vice.com/fr_ca/article/433ndn/black-lives-matter-denonce-la-complaisance-de-fierte

Evans, Elizabeth. 2015. *The Politics of Third Wave Feminism: Neoliberalism, Intersectionality, and the State in Britain and the US*. New York, NY: Palgrave Macmillan.

Evans, Elizabeth. 2016. "Intersectionality as Feminist Praxis in the UK." *Women's Studies International Forum* 59 (November): 67–75. https://doi.org/10.1016/j.wsif.2016.10.004

Giwa, Sulaimon, and Cameron Greensmith. 2012. "Race Relations and Racism in the LGBTQ Community of Toronto: Perceptions of Gay and Queer Social Service Providers of Color." *Journal of Homosexuality* 59 (2): 149–185. https://doi.org/10.1080/00918369.2012.648877

Hage, Ghassan. 2000. *White Nation: Fantasies of White Supremacy in a Multicultural Society*. London: Routledge.

Hancock, Ange-Marie. 2007. "When Multiplication Doesn't Equal Quick Addition: Examining Intersectionality as a Research Paradigm." *Perspectives on Politics* 5 (1): 63–79. https://doi.org/10.1017/S1537592707070065

Higgins, Ross. 2011. "La Régulation Sociale de l'homosexualité: De La Répression Policière à La Normalisation." In *La Régulation Sociale Des Minorités Sexuelles: L'inquiétude de La Différence*, edited by Patrice Corriveau and Valérie Daoust, 67–102. Québec: Presses de l'Université du Québec.

Hill Collins, Patricia. 2000. *Black Feminist Thought: Knowledge, Consciousness, and the Politics of Empowerment* (2nd ed.). New York, NY: Routledge.

Hill Collins, Patricia, and Sirma Bilge. 2016. *Intersectionality*. Cambridge, UK: Polity Press.

Hodzić, Amir, J. Postić, and Arian Kajtezović. 2016. "The (In)Visible T: Trans Activism in Croatia (2004–2014)." In *Intersectionality and LGBT Activist Politics: Multiple Others in Croatia and Serbia*, edited by Bojan Bilić and Sanja Kajinić, 33–52. London: Palgrave Macmillan.

hooks, bell. 1981. *Ain't I a Woman: Black Women and Feminism*. Boston, MA: South End Press.

Laperrière, Marie, and Eléonore Lépinard. 2016. "Intersectionality as a Tool for Social Movements: Strategies of Inclusion and Representation in the Québécois Women's Movement." *Politics* 36 (4): 374–382. https://doi.org/10.1177/0263395716649009

Laws, Judith Long. 1975. "The Psychology of Tokenism: An Analysis." *Sex Roles* 1 (1): 51–67. https://doi.org/10.1007/BF00287213

Lenon, Suzanne. 2011. "'Why Is Our Love an Issue?' Same-Sex Marriage and the Racial Politics of the Ordinary." *Social Identities* 17 (3): 351–372. https://doi.org/10.1080/13504630.2011.570975

Lenon, Suzanne, and Omisoore H. Dryden. 2015. "Introduction: Interventions, Iterations, and Interrogations That Disturb the (Homo)Nation." In *Disrupting Queer Inclusion: Canadian Homonationalisms and the Politics of Belonging*, 3–18. Vancouver: UBC Press.

Lépinard, Éléonore. 2014. "Doing Intersectionality: Repertoires of Feminist Practices in France and Canada." *Gender & Society* 28 (6): 877–903. https://doi.org/10.1177/0891243214542430.

Maillé, Chantal. 2007. "Réception de La Théorie Postcoloniale Dans Le Féminisme Québécois." *Recherches Féministes* 20 (2): 91–111.

McCall, Leslie. 2005. "The Complexity of Intersectionality." *Signs: Journal of Women in Culture and Society* 30 (3): 1771–1800. https://doi.org/10.1086/426800

McCaskell, Tim. 2018. *Queer Progress: From Homophobia to Homonationalism*. Toronto: Between the Lines.

Melucci, Alberto. 1995. "The Process of Collective Identity." In *Social Movements and Culture*, edited by Hank Johnston and Bert Klandermans, 41–63. Minneapolis, MN: University of Manitoba Press.

Namaste, Viviane. 2000. *Invisible Lives: The Erasure of Transsexual and Transgendered People*. Chicago, IL: University of Chicago Press.

Podmore, Julie. 2015. "From Contestation to Incorporation: LGBT Activism in Urban Politics in Montreal." In *Queer Mobilizations: Social Movement Activism and Canadian Public Policy*, edited by Manon Tremblay, 187–207. Vancouver: UBC Press.

Podmore, Julie A., and Line Chamberland. 2015. "Entering the Urban Frame: Early Lesbian Activism and Public Space in Montréal." *Journal of Lesbian Studies* 19 (2): 192–211. https://doi.org/10.1080/10894160.2015.970473

Polletta, Francesca, and James M. Jasper. 2001. "Collective Identity and Social Movements." *Annual Review of Sociology* 27 (1): 283–305. https://doi.org/10.1146/annurev.soc.27.1.283

Puar, Jasbir K. 2007. *Terrorist Assemblages: Homonationalism in Queer Times*. London: Duke University Press.

Radio-Canada. 2016. "Québec adopte la loi 103 qui renforce la lutte contre la transphobie." *Radio-Canada.ca*. https://ici.radio-canada.ca/breve/58278/quebec-adopte-loi-103-qui-renforce-lutte-contre-tr

Radio-Canada. 2017. "40e de la descente policière du barTruxx: un tournant pour les droits des homosexuels." *Radio-Canada*. https://ici.radio-canada.ca/nouvelle/1062535/40e-de-la-descente-policiere-du-bar-truxx-un-tournant-pour-les-droits-des-homosexuels

Reger, Jo. 2002a. "More Than One Feminim: Organizational Structure and the Construction of Collective Identity." In *Social Movements: Identity, Culture, and the State*, edited by David S. Meyer, Nancy Whittier, and Belinda Robnett, 171–184. Oxford: Oxford University Press.

Reger, Jo. 2002b. "Organizational Dynamics and Construction of Multiple Feminist Identities in the National Organization for Women." *Gender & Society* 16 (5): 710–727. https://doi.org/10.1177/089124302236993

Robnett, Belinda. 1997. *How Long? How Long? African-American Women in the Struggle for Civil Rights*. New York, NY: Oxford University Press.

Robnett, Belinda. 2002. "External Political Change, Collective Identities, and Participation in Social Movement Organizations." In *Social Movements: Identity, Culture, and the State*, edited by David S. Meyer, Nancy Whittier, and Belinda Robnett, 266–285. Oxford: Oxford University Press.

Roy, Olivier. 2012. "The Colour of Gayness: Representations of Queers of Colour in Québec's Gay Media." *Sexualities* 15 (2): 175–190. https://doi.org/10.1177/1363460712436541

Scott, Ellen K. 2005. "Beyond Tokenism: The Making of Racially Diverse Feminist Organizations." *Social Problems* 52 (2): 232–254. https://doi.org/10.1525/sp.2005.52.2.232

Smith, Miriam. 2019. "Homophobia and Homonationalism: LGBTQ Law Reform in Canada." *Social & Legal Studies*, January, 1–20. https://doi.org/10.1177/0964663918822150

Strolovitch, Dara Z. 2006. "Do Interest Groups Represent the Disadvantaged? Advocacy at the Intersections of Race, Class, and Gender." *The Journal of Politics* 68 (4): 894–910. https://doi.org/10.1111/j.1468-2508.2006.00478.x

Taylor, Verta, and Nancy Whittier. 1992. "Collective Identity in Social Movement Communities: Lesbian Feminist Mobilization." In *Frontiers in Social Movement Theory*, edited by Aldon D. Morris and Carol Mueller, 104–129. New Haven, CT: Yale University Press.

Trawalé, Damien, and Christian Poiret. 2017. "Black Gay Paris: From Invisibilization to the Difficult Alliance of Black and Gay Politics." *African and Black Diaspora: An International Journal* 10 (1): 47–58. https://doi.org/10.1080/17528631.2015.1085669

Tremblay, Manon. 2013. "Mouvements Sociaux et Opportunités Politiques: Les Lesbiennes et Les Gais et l'ajout de l'orientation Sexuelle à La Charte Québécoise Des Droits et Libertés." *Canadian Journal of Political Science/Revue Canadienne de Science Politique* 46 (2): 295–322. https://doi.org/10.1017/S0008423913000656

Tremblay, Manon. 2015. *Queer Mobilizations: Social Movement Activism and Canadian Public Policy*. Vancouver: UBC Press.

Walcott, Rinaldo. 2006. "Black Men in Fricks: Sexing Race in a Gay Ghetto (Toronto)." In *Claiming Space: Racialisation in Canadian Cities*, edited by C. Teelucksingh, 121–133. Waterloo: Wilfrid Laurier University Press.

Ward, Jane. 2008. "White Normativity: The Cultural Dimensions of Whiteness in a Racially Diverse LGBT Organization." *Sociological Perspectives* 51 (3): 563–586. https://doi.org/10.1525/sop.2008.51.3.563

Warner, Tom. 2002. *Never Going Back: A History of Queer Activism in Canada*. Toronto: University of Toronto Press.

Weldon, S. Laurel. 2006. "Inclusion, Solidarity, and Social Movements: The Global Movement Against Gender Violence." *Perspectives on Politics* 4 (1): 55–74. https://doi.org/10.1017/S1537592706060063

Weldon, S. Laurel. 2011. *When Protest Makes Policy*. Ann Arbor, MI: University of Michigan Press.

Yuval-Davis, Nira. 2006. "Intersectionality and Feminist Politics." *European Journal of Women's Studies* 13 (3): 193–209. https://doi.org/10.1177/1350506806065752

Chapter 11

Paradoxes of intersectional practice

Race and class in the Chicago anti-violence movement

Marie Laperrière

Introduction

Prior to the 1960s–1970s, domestic violence was typically understood to be a relatively rare occurrence that should be addressed within the private sphere (Schneider 2000). Reconstructing domestic violence as a pervasive social problem requiring state intervention was without doubt one of the main contributions of the American anti-violence movement (Schechter 1982). This work involved challenging cultural ideas about domestic violence as well as sexist stereotypes that supported state inaction. Half a century later, the impact of the movement is significant: the term domestic violence has gained widespread usage, and surveys show that most Americans support state interventions aimed at protecting victims. However, anti-violence activists are still confronted with the resilience of cultural ideas about domestic violence that limit the movement's ability to foster social change. In this context, most see redefining domestic violence and educating the public as central to their role.

In recent years, the anti-violence movement has progressively integrated the concept of intersectionality into its work – an important development in the broader American social movement landscape (Hancock 2016). Many anti-violence activists claim a commitment to 'recognising,' 'taking into account,' or 'practicing' intersectionality. This turn in anti-violence work impacts how they redefine domestic violence as well as the specific goals that they choose to focus on. In fact, a recognition of intersectionality pushes them to address issues of race and class in ways that the movement has historically been resistant to do. The history of the movement's engagement with those issues as well as the resilience of racialised and classed narratives about domestic violence complicate this work by limiting activists' capacity to imagine new ways of addressing and talking about domestic violence. In this context, they often struggle to determine what recognising intersectionality means for their work.

In this chapter, I analyse intersectional practices in the Chicago anti-violence movement, focusing on the challenges that activists face when attempting to address issues of race and class. Building on data from interviews and ethnographic observations that I conducted between 2014 and 2016, I show that the strategies that activists develop to practice intersectionality are constrained by persistent narratives about race and class and the ways in which they have shaped the practices of the anti-violence movement in the past. I start by discussing how conceptions of domestic violence and of the legitimate ways to address it have historically been entangled with ideas about race and class. Then, I explore how an explicitly articulated commitment to intersectionality encourages activists to reflect on inequalities and privilege and to adapt their interventions with survivors and perpetrators. Finally, I analyse specific spaces where a commitment to intersectionality fails to translate into practices that call privileges into question. I conclude by discussing how gendered, racialised, and classed narratives about domestic violence shape the political imagination of activists and their capacity to truly confront issues of privilege inside the movement.

Race, class, and domestic violence in the American context

In the United States, conceptions of gender-based violence have always been entangled with ideas about race and class. In fact, racialised and classed narratives have shaped how gender-based violence is inscribed in the law, studied and analysed by academics, and addressed by social movements. In particular, the association of violence with blackness and poverty has long served to maintain an unequal social order. For example, in *Rape, Racism and the Myth of the Black Rapist* (1983b), Angela Davis traces how the myth that Black men are sexual predators and, in particular, threats to white women – which she describes as 'one of the most formidable artifices of racism' – was developed as a tool to justify terror against the Black community. Davis explains how the myth of the Black rapist was evoked to provide a moral justification for lynching in the aftermath of the Civil War – a period of growing concern with the maintenance of the racial order. She argues, furthermore, that the association of blackness with violence pervades the writings of several feminist scholars and that the centrality of the myth to the American psyche is reflected in its resurgence at times of heightened racial conflict.

Scholars have also argued that the association of blackness with criminality has been an important narrative serving to support the rise of the carceral state. Activists who mobilised in the early years of the anti-violence movement were aware of this reality and divided over the issue of whether they should demand that the state intervenes to sanction perpetrators. In a context in which social provision remained limited in comparison to other Western democracies, and with the emergence of the anti-violence movement coinciding with the development of a broader crime control agenda (Garland 2001; Simon 2007), the sanctioning of perpetrators rapidly came to dominate the political agenda of the movement. Scholars have argued that the anti-violence movement was co-opted by the state while its political project was distorted to fit the crime control agenda (Bumiller 2010). Others go a step further by contending that the anti-violence movement – as well as the feminist movement as a whole – has been an important ally in the state's project of mass incarceration (Gottschalk 2006).

Several scholars have described how the criminal justice response to domestic violence has negatively affected communities of colour. For example, Beth Richie argues that the work of the anti-violence movement has contributed to the build-up of a 'prison nation' that fosters the marginalisation of poor men and women (2012a). Similarly, Bumiller posits that by becoming an ally of a 'criminalised society,' the feminist movement has contributed to the criminalisation of minority and immigrant men and subjected women to increased scrutiny from the state (2008). Others contend that criminal justice interventions, especially mandatory arrest policies, have resulted in more aggressive policing in communities of colour, which can further impede the safety of survivors and other women (Richie 1996, 2000, 2012a) and increase women's contact with the criminal justice system (Gondolf 1998, 2001, 2002). Finally, despite state intervention, rates of domestic violence victimisation remain notably higher among racial minorities and in communities plagued by poverty, unemployment, and low education levels (e.g. Cunradi, Caetano, and Schafer 2002; Benson et al. 2004).

Racialised and classed narratives about domestic violence, as well as the legacy of the state and anti-violence movement's engagement with issues of race and class, still weigh heavily on the practices of the movement. Like other social movements, the anti-violence movement is situated in a broader culture (Horowitz 1977; Fine 1995) that shapes the interactive process of collective definition through which domestic violence is identified as a social problem requiring specific interventions (Blumer 1971; Spector and Kitsuse 1973, 1977; Hilgartner and Bosk 1988). As social movement scholars have argued, it is precisely the inconsistencies and contradictions that characterise the dominant culture that allow activists to develop and promote alternative ideas and values (Billig 1995; Jenson 1995; Swidler 1995). Indeed, there is ample evidence that anti-violence activists throughout American history have developed political strategies in response to conceptions of domestic violence that they perceived as problematic. For instance, activists have attempted to avoid issues of race and class by focusing on the notion that domestic violence 'can happen to anyone' – an idea that served to highlight the experiences of white, middle-class survivors (Richie 2000). Scholars have also described how concerns with supporting the carceral state and reinforcing negative stereotypes has led to the prioritisation of the needs of Black men over that of Black women, the tendency to refuse to collect or share statistics about victimisation among women of colour, and pressures on Black women not to bring attention to the issue (Crenshaw 1993; Richie 2012b).

Its pervasiveness as well as the complexity of its politics and significance to the feminist project explain why gender-based violence has come to represent the quintessential manifestation of both structural and political intersectionality. Several of intersectionality theory's foundational texts discuss the challenges involved in building an intersectional political project around the issue (hooks 1981; Davis 1983a, 1985; Crenshaw 1989, 1991; Collins 1998). For example,

Kimberlé Crenshaw's analyses of the way in which cases of domestic violence are addressed by the American legal system and the failure of feminist legal mobilisation to recognise the impact of pervasive racist practices on African-American women have strongly shaped the field of intersectional research. In many ways, the challenges identified by these scholars still face anti-violence activists today – in a context in which the rising popularity of intersectionality as a guiding principle for activism has brought a renewed commitment to challenging inequalities of race and class. In fact, my analysis shows that hegemonic narratives about race and class continue to constrain activists' ability to develop new strategies to confront issues of privilege.

The Chicago anti-violence movement

The anti-violence movement emerged in the 1960s–1970s, a period of peak activism in American history. Activists, many of whom were involved in the women's movement, initially organised at the grassroots level to provide services to survivors (e.g. shelters, survivors' groups, emergency hotlines, legal advocacy services). They also developed partner abuse intervention programmes (PAIPs), which are meant to help perpetrators develop non-violent behaviour, and mobilised to demand legal reforms. By the early 1990s, all 52 states had adopted laws criminalising domestic violence. The 1994 Violence Against Women Act (VAWA), enacted during the Clinton presidency, guaranteed state funding for victim services while strengthening the criminal justice response. As state funding became available, anti-violence organisations increasingly focused on advocacy work and service provision while PAIPs were integrated into the criminal justice apparatus.

Because it is home to a very active and well-established anti-violence movement that includes both state-funded and grassroots organisations, Chicago represented an ideal site to conduct this research. While anti-violence organisations emerged in the city in the 1960s, their number multiplied in the 2000s. Organisations provide a range of services to victims and also engage in advocacy, prevention, and outreach activities. Domestic violence programmes are also present in the courts, hospitals, schools, social service agencies, and police department. Finally, Chicago has a network of about two dozen PAIPs working under the supervision of the Illinois Department of Human Services as well as a specialised domestic violence courthouse established in 2005. The movement is spearheaded by a large umbrella organisation created in the late 1970s, which provides trainings and workshops and runs an emergency hotline. It enjoys a certain level of governmental recognition and was invited to participate in the debates that led to the adoption of the Illinois Domestic Violence Act of 1982, the development of violence prevention programmes in Chicago public schools, the Chicago Police Department anti-violence initiative, and other state-sponsored programmes. Serving as a spokesperson for the movement, it also connects anti-violence organisations with different governmental agencies.

Data and methods

Data analysed in this chapter consist of semi-conducted interviews and ethnographic observations. Between 2014 and 2016, I conducted 40 interviews with activists involved in the Chicago anti-violence movement. The activists I interviewed worked or volunteered for organisations focusing on domestic violence intervention and/or prevention. Some organisations were state-funded and followed state protocols. Others operated at the grassroots level. Activists engaged in a range of activities including community outreach, prevention programmes, service provision for survivors, partner abuse intervention and advocacy work. The large majority identified as women ($n = 37$) and half as women of colour ($n = 20$), and most held a bachelor's or master's degree. The interviews lasted between 45 and 90 minutes and questions focused on activists' work, goals, and general understanding of domestic violence. Because of the historical legacy of ideas about race, class, and domestic violence in the American context, I avoided asking about them directly. This allowed me to observe when and in which particular context activists chose to refer to race and class explicitly. Similarly, I opted not to ask specific questions about intersectionality or intersectional practice, preferring to observe whether they would come up during conversations. However, when activists did mention intersectionality, I asked them to explain what the term meant to them as well as when and where they remembered first encountering it. Similarly, when they described situations in which they had to address issues of race and class, I asked extensive follow-up questions about the strategies that they chose to employ and the rationale behind them.

I conducted ethnographic observations of spaces where activists define domestic violence, discuss strategies for service provision, and negotiate goals for the movement. I observed two 40-hour domestic violence trainings and two 20-hour partner abuse intervention trainings.[1] I also attended a series of trainings and workshops provided by different organisations and covering a range of topics such as safety planning, trauma-based approaches to intervention, and strategies for effective legal advocacy. Finally, some of my interviewees gave me permission to observe staff meetings at their organisation. In all of these spaces, I paid particular attention to the ways in which ideas about how to address issues of race and class shape activists' interventions and strategies. Conducting ethnographic observations allowed me to observe discrepancies between some of the claims that activists made during interviews regarding their work and the ways in which they discussed issues on the ground (Jerolmack and Khan 2014).

Practicing intersectionality in anti-violence work

Originally a theoretical tool, intersectionality has become a guiding principle for activism. Although the term is used unevenly, it has become part of the collective language of several social movements. Activists can invoke it to refer to broad political commitments, specific intervention practices, or a general framework for understanding social problems. The language of intersectionality has had a particular impact on movements rooted in feminist ideas such as the anti-violence movement. In fact, the majority of activists whom I interviewed throughout the course of my research routinely used the term. Those who didn't refer to *intersectionality* specifically still described the different ways in which their work has evolved over time to respond to a new imperative of 'inclusion,' 'recognising diversity,' or thinking about 'different systems of power.' Hence, even when activists didn't use the term, it was clear that their practices had been impacted by the integration of intersectionality into the discourse of the movement. Most believed this shift to represent an important development in anti-violence work: one that has taken 'way too much time historically' or that 'still has a long, long way to go.' Some also explained how although their organisations have always served a diverse constituency, discussions of the necessity to address specific needs related to race, class, immigration, or disability have only taken centre stage in the last 10 to 20 years.

While activists mobilised intersectionality to describe practices related to service provision or advocacy, most thought of the integration of intersectionality into the work of the anti-violence movement as part of a collective project. In recent years, intersectionality has become a topic of major interest in the trainings, workshops, and roundtables that anti-violence organisations frequently organise and that serve as spaces where activists can work to develop a common theoretical framework to better understand domestic violence and guide the work they do on the ground. For example, discussions of intersectionality have become an integral part of the 40-hour domestic violence training that all individuals who wish to volunteer or work with survivors or perpetrators of domestic violence in Illinois have to complete. The state-approved training, which is provided by different anti-violence organisations, has a curriculum that varies slightly from one training to the next. However, all the trainings that I observed – as well as those that were described to me during interviews – included topics related to intersectionality such as 'Intersectionality and Inclusion,' 'The Anti-Oppression Framework,' 'Being an Ally,' or 'History of the Domestic Violence Movement.'

Sessions focused on intersectionality served different purposes. For example, sessions on intersectionality as a theoretical concept or on the history of the anti-violence movement were used to construct a collective identity among activists. As Joanna, who facilitated a session on the history of the anti-violence movement, explained at the end of the day:

> We wanted to have this conversation today because we need to remember where we come from as a movement. We are very much rooted in a feminist framework. And that needs to include intersectionality. It helps us to remember things we sometimes forget when we do our work with victims. What do we want as a movement? For example, we have been working hand in hand with the criminal justice system. Is this still what we want as a movement? We need to keep this in mind.

When she affirmed that 'we need to remember where we come from,' Joanna expressed a common concern among individuals involved in anti-violence work: that the focus on service provision depoliticised the movement. She invoked intersectionality to remind activists of – or to encourage them to 'keep in mind' – the potential tensions between the day-to-day demands of service provision and the broader goals of the movement. This type of session is also used to reaffirm the centrality of feminist thinking to the movement. Like many others, Joanna associated intersectionality with feminism – and thought of intersectionality not as a critique or as an alternative to feminist thought, but as central to it. Hence, she presented intersectionality as a tool that can help activists identify goals for the movement by 'remembering' what activists of the 1960s–1970s envisioned.

An important number of sessions on intersectionality are devoted specifically to the work of service provision. For example, trainings include sessions on how to work with specific populations such as immigrant, LGBTQ, poor, or elder survivors. These sessions usually invite participants to explore and challenge their own beliefs and prejudices about survivors and perpetrators of domestic violence. They often highlight the necessity to fight stereotypes and reverse the historical process by which domestic violence has been used to marginalise racial minorities, immigrants, and the poor. For example, one of the 20-hour PAIP trainings that I attended started with a 90-minute session called 'Intersectionality and Privilege.' After offering a broad theoretical definition of intersectionality and reading extracts from Kimberlé Crenshaw's work, Mark, the presenter, explained what he believed intersectionality should mean in the context of PAIP:

> Being able to know who you are, where you stand and what advantage you have compared to those with whom you work is central to doing PAIP work. This is very difficult work. It's uncomfortable. It takes personal change and reflection. But it's very important.

Just like Mark, many activists associated intersectionality with a commitment to reflection and individual change, as well as with the broader goal of fighting stereotypes. Whether activists invoked intersectionality as a guiding principle to identify goals for the movement, or whether they used it to reflect on practices related to service provision, it allowed them, to some extent at least, to recognise how certain forms of privilege operate inside the anti-violence movement. However, when they attempted to practice intersectionality in their day-to-day activities, they were often confronted with the uncertainties that characterise anti-violence work. Hence, many were still struggling to figure out what intersectionality means for their practices and for the movement as a whole. Activists seemed to be particularly hesitant to change the way in which the movement has addressed issues of race and class and were concerned with the possibility of reinforcing existing stereotypes. This sometimes led them to practice intersectionality in a way that reinforced different forms of privilege. In the next three sections, I explore some of the ways in which activists address issues of race and class in their work, paying particular attention to the spaces where intersectionality fails to become a tool that challenges power and privilege.

'You give them options and you let them choose': race and class in the provision of services to survivors

Most anti-violence organisations situated in Chicago serve a clientele composed in majority of poor women and women of colour. The activists I interviewed who had been working at a domestic violence agency for over ten years described a shift in how their organisation addresses issues of race and class, even though the demographics of their clientele had not changed. For example, many organisations now provide services in languages other than English, translate educational material and legal documents, and do targeted outreach in migrant communities. They also provide or help survivors access a broad range of services. Historically, funding restrictions have limited organisations' capacity to provide services that were not considered directly related to domestic violence. Services considered as belonging to this category have usually been those needed the most by white, middle-class women, while services of importance to poor women and women of colour have often been constructed as something other than domestic violence services (Richie 2000). In order to provide job placement, childcare, or financial literacy services, for example, activists had to reconstruct them as central to survivors' capacity to achieve safety. Hence, broadening the range of services that organisations provide involved redefining survivors' needs.

Many activists also discussed how addressing issues of race and class in their work meant rethinking the relationship between service provider and client. They described having adapted their work to serve a diverse clientele by becoming 'more open-minded,' 'less rigid about what the right solutions are,' or 'work[ing] actively against [our] own stereotypes.' Challenging the stereotypes or prejudices that service providers have towards survivors was also emphasised during workshops and trainings on intersectionality and social provision. As Annie, the director of a large anti-violence organisation, explained:

> If you want to work with survivors, you have to leave all of your preconceived ideas at the door. You never know a woman until you really talk to her and listen to her . . . or until you walk a mile in her shoes. No two women need the same things. You have to be really careful with stereotypes. So how do you do that? You give them options. You give them options and you let them choose. And you try to respect their choices, even when you don't agree.

Critiques of the anti-violence movement have often argued that activists tended to only offer solutions that reflected the needs of white, middle-class women (e.g. INCITE! Women of Color Against Violence 2006). By 'respecting [survivors'] choices' and 'giv[ing] them options,' Annie recognises the diversity of women's needs. This approach to service provision – which is in line with the way in which intersectionality is defined during trainings – can be beneficial to survivors who have specific needs that can be addressed through available services. However, reconstructing needs that derive from different social positions as 'individual choices' erases disadvantage. By arguing that 'no two women need the same things,' Annie distances needs from inequalities. Most importantly, activists often emphasise individual 'preferences' or 'choices' when discussing issues that have historically been highly divisive for the movement, such as addressing domestic violence through criminal justice interventions, an issue that has been widely criticised by women of colour. When activists frame divisive issues as matters of individual 'choices,' they also argue that these issues don't need to be critically examined. For example, during a training session focused on legal advocacy, Maggie, an advocate in her thirties who works at a specialised domestic violence court, argued:

> My work is to help women take control of their own safety. This is what safety planning is really about. It's not about telling a woman what I think she should do, or what you think she should do. I give them options. I can help her file a police report. I can help her apply for an order of protection. But of course, if this is not what she wants, then she doesn't have to. Some women are not comfortable with involving the police . . . and that belongs to them. It might be because of their own history. So, we have to accommodate. It might take a little extra work, but we will find a way to make her safe.

Throughout my interviews with activists, a refusal to involve the police or to prosecute an abusive partner was the most common example of accommodation that service providers had to make for poor women and women of colour. Maggie's claim that a survivor's resistance to involve the police reflects 'their own history' or 'belongs to them' negates the social conditions that produce individual choices – but it also fails to acknowledge the long history of anti-violence activism that criticised this approach to addressing domestic violence. Finally, the recognition that survivors have different needs has not led to a discussion of the cost on poor women and women of colour when the movement continues to privilege some strategies over others – in particular those that contribute to the rise of the carceral state or to the widespread belief that 'real' victims collaborate with the police and courts to prosecute offenders.

The way in which activists define survivors' needs – as well as the specific options that they provide them with – has a major impact on the strategies to address domestic violence that come to dominate. In fact, while victim services have always been central to the work of the anti-violence movement, the availability of state funding and the integration of domestic violence services into the state apparatus has created an opportunity for activists to acquire legitimacy as individuals possessing knowledge and expertise recognised by the state (Gottschalk 2006). This provides them with opportunities to shape the state response to domestic violence. In fact, service providers are able to advocate for survivors with different governmental agencies. For instance, legal advocates have established offices inside courthouses and are able to intervene and provide expertise in domestic violence cases. Similarly, caseworkers and counsellors at domestic violence agencies can be called to provide expertise in custody issues or support survivors' access to social services and benefits. Most importantly, activists involved in service provision often sit on committees where they provide expertise that can shape public policies. Hence, activists' inability to confront privilege shapes interventions in ways that carry material consequences for survivors.

While trainings on applying intersectionality in the context of social provision instruct activists to think about their own privilege, it is mainly to encourage them to see how survivors of different social backgrounds might want different things. Intersectionality is hence used in a way that allows activists not to question the established strategies of the movement and reinforces a discourse that equates needs with choices, and thus makes the needs of poor women and women of colour invisible. Despite a commitment to take into account inequalities, activists remain unable to interrogate relational privileges between survivors whose needs are perceived as being outside of the norm and service providers who dictate which strategies come to dominate.

'Please don't let race come into it': race and class in interventions with perpetrators

PAIPs constitute the main space where activists interact with perpetrators of domestic violence. The majority of their clientele consists of individuals who were court-mandated to complete 24 to 26 weeks of partner abuse intervention after being charged with domestic battery. PAIPs are mainly provided by nonprofit organisations and, while state protocols establish broad guidelines for the structure of meetings and content of educational material, PAIP facilitators have a lot of leeway in how they do their work. Most organisations follow a curriculum inspired by the Duluth curriculum, which was developed by a group of feminist activists and survivors in the 1970s and focuses on male privilege, gendered patterns of power and control, and sexist beliefs as the roots of abusive behaviour (Pence and Paymar 1993). Agencies that offer PAIPs are often able to connect perpetrators with different services, and the evaluations they do of their clients can have a major impact on the outcome of their court cases, which means that facilitators are also in a position to shape the state response to domestic violence.

PAIPs attempt to change behaviour by encouraging participants to reflect on their experiences and on how they learned to use violence as a way to resolve conflict in their relationships. Because facilitators help perpetrators process their experiences, PAIPs constitute an important space where activists work to redefine domestic violence and the social conditions that foster violent behaviour. With poor men and men of colour representing the majority of the clientele in most organisations providing PAIP, issues of race and class often come up during group meetings. In fact, race and class are often central to the way in which individuals understand their childhood experiences, the dynamics of their relationships, as well as their experiences with the criminal justice system. While there is a lot of variation in how facilitators chose to address issues of race and class, a majority of my interviewees agreed that this was a topic that was often 'difficult,' 'sensitive,' or had the potential to be 'disruptive to the group.' Many expressed a concern that discussing race and class could only serve to reinforce existing stereotypes associated with violent behaviour and, hence, believed that the topic should be avoided when possible.

One of the strategies that facilitators employed to avoid discussing race and class during group meetings was to reconstruct them as irrelevant to discussions of domestic violence. For example, Matthew, who facilitates a group on the Chicago Southside, explains how he handles situations in which perpetrators discuss how race has shaped their experience:

> Please don't let race come into it because it doesn't matter. It's just another way to deflect. If you have people in your group who are Black, they will always use it. Especially if it's two Caucasian facilitators. They tell you: 'You don't understand what it's like' or 'It's our culture.' Perpetrators truly believe that the system is there to get them.

Matthew's comment reflects how facilitators are able to position themselves as experts of the dynamics of domestic violence. As such, they can impose a framework in which only gender matters as an explanatory variable. Even when domestic violence perpetrators themselves understand race and class as central to their experiences, they are constructed as irrelevant – something that 'doesn't matter.' Moreover, Matthew describes race as something that group participants 'use' to 'deflect.' Doing so, he reconstructs participants' identities as characteristics inherent to violent individuals who 'believe that the system is there to get them.' As the expert, Matthew has the authority to interpret perpetrators' beliefs. He constructs Black participants' 'use' of race as a reaction to a group run by white facilitators. Similarly, Manuel, a Latino facilitator in his forties, explains how his own position can help him confront participants who bring up issues of race and class:

> As a Latino man who grew up on the West Side, I am able to use my culture to relate to them, but also to show them that it didn't make them do things they didn't want to do. It didn't make them choose to be abusive. It didn't make them fail in all their relationships. When they are with Brian and Julie, it's easier for them to blame it all on the culture, on their family, on the whole community. But with me, they know they can't do that. I am a Latino man and I am not violent. My father was a Latino man and he is not violent. Domestic violence doesn't see culture.

Manuel positions himself as an expert just like Matthew, but he also uses his own racial identification as a proof that domestic violence 'doesn't see culture.' While not all facilitators interpreted perpetrators' discussions of how race shaped their experience as an 'excuse' or something without importance, the tendency to avoid the topic when possible was widespread. Some facilitators described participants' desire to speak about race or class as 'a way to change the topic,' a 'refusal to be accountable,' or something that 'they are not here to discuss.' Hence, facilitators' focus on accountability and gendered power led them to silence group participants and to misrecognise the structures of power that shape their lives. While many activists claimed to be deeply concerned with the rise of the carceral state and the different ways in which it broadens inequalities of race and class, they refused to let perpetrators discuss the issue. Other facilitators insisted that focusing on inequalities of race and class during group discussions would reinforce negative stereotypes of domestic violence perpetrators. However, they always prioritised this strategy even when it went against the desire of participants and didn't attempt to think of ways in which they could include race and class in their analysis of domestic violence without reinforcing negative stereotypes.

Even when PAIP facilitators are invested in integrating intersectionality into their work, they often do so in ways that fail to challenge privilege. In fact, the position of power that they occupy vis-à-vis PAIP participants – whose presence in the programme is in most cases mandated by the courts – can encourage them to position themselves as experts who can determine the 'right' way of addressing issues of race and class. This limits their capacity to support perpetrators by helping them understand their experiences and discussing specific needs that they might have in terms of services, but also to develop an analysis of domestic violence that takes into account the experiences of perpetrators.

Expertise and the subjects of intersectionality

Scholars have argued that the potential of intersectionality for feminist theory lies in its open-endedness: in the ways in which it keeps us looking for new ways of understanding the social world (Davis 2008; Collins and Bilge 2016). This can also be said of the potential of intersectionality to transform social movements and challenge relations of power. When anti-violence activists adopt intersectionality as a broad principle, they are pushed to constantly question established practices, assumptions about survivors and perpetrators, as well as their own privilege. However, as specific ways of practicing intersectionality become integrated into the day-to-day work of the movement, activists develop rigid beliefs about the right ways to address issues of race and class. In this context, intersectionality fails to challenge privilege and might be used in ways that reinforce inequalities inside the movement.

In the early years of the anti-violence movement, survivors of domestic violence were constructed as an important source of knowledge about the dynamics of domestic violence. In fact, activists as well as scholars believed that analyses of domestic violence should centre the experiences and perspectives of survivors. As the movement professionalised, became integrated into the state apparatus, and gained legitimacy in the eyes of the public, a new class of individuals emerged as recognised experts. Domestic violence professionals replaced survivors as leaders of the movement and progressively became the legitimate authority on domestic violence. To some extent, when intersectionality becomes a prominent tool in the discourse of the movement, it also becomes an object of expertise. In fact, intersectionality – as well as the right ways to integrate it in anti-violence work – is increasingly becoming an object that is taught during trainings and workshops by individuals claiming the status of experts. This allows the language of intersectionality to spread inside the movement and encourages activists to perceive practicing intersectionality as a fundamental part of their work. However, it also contributes to a narrowing of ideas about the right ways to practice intersectionality, which can limit the potential of the concept to foster activists' political imagination. Moreover, it creates new forms of epistemic privilege by prioritising the perspectives of 'experts' at the expense of the voices of survivors. Hence, the growing centrality of intersectionality to the discourse of the movement, combined with its construction as a tool that requires expertise, provides some individuals with the privilege to dominate the discourse and to dictate the strategies of the movement.

When domestic violence professionals position themselves as experts, they also construct some individuals as the primary subjects of intersectionality. When the activists whom I interviewed described what intersectionality meant to them, it was clear that they considered survivors – and in particular poor women and women of colour – as the main and perhaps only subjects of intersectionality in anti-domestic violence work. They conceived of intersectionality as a tool to help them identify individual needs. Doing so, they built on and reinforced cultural ideas about men and women of colour. For example, by arguing that survivors of colour had specific needs that might require 'extra work,' they reconstructed women of colour as the quintessential receivers of service provision in need of accommodation. Moreover, by making survivors the primary subjects of intersectionality and describing as irrelevant analyses of race and class in discussions of perpetrators, they contributed to making perpetrators of colour, as well as their needs and the social conditions that can foster violence, invisible. Finally, it is worth noting that activists never considered themselves or the anti-violence movement as a potential subject of intersectionality. In fact, during the time that I conducted my research, I never heard discussions about representation inside the movement. Women of colour were always discussed as survivors, but never as activists or leaders of the movement. Hence, while intersectionality allowed activists to identify specific forms of disadvantage that shape the lives of survivors, it didn't challenge the privileged position that allowed them to control the narrative of the movement.

Conclusion

The concept of intersectionality has become central to trainings and workshops focused on anti-violence intervention. Many activists regularly use the term to refer to their work. Some invoke intersectionality to describe the ways in which they have changed how they think about service provision. Others explain how it has shaped their understanding of domestic violence as a social problem or guides how they envision the broader goals of the movement. The impact of this development in anti-violence work is difficult to assess. In fact, intersectionality is used in many ways: some that challenge privilege and others that deepen existing inequalities. The strategies that activists have adopted to integrate intersectionality into their work – and in particular to address issues of race and class – were not developed in a vacuum. They were shaped by the way in which the anti-violence movement has addressed issues of race and class historically, and by existing narratives about race, class, and domestic violence. My analysis shows that intersectional practices can only be understood in the historical and cultural contexts that shaped their development. In fact, the ways in which activists understand what practicing intersectionality means reflect the unique history of the anti-violence movement and the complex ways in which it was shaped by racial and class relations. However, it also sheds light on conditions that can lead social movements to co-opt or use intersectionality in ways that fail to challenge privilege. Some of the problematic uses of intersectionality that I identified are unlikely to be unique to the anti-violence movement, even though they might take different forms in other contexts.

Because social movement practices become institutionalised over time, they are particularly difficult to change. While intersectionality can be used as a tool to challenge established practices, activists can also invoke it to legitimise strategies that they are resistant to rethink. For example, activists invoke intersectionality to explain why they should avoid discussing issues of race and class during PAIP by referring to the ways in which they could risk reinforcing negative stereotypes. By doing so, they continue to privilege a discourse that centres the experiences of white, middle-class survivors. In this case, reinforcing the belief that there is only one right way to address a specific issue constrains activists' ability to imagine other ways to practice intersectionality. Hence, intersectionality fails to challenge privilege when some activists are able to dictate the right ways to practice it. This is particularly likely to happen when intersectionality is constructed as an object of expertise, i.e. as a tool that is only accessible to those with specific knowledge. Individuals who can claim the status of experts can use their privilege to silence the perspectives of others and to create new spaces of exclusion, as when PAIP facilitators reconstruct a desire to speak about experiences related to race and class as a refusal to be accountable for violent behaviour.

Intersectionality can also be used to shed light on tensions between conflicting interests, needs, and political goals. For example, scholars have used intersectionality as a theoretical lens to analyse the complicated relationship between the goals of the anti-violence movement and the rise of the carceral state and to highlight how the interests of poor women and women of colour have been in conflict with those of middle-class, white women. But when activists equate practicing intersectionality with respecting survivors' individual choices, they erase how the issue of criminal justice responses to domestic violence has historically divided the anti-violence movement. In this case, intersectionality is used to resolve conflict by depoliticising interests. These examples show that while scholars can remain optimistic about the potential of intersectionality to foster social justice, they should be critical of the ways in which intersectional practices can fail to truly challenge privilege.

Note

1 All individuals who wish to volunteer or work with survivors or perpetrators of domestic violence in Illinois have to complete a state-approved 40-hour domestic violence training provided by different non-profit organisations. Individuals who facilitate PAIPs also need to complete a 20-hour partner abuse intervention training.

References

Benson, Michael L., John Wooldredge, Amy B. Thistlethwaite, and Greer Litton Fox. 2004. "The Correlation Between Race and Domestic Violence Is Confounded With Community Context." *Social Problems* 51 (3): 326–342.

Billig, Michael. 1995. "Rhetorical Psychology, Ideological Thinking, and Imagining Nationhood." In *Social Movements and Culture*, edited by Hank Johnson and Bert Klandermans, 64–84. Minneapolis, MN: University of Minnesota Press.

Blumer, Herbert. 1971. "Social Problems as Collective Behavior." *Social Problems* 18: 298–306.

Bumiller, Kristin. 2008. *In an Abusive State: How Neoliberalism Appropriated the Feminist Movement Against Sexual Violence.* Durham, NC: Duke University Press.

Bumiller, Kristin. 2010. "The Nexus of Domestic Violence Reform and Social Science: From Instrument of Social Change to Institutionalized Surveillance." *Annual Review of Law and Social Science* 6: 173–193.

Collins, Patricia Hill. 1998. "It's All in the Family: Intersections of Gender, Race, and Nation." *Hypatia* 13 (3): 62–82. doi:10.2307/3810699

Collins, Patricia Hill, and Sirma Bilge. 2016. *Intersectionality.* Cambridge, UK: Polity Press.

Crenshaw, Kimberle. 1993. "Mapping the Margins: Intersectionality, Identity Politics, and Violence Against Women of Color." *Stanford Law Review* 43: 1241–1299.

Crenshaw, Kimberlé Williams. 1989. "Demarginalizing the Intersection of Race and Sex: A Black Feminist Critique of Antidiscrimination Doctrine, Feminist Theory and Antiracist Politics." *The University of Chicago Legal Forum* 139–167.

Crenshaw, Kimberlé Williams. 1991. "Mapping the Margins: Intersectionality, Identity Politics and Violence Against Women of Color." *Stanford Law Review* 43: 1241–1299.

Cunradi, Carol B., Raul Caetano, and John Schafer. 2002. "Socioeconomic Predictors of Intimate Partner Violence Among White, Black, and Hispanic Couples in the United States." *Journal of Family Violence* 17 (4): 377–389.

Davis, Angela Y. 1983a. *Women, Race, & Class*. New York, NY: Vintage.

Davis, Angela Y. 1983b. "Rape, Racism and the Myth of the Black Rapist." In *Women, Race, & Class*, edited by Angela Y. Davis, 172–201. New York, NY: Vintage.

Davis, Angela Y. 1985. *Violence Against Women and the Ongoing Challenge to Racism*. New York, NY: Kitchen Tables.

Davis, Kathy. 2008. "Intersectionality as Buzzword: A Sociology of Science Perspective on What Makes a Feminist Theory Successful." *Feminist Theory* 9: 67–85.

Fine, Gary A. 1995. "Public Narration and Group Culture: Discerning Discourse in Social Movements." In *Social Movements and Culture*, edited by Hank Johnson and Bert Klandermans, 127–143. Minneapolis, MN: University of Minnesota Press.

Garland, David. 2001. *The Culture of Control: Crime and Social Order in Contemporary Society*. Chicago, IL: University of Chicago Press.

Gondolf, Edward W. 1998. "Victims of Court-Mandated Batterers: Their Victimization, Helpseeking, and Perceptions." *Violence Against Women* 4: 659–676.

Gondolf, Edward W. 2001. *Civil Protection Orders and Criminal Court Actions: The Extent and Impact of "Overlap' Cases*. Harrisburg, PA: Pennsylvania Commission on Crime and Delinquency.

Gondolf, Edward W. 2002. *Batterer Intervention Systems: Issues, Outcomes, and Recommendations*. Thousand Oaks, CA: Sage Publications.

Gottschalk, Marie. 2006. "The Battered-Women's Movement and the Development of Penal Policy." In *The Prison and the Gallows: The Politics of Mass Incarceration in America*, 139–164. Cambridge, UK: Cambridge University Press.

Hancock, Ange-Marie. 2016. *Intersectionality: An Intellectual History*. New York, NY: Oxford University Press.

Hilgartner, Stephen, and Charles L. Bosk. 1988. "The Rise and Fall of Social Problems: A Public Arenas Model." *American Journal of Sociology* 94 (1): 53–78. doi:10.2307/2781022

hooks, bell. 1981. *Ain't I a Woman: Black Women and Feminism*. Boston, MA: South End Press.

Horowitz, Donald L. 1977. "Cultural Movements and Ethnic Change." *Annals of the American Academy of Political and Social Science* 433: 6–18.

INCITE! Women of Color Against Violence. 2006. *The Color of Violence: The Incite! Anthology*. Cambridge, UK: South End Press.

Jenson, Jane. 1995. "What's in a Name? Nationalist Movements and Public Discourse." In *Social Movements and Culture*, edited by Hank Johnson and Bert Klandermans, 107–126. Minneapolis, MN: University of Minnesota Press.

Jerolmack, Colin, and Shamus Khan. 2014. "Talk Is Cheap: Ethnography and the Attitudinal Fallacy." *Sociological Methods & Research* 43 (2): 178–209.

Pence, Ellen, and Michael Paymar. 1993. *Education Groups for Men Who Batter: The Duluth Model*. New York, NY: Springer.

Richie, Beth E. 1996. *Compelled to Crime: The Gender Entrapment of Battered Black Women*. London: Routledge.

Richie, Beth E. 2000. "A Black Feminist Reflection on the Antiviolence Movement." *Signs* 25 (4): 1133–1137.

Richie, Beth E. 2012a. *Arrested Justice: Black Women, Violence, and America's Prison Nation*. New York, NY: New York University Press.

Richie, Beth E. 2012b. "The Problem of Male Violence Against Black Women." In *Arrested Justice: Black Women, Violence, and America's Prison Nation*, 23–64. New York, NY: New York University Press.

Schechter, Susan. 1982. *Women and Male Violence: The Visions and Struggles of the Battered Women's Movement*. Cambridge, MA: South End Press.

Schneider, Elizabeth M. 2000. *Battered Women and Feminist Lawmaking*. New Haven, CT: Yale University Press.

Simon, Jonathan. 2007. *Governing Through Crime*. Oxford: Oxford University Press.

Spector, Malcolm, and John I. Kitsuse. 1973. "Social Problems: A Re-formulation." *Social Problems* 21: 145–159.

Spector, Malcolm, and John I. Kitsuse. 1977. *Constructing Social Problems*. Menlo Park, CA: Cummings.

Swidler, Ann. 1995. "Cultural Power and Social Movements." In *Social Movements and Culture*, edited by Hank Johnson and Bert Klandermans, 25–40. Minneapolis, MN: University of Minnesota Press.

Chapter 12

Intersectional politics on domestic workers' rights

The cases of Ecuador and Colombia

Daniela Cherubini, Giulia Garofalo Geymonat and Sabrina Marchetti

1 Introduction

This chapter focuses on organising for domestic workers' rights as a telling case in relation to the uses of intersectionality as a social movement strategy[1] (Chun, Lipsitz, and Shin 2013; Evans 2016; Lapèrriere and Lépinard 2016). As we will show through the analysis that follows, this case represents an example of self-organising based on multiply-marginalised identities, which has been described in the introduction of this volume as a first possibility in the use of intersectionality in social movements.

We take the case of two domestic workers' organisations in Ecuador and Colombia and, through the analysis of their discourses and activities between 2011 and 2018 we explore the different 'intersectional politics' that these two collective actors have developed 'on the ground' with the aim of making sense of the specific experience of marginalisation lived by domestic workers, as well as building their collective identity, putting forward their claims, and dealing with other potentially converging social struggles that surround the promotion of domestic workers' rights – in particular, feminist, anti-racist, and labour struggles.

Throughout this analysis we propose a heuristic model for the application of intersectionality to the study of the collective action carried out by multiply-marginalised groups. In particular we use a multilevel approach which looks into (1) the collective identity of the organisations, (2) the claims, activities, and frames that they mobilise, and (3) the alliances they establish with institutional and non-institutional actors in related fields. Such a multilevel reading allows us to show how in different aspects and moments of their mobilisations, the organisations under study can embrace different approaches to intersectionality, and their strategies and positioning in this field change when moving from discourses to actions, from compositions to claims, to address (or not) privileges and inequalities rooted in gender, class, and race relations.

In this chapter we illustrate our multilevel analysis of domestic workers' movements by offering a comparative study of two organisations mobilising for domestic workers' rights in Colombia and Ecuador, which have been chosen both for their visibility and for the impact of their actions at the national level. The study of these two organisations is part of a broader comparative study on the transformations of paid domestic workers' rights and conditions in Europe, Latin America, and Asia from 1950 to the present day. Local research-ers[2] gathered data between April 2017 and March 2018, while the authors made ethnographic visits and conducted workshops between September 2017 and January 2018.

The analysis presented in this chapter is based primarily on a total of 46 quali-tative in-depth interviews held in both countries with key informants includ-ing representatives from domestic workers' grassroots organisations, women's and feminist groups, ethnic minorities' organisations, trade unions and workers' organisations, human rights and non-governmental organisations, governmen-tal and state actors, and international organisations (in particular the ILO-International Labour Organization regional offices), as well as with academic experts. These interviews are complemented by written documents produced by organisations of domestic workers and other relevant actors and by ethno-graphic observations during meetings and workshops with local stakeholders. The analysis we propose does not aim to be representative of the complexity of the processes at stake, as we use an interpretative approach of the materials that are looked at as situated accounts produced in a particular context and time. Finally, we used statistical data gathered mainly from Population Censuses of 2005 (Colombia) and 2010 (Ecuador) describing the sociodemographic charac-teristics of people employed in paid domestic work.

In what follows we first provide a short review of the literature on inter-sectionality and social movements, indicating how our work may be seen as engaging with some of the open conceptual and methodological questions and empirical shortcomings in the current debate. In the next section we describe the composition of domestic workers' labour forces in Ecuador and Colombia, both of which largely show similar patterns of a strongly gendered and eth-nicised labour force. In addition to this, we describe how both countries find themselves, since the late 2000s, in a period of emergent mobilisation in the field, with the creation or strengthening of paid domestic workers' organisa-tions, and pivotal legislative reforms – such as the ratification of the ILO Con-vention No. 189 - that are regarded as special achievements of the movements we discuss. Such a contextual analysis demonstrates the relative comparability of the two organisations[3] that we take as case studies in the following of the chapter: ATHE – Asociación Trabajadoras de Hogar Ecuatorianas (Ecuadorian Domestic Workers' Association) and UTDC – Unión de Trabajadoras Domés-ticas de Colombia (Colombian Domestic Workers' Union). Our analysis of the organisations through intersectional lenses focuses on two at least partly distinct levels: on the one hand, we consider their composition and collective identity, and on the other hand, we look into their most important recent campaigns, tak-ing into consideration the claims, actions, discursive frames, and alliances they mobilised.

2 Intersectionality in social movements

As illustrated in the introduction to this book, in the last decades an expanding body of studies has drawn upon the concept of intersectionality as a critical tool to explore a vast array of political projects and social movements (Evans and Lépinard, this volume). Intersectionality has been used as an analytical tool to investigate social movements in relation to the construction of their collective identity (Carastathis 2013; Maddison and Partridge 2014; Okechukwu 2014), agendas, representation and recruitment strategies (Strolovitch 2007; Alberti, Holgate, and Tapia 2013), as well as the framing processes and cultural repertoires they adopt (Cruells López and Ruiz García 2014; Lépinard 2014; Okechukwu 2014), and the conflicts, coalitions, and alliances they establish (Ferree and Roth 1998; Cole 2008; Townsend-Bell 2011; Predelli and Halsaa 2012; Verloo 2013; Coley 2014; Rothman 2014). This literature suggests that intersectionality is an inspiring concept to be applied to a vast array of social movements – not limited to feminist movements – that can be understood, articulated, and used in different ways, for different purposes, and that may encounter various forms of resistance – to which correspond a variety of possible consequences for movements' struggles and constituencies. Several authors suggest that mapping the different uses, resistances, and outcomes of intersectionality 'on the ground' is a relevant task that deserves further elaboration (Townsend-Bell 2011; Bassel and Lépinard 2014; Evans 2016; Evans and Lépinard, this volume). There is no agreement, however, on how to carry out this analysis at the methodological level. Where should we look in order to understand the specific ways in which collective actors engage with intersectionality as a cognitive and political strategy to carry on their struggle? And crucially, how can we account for the dynamic and situated character of individual and collective actors' positioning processes, while carrying out this analysis?

This chapter engages with these questions by employing a multilevel intersectional approach to the study of social movements, separating the analysis into different levels – namely the collective identity of organisations; their claims, activities, and discursive frames; and the alliances they establish – without postulating a coherence in the way intersectionality takes place at each level.

In applying this analytical model, we pay special attention to how categories such as gender, race, and class convey different meanings and have different relative power in structuring domestic workers' struggle in different spaces, at different scales, and at different moments in time – thus drawing on the ideas of 'translocality,' 'transcalarity,' and 'transtemporality' of social divisions developed by Nira Yuval-Davis (2015) and Floya Anthias (2012). We show how intersectional identities are forged by different movements with different emphasis on gender, race, and class, we investigate how these intersectional identities are in turn translated into organisations' activities and claims directed to their members and to external actors, and finally we explore the ways in which the construction of alliances may imply downplaying or integrating the categories they emphasise in their collective identity-making.

Finally, when looking at the empirical cases addressed so far by the literature on intersectionality in social movements, one can see that most studies concentrate on feminist movements, take place in Western contexts, and are developed on a national basis. Within this scenario, little attention is given to other kinds of women's movements that may not define themselves as feminist (Molyneux 2001), as it is often the case with women workers' movements (Cobble 2005) and in particular with movements for informal, precarious, and mostly female workforce, such as domestic workers (relevant exceptions, among others, are Alberti et al. 2013; Bernardino-Costa 2014). Our chapter addresses these shortcomings by looking at the kind of women's labour movement that is rarely researched in this literature, focusing on non-Western contexts, and using a large comparative analysis.

3 The international movement for domestic workers' rights and the case of Ecuador and Colombia

At the global level, domestic workers have been seen as the quintessential example of low-skilled, low-valued, precarious, hidden, and unorganised labourers (Boris and Fish 2014; Sarti 2007; Schwenken 2016). They are partly or fully excluded from labour laws and protections in several countries, and they usually belong to the most impoverished and socially stigmatised groups in each context: migrants, low-caste people, black and indigenous women, and so on, depending on the context. Moreover, their situation across countries has increasingly been impacted by the multidimensional transformations induced by globalisation, such as the intensification of international migration, reorganisation of social classes, the urbanisation of rural and indigenous populations, and changes in gender norms, lifestyles, household organisation, and welfare regimes.

In recent decades, the condition of these workers has become an object of general concern, and several local and global actors have undertaken actions to promote rights and better working conditions in the sector. Among these actors are international organisations such as the ILO and the UN Commission on the Status of Women, as well as NGOs, trade unions, and domestic workers' organisations active at national, regional, and transnational levels (Fish 2017; Marchetti and Garofalo Geymonat 2017). The increased relevance of domestic work as a global governance issue and as a matter of contention parallels the increasing visibility and mobilisation of this category of workers, the strengthening of their organisations and campaigns, and the improvement of normative frameworks that influence their conditions. Key examples – at the transnational level – are the promulgation of the ILO 'Convention No. 189 on decent work for domestic workers' (C189) in 2011[4] and the creation of the International Domestic Workers Federation (IDWF-FITH) in 2012, which has been promoting the global campaign for the ratification of C189 since its founding.[5] These key events have variously affected different national contexts, where international standards and global campaigns on the issue have been received, appropriated, or resisted in different ways by institutional and non-institutional actors, including domestic workers' organisations (Cherubini, Garofalo Geymonat, and Marchetti 2018).

In Ecuador and Colombia, paid domestic work has become an object of increasing attention from both institutional and non-institutional actors in the last decade. During the late 2000s and the 2010s, newly emergent mobilisations in the field have led to the creation or strengthening of paid domestic workers' organisations and to pivotal legislative reforms (among them, the ratification of C189) that are regarded as special achievements of these movements. As we will later discuss, these achievements have been possible partly thanks to the support of institutional actors, as well as national and international NGOs, that have recognised C189 as a strategic opportunity for achieving their goals and have integrated this exogenous factor, its logic and language, into their actions. In general terms, we can say that the struggles for domestic workers' rights have been favoured by the progressive politics in both countries in the last decade, related in Ecuador to Rafael Correa's administration (2007–2017) and in Colombia to the end of the war and subsequent peace process (since 2012). Under these conditions, we see the expansion of rights for domestic workers as part of larger political projects working towards a more egalitarian society and the inclusion of historically marginalised groups as essential to the formation of a renewed national identity (Marchetti 2018).

Other relevant similarities between the two countries have to do with the main characteristics and the composition of the domestic workforce. According to the latest available data, around 681,000 people were employed as domestic workers in Colombia in 2017 and 214,000 in Ecuador in 2018, representing three percent of all workers in both countries.[6] Qualitative accounts collected in interviews with key informants in both countries describe domestic work as a highly feminised sector, mainly employing women from lower social classes and with low educational levels, often coming from the most impoverished regions of the countries, and whose working conditions vary greatly according to their age, ethnicity, and rural or urban residence. Our interviewees agree that the majority of paid domestic workers are Colombian or Ecuadorian nationals, although international migrants from other Latin American countries are also present and include, notably, Colombian refugees and Peruvian migrants in Ecuador, and, more recently, Venezuelan refugees in both countries.

An analysis of quantitative data helps to refine this description. Data show, first, how in both countries internal movements from rural to urban areas and from poor to rich regions – as well as, for the case of Colombia, from the regions most affected by internal war – have long determined the current composition of this workforce.[7] They also show how the composition of this workforce reflects the ethnic and racial diversity of these countries – a key feature of their social stratification and national identity, categorised in terms of relations between 'white,' 'mestiza,' 'black/Afro-descendant,' and 'indigenous' populations.[8] Finally, in both countries domestic workers are more likely to be women, aged over 30, and with a low level of education.[9]

To sum up, Colombia and Ecuador show relevant similarities when it comes to the legal frame regulating domestic worker's labour rights, recent trends in domestic workers' organising, and in the composition of the sector, which appears to be fundamentally shaped by internal migrations, ethnic and racial diversity, and gender-race-class relations rooted in colonial legacy. Despite specific differences that will become clear in the analysis that follows, we are confronted with two national contexts that can be considered as a comparable background for the analysis of the identity and activities of the two selected domestic workers' organisations, which we will discuss in the following sections.

4 The Ecuadorian Domestic Workers Association (ATHE)[10]

ATHE was created in the late 1990s in one of the country's largest cities.[11] It mostly operated at the local level until the mid-2000s, when it expanded its activities and visibility beyond its province of origin and started to articulate claims at a national scale, focusing upon the transformation of the legal and policy frameworks regulating domestic work.

4.1 'We are all domestic workers': gender and class in the construction of collective identity

Since its creation, ATHE has been not only composed but also led by women who work or have worked for many years as domestic workers. According to the narratives these leaders offered in interviews and at public events, ATHE articulates the specific interests and identity of the 'trabajadoras remuneradas de hogar,' meaning the (women employed as) domestic workers. From analysis of the interviews, it can be seen that the term serves to describe a type of labour *and* a social category created by the interplay between two main dimensions of inequality: gender and class position. Indeed, according to ATHE leaders, the specific form of oppression lived by domestic workers seems to be rooted in the gendered and classist construction of (paid and unpaid) domestic work. The idea of reproductive work as a female responsibility and its social, economic, and symbolic devaluation are portrayed as strongly related, and the dominant representation of domestic work as a job for women from lower social classes is reflected in the lack of both labour rights and social respect. For instance, one of the leaders of the association explains the following:

> The social classes that we come from, we are low social classes, whether black, white, indigenous, mestizo or whatever. . . . It is a hard job, it is not recognized, rights are always violated, here we can see the patriarchal system . . . that women in general are considered . . . just because you are a woman, you must be related to reproduction.
>
> (ECU04, ATHE leader)

Along this line of analysis, ATHE leaders seem to think that domestic workers' struggles for labour rights cannot be considered as similar to those of other workers or to be related to the 'universal' interests of the working class. Likewise, the way in which gender, in its interplay with class, applies to the case of domestic workers is understood as significantly different from what happens in the case of other women and other female workers. For this reason, rather than general unions, women's and feminist groups, or gender equality bodies, it is necessary that ad hoc organisations with the specific purpose of addressing the problems of domestic workers are set up. This discourse seems to indicate that the organising process leading to the formation of ATHE may be exemplary of practices of political subjectification that domestic workers activate in reacting to their intersectional marginalisation, at the structural and political levels, through collective action and through the construction of a 'multiple-axes' organisation. This echoes the ethos of 'organising on one's own' described by Benita Roth (2004) in relation to black and chicana feminisms in the United States, as well as what Éléonore Lépinard (2014) has called 'intersectional representation,' defined as one of the possible ways of practicing intersectionality in social movements.

The quote above also shows the specific construction of race differences within ATHE's discourse and collective identity. The organisation presents itself as being inclusive of and representing the interests of all domestic workers, no matter the sector of society they belong to, and in particular, their racial and ethnic background. In other words, while the intersection between class and gender receives most of the political emphasis in the self-representation developed by ATHE leaders, the same cannot be said of other intersections between categories of difference such as race/ethnicity, age, and migration status. On these other issues, the organisation offers a more variegated approach, according to the situation and the level of action. In fact, although forms of discrimination based on race, gender, age, and nationality are often mentioned and denounced by leaders during the interviews and in their internal activities, they are granted less relevance in the formulation of claims directed to external actors, as we explain in the following section.

4.2 ATHE actions and claims

> On the issue of racism, those who suffer from discrimination in paid domestic work are the *compañeras* of Esmeralda,[12] the afros. . . . The *compañeras* who are indigenous, too. . . . Somehow it affects us, because you should put yourself in the other's shoes. For example, in training and empowerment. . . . In fact, we had to work on the strengthening of recognizing ourselves as a woman, as an afro, as a mestiza, as an indigenous woman. Definitely we have worked on these aspects, yes.
>
> (ECU08, ATHE leader)

These words from another leader of the association exemplify the way in which different forms of racial discrimination – intertwined in this case with gender-based discrimination – are addressed in internal activities acting for the empowerment of members (e.g. information and training). Through these internal activities ATHE explicitly addresses the risk of discrimination, exploitation, violence, and abusive behaviour from employers to which specifically Afro-Ecuadorian, indigenous, or migrant domestic workers are exposed to. At the same time, the narrative quoted above implicitly recognises the relative privilege that *mestizas* domestic workers may have, in comparison to domestic workers belonging to other racialised social groups. At this level of action ATHE promotes an intersectional understanding encompassing domestic workers' social position, their possible pathways toward empowerment, and the power asymmetries within their own group.

However, such intersectional awareness with respect to race issues seems to be set aside when it comes to activities directed towards external actors, such as those aimed at influencing government interventions, for example to improve the legal framework for the sector, or to alter the public image of 'domestic work as work.' In this case, the interests and needs of specific sub-groups of domestic workers are subsumed into the general struggle for equality between domestic workers and other workers both in the legal and in the cultural field. In our inter-pretation, this level of ATHE action with regard to ethnic, racial, and other differ-ences can be understood as a case of an additive or 'multiple' approach (Hancock 2007). In other words, race-based discriminations are seen as an additional burden worsening the condition of racialised domestic workers, but not as an intrinsic feature of the social organisation of domestic work.

4.3 'Yo apoyo al Convenio 189, y tu?' Campaigning and strengthening alliances in the labour field

The framing processes described so far emerge more clearly in considering the campaign for the ratification of C189 run by ATHE and its allies from 2011 to 2013. After the promulgation of the convention in Geneva in June 2011, a committee for ratification was formed in Ecuador and the campaign 'Yo apoyo al Convenio 189, y tu?' ('I support Convention 189, and you?') was launched. The campaign developed through a series of awareness-raising interventions in public spaces and in the media and through the participation of technical and political working groups within state institutions and the government, in particular in the Ministries of Labor and Social Security. Key actors on the com-mittee were ATHE, two international NGOs that are long-term allies of ATHE, and other international organisations (including the local office of the ILO). The support of individual policymakers from the governmental party Alianza Pais also proved crucial to this phase, especially in preparing the debate in the National Assembly and creating a large consensus for the ratification, which crossed all political groups. In September 2013, the ratification was approved unanimously by the National Assembly. ATHE and other supporters attended the debate as audience members wore yellow t-shirts with the campaign logo – as did the supportive parliamentarians in their stalls.

The ratification of C189 was portrayed by informants from ATHE as a strategic objective in order to consolidate their position as workers on an equal footing with other workers. The claim for 'equal rights and decent work,' which is central to C189, brings together the ideals of labour equality and human dignity in order to promote the inclusion of domestic workers in the general labour force on equal grounds. In the context of ATHE's interventions, the support for C189 was framed in relation to the need for a new cultural and economic approach to the role of domestic workers in society, considered primarily as a category of vulnerable and discriminated workers.

Within this framework, C189 claims provided an opportunity for the convergence of the organization's objectives and governmental politics relating to labour and class equality. C189 was portrayed as giving expression to the ideals of equality, social progress, and modernisation that, notwithstanding existing limitations, the Correa government fiercely proclaimed to be in the national interest. According to some key informants, the ratification of C189 represented the 'cherry on top' of a period of legal reforms originating with the constitutional process.

ATHE and the Correa government both aimed at the full integration of domestic work into the general labour code, removing all existing normative bias and legislative exceptions concerning minimum wage, working hours, social security coverage, and unionisation rights. In the words of a congresswoman supportive of the campaign:

> The recognition of workers has always been there in Correa's discourse, and this included women domestic workers. . . . For that reason before the approval of Convention 189, the government of the Republic implemented a public policy. . ., to put (domestic workers) on the same level of other workers. . . . What the Convention did, was simply . . . it was like the cherry on top: and the public policy made much earlier was the cake
>
> (ECU14, congresswoman and feminist activist)

These words align with a similar stance on the part of ATHE representatives, as in the following statement:

> Well, I think that we have had this progress in recent years . . . Now, with the Revolución Ciudadana,[13] we achieved at least the unified basic salary, which domestic workers are also entitled to, like any other worker.
>
> (ECU08, ATHE leader)

In observing the campaign for ratification, the advantages of having such a sharply defined agenda in the field of labour rights are evident. These are, firstly, the capacity to formulate pragmatic objectives and, secondly, the possibility of establishing long-term alliances. In fact, the synergy and alignment between ATHE, international NGOs, and the government led to the successful ratification of C189 and to other key achievements in the legal field, which established full equal labour rights for domestic workers in Ecuador. However, pursuing such a sharply defined agenda appears to have come at the cost of simplifying the intersectional approach that ATHE developed in their internal actions and claims. However, rather than constituting a 'failure' or lack of ability to put intersectionality into practice, this may represent a strategic reading of the political situation, on the part of ATHE, and its need to find common ground with potential allies, particularly with the government.

5 The Colombian Domestic Workers Union (UTDC)

UTDC was founded in the early 2010s in one of the largest cities in Colombia by a group of Afro-Colombian domestic workers – most of them internal war refugees. At the time of our fieldwork (2018), the organisation had gathered around 200 members and was one of the most visible domestic workers' associations in the country.

5.1 'The first ethnic-based domestic workers' union of the country': collective identity and interests between gender, class, and race

Similar to what we have described in relation to ATHE, UTDC can be considered an example of organising which responds to an 'intersectional representation' strategy (Lépinard 2014), through which a social group subjected to social and political marginalisation organises on their own (Roth 2004) and creates a new collective actor representing its own voice and interests. In the case of UTDC, however, the element of race is integrated into the collective identity and enters, along with class and gender, in the analysis of domestic workers' conditions developed by the organisation. Domestic work is addressed not solely as a gendered but also as a racialised sector; the specific experiences of gendered racism and racialised economic exploitation lived by Afro-Colombian women employed as domestic workers are recognised and lead to the construction of what the activists describe as 'the first ethnic-based domestic workers' union of the country,' as their website clearly states.

UTDC openly relies on an intersectional discursive repertoire based on the articulation of gender, class, and race – where the dimension of race and racism is mostly shaped around the experience of black women working in the sector – and, more specifically, the experience of internally displaced Afro-Colombian women. Other experiences of racism that are in place in domestic work and in Colombian society are discursively acknowledged by the leaders, for instance those lived by indigenous or migrant domestic workers. However, this does not lead to the articulation of specific claims for each of these subgroups. In fact, this is how one of the leaders describes the union's aims and organising process:

This process [the organizing process that led to the creation of the UCDW] brought positive results for us as domestic workers[14] and in particular, for black women, women victims of armed conflict, displaced women, female heads of households, abused women, raped women, discriminated women, women who have gone, as domestic workers, through all kind of things that this country cannot even imagine. And why have we arrived at domestic work? Because we are not asked 'what do you know? What is your (job) experience?' But the color, the race, this marks me in a way that I have to be a domestic worker, to clean floors, to mop and to be in that place, only for this color. However, UTDC is an inclusive, not exclusionary, union; even if its name says Afro women, there are mestizas and indigenous women in the union . . . The advocacy is not only for Afro women, women from Antioquia or Chocó[15] . . . We do this for the benefit of all women nationwide.

(COL03, UTDC leader)

As this excerpt suggests, UTDC leaders present the union as being at the same time rooted in the black and Afro-descendant identity and open to all domestic workers – black, mestizas, and indigenous – and concerned simultaneously with the end of racist discrimination against Afro-Colombian women and with the advancement of labour rights for all domestic workers. In other words, they present the organisation as representative of both the specific interests of black domestic workers and the general interests of the category of labourers. This kind of articulation of collective identity within the union should be framed in the broader political context, characterised by a long-term trend towards the re-integration of historically marginalised ethnic communities (among them, Afro-Colombians) within the national identity since the 1991 constitution, by restorative policies targeting displaced people (most of them belonging to the black minority) deployed by state and civic society actors, and by the rising awareness of women's rights and the conditions of racial minorities, in the context of the peace process. Within this framework, C189 provided opportunities for a renewed politicisation of paid domestic workers' rights, after decades of low mobilisation and low visibility due to the internal war, political violence, and the repression of social and labour movements.

5.2 UTDC actions and claims

The objective of UTDC, its desire, its aspiration is that all . . . first of all, to show the government and society that we are here in this world, we are present, we are domestic workers women, that we also have the same value, the same rights as other workers. . . . God, we have to raise the alarm to the government, the State, that here we are domestic workers, that we also exist and that we also are Colombian. . . . Our message? Domestic workers [feminine form used] give value to your work and do not wait for others to do that, do it right but give it the right price too. The point is, I do my job well and I demand decent treatment, because domestic work is not a favor, domestic work, as Convention 189 states, is work. It is like the nurse, like the professor, the gardener, domestic work is a job and a profession.

(COL03, UTDC leader)

This quotation from the interview with a UTDC leader exemplifies the main claims of the organisation, which aims at transforming the conditions of domestic workers with respect to the economic and cultural terrain and at fostering their recognition as part of the Colombian society, economy, and national identity. According to our observations and interviews, the union pursues these objectives both through training and sensitising activities directed towards its members and through political pressure targeting state institutions in order to improve the legal frame regulating domestic workers' labour rights.

Similar to what we described in the Ecuadorian case, the internal activities seem to draw on a complex and intersectional reading of the reality and needs of domestic workers, whose pathways towards empowerment encompass the overcoming of multiple processes of marginalisation and require the reconstruction of a positive self-image.

For instance, within the actions that we do internally, we do training in gender equality, we do training in labor rights, ethnic training, these are the activities we have designed and that we emphasize, because we know that on the issue of gender equality . . . all this inequality for being a woman . . . and it is not the same to be a woman, in Colombia, and to be a black woman, neither the same to be a black woman as to be a poor woman, so . . . all this makes the difference, it makes everything harder. . . . We also have sexual and reproductive education workshops, that are very important because as women, all these things are going to help us, because we cannot go on with this mindset that black women are just there to give birth and to work in a house . . . So all those programs are designed with our characteristics in mind.

(COL03, UTDC leader)

What happens at the level of the activities directed towards external and institutional actors is, once again, quite different. As with ATHE, the central goal is the achievement of equal labour rights. However, as we will show in the next section, UTDC articulates the struggle in the labour field in a unique manner, in which feminist discourse converges with the field of action of the care economy.

5.3 The Ley de Prima campaign: convergence between domestic workers' rights and feminist views on the value of care

UTDC began its activities when the main issue at stake for domestic workers' struggles was the implementation of C189 – which had earlier been ratified by the government without major opposition – and the transformation of the legal frame regulating labour rights and access to social security for domestic workers, in compliance with the principle set by the convention. In fact, Colombia ratified C189 in 2012 (Law 1595 of 2012)[16] and thereafter adopted a number of measures that included this category of workers within the social security system (Decree 2616 of 2013 expanding access to social security to 'per days' domestic workers; Decree 721 giving access to family benefits). In this frame, UTDC engaged in its first and most relevant campaign, for the so-called Ley de Prima (Law on Bonus).

The campaign started at the end of 2013 and was promoted by UTDC in alliance with two non-profit organisations providing technical support to UTDC activities since its creation – one involved in the labour field and another in the promotion of social communication, well-being, and education – and with two feminist congresswomen from the Green Party who played a key role in the process. The building of this coalition was facilitated by the fact that during the same period these UTDC allies were also involved in a feminist debate on the value of reproductive work and on the so-called care economy (Folbre 2001; Boris and Parreñas 2010; Lutz 2011) and in the Comité para la Economía del Cuidado (Care Economy Committee),[17] a space for planning and negotiation composed of institutional and non-institutional actors created in 2010. The campaign developed through several public events, communication interventions in traditional media and social networks, and lobbying activities. It culminated in parliamentary debates through which the law was finally approved in June 2016 (Law 1788).

The law extended the right to receive the 'prima de servicio' (that is, the thirteenth check given to all workers in 'productive' sectors) to domestic workers, who were previously excluded from such provision. Notably in this case, the argument at the centre of this historical exclusion – the fact that (paid and unpaid) domestic work does not produce any profit, in other words it is *reproductive* as opposed to *productive* – was overturned through this campaign, drawing on feminist debates around the value of care. In fact, since the late 2000s, feminist groups and individuals – most of them coming from the academy and public sector institutions – were promoting a debate on the care economy in Colombia. One of their main achievements was the National Law on the Care Economy approved in 2010 (Law 1413 of 2010), which gives full recognition to the social and economic value of unpaid care and domestic work and lays the basis for its financial and economic measurement in official statistics, as part of the national GDP. UTDC and the other actors campaigning for the bonus used these tools for making the value of paid domestic work visible. This in turn opened the possibility of correcting what domestic workers and their allies reframed as discrimination of a valuable category of workers who actively contribute to the national economy and to Colombian society. This is how the spokesperson of one of the allied NGOs and participant in the Committee describes the process:

> Definitely in recent years the care economy is what has given the feminist movement the figures that economists require when making public

policies . . . I can tell you that in almost all the more or less serious discussions and analyses on the matter of gender equality, in Colombia we can make use of the figures coming from sectors of the Care Economy, and in this way the discussion is among peers; before it was a bit romantic and abstract.

(COL18, member of an NGO supporting UTDC)

Therefore, the campaign developed by UTDC may be seen as an example of convergence between domestic workers' struggle for labour rights and feminist struggles for the transformation of the socio-cultural representation of reproductive work and recognition of the value of women's work and of their contribution to the economy and society. In the Colombian case, the legal and discursive frame on the social and economic value of reproductive work has transformed into one which is favourable to domestic workers' struggles, even if it was primarily related to unpaid work performed by women for their families. By stretching the original scope of the care economy framework to include paid work, UTDC has revealed – and challenged – the epistemic and institutional privileges embedded in the social organisation of care and domestic work, exposing the problematic assumptions present in the division between paid/unpaid, skilled/unskilled, and productive/reproductive labour.

6 Discussion

Both organisations studied in the present chapter, ATHE and UTDC, since their creation, have been composed and led by women employed as domestic workers, who have reacted to the lack of rights and social recognition experienced by their category in society at large as well as to the situation of political marginalisation they live in institutional politics, in the local civil society, and within existing social movements. According to our analysis, both organisations exemplify processes of political subjectification and organising that come from multiply-marginalised groups and lead to the construction of 'multiple-axis' organisations, to complex collective identities, and to forms of intersectional praxis. Yet, the kinds of intersectional politics developed by the two organisations diverge in relation to several aspects, namely (a) in relation to the categories and experiences of inequality that are emphasised in the building of collective identity and in the pursuit of inclusivity and unity and (b) in their alliances with other actors.

First, we have seen that the two organisations define the specific form of marginalisation lived by domestic workers differently, as resulting from 'intersectional' or 'multiple/additive' relations between different sources of inequality. According to our analysis of the self-presentation of the leaders of the two organisations, the Colombian organisation appears to propose an intersectional understanding of the interplay between gender, class, and race in shaping domestic workers' experience of discrimination, while the Ecuadorian organisation points out the intersectional relationship between class and gender, but is less keen to identify the intersection with race as constitutive of their subordinated condition. ATHE sees race-based discrimination as something that contributes to increased levels of exploitation suffered by non-white and not-mestiza domestic workers, but they do not make this into a central feature of their collective identity, thus maintaining an 'additive/multiple' approach to racism and racial difference. Second, we have seen that both organisations portray themselves as representing the interests of *all* domestic workers, but they rely on different arguments to sustain this claim. ATHE purports to be inclusive of all domestic workers *despite* ethnic and racial differences: its strategy consists of transcending such differences in order to include the needs of all categories of domestic workers into its general struggle. By contrast, UTDC claims to represent the interests of the entire category (including white and indigenous workers) *on the ground of* racial differences: since Afro-Colombians are 'the ones who suffer the most,' i.e. the most stigmatised and vulnerable group, they can embrace the perspective of all other vulnerable groups. Moreover, we have shown that the two organisations have different strategies in their campaigns in the field of labour rights and in establishing alliances with different types of actors: in Ecuador, the left-wing government that promotes favourable politics towards the working class, and in Colombia the feminist movement engaged in the debate on the social and economic value of care work. Last, we have seen how, in the Colombian case, such an alliance entails a challenge to the epistemic and institutional privileges often present in the care economy discourse mobilised by feminist actors. Indeed, the alliance produced around the campaign for the Ley de Prima was able to overcome the initial exclusive focus on unpaid reproductive work that feminists had developed, by exposing how it problematically reproduces the divisions between women based on class and race.

Conversely, the analysis of the claims and actions carried out by the two organisations has shown relevant similarities. Importantly, we have seen that, while complex and intersectional views seem to inform the internal activities of both organisations, when it comes to the campaigns and lobby activities directed at external actors, they seem to adopt a rather simplified (often quite unitary, single-axis) strategy, mostly focused on labour issues. This apparent move towards the simplification of the issues at stake may be understood as a result of the convergence between actors' strategic choices and the opportunities given to them in a specific setting. Notably, the adoption of simplified claims in the organisations' lobbying activity and campaigns should not obscure the relevance of intersectional orientation and practices at other levels of their activity and collective identity.

7 Conclusion

In this chapter, domestic workers' movements are seen as forms of collective action developed by the multiply-marginalised social groups employed in the sector such as migrant, low-class, racialised, and rural women. We have shown how domestic workers' mobilisations may offer a space where several usually separated social struggles converge, such as those for equal labour rights and class equity, women's rights, and recognition for ethnic and racialised minorities. At the same time, the regulation of domestic work is a contentious issue, able to reveal conflicting interests and power asymmetries based on gender, class, race, and so on. For these reasons, the analysis of these movements allowed us to look at how the intersections of gender, class, race, ethnicity, and other relevant categories in each context are enfolded in, and in turn shape, the processes taking place within these movements, their identity-making activities, their strategies and actions, and their alliances.

Overall the results of our analysis show how, when using intersectionality as an analytical tool, it is particularly important to unpack the various aspects involved in the mobilisation process, such as collective identity, elaboration of agenda and claims, strategies and actions, and alliances and conflict with other actors, in order to avoid assuming a spontaneous coherence between the different levels of analysis. As our case studies reflect, intersectionality might emerge as a key element in some moments of a mobilisation process, while being a marginal one in others. For instance, it may be present in the discourse produced by the movement but not reflected in its action; it may be a central issue in some campaigns and not in others; it may shape the movement's composition but not its claims; it may be a central concern in members' recruitment but not be reflected in alliances built with other movements, and so on. Movements' strategies and positioning with respect to this terrain may change when moving from one field of action to another (for example between the separate fields of labour rights, anti-racism, and human rights), from one scale to another (such as local, national, and transnational organising), as well as over time – depending on both the power relations affecting the field and the strategic choices of the movements. Moreover, in distinct aspects and moments of their activity, social movements may address some forms of inequality, some intersections between social categories and social groups, while silencing or failing to address some others. The meaning and political salience assigned to gender, race, class, and other social categories vary not only between different national contexts and in different domestic workers' organisations, but also within the same organisation in relation to different aspects of its activity.

Notes

1 The present chapter is the result of the authors' shared analyses and writing. Daniela Cherubini is the author of sections 2 and 5, Giulia Garofalo Geymonat is the author of sections 1 and 6, Sabrina Marchetti is the author of sections 3 and 4. This publication has received funding from the European Research Council (ERC) under the European Union's Horizon 2020 Research and Innovation Programme, under Grant Agreement n. 678783 (DomEQUAL). Principal Investigator Prof. Sabrina Marchetti, Ca' Foscari University of Venice. www.domequal.eu.

2 We thank our country experts Gabriela Alvarado Perez (Ecuador) and Maria Fernanda Cepeda Anaya (Colombia) for their contribution to gathering data for our analysis.

3 The names of these organisations have been modified to ensure the anonymity of participants.

4 Convention No. 189 and the relative Recommendation No. 201 set international labour standards for the paid care and domestic work sector, equating labour rights for these

workers to those of other workers in ratifying countries. At the time of writing 25 countries in the world have already ratified the convention. www.ilo.org/dyn/normlex/en/f?p= NORMLEXPUB:11300:0::NO::P11300_INSTRUMENT_ID:2551460 [accessed 31 October 2018].

5 From webpage information at http://idwfed.org/en/campaigns/ratify-c189 [accessed 31 October 2018].

6 Data are taken from the *Gran Encuesta Integrada de Hogares* of the *Departamento Administrativo Nacional de Estadística* (Colombia) and the *Encuesta Nacional de Empleo, Desempleo y Subempleo* of the *Instituto Nacional de Estadística y Censos* (Ecuador).

7 According to available census data, in Colombia (2005) 41 percent of domestic workers were internal migrants and/or refugees. In the regions of Bogotá, Valle del Cauca, and Antioquia – where four out of ten domestic workers were employed, most of them in the cities of Bogotá, Cali, and Medellin – this percentage stood at 87 percent, 57 percent, and 23 percent respectively. Similarly, in Ecuador (2010) internal migrants represented 31 percent of the domestic workforce. These shares peaked at 56 percent and 44 percent in Pichincha and Guayas, two provinces that alone host more than half (56 percent) of domestic workers living in the country, most of them in the main cities of Quito and Guayaquil. In both countries internal migrants (or refugees) are counted as those who work in a region or province other than their birth region/province.

8 In Colombia the vast majority of domestic workers define themselves as 'white' (85%), followed by 'black' (12%), and 'indigenous' (3%); similar percentages are found in the total population (85%, 10%, and 3%respectively). In Ecuador domestic workers are 'mestizas' (69%), 'montubias' (7.6%), Afro-Ecuadorian (7%), 'indigenous' (6%) and 'white' (5%). Afro-Ecuadorian people are overrepresented in domestic work (accounting for 7% vs. 4% among all workers), while other groups account for similar percentages in domestic work and in the total population.

9 Women represent 95 percent of domestic workers (vs. 50 percent of 'all workers') in Ecuador and 91 percent (vs. 51 percent of 'all workers') in Colombia. Of those, 84 percent have an educational level lower than secondary school vs. 72 percent of 'all workers' in Ecuador; 81 percent vs. 74 percent of 'all workers' in Colombia.

10 Names of the organisations have been modified to ensure the anonymity of participants.

11 Name removed to ensure anonymity.

12 One of the regions with a large Afro-descendant population, from which many internal migrants come and are employed as domestic workers in the main cities.

13 The Citizens' Revolution, the political and socio-economic project at the basis of Rafael Correa's government and the 2008 Constitution.

14 'Trabajadoras domésticas' in the original. The feminine form is used throughout the sentence.

15 The region with the highest percentage of black and Afro-Colombian groups (75.68%); also one of the poorest regions of the country.

16 The Convention entered into force in 2014.

17 Fictional name.

References

Alberti, Gabriella, Jane Holgate, and Matie Tapia. 2013. "Organising Migrants as Workers or as Migrant Workers? Intersectionality, Trade Unions and Precarious Work." *The International Journal of Human Resource Management* 24 (22): 4132–4148.

Anthias, Floya. 2012. "Hierarchies of Social Location, Class and Intersectionality: Towards a Translocational Frame." *International Sociology* 28 (1): 121–138.

Bassel, Leah, and Éléonore Lépinard. 2014. "Introduction." *Politics & Gender* 10 (1): 115–117.

Bernardino-Costa, Joaze. 2014. "Intersectionality and Female Domestic Workers' Unions in Brazil." *Women's Studies International Forum* 46: 72–80.

Boris, Eileen, and Jennifer N. Fish. 2014. "'Slaves No More': Making Global Labor Standards for Domestic Workers." *Feminist Studies* 40 (2): 411–443.

Boris, Eileen, and Rhacel Salazar Parreñas. 2010. *Intimate Labors: Cultures, Technologies, and the Politics of Care.* Stanford, CA: Stanford University Press.

Carastathis, Anna. 2013. "Identity Categories as Potential Coalitions." *Signs* 38 (4): 941–965.

Cherubini, Daniela, Giulia Garofalo Geymonat, and Sabrina Marchetti. 2018. "Global Rights and Local Struggles: The Case of the ILO Convention n. 189 on Domestic Work." *Partecipazione e Conflitto* 11 (3): 717–742.

Chun, Jennifer Jihye, George Lipsitz, and Young Shin. 2013. "Intersectionality as a Social Movement Strategy: Asian Immigrant Women Advocates." *Signs* 38 (4): 917–940.

Cobble, Dorothy Sue. 2005. *The Other Women's Movement: Workplace Justice and Social Rights in Modern America.* Princeton, NJ: Princeton University Press.

Cole, Elizabeth. 2008. "Coalition as a Model for Intersectionality: From Practice to Theory." *Sex Roles* 59 (5–6): 443–453.

Coley, Jonathan S. 2014. "Social Movements and Bridge Building: Religious and Sexual Identity Conflicts." In *Intersectionality and Social Change*, edited by Lynne. M. Woehrle, 125–151. Bingley, UK: Emerald.

Cruells López, Marta, and Sonia Ruiz García. 2014. "Political Intersectionality Within the Spanish Indignados Social Movement." In *Intersectionality and Social Change*, edited by Lynne M. Woehrle, 325. Bingley, UK: Emerald.

Evans, Elizabeth. 2016. "Intersectionality as a Feminist Praxis in the UK." *Women's Studies International Forum* 59: 67–75.

Ferree, Myra Marx, and Silke Roth. 1998. "Gender, Class and the Interaction Between Social Movements: A Strike of West Berlin Day Care Workers." *Gender and Society* 12 (6): 626–648.

Fish, Jennifer. N. 2017. *Domestic Workers of the World Unite! A Global Movement for Dignity and Human Rights.* New York, NY: New York University Press.

Folbre, Nancy. 2001. *The Invisible Heart: Economics and Family Values.* New York, NY: New Press.

Hancock, Ange-Marie. 2007. "When Multiplication Doesn't Equal Quick Addition: Examining Intersectionality as a Research Paradigm." *Perspectives on Politics* 5 (1): 63–79.

Lapèrriere, Marie, and Eléonore Lépinard. 2016. "Intersectionality as a Tool for Social Movements: Strategies of Inclusion and Representation in the Québécois Women's Movement." *Politics* 36 (4): 374–382.

Lépinard, Éléonore. 2014. "Doing Intersectionality: Repertoires of Feminist Practices in France and Canada." *Gender & Society* 28 (6): 877–903.

Lutz, Helma. 2011. *The New Maids: Transnational Women and the Care Economy.* London: Zed Books.

Maddison, Sarah, and Emma Partridge. 2014. "Agonism and Intersectionality: Indigenous Women, Violence and Feminist Collective Identity." In *Intersectionality and Social Change*, edited by Lynne M. Woehrle, 27–52. Bingley, UK: Emerald.

Marchetti, Sabrina. 2018. "The Global Governance of Paid Domestic Work: Comparing the Impact of ILO Convention No. 189 in Ecuador and India." *Critical Sociology* 44 (7–8): 1191–1205.

254 Daniela Cherubini et al.

Marchetti, Sabrina, and Giulia Garofalo Geymonat, eds. 2017. *Domestic Workers Speak: A Global Fight for Rights and Recognition*. London: Open Democracy.

Molyneux, Maxine.2001. *Women's Movements in International Perspective: Latin America and Beyond*. London: Springer.

Okechukwu, Amaka. 2014. "Shadows of Solidarity: Identity, Intersectionality, and Frame Resonance." In *Intersectionality and Social Change*, edited by Lynne M. Woehrle, 153–180. Bingley, UK: Emerald.

Predelli, Line Nyhagen, and Beatrice Halsaa, eds. 2012. *Majority-Minority Relations in Contemporary Women's Movements: Strategic Sisterhood*. Houndmills, Basingstoke: Palgrave Macmillan.

Roth, Benita. 2004. *Separate Roads to Feminism: Black, Chicana, and White Feminist Movements in America's Second Wave*. Cambridge, UK: Cambridge University Press.

Rothman, Jay. 2014. "From Intragroup Conflict to Intergroup Cooperation." In *Intersectionality and Social Change*, edited by Lynne M. Woehrle, 107–123. Bingley, UK: Emerald.

Sarti, Raffaella. 2007. "The Globalisation of Domestic Service in a Historical Perspective." In *Migration and Domestic Work: A European Perspective on a Global Theme*, edited by Helma Lutz, 77–98. Aldershot: Ashgate.

Schwenken, Helen 2016. "The Emergence of an Impossible Movement: Domestic Workers Organize Globally." In *Transnational Struggles for Recognition: New Perspectives on Civil Society Since the 20th Century*, edited by Dieter Gosewinkel and Dieter Rucht, 205228. New York, NY: Berghahn Books.

Strolovitch, Dara Z. 2007. *Affirmative Advocacy: Race, Class, and Gender in Interest Group Politics*. Chicago, IL: University of Chicago Press.

Townsend-Bell, Erica. 2011. "What Is Relevance? Defining Intersectional Praxis in Uruguay." *Political Research Quarterly* 64 (1): 187–199.

Verloo, Mieke. 2013. "Intersectional and Cross-Movement Politics and Policies: Reflection on Current Practices and Debates." *Signs* 38 (4): 1893–8915.

Yuval-Davis, Nira. 2015. "Situated Intersectionality and Social Inequality." *Raisons Politiques* 2: 91–100.

Chapter 13

Queer Muslims, autonomous organising, and the UK LGBT+ movement

Abbie Bonane

Introduction

LGBT+ movements across Europe[1] have made significant progress over the past couple of decades (Ayoub 2016). Specific goals, such as same-sex marriage and adoption rights, have been achieved in some countries, although LGBT+ movements remain vigilant in the face of threats to hard-won gains (Verloo 2018). Thus far, the juridical successes of the international movement has enabled some activists and organisations to focus on a wider range of issues, for instance biphobia or transphobia (Weiss 2011), as well as exploring dynamics of power and privilege within the movement (Alimahomed 2010; Logie and Rwigema 2014). However, despite the well-documented rise in Islamophobia across the West (Morgan 2016), there remains relatively little attention paid to queer Muslims, whose very identities are coded as diametrically opposed (Rahman 2010; El Tayeb 2012). Queer Muslims experience the intersection of homophobia and Islamophobia, as well as patterns of Islamophobia within some queer spaces and homophobia within some religious spaces. Indeed, structural and cultural patterns of privilege, which produce and exacerbate both homophobia and Islamophobia, render the very idea of a queer Muslim as an abject and, thus, marginalised identity.

Research into the process of 'coming out' for British gay Muslim men has found that they face a 'bi-dimensional homophobia from ethno-religious ingroup members and the general population,' which poses an existential threat to their identity (Jaspal and Siraj 2011). Studies from the US have also identified that gay Muslims have to negotiate social dynamics within a gay culture dominated by white privilege, and that this poses a difficult obstacle to full integration within the LGBT+ movement (Minwalla et al. 2005). Strategies that individuals adopt in order to reconcile, and legitimise, being both queer and Muslim, include queering religious texts (Peumans 2014) and creating support structures of solidarity (Kugle 2014), a strategy which this chapter explores in greater detail later.

For queer Muslims, the post 9/11 context has proven to be a particularly dangerous time. Indeed, Jasbir Puar conceptualised homonationalism to identify and analyse the conflagration between LGBT+ and nationalist discourse and policies, especially in the areas of immigration and foreign policy, which reinforced a binary distinction between the West and Islam (2007, 2017). Puar argued that the downward trajectory of Muslims post 9/11 has to be seen in relation, and direct contrast to, the upward trajectory of (some) queer people who sought to distance themselves from queer Muslims in order to achieve landmark legislative goals (2007, 2017). While Puar's work on homonationalism centres mostly on a US context, she notes its applicability for the UK, identifying LGBT+ activist groups such as OutRage! as an example of a group which utilised homonationalist rhetoric to paint a divide between being queer and Muslim. Moreover, she observes that white, nationalist queers in the UK draw upon the post-9/11 'war on terror' era imagery of the Middle Eastern 'terrorist' as a significant threat to the LGBT+ community. This chapter aims to examine the UK homonational scene more closely, using Puar's concept of homonationalism in order to provide an analysis of the (lack of) inclusion of queer Muslims in LGBT+ activism in the UK, and to identify an upwards trajectory in what has been a nominally homonational LGBT+ scene, one that constructs and upholds monolithic images of queerness and resists notions of inclusivity, to a more intersectional movement that has slowly begun to welcome queer Muslims.

The de-homonationalisation of the movement has been staggered, with mainstream LGBT+ movements opting for more generalised notions of solidarity over explicitly denouncing specific facets of homonationalism (i.e. decrying 'discrimination' when 'transphobia' or 'Islamophobia' would have been applicable). Consequently, because of this generalised push for inclusion, there has been a rise in autonomous organising amongst queer Muslims in the UK who have sought to tackle Islamophobic-homonational rhetoric directly. Mainstream organisations such as Stonewall have sought to provide help and visibility to autonomous organisers, through coalitional intersectionality (Evans and Lépinard, this volume) which demonstrates a commitment to engaging with and supporting the queer Muslim community, although as noted earlier this has mainly been addressed through general calls for inclusion rather than through a direct rebuttal of homonationalism.

Drawing upon interviews, participant observation at an autonomous conference for queer people of colour, and an analysis of leading national LGBT+ organisation Stonewall, the chapter argues that despite the best efforts of mainstream LGBT+ activism to adopt, or promote, intersectional activist strategies which resist the marginalisation of historically oppressed groups within the community, this has not been a key priority. The chapter begins with an overview of homonationalism as a concept, exploring how it speaks to, and is an integral part of, intersectional analysis; the chapter then sets out the methods before turning to the empirical analysis.

Homonationalism and intersectionality

Much of the debate concerning intersectionality within the queer movement has been considered through the lens of homonationalism, thus closely linking the actions and discourse of social movement activists and the nation state in various parts of the world, especially in their approaches to the war on terror (Puar 2007; Haritaworn 2008; Kuntsman 2008). Historically, far-right ideology has been at odds with gender and sexual diversity; both are considered antithetical to the patriarchal nationalist ideal of what it means to be part of a nation state (Nagel 1998). LGBT+ communities were often easy targets for nationalist governments, with minority groups and individuals depicted as 'enemies' of the state, alongside racial minorities and ideological opponents.

However, post-9/11 nation states have been paying increasing attention to gay rights. The growing acceptance of LGBT+ people has created a progressive consensus surrounding gender and sexual diversity, one which reinforces, and indeed relies upon, the Arab Muslim 'other' who opposes this consensus (Ritchie 2015). This has led to a partial realignment within populist and far-right ideology, wherein the inclusion and safeguarding of LGBT+ people and culture is equated with Western ideals of modernity (Puar 2007, 2017). LGBT+ rights have now been reframed as Western democratic rights, and defending those rights has become a strategic objective for both the nation state as well as for, traditionally homophobic, nationalists. In the UK, for example, the far-right English Defence League established an 'LGBT division' in 2010, which eventually spawned the 'Gays Against Sharia' campaign.[2] This shift, which celebrates white heteronormative forms of queerness, should also be understood within what Lisa Duggan refers to as the 'new homonormativity' (2002), whereby gay movements seek to uphold, rather than contest, heteronormative institutions and cultures, as well engage in and promote the imperialist framing of Islam and Islamic countries as antithetical to gay rights.

When some Western governments began including, and even celebrating, LGBT+ people as part of their national fabric, they also started to use gay rights as a barometer of a nation's progressiveness. The populist and far right, to some extent, followed suit, which created new forms of solidarities amongst unlikely allies (Binnie and Klesse 2012). The turn towards including LGBT+ people within national and nationalist politics also resulted in a desire to defend those communities, principally from the threats posed to their existence by the nation's immigrant and racial and religious minority populations. Great emphasis was placed upon the incompatibility of religious or cultural approaches to gender and sexuality, for that typically read Islam, with the very existence of the LGBT+ community. A binary was established whereby religious minorities were framed as hostile to, or unwilling to accept, the nation's democratic and progressive values. By reinforcing this narrative, Islamophobic rhetoric was given greater legitimacy, and notably amongst some LGBT+ people.[3] In short, the progressive, homo-inclusive West was positioned against the backwards, homophobic 'others' of the East.

It is within this context that queer assimilation was achieved through working within the framework of a white, heteronormative hierarchy, one which excluded, amongst others, queer Muslims. Hence, those LGBT+ individuals given a national profile, or those who took on the role of spokesperson, were typically those who most closely resembled white heteronormative sensibilities. As a result, scholars and activists have called for greater attention to be paid to the 'lived realities' of queer Muslims (Jivraj and De Jong 2011). Questioning structural issues, which reinforces the privilege of some within the LGBT+ movement, is a difficult process and is perhaps a somewhat nebulous goal. Finally, and more broadly, Muslims are called upon to present themselves as 'loyal citizens' in the face of terrorism (Van Es 2019).

This chapter provides a case study analysis of the extent to which queer Muslims are included within mainstream campaigns and discourse of the LGBT+ movement in the UK. The turn towards homonationalism within queer scholarship has brought the issue of inclusion to the fore, despite ongoing theoretical disagreements about the precise contours and utility of homonationalism as a concept (Heike Schotten 2016). Intersectionality, and in particular the acknowledgement of the queer Muslim community, is an issue that was neglected during the whitewashed early decades of the LGBT+ rights movement (Rahman 2010), and then actively resisted in the post-9/11 homonational arena. More recently, there has been a noticeable attempt to undo constructed monolithic images and hierarchies of how the modern queer in the Western world 'should be' (Alimahomed 2010). Accordingly, intersectionality has an important role to play in revealing and contesting patterns of marginalisation and privilege within the LGBT+ movement vis-à-vis the queer Muslim community.

This chapter speaks to the wider literature on LGBT+ activism, homonationalism, and intersectionality. The research finds that there has been a rise in queer Muslim autonomous organising over the past few years, and that this has, at least in part, been a result of marginalisation within the broader movement and an outward rejection of the homonationalist construction of the 'anti-queer terrorist' Muslim that featured within the discourse of prominent UK LGBT+ rights actors like Peter Tatchell (Puar 2007).

Methods

Queer Muslims arguably constitute a hard-to-reach group, not least when we consider the homonationalist context. Indeed, Asifa Siraj has reflected on the specific difficulties of undertaking research on Muslim lesbians who are 'isolated and 'invisible' (2011, see also Yip 2008). Recent media coverage in the UK has explored the anonymous and discreet lives that queer Muslims are forced to lead, as they negotiate their identity within the spaces between Islamophobia and homophobia.[4] As a result, queer Muslim activism has the potential to be difficult to identify, especially if it consists of informal and/or highly private groups. However, as a queer Muslim, my own social location has enabled me to access spaces and be aware of issues that may otherwise have flown beneath the radar.

This chapter explores queer Muslims within the UK LGBT+ movement. The UK is a particularly useful case study for this topic given that it has a vibrant and high-profile LGBT+ movement, as well as a sizeable Muslim community.

The chapter has two key empirical foci: analysis of the leading LGBT+ rights organisation Stonewall and a study mapping and analysing autonomous organising amongst queer Muslims. Founded in London in 1989 as a response to the UK government's Section 28 legislation, which forbade the 'promotion' or even discussion of LGBT+ people in schools, Stonewall aims to combat homophobic stigma and raise awareness of LGBT+ issues in the UK and abroad. In the 30 years since its inception, Stonewall has campaigned and lobbied for LGBT+ employment rights, parenting rights, partnership rights, marriage equality, and equalising the age of consent for LGBT+ people.[5] The research highlighted later explores Stonewall's recent activism and includes analysis of their website, materials, campaigns, and speeches by the current chief executive. The research sought to identify whether, how, when, where, and in what ways Stonewall had engaged with issues of Islamophobia and whether they had explicitly tried to include queer Muslims in their activism.

The second empirical element is focused on autonomous organising amongst queer Muslims in the UK. Participant observation was used to gather data at an activist conference entitled 'LGBTIQ+, Intersectionality and Islam.' The conference was the first of its kind to be held in the UK, and occurred on 23 February 2019 in Birmingham – full field notes were taken and analysed. I undertook a number of informal interviews throughout the day, as well as attending panel sessions to hear from activists and listen to discussions. As noted previously, my own particular social location played a critical part in enabling me to gain access to this space, but it also meant that activists and attendees were happy to engage with me and this research project. Finally, the research on autonomous organising presented in this chapter also includes analysis of the activities, campaigns, and websites of two new explicitly intersectional groups – Hidayah and London Queer Muslims.

Social media has undoubtedly lent a voice to many marginalised and 'non-homonormative' queers, i.e. those who are not white, cis, able-bodied, and affluent. It offers an insight into the unique prejudices queer Muslims experience, both within their own religious communities and from LGBT+ spaces; the chapter does not present an exhaustive nor systematic analysis of social media activism but will, at times, make reference to online debates which have been particularly important for thinking about the role of queer Muslims within the LGBT+ community. Of course, the research presented in this chapter only tells half of the story; indeed, the wider project of which this chapter forms a part also explores the homophobia experienced by queer Muslims in religious spaces.

Stonewall

Stonewall is the UK's largest, and most high-profile, LGBT+ civil society organisation. Over the last few years, and specifically under the leadership of Ruth Hunt (who took over as chief executive in 2014), Stonewall has sought to become more inclusive and intersectional in their priorities and campaigning.[6] Indeed, during the last five years Stonewall has pivoted to a strategy that is best understood as intersectionality as inclusivity (Evans and Lépinard, this volume) – seeking to abandon a politics that has been described as 'catering for white, middle-class gay male dominance.' In order to analyse the extent to which Stonewall promotes an intersectional form of organising which includes queer Muslims and the specific intersections between Islamophobia and homophobia, this section of the chapter considers their mission statement; a report they produced on discrimination within the movement; their 'Come Out for LGBT' campaign; and their responses to a recent row over the teaching of LGBT+ issues within UK schools.

Stonewall's mission statement illustrates the ways in which they incorporate intersectionality within their priorities. For instance, one of their key concerns is ensuring the safety of all within the LGBT+ community, and they explicitly state that they are committed to improving inclusion and visibility both in the mainstream and within LGBT+ spaces, specifically mentioning the need to tackle prejudices and discrimination within LGBT+ communities. This emphasis on inclusion is promising; however, searching through the organisation's website reveals that they have only actually addressed the issue of Islamophobia on one occasion. In December 2016 Stonewall released a statement in response to Kelvin Mackenzie, editor of *The Sun* (a daily tabloid paper with a high circulation in the UK), who called upon Stonewall to 'fight Islam' because it posed an existential threat to queer people and to 'western' values of tolerance.[7] Mackenzie's homonationalist rhetoric could not be clearer and Stonewall's response, quoted here, is notable in its intersectional framing:

> By suggesting that we should 'fight Islam' Kelvin Mackenzie yet again spreads the false idea that religion and LGBT equality are not compatible. At Stonewall, we work with many people of faith and faith leaders – including many Muslims – who are LGBT or who believe in and support LGBT equality. The atrocities committed by terrorist organisations cannot be ignored but nor can they be conflated or confused with the Muslim faith. That is Islamophobia.

Importantly, Stonewall argues explicitly and emphatically that Muslims can both *be* LGBT+ and *support* LGBT+ equality. Stonewall's statement rejects the harmful constructed binary of the Western queer and the homophobic Muslim. Mackenzie, who is not widely recognised for his activism on behalf of the LGBT+ community, cynically deploys homonationalist rhetoric in order to pursue an attack on Islam and Muslims. Moreover, his attempt to enlist the aid of Stonewall in order to vilify Muslims suggests that for him, at least, a queer Muslim identity is unthinkable. Of course, it is reassuring for queer Muslims that Stonewall issued a direct rebuke to Mackenzie; however, it is also notable because it is the only time that they have explicitly sought to address Islamophobia and indeed, they arguably only did so on this occasion because the organisation was dragged into the fray by Mackenzie himself.

In 2018 Stonewall produced a report which concluded that racism is 'rife' in the LGBT+ community. The report, which surveyed over 5,000 LGBT+ people, revealed that half of BAME (black and ethnic minority) LGBT+ people (51%) face discrimination within the community – with black queer people in particular facing higher instances of discrimination (61%). Respondents highlighted witnessing and being the victim of racist language and behaviour, as well as feeling unwelcome in LGBT+ spaces. The report revealed examples of the racist language commonly found in queer dating apps, often an important avenue for LGBT+ people, and especially queer Muslims, to find dates and potential partners; for example, some profiles featured racial epitaphs such as 'no blacks, no spice, no curry, no rice.' The report cited figures indicating high instances of discrimination based on race, transphobia, biphobia, and disability, and features testimonials from marginalised queer people. On launching the findings of the report, Ruth Hunt released a statement denouncing racism:

> This is unacceptable and it causes damage and mistrust. If real change for BAME LGBT people is to occur, we as a community need to hold a mirror to ourselves and have open conversations about how to change. This means learning to recognise our own privileges and to be active allies to each other. The same is true for Stonewall: we are absolutely aware that we too are on a journey and we have a long way to go. But we are committed to learning and getting it right going forward – both internally within Stonewall, and externally.[8]

As we can see from the statement, Hunt explicitly draws upon the language of privilege (albeit one in which actors are not ascribed any active form of agency) as a strategic means by which to contest racism. Moreover, she acknowledges that this is a long-term, or indeed permanently ongoing, process.

Partly in response to this report, Stonewall launched the 'Come Out For LGBT' campaign which encouraged those outside of the LGBT+ community to 'come out' and support the movement through 'small, everyday life actions,' in order to confront stigma where they see it.[9] They also acknowledged that an intersectional approach towards LGBT+ inclusion frameworks have traditionally been lacking in the LGBT+ rights movement, as the following quotation from the campaign illustrates:

> To truly work with and for all LGBT communities, we have to be an active part of the solution to many of the issues outlined in this report. Our 'Come Out For LGBT' campaign is all about being visible and doing something to stand up for others. This research shows just how much those voices are needed if we are to get to a point where everyone in our community is included as an equal.

The campaign calls upon allies to sign a pledge promising that they will 'take action,' tell their friends to get involved, speak up for trans rights, and share their support on social media so that it spreads to other people's feeds and they too can participate. The campaign included testimonials from LGBT+ people not normally 'coded' as being queer – athletes, people of colour, people of faith; promotional media, through billboard and television advertising; a social media campaign, #ComeOutForLGBT[10]; and 'Equali-tea' fundraisers. The campaign also offered safe spaces (such as Equali-tea, and also an annual Pride Breakfast) for queer-focused meet-ups for socialising and being 'out' – something the campaign acknowledges might not be a privilege always afforded to some members of the community.

Overall, the campaign has sought to demonstrate that whilst the 'fight' for LGBT+ emancipation has been achieved for some (homonormative) queer people, it has not been achieved for all, especially trans people and BAME individuals. While the campaign does not give a full-throated indictment of homonationalism or Islamophobia within the queer community, it does briefly touch upon it under the umbrella of 'racism and discrimination within the LGBT+ community.' Similarly, the campaign enlists an array of celebrities and testimonials from both straight and queer individuals alike, though one can't help but notice the overwhelming whiteness of the celebrities. Moreover, the testimonials themselves offer no real attempt to engage with what it might mean to be a queer marginalised within the LGBT+ movement, besides providing a cursory acknowledgement that it is difficult to be both queer and, for example, a 'person of colour.'

The testimonies, and indeed the wider campaign, demonstrate how recent discussions within the LGBT+ community with regards the 'push' for intersectionality and inclusion lack any substance with regards to being queer and black, or queer and Muslim. Indeed, the term 'discrimination' tended to be used when 'Islamophobia,' 'racism,' or 'transphobia' would have been more applicable, and arguably more useful to tackle structural forms of oppression and dynamics of privilege within the LGBT+ movement. As such, any push for a more inclusive, intersectional dialogue still shies away from naming, and therefore addressing, the problems queer Muslims face. Indeed, the failure to use the term Islamophobia denies the specificity that would strengthen an intersectional framework.

One important step that Stonewall has taken to provide some visibility for queer Muslims came in 2019, when they named queer Muslima and LGBT+ activist Hafsa Qureshi as 'Bi Role Model of the Year 2019.' Qureshi is well known in LGBT+ activist spaces for giving a voice and platform to issues related to being queer and Muslim; for instance, she has addressed the stigma related to the hijab. She has worked with queer Muslim groups such as Hidiyah (discussed in greater detail later) to raise awareness regarding the intersections between Islamophobia and homophobia, and she has proven to be an important role model for highlighting the discrimination faced by queer Muslims within the LGBT+ community and the Muslim community. By featuring Qureshi, Stonewall has enabled her to have a higher profile and voice in the media; this platform has allowed her to spread awareness on the issues queer Muslims face, and in particular to highlight the difficult struggle to reconcile both identities within a homonational landscape.

Importantly, Quershi provides a visible role model for other queer Muslims who are presented with an unapologetic queer Muslima and hijabi; her presence on their screens, and social media feeds, helps dismantle the homonationalist-Islamophobic construct that one can only be queer or Muslim but never both.

The perceived 'impossibility' of being both queer and Muslim recently gained mainstream attention with the onset of what has been dubbed the 'Birmingham school row,' in which Muslim parents of students at Parkfield Community School objected to the government curriculum teaching their children about LGBT+ people. Parents opted to withdraw their children from classes, claiming it was their right as parents to be able to vet what their students learned about, and that LGBT+ 'lessons' were against their beliefs as Muslims. The dispute has lasted months, indeed at the time of writing it is still ongoing, with media figures and politicians weighing in on behalf of both sides. Whilst some argue that the learning environment was designed to be inclusive and reflective of modern society, there are also those who believe that parents have the right to object to material that goes against their own personal or religious beliefs. This school row resulted in a deluge of homonationalist-Islamophobic rhetoric from well-known nationalist actors, for examples Katie Hopkins,[11] as well as from those within the LGBT+ community who feel that hard-won gains are being threatened by Muslims.[12]

This controversy can easily be framed within a homonationalist narrative. Muslims refusing to integrate, and rejecting the egalitarian and progressive society of the West, are seeking to promote their regressive views on sexuality. Concomitantly, the row has fuelled homophobic rhetoric that has alarmed some within the LGBT+ community. Member of Parliament Esther McVey has gone on record to show support for the parents, stating that they have a right to object to material they deem 'inappropriate' – implying that there was a sexualised or corrosive element to LGBT+ lessons which impressionable children need to be protected from.[13] Such a position obviously recalls Thatcher's Section 28, which prevented the 'promotion' of LGBT issues in schools (Richardson 2000). The Birmingham school row has also re-energised debates on how the 'gay agenda' is curtailing religious freedoms, in which LGBT+ issues are forced onto people of faith by the government. Hence, questions are raised regarding where the line falls between being 'tolerant' of LGBT+ issues and the perception that religious freedoms are being threatened by said 'tolerance.'

As the leading LGBT+ organisation in the UK, the views of Stonewall were obviously sought. The statement which they released in March 2019 argued that the row was being used to further Islamophobic attitudes, and to further ingrain the imagined binary between Muslim/queer. Calling for solidarity, Stonewall highlighted instances in which the Muslim community had been an ally of the LGBT+ community; moreover, they included the views of prominent queer Muslims such as Benali Hamdache[14] and Ezra Stripe, as quoted here[15]:

> Amid the protests taking place at Parkfield Community School in Birmingham, it's been incredibly powerful to see and hear LGBT Muslims and

allies standing up to affirm their support for LGBT-inclusive education. As Masuma Rahim rightly put it: 'Schools do, however, have a responsibility to teach children how to live in a society that is made up of people who will have some similarities to them, as well as those who will have differences. It's vital children from all faith backgrounds learn about and celebrate diversity at all ages.' As Ezra Stripe, diversity and inclusion officer at Hidayah, said: 'Some children have no idea that it's even possible to be both gay and Muslim. They've never been given space to explore these topics, and no one has ever sat them down and told them "actually, being LGBT is okay." '

Stonewall provided an intersectional unpacking of the incident, mindful of the homonationalist politics at play, identifying how queer Muslims are the ones who are made most vulnerable by this situation and that there are bad faith actors only wishing to sow division and discord.

The previous analysis has explored the extent to which Stonewall has sought to recognise the identity of queer Muslims and to address the explicit and implicit forms of Islamophobia that queer Muslims face within the LGBT+ movement. The organisation has taken opportunities, when they have presented themselves, to explicitly reject the idea that Muslims are inherently homophobic. Indeed, their responses to specific controversies has enabled them to acknowledge and amplify the identity and voices of queer Muslims. However, in terms of their broader focus, it is clear that they have yet to seriously address the specific concerns of queer Muslims, nor has their intersectional analysis sought to identify forms of privilege which are particularly harmful for queer Muslim identities.

There has been a conscious refusal of homonationalism within Stonewall, which has paved the way for intersectionality to be incorporated into their activism – specifically a heightened awareness of the need to be more inclusive. However, these measures have hitherto been broad and somewhat ineffective in highlighting specific issues facing queer Muslims or addressing them efficiently and appropriately (see also Labelle, this volume). This leaves those with marginalised identities in the LGBT+ community still feeling voiceless and unheard, despite the added visibility of more (for example) people of colour in queer-centred imagery, media, organisational roles and queer spaces, and a more refined vocabulary with which to discuss intersectional queer issues. Perhaps because of the lack of attention provided to either queer Muslims or the intersections between homophobia and Islamophobia, as well as the desire for self-organisation, the past few years have seen a rise in autonomous forms, a theme to which the chapter now turns.

Autonomous organising

As previous research has identified, autonomous organising is a strategy that queer Muslims have adopted in order to reconcile their religious and sexual identity and to create structures of support (Kugle 2014). Organisations such as London Queer Muslims and Hidayah have been founded in the UK within the last several years, and whilst they are principally focused on autonomous organising they often also enjoy a symbiotic relationship with the more established mainstream organisations such as Stonewall, which can provide resources for those in the community that have been historically neglected. Stonewall offers these groups better visibility and a stronger platform on which to campaign, and these autonomous organisations provide Stonewall with more specialised outlets in which to better realise their push for a more intersectional LGBT+ community, acknowledging that their own framework is inherently generalised and constrained by its structural origins and designs.

London Queer Muslims was founded in 2017 and is the first Islamic theology group run 'for and by' queer Muslims. Their website outlines their mission statement as seeking to empower queer Muslims through community building, aiming to 'transcend the binaries of faith vs LGBTQIA+ identities and facilitate self-acceptance across religious and queer spectrums.' The group identifies a lack of intersectional organising in established LGBT+ organisations, arguing that the wider turn to intersectionality can offer queer Muslims the tools to help them navigate their specific marginalised identities. The organisation delves into far more nuanced language than anything offered by the more established LGBT+ groups. They identify that queer Muslims are 'excluded' from 'heteronormative Muslim spaces and simultaneously excluded from homonormative 'LGBT' spaces.'[16] The language that they adopt indicates their frustration with the mainstream movement; moreover, they use the language of exclusion repeatedly in order to name a more active process of marginalisation. Their discourse is also far more wide-ranging than that used by Stonewall in terms of promoting an inclusive approach to gender and sexuality, as the following quotation taken from their website demonstrates:

> Rather than accept 'inclusion' or 'integration' into endo-cisgendered and heteronormative spaces, we place a strong emphasis on trans, intersex, non-binary, homosexual, bisexual, pansexual and asexual leadership and participation. Our cisgendered and heterosexual allies are welcome too! By centralising the intersection of Queer and Muslim experiences in our group, we address some of the solutions queer Muslims seek. We affirm our queerness, sexualities and non-normativity as a source of empowerment. Our identities are fully realised through the practice of an expression of Islam that is accepting and loving and where queerness is pivotal to our faith.

The statement explicitly draws upon the language of intersectionality to stress the importance of centralising the specific intersection of queer and Muslim identities. Moreover, they seek to tie the very idea of queerness to Islam, with the group's website providing access to further religious sources.

Hidayah, a nation-wide organisation for LGBTQI+ Muslims, was set up in order to 'defeat stigma, taboo and discrimination' and was founded in Birmingham in 2017.[17] It provides support groups, campaigns for queer Muslim visibility, and runs educational workshops in schools in order to better promote the notion that queerness and Islam are compatible. The organisation is made up of a mixture of practicing, non-practicing, and secular queer Muslims, acknowledging that the 'Muslim' label is nebulous and straddles the line between being racialised and politicised as strictly religious. Their website offers what is perhaps lacking in Stonewall's 'Come Out for LGBT' campaign – testimonials and a regularly updated blog that provides queer Muslim perspectives on navigating the world and the LGBT+ community.

Perhaps one of the most important forms of activism undertaken by Hidayah is its role in promoting the visibility of queer Muslims through community building. It regularly organises events around the UK and has 'contact points' to enable individuals to reach out for support and to engage with their work. The group also produced an online video to launch 'Muslim Pride' in order to provide a visual introduction to the 'lived realities' of LGBTQI+ Muslims. The group has also sought to broaden its social justice activism by collecting, cooking, and delivering food to the homeless in London.

Hidiyah and London Queer Muslims, with additional support from Stonewall, organised the LGBTIQ+, Intersectionality and Islam conference in March 2019.[18] The conference was intended to provide a safe space for queer Muslims to discuss political issues which they face specifically as queer Muslims: the vast majority of those in attendance (which numbered around 200) had never had the opportunity to experience such a space – myself included. Panels featured queer Muslim speakers ranging from faithful to secular; South Asian to Middle Eastern; and those that identified as cisgender, transgender, and non-binary. Substantive topics included self-acceptance; gender and sex diversity affirmation within Islam; allyship through secularism; navigating institutionally Islamophobic and homophobic environments, for example the UK immigration system is particularly difficult for bisexuals who often face a more rigorous process to 'prove' their queerness to immigration officials; deconstructing the notion that being queer and Muslim are paradoxical ('not "or," but "and"'); and in-depth discussions on the importance and ways of showing solidarity to trans people as queer Muslims.

During the day there was explicit engagement with the ideas, discourse, and politics of intersectionality, for example one talk was titled 'A Journey of Intersectionalities.' Significant attention was paid to how to better support particularly marginalised groups within the queer Muslim community. The conference provided an important example of the more granular levels of analysis which (mainly) autonomous organising affords those often marginalised within wider social movements (see for instance the discussion of bisexuality and immigration). Moreover, organising such a well-attended conference provides an often-hidden community with an important opportunity to display visibility; this was further supported by the hashtag #QueerIslam2019.

The pervasive feeling expressed at the conference was that queer Muslims are addressed only in brief acknowledgements of their existence, and that such an existence is difficult and deserves solidarity. Several people highlighted that even when such acknowledgements are made, they are usually vague or enveloped into catchall terms such as 'people of colour' – which does little to highlight the differences in stigma and discrimination that, for example, black queer people face compared to Asian queer people or Middle Eastern queer people. Trickier still is, where do Muslim queers fall under this generalised framework? Indeed, at the conference some repeatedly stressed that being 'Muslim' is a religious and not racialised identity, and hence requires a different set of discursive and analytic frameworks.

Discussions with attendees revealed that whilst they recognised that there has been a generalised push towards 'inclusion' and 'awareness' amongst the LGBT+ community and its principal advocates, many of those for whom such strategies are intended to address feel unheard. There was a sense amongst the delegates that by attempting to address all diverse identities and intersections at play within the community, that racial and ethnic framing lacked the specificity of focusing on the challenges presented by homonationalist discourse and politics. Furthermore, one attendee noted that there was a dominant binary between 'queer people' and 'queer people of colour,' with other marginalised groups such as the disabled, and those outside the gender binary, often acknowledged as part of a list to demonstrate the diversity of the community.

Of course, the affective dynamics that result from these types of autonomous organising are critical. For those who attended the conference it was a revelatory introduction to a wider community of queer Muslims. To *feel* part of a community, which certain sections of society do not even believe exists, is a powerful political act. Indeed, these initial stages of community building are playing an important role in consciousness raising amongst queer Muslims as they begin to navigate, and contest, the various issues that affect their lives. The importance of community and intersectional solidarity offers an opportunity to name, identify, and critique patterns of privilege which intersect in ways that marginalise and disempower queer Muslims.

The rise of these specialised autonomous groups, in tandem with the mutual support from more established organisations, such as Stonewall, that have also begun to develop a more intersectional platform is a welcome trajectory for marginalised groups. They provide visibility, support networks, and an opportunity to engage in more detailed analysis of specific issues that affect their daily lives. Moreover, they also provide a space within the LGBT+ community to better reconcile their own identities, after years of being told their very existence is a paradox or an affront. Thus far, the autonomous groups and events have focused on visibility, community building, and raising awareness of the specific blend of homophobia and Islamophobia that affects queer Muslims. It is hoped, therefore, that the conference will have acted as a spur to more high-profile and sustained forms of political engagement with the issues.

Conclusion

In a post-9/11 world, a (whitewashed) Western LGBT+ movement was increasingly securing social currency, at the same time Muslims were vilified and presented as inherently homophobic (Puar 2007). Hence, queer Muslims felt themselves left behind by a movement keen to pursue legitimacy within in a main-stream, Islamophobic landscape, as well as simultaneously cast out by their own religious or racial communities. More than a decade on, the LGBT+ community has begun to move away from constructed images of the 'homonormative queer' by unpacking the whitewashed origins of the movement. Stonewall, the de facto face of mainstream LGBT+ activism in the UK, has increasingly sought to adopt an intersectional lens, for example using the language of privilege and elevating non-normative queers – such as a Muslima in a hijab – to visible roles within their campaigns. Moreover, they have been keen to engage in coalitional forms of intersectionality by offering support to autonomous queer Muslim activism: they have raised their profile and visibility in campaigns and platforms. Stonewall has seemingly acknowledged that an intersectional reworking of the LGBT+ move-ment must include specialised and diversified voices, and that their own politics are inherently constrained by their institutional privilege and historical whiteness.

Hidayah and London Queer Muslims are both examples of autonomous organi-sations, created as a response to the lack of attention paid to queer Muslims by the wider LGBT+ community. Both groups were emboldened by the recent push towards intersectionality but frustrated by the slow and incremental progress being made. Now they exist in a cooperative relationship with a movement that had historically neglected them. Creating queer Muslim organisations has been an important step towards realising a sense of political, and collective, identity and belonging. The lessons learned in terms of the importance of autonomous organis-ing is critical and perhaps will be replicated by other marginalised groups as the wider LGBT+ movement continues to grapple with intersectionality and privi-lege. Specifically, autonomous organising will likely prove an important strategy for other non-homonormative queers, in particular trans women of colour, disa-bled queers, queers of colour, and those outside the gender binary.

Notes

1 Queer in this chapter refers to non-normative or singular instances of LGBT+ people, such as 'queer Muslim,' whereas LGBT+ is used to refer to normative and mainstream actors and organisations, the emancipation movement and the community as a whole.
2 See Wilkinson, Sophie. 2018. March 12 "Is It Okay to Be Gay (and in the Far-Right?)"www.vice.com/en_uk/article/ywqd55/is-it-okay-to-be-gay-and-in-the-far-right [accessed 9 July 2019].
3 See Chalk, Will. 2017. April 20 "Why gay French men are voting far right." www.bbc.co.uk/newsbeat/article/39641822/why-gay-french-men-are-voting-far-right
4 See Holmes, Jonathan. 2019. 14 January. "It is possible to be Muslim and a lesbian." www.bbc.co.uk/news/uk-england-bristol-46567505 [accessed 18 June 2019].
5 For details of Stonewall including their mission statement, see www.stonewall.org.uk/ [accessed 14 June 2019].
6 Stonewall received criticism for failing to include transgender people in their equality campaigns prior to Hunt's tenure as chief executive; see a *Guardian* interview with Ruth Hunt about her decision to shift the direction of Stonewall. www.theguardian.com/society/2019/may/19/ruth-hunt-stonewall-moral-responsibility-fight-trans-peo-ple [accessed 10 July 2019].

7 See MacKenzie, Kelvin. 2016. December 29. www.thesun.co.uk/news/2498980/gay-charity-should-fight-islam-not-pick-on-soft-target-like-tvs-richard-hammond/ [accessed 21 June 2019].
8 For a full copy of the Stonewall report, see www.stonewall.org.uk/i-will-bring-any-one-and-everyone-out-lgbt [accessed 21 June 2019].
9 For a full copy of the Stonewall report see www.stonewall.org.uk/i-will-bring-anyone-and-everyone-out-lgbt [accessed 21 June 2019].
10 See https://twitter.com/hashtag/comeoutforlgbt?ref_src=twsrc%5Egoogle%7Ctwcamp%5Eserp%7Ctwgr%5Ehashtag [accessed 21 June 2019].
11 See https://twitter.com/KTHopkins/status/1135842548176625664 [accessed 30 June 2019].
12 See "Parkfield school protests are exposing bigotry of gay people, too." www.pinknews.co.uk/2019/03/08/parkfield-protests-bigotry-gay/ [accessed 30 June 2019].
13 See Smith, Reiss. 2019. May 30. "Tory leadership: Esther McVey says 'parents know best' on LGBT lessons." www.pinknews.co.uk/2019/05/30/esther-mcvey-lgbt-lessons-birmingham-tory-leadership/ [accessed 21 June 2019].
14 See Hamdache, Benali. 2019. March 05. "Pupils shouldn't be denied LGBT lessons – whatever their parents say." www.theguardian.com/commentisfree/2019/mar/05/pupils-lgbt-lessons-parents-gay-muslim-parkfield-school [accessed 30 June 2019].
15 See Stripe, Ezra. 2019. February 25. "I'm Muslim and LGBT, and I teach children it's OK to be both." https://metro.co.uk/2019/02/25/im-muslim-and-lgbt-and-i-teach-children-its-ok-to-be-both-8713922/
16 For details of London Queer Muslims see https://londonqueermuslims.com [accessed 10 July 2019].
17 For details of Hidayah see www.hidayahlgbt.co.uk [accessed 10 July 2019].
18 For details of the conference see https://lgbtqfaithuk.com/2019/02/27/lgbtiq-intersectionality-and-islam-conference/ [accessed 24 June 2019].

References

Alimahomed, Sabrina. 2010. "Thinking Outside the Rainbow: Women of Color Redefining Queer Politics and Identity." *Social Identities* 16 (2): 151–168.
Ayoub, Phillip M. 2016. *When States Come out: Europe's Sexual Minorities and the Politics of Visibility*. New York, NY: Cambridge University Press.
Binnie, Jon, and Christian Klesse. 2012. "Solidarities and Tensions: Feminism and Transnational LGBTQ Politics in Poland." *European Journal of Women's Studies* 19 (4): 444–459.
Duggan, Lisa. 2002. "The New Homonormativity: The Sexual Politics of Neoliberalism." In *Materializing Democracy: Towards a Revitalized Cultural Politics*, edited by Russ Castronova and Dana D. Nelson, 175–194. Durham, NC: Duke University Press.
El-Tayeb, Fatima. 2012. "'Gays Who Cannot Properly Be Gay': Queer Muslims in the Neoliberal European City." *European Journal of Women's Studies* 19 (1): 79–95.
Haritaworn, Jin, Tamsila Tauqir, and Esra Erdem. 2008. "Gay Imperialism: Gender and Sexuality Discourse in the War on Terror." In *Out of Place: Interrogating Silences in Queerness/Raciality*, edited by Adi Kuntsman and Esperanza Miyake, 71-95. York, England: Raw Nerve Books.
Heike Schotten, C. 2016. "Homonationalism: From Critique to Diagnosis, or Are We All Homonational Now." *International Feminist Journal of Politics* 16 (3): 351–370.
Jaspal, Rusi, and Asifa Siraj. 2011. "Perceptions of 'Coming out' Among British Muslim Gay Men." *Psychology & Sexuality* 2 (3): 183–197.

Jivraj, Suhraiya, and Anisa De Jong. 2011. "The Dutch Homo-Emancipation Policy and Its Silencing Effects on Queer Muslims." *Feminist Legal Studies* 19 (2): 143.

Kugle, Scott Siraj-al Haqq A. 2014. *Living out Islam: Voices of Gay, Lesbian, and Transgender Muslims*. New York, NY: New York University Press.

Kuntsman, Adi. 2008. "Genealogies of Hate, Metonymies of Violence: Immigration, Homophobia, Homopatriotism." In *Out of Place: Interrogating Silences in Queerness/ Raciality*, edited by Adi Kuntsman and Esperanza Miyake. York, England: Raw Nerve Books.

Logie, Carmen H., and Marie-Jolie Rwigema. 2014. "'The Normative Idea of Queer Is a White Person': Understanding Perceptions of White Privilege Among Lesbian, Bisexual, and Queer Women of Color in Toronto, Canada." *Journal of Lesbian Studies* 18 (2): 174–191.

Minwalla, Omar, B. R. Simon Rosser, Jamie Feldman, and Christine Varga. 2005. "Identity Experience Among Progressive Gay Muslims in North America: A Qualitative Study Within Al-Fatiha." *Culture, Health & Sexuality* 7 (2): 113–128.

Morgan, George. 2016. *Global Islamophobia: Muslims and Moral Panic in the West*. New York, NY: Routledge.

Nagel, Joane. 1998. "Masculinity and Nationalism: Gender and Sexuality in the Making of Nations." *Ethnic and Racial Studies* 21 (2): 242–269.

Peumans, Wim. 2014. "Queer Muslim Migrants in Belgium: A Research Note on Same-Sex Sexualities and Lived Religion." *Sexualities* 17 (5–6): 618–631.

Puar, Jasbir K. 2007. *Terrorist Assemblages: Homonationalism in Queer Times*. Durham, NC: Duke University Press.

Rahman, Momin. 2010. "Queer as Intersectionality: Theorizing Gay Muslim Identities." *Sociology* 44 (5): 944–961.

Richardson, Diane. 2000. "Constructing Sexual Citizenship: Theorizing Sexual Rights." *Critical Social Policy* 20 (1): 105–135.

Ritchie, Jason. 2015. "Pinkwashing, Homonationalism, and Israel – Palestine: The Conceits of Queer Theory and the Politics of the Ordinary." *Antipode* 47 (3): 616–634.

Siraj, Asifa. 2011. "Isolated, Invisible, and in the Closet: The Life Story of a Scottish Muslim Lesbian." *Journal of Lesbian Studies* 15 (1): 99–121.

Verloo, Mieke, ed. 2018. *Varieties of Opposition to Gender Equality in Europe*. London: Routledge.

Weiss, Jillian. 2011. "Reflective Paper: GL Versus BT: The Archaeology of Biphobia and Transphobia Within the US Gay and Lesbian Community." *Journal of Bisexuality* 11 (4): 498–502.

Yip, Andrew K. T. 2008. "Researching Lesbian, Gay, and Bisexual Christians and Muslims: Some Thematic Reflections." *Sociological Research Online* 13 (1): 1–14.

Chapter 14

Generational conflict and the politics of inclusion in two feminist events

Pauline Stoltz, Beatrice Halsaa
and Christel Stormhøj

Introduction

In 2014, two related feminist events in the Nordic region created controversies among feminist, LGBT*QI, and anti-racist activists: *Nordiskt Forum Malmö* (or NF) and *Feministiskt Festival* (or FF), which took place in Malmö, Sweden. NF was organised by a steering group of national feminist and women's movement umbrella organisations from the Nordic region and FF by a local feminist network of individuals and organisations. Both events were huge successes, but FF initially emerged as a protest against NF. The in/exclusion of LGBT*QI and anti-racist activists, issues, and ideas, and the perceived high costs of attending NF, were at the core of the contentions within NF and between NF and FF. Based on extensive fieldwork, we have determined that the events have had a profound legacy, both stimulating feminist activism and nurturing conflict.

We can understand these conflicts in two ways: firstly as a generational conflict between an older generation of more institutionalised and policy-oriented women's movement activists (the steering group of NF) and a younger generation of non-institutionalised and activism-oriented feminists (partly NF and FF) (see Manga and Vinthagen 2015, p. 12 for the division between policy-oriented and activism-oriented feminism). In this generational approach, the categories of age and generation are central and can be related to each other via theories about generations, history, and social change (see Mannheim 1927/1952; Reger 2015). Secondly, and not necessarily contradicting the first, we can use an intersectional approach to the politics of privilege and inclusion within and between movements. Sometimes this approach includes categories of age and generation (here understood as a group of people of similar age), but more often other categories, such as gender, 'race,' ethnicity, class, and sexuality, are the focus of analysis (Hill Collins 2015; Hancock 2016).

We ask, what are the advantages of using generational and intersectional approaches if we want to explain the controversies around these events? This is interesting, since the nexus between how we use an intersectional approach in the analysis of controversies around the politics of inclusion and privilege and how activists use the concept of intersectionality in their mobilisations can create confusion in the study of conflicts over feminist events. We can also consider whether we should treat generation as one category amongst others within an intersectional analysis and/or whether intersectionality is an issue about which generations of activists can be in conflict with each other.

We use a bottom-up approach to the study of these conflicts and thereby emphasise the importance of context. We start by introducing theories on generations and intersectionality. The argument then proceeds as follows. In the first step, we ask how organisers and participants represent what the respective conflicts over NF and FF were about and what related them to each other. Secondly, taking a generational perspective, we ask if we can identify any generations and, from an intersectional perspective, what inequalities in power and privilege within and between the two groups of organisers of NF and FF, it is possible to identify. Thirdly, we discuss the use of intersectional approaches in the politics of inclusion of the two events and the articulation of generation and intersectionality in our analysis of the controversies. The results will illuminate the debates, antagonisms, and alliances that characterised both events and, notably, will illustrate how perceptions of privilege – including both internal and external criticisms of the reproduction of privilege in the organisation of these events – concentrated on institutionalised privileges.

Theorising gender, age and generation

In the following, we want to provide a broader perspective than simply equating categories of age and generation to the power to influence social change towards gender equality (a young generation of less-privileged feminist activists versus an older generation of privileged women's activists) in order to understand intersectional inequalities in controversies over the politics of inclusion at these two events.

The radicalisation of youth and generational conflict

One of the most frequently cited scholars on the notion of generation is Mannheim. In *The Problem of Generations* (1927/1952), he argues for a socio-historical concept of generations. According to him, these become both subject to history and the markers of it. Mannheim distinguishes between different aspects of the concept of generation. Firstly, a generation is a location in time (a historical process) and space (a specific social structure) (Mannheim 1952, p. 290). This *location* exposes individuals of approximately the same age to certain experiences, opportunities, and crises and excludes them from others. Mannheim claims that this exposure is 'predisposing them to a certain characteristic mode of thought and experience and a characteristic type of historically relevant action' (Mannheim 1952, p. 291).

Importantly, he emphasises that the individuals under study need to be of approximately the same age. For example, we could suggest that we can describe those who lived in the Nordic countries and became adults during the 1970s, 1980s, and early 1990s as being exposed to experiences and opportunities of social democratic state feminism (Hernes 1988, 1987) and widely used euphemisms such as 'women-friendly' or 'gender-sensitive' policies (Kantola and Verloo 2018). Likewise, we could suggest that those who grew up after 2000 can be described as being exposed to the political opportunities of neoliberal and conservative gender-equality policies (Elomäki and Kantola 2018) or to a time in which intersectionality has gained legitimacy and is seen as a motivation for mobilisation (see 'Intersectionality' section later in this chapter).

Secondly, for a generation to become conscious of itself, 'to share the same generation location' and develop into 'an actuality,' members need to interact and develop a sense of their own place in society, a sense of a 'we' (Mannheim 1952, p. 303). They need to reflect on the ideas they have inherited and internalised from their communities, peers, and families. Whereas location figures as a structure of opportunities (and a macro-sociological perspective), generation as actuality refers to the actor-related aspects of the concept (a micro-sociological perspective). Here, the shared lived experiences of the group become a politicised frame of reference and constitute a political generation, a generation which sees itself as capable of creating social change.

Thirdly, an actual generation often contains what Mannheim calls *generational units*. These units are concrete groups who develop different and often antagonistic outlooks and identities as responses to the same socio-historical conditions (Mannheim 1952, pp. 304–306). Mannheim assumes that the biographical phase of adolescence is the only formative period for developing a *political generation* that can function as an agent of change (1952, pp. 293, 300–301). That is, he assumes that when we are older, this does not apply.

In contrast, feminist scholars regard engagement in political activism as transformative at any age (Schneider 1988; Whittier 1997). Individuals of varying ages enter a social movement during a given period of protest and then internalise a new self-definition as part of a new collective that interprets the world politically. These then form a new *political generation* (Schneider 1988). Consequently, it becomes an empirical question as to whether the same or different *political generations* initiated the *Nordiskt Forum* and the *Feministiskt Festival* and if these generations mainly included middle-aged or older participants, or if young women, men and trans*persons were part of the generation who organised one or both of these events.

Scholars have introduced the notion of *generational conflict* to indicate the phenomenon of activists highlighting their distinctiveness from, and often superiority to, previous or subsequent generations. Feminist scholars distinguish between the concepts of *identification* and *dis-identification* as referring to processes of distinguishing one's own generation from another feminist generation through acts of self-assertion and self-identity construction (Cullen and Fischer 2014; Reger 2014; see also Henry 2004; van der Tuin 2009). Additionally, they have introduced the concept of *inverted dis-identification* (Reger 2015, p. 90ff.).

Here, an older generation actively works to separate itself from younger generations, not only to define who it is, but also to define what 'real' feminism looks
like. Processes of identification, dis-identification, and inverted dis-identification
are thus power struggles between generations – *generational conflicts* – over who
can define and represent 'real' feminism.

That is, we can raise questions about the link between *generational conflicts,
political generations*, and *generational locations*. Mannheim focuses on the relation between generation and history. With him, we can ask (this is due to the fact
that Mannheim himself never reflected on the impact of gender) how historically
specific (gender) arrangements and historical conditions of (gender) politics may
illuminate *generational location* and trigger the development of *generation in
actuality*. However, as feminist scholars have pointed out, Mannheim's explanation of antagonism and conflict is perhaps too simplistic. There is no single way to
understand the relation between the political and historical context (location) and
the politicisation and mobilisation of a generation (actuality).

Intersectionality

Age and generation – understood as both a political generation and a generation that is representative of a certain age – might matter less to activists than
categories of 'race'/ethnicity, class, sexuality, disability, or indigenousness. Studies on feminist movements have indeed stressed that conflicts and divisions run
along the lines of race, class, or sexuality (see Nyhagen Predelli and Halsaa 2012;
Springer 2005). Here, notions of intersectionality become of interest.

Originally, intersectional approaches focused on the analysis of social categories of gender, 'race'/ethnicity, and class (Crenshaw 1989; de los Reyes, Molina,
and Mulinari 2002). Later, researchers discussed whether intersectional analysis
should engage with one or several *specific* categories in order to achieve the normative political potential of the approach (Mügge et al. 2018; Hancock 2016; Hill
Collins 2015). Inequalities due to categories of age and generation are not always
part of these discussions and many researchers treat them as irrelevant, but they
can become relevant in combination with more frequently used categories, such
as gender, ethnicity, class, sexuality, nationality, and religion. Questions about
the roles of age and generation in the conflicts over NF and FF highlight the need
to analyse privilege and power relations amongst feminists and to examine how
inequalities amongst them influence how different feminists think about feminism as a project (see Walby 2011, p. 6). Privilege and power may follow age and
generation – as well as gender, race, and class – but other categories may also be
relevant if we want to gain a fuller understanding of the conflicts.

Following Patricia Hill Collins' theory on intersectionality, we could differentiate between two understandings of intersectionality: first, intersectionality as
an analytical approach to analysing social inequalities, emphasising contexts of
time, place, and space in the analyses of power relations within feminist mobilisations and communications. Second, we could understand intersectionality as a

normative political approach and critical praxis that reacts to social inequalities in pursuit of social justice (Hill Collins 2015). A relationship between intersectionality theory and activism runs both ways. Intersectionality is increasingly taught in the academy and made available on the Internet and has thus gained legitimacy among young activists entering social movements. These activists refer to intersectionality as a motivation for their political organising (Hancock 2016, chapter 2).

Let us now consider the articulation between a generational approach and an intersectional one. Generational theories such as Mannheim's focus on explaining divergences between generations and generational conflicts through politicisation at different points in time. This provides a rather simplistic understanding of conflict. Feminist approaches to Mannheim are more sensitive to differences in power and privilege and are suitable for combining with an intersectional approach. This articulation between generational and intersectional approaches suggests that both researchers and activists should take into account generation as one of the axes of power, alongside 'race,' sexuality, etc. in their feminist analyses and mobilisations.

Controversies over *Nordiskt Forum Malmö* and *Feministisk Festival*

How did organisers and participants present the controversies over Nordiskt Forum Malmö and Feministiskt Festival? We base the answer to this question and our remaining argument upon our extensive fieldwork. Between 2014 and 2018, we conducted participatory observations during the events and 53 interviews with organisers and participants whom we visited in Denmark, Finland, Iceland, Norway, and Sweden. In order to respect the anonymity of the interviewees, we have applied numbers to every interview. We collected documents related to both events, including the printed programme and the final document produced by NF as well as reactions to the events in both social and traditional media.

Nordiskt Forum Malmö

In June 2014, approximately 20,000–30,000 people gathered in Malmö, Sweden, at *Nordiskt Forum Malmö*. It was the third Nordiskt Forum, after Oslo, Norway, in 1988 and Åbo, Finland, in 1994. The Nordic Council initiated the first two, and both the Council and the host countries provided generous funding in order to stimulate women's organisations. This was due to the part that the forums played in the global governance of gender equality. The first two events took place at the peak of what is sometimes called 'state feminism' (Hernes 1987). Nordiskt Forum Oslo in 1988 was a follow-up to the Third World Conference on Women in Nairobi in 1985 and the end of the United Nations Decade for Women: Equality, Development and Peace 1975–1985 (Pietilä and Vickers 1994). The organisers of NF Oslo modelled the event after the three previous UN world conferences

(Knudsen and Moen 1989). NF Oslo also set out to assess the implementation of the Nairobi Forward-looking Strategies for Women: Equality, Development and Peace (Planlægningsgruppen 1988). Nordiskt Forum Åbo in 1994, in turn, was a kick-off for the UN Fourth World Conference on Women held in Beijing in 1995. In Beijing, the governments of UN member states adopted the *Beijing Platform for Action* and undertook to implement CEDAW – the Convention on the Elimination of All Forms of Discrimination Against Women from 1979 onwards, through more active and transparent actions.

It was, however, not the Nordic Council but Icelandic activists who took the initiative for the third NF. This was at the beginning of the century, at a time when there was still reason to believe there would be a fifth UN women's conference. They soon realised that it was too big for them to organise (interviews 23 and 37). In 2011, the Swedish Women's Lobby (*Sveriges Kvinno Lobby* or SWL) took the lead in the planning and organised a preparatory conference. This resulted in the creation of a Nordic Steering Group consisting of eight major umbrella organisations of the women's movements from all the Nordic countries (two from Norway, two from Iceland, one from Sweden, one from Denmark, one from Finland, and one from Åland). The SWL established a Chancellery in Stockholm, Sweden. Together, the Nordic Steering Group and the Chancellery were the organisers of NF Malmö. A conference agency organised many of the practicalities, including the basic task of generating sponsors.

The programme for NF consisted of three streams: the Arena programme, the Nordic programme, and the Open programme. (1) The Arena programme presented famous researchers, top politicians and activists, performers, and cultural celebrities. (2) The Nordic programme provided opportunities to discuss the challenges facing the Nordic countries and globally in order to fulfil CEDAW and the Beijing Platform for Action. (3) The Open programme was a meeting place for 280 civil society organisations, activist networks, political authorities from different levels, universities, unions, companies, and others to attend hundreds of programme activities. The Open programme was free of charge, whereas a fee was charged for the two other programmes and for having a stand.

NF Malmö was an effort to formulate demands and proposals directed towards the Nordic governments and politicians, to promote debate on women's rights, and to energise women's movements. The UN played a prominent role in Malmö. Instead of remaining quiet in fear of a global gender backlash, the Nordic organisers insisted on assessing the actual status of gender equality and to voice their claims in the hope of inspiring feminists elsewhere to do the same. In addition to explicitly providing information on the follow-up to CEDAW (1979) and the Beijing Platform for Action (1995), the goal in Malmö was to formulate recommendations for strategies to implement gender-sensitive sustainable development and for the global agenda that was to replace the *UN Millennium Development Goals* in 2015. The Steering Group prepared a draft document and presented this to the participating organisations and individuals, who were invited to comment during the conference. This resulted in a final document containing 63 demands, which was handed over to the Nordic Ministers of Equality, the Nordic Council of Ministers, and the Executive Director of UN Women during the Closing Ceremony – closely mirroring the procedure at the two previous NFs.

The funding of NF Malmö was problematic from the start. The Nordic Council of Ministers did not contribute as it had done on the two previous occasions, when it was the initiator of the events, and the Nordic governments were reluctant to fund the event, with the exception of Sweden. This created an imbalance amongst the organisers. SWL managed to secure a large part of the funding for NF from the Swedish government, whereas other umbrella organisations in the Nordic countries turned out to have scarce and uneven means of accessing funding. This, in addition to expensive conference sites in Malmö – a trade fair and convention centre – resulted in participation fees for individual participants and fees for stands. This situation resulted in a financial surplus, which ended up almost in its entirety at the SWL.

The controversies

We can describe the criticism of *NF* as occurring at different stages: firstly, internally in the Nordic Steering Group; secondly, externally during the planning of the event (this was primarily in Sweden). Finally, there were external criticisms in both traditional and social media during and after the event throughout the Nordic region. The controversies concerned issues ranging from the planning to the evaluation and follow-up and disclosed both privileges and inequalities between the movements in the Nordic countries.

There were internal tensions amongst the organising umbrella organisations over the composition of the Nordic Steering Group, relating to the unequal composition and strengths of Nordic women's movement umbrella organisations (see Seibicke 2019; Borchorst and Siim 2008). There were disagreements both within the Steering Group and between the Steering Group and the Chancellery regarding the financing and agenda of the event. This related to the lack of adequate public funding for NF from all the Nordic countries except Sweden. The cost of the event was criticised by some of the organisers for preventing poor or underfunded groups from participating (interviews 9 and 11, organisers). The costs were high in comparison to previous NFs, which many organisers and participants remembered, but some asserted that it was in no way expensive (interview 49, organiser). Some of the organisers considered it to be in violation of national traditions to charge a fee for feminist events (interview 11, organiser; interviews 21 and 22, participants).

Despite general agreement about the actual content of the event, some of the organisers claimed that they did a lot of 'non-work'; for example, making lists of potential speakers that were never considered by the Secretariat who actually decided (11, organiser). The absence of activists, organisations, and issues of anti-racism and homosexual and trans* inclusion was addressed at an early stage of the planning and triggered frustration among many activists, particularly in Sweden.

Despite various initiatives within the Steering Group and from organisations and activists, the organisers never managed to silence this critique. This led the Swedish anti-racist feminist think tank Interfem to decline to participate in the Forum.

The closing ceremony was critiqued for including the Norwegian nationalist right-wing populist Minister of Equality, who was controversial for statements which have been characterised in Sweden as transphobic, homophobic, and racist (see Liinason 2018, p. 186; Manga and Vinthagen 2015). Harsh criticisms flourished in public media, including controversies between (mainly) the Norwegian and Swedish organisers and the Chancellery regarding the invited minister.

After the event, NF found itself with a considerable profit, which SWL mainly kept for its own use. This led to internal tensions (interview 49, organiser) within the Nordic Steering Group. Co-organisers were irritated, and the situation resulted in a breakdown of the established network of organisers, the Nordisk Feministisk Forum (interviews 36, 37, and 49, organisers).

The public controversies surrounding the planning of NF resulted in the organisation of the Feministisk Festival. Malmö Feminist Network (MFN), a network of private individuals and organisations working with feminism in the city of Malmö, organised this festival. According to the organisers of FF, NF Malmö represented mainstream feminism in the Swedish capital of Stockholm in ways that did not reflect what was going on in multicultural Malmö, in the south of the country. According to the organisers, FF was anti-racist, inclusive, and free of charge. The festival was presented on Facebook as addressing itself to both those who had been engaged feminists for 20 years and those who were young and curious. FF took place at the Malmö Folkets Park [The Malmö People's Park] and became an annual event.

There also turned out to be some controversy over issues of privilege and lack of inclusion at FF. An evaluation of the second festival, which partly covered what had happened at the first (interviews 44 and 47), indicated that organisers and participants were mainly white, middle-class, cis women and young people under the age of 35. Interviewees mentioned disability as an issue, since disabled participants had problems accessing the venue (interviews 21 and 22, participants). Over the years, organisers addressed these privileges and the politics of inclusion on a regular basis. After four years, more than 50 grassroots organisations and several individuals had become included in the organisation.

Generations and intersectional inequalities

If we want to identify a political generation, the generational approach encourages us to concentrate on the *(dis)identification* of its members. Do the organisers of NF identify as similar kinds of feminists or not, and do they *dis-identify* with the organisers of FF? We can ask the same of the organisers of FF. Using an intersectional approach, we can ask which, if any, inequalities in power and privilege within and between the two groups of organisers of NF and FF were identified in the interviews with the organisers.

Identification and dis-identification of generations

A Nordic Steering Group, a Chancellery, and a conference agency organised NF Malmö, as described previously. We leave the conference agency out of this equation, given that it was mainly an object but not a subject in the conflicts. In Mannheim's generational approach, the category of age is important: individuals of approximately the same age are exposed to certain experiences, opportunities, and crises in common. That is, the age of the organisers becomes relevant.

The Nordic Steering Group and the Chancellery consisted of both younger and older women. Whilst several members of the Nordic Steering Group were young, one interviewee described most of the members as experienced women 'past their prime,' who had been working for women's organisations for decades (interview 49). Gertrud Åström, who was the Chair of SWL at the time of NF Malmö (2009–2015) as well as the Chair of the Nordic Steering Group, was aged 64 in 2014, and two of the three women who represented Norway were also older than 50. The members of the Nordic Chancellery were much younger. In all, the organisers of NF were not individuals of approximately the same age.

Additionally, Mannheim claimed that individuals need to interact and develop a sense of 'we' in order to develop a political generation *in actuality* (Mannheim 1952, p. 303). We could suggest that some organisers identified themselves as belonging to the political generation of state feminists, analytically speaking, while others were more prone to see feminism as a business event (interview 11), or wished NF to be more intersectional and organised from what they called 'a movement' perspective (interviews 39 and 42). The conflicts *within* the organisation of NF make the identification of the organisers as a common political generation difficult to justify. These conflicts do not indicate any sense of a 'we' or a political generation *in actuality*. Interviewees described frustrations and conflicts, both amongst the members of the Nordic Steering Group and between the Nordic Steering Group and the Chancellery. They mentioned that these frustrations concerned power struggles over the presence of 'female patriarchs' and the application of 'master suppression techniques' (Ås 1981) (interview 42).

Another way of looking at the issue of political generations would be to stress the general agreement among the organisers about the actual overarching *aim* of the event: the production of a policy document. This is despite disagreements about whom to include in different aspects of the organisation (interviews 36 and 37, organisers). We agree with Schneider and Whittier that radicalisation can come at any age (Schneider 1988; Whittier 1997), which makes the particular information about age less important.

Agreement about the general content of the event would instead indicate the occurrence of many *generational units*, which can all be part of the same political generation. The question of what characterises the political generation of the organisers of NF would then lead us to an identification of the reasons for organising NF in the first place. This was related to the fear of a global gender equality backlash, in the wake of an alliance of conservative Catholic, Protestant, and

Muslim forces to combat the UN's policy on women's sexual and reproductive rights (we turn to the background of Nordiskt Forum 2013, see 'Generational conflicts about 'real feminism' and transnational solidarities' subsection), and to the desire to make claims on Nordic governments.

In terms of dis-identification from other feminists, there was little specific or collective dis-identification on the part of the organisers of NF from the organisers of FF. Quite the contrary, most of the interviewees expressed positive attitudes towards FF. The focus of attention of the Steering Committee seemed to be on the organisation of NF, rather than on creating a dialogue with local activists in Malmö about how to organise the event. The Chancellery was responsible for this dialogue, and its approach was rather to cooperate than to create or sustain conflict (interviews 38, 39, and 42).

The social composition of the organisers of FF was, as mentioned previously, mainly white, middle-class, cis women and young people under the age of 35. Ironically, the organisers soon considered themselves an older generation in relation to younger feminists who were teenagers and in their early twenties. Although there were internal discussions within FF about strategies of separatism, anarchism, and working together with (which) political parties during this election year, the organisation of FF was horizontal and the decision-making procedure was consensual.

At the same time, FF organisers clearly *dis-identified* from NF by describing this group as representing 'mainstream feminism' from the capital of Sweden. This (negative) identity was contrasted with their own, locally based feminism, self-characterized as anti-racist and inclusive because the events were free of charge (interviews 44, 46, and 47). In this *inverted dis-identification* in relation to NF, we can therefore recognise a reference to what the organisers of *Feministiskt Festival* considered to be 'real' feminism.

Inequalities in power and privilege

Interestingly, during our fieldwork, the interviewees mention different intersectional inequalities and problems with power and privilege in relation to all the conflicts and controversies we have identified: in the internal conflict within the NF organisation, in the external conflict over the organisation of NF, and in the conflict between NF and FF. Even the previously described internal controversies within the organisation of FF addressed the intersectionality of gender with other categories.

The organisers of NF Malmö held different positions of power, relative to each other and to the smaller event of FF. Four issues are relevant to highlight in relation to the explanation of the controversies: (1) the importance of funding for gaining positions of power and privilege; (2) the importance of inequalities in power and privilege for *what* is on the programme, or *how* topics should be included in the programme; (3) who should be included on the steering committee; and (4) the process of drafting the final document.

Power and money are closely related. This meant that the generous funding provided by the Swedish government for NF Malmö implicitly gave the SWL a position of power and privilege in relation to representatives from umbrella organisations from other Nordic states (see Nordiskt Forum Malmö, previously in this chapter; interview 49). One interviewee claimed that the SWL insisted on having the final say, due to its major contribution to the funding. This led to internal tensions within NF, both during and after the planning process (interviews 36, 37, and 49).

High aspirations – for instance to invite 'feminist stars' and to have at least 15,000 participants (Focus interview 8) – combined with insufficient public funding, led to the decisions to introduce a relatively high charge for hiring a stand in the exhibition area and to charge a registration fee for participants. The combined costs of travel, accommodation, and the NF itself became too expensive for many potential participants. Budget issues became an ongoing issue of contention and strengthened the role of the SWL and the Swedish Chancellery, which feared bankruptcy. The high ambitions for the programme clashed with the desire to have numerous participants from all over the Nordic region, and the (self-)financing of participants attracted external criticism. Nevertheless, external critics of the cost of the event rarely addressed the internal power struggles over funding. This is probably because these were not widely known.

The feminist festival was free of charge, but a location had to be booked and other expenses paid. The financing of FF was eventually covered by the City of Malmö, on the condition that the organisers of FF promised to lower the profile of their protest against NF. In effect, this contributed to the situation in which FF became a parallel event, as opposed to a counter festival to NF (interview 44, organiser FF). The dynamic between NF and FF was thus constrained on the part of FF, but in the long term, and especially as the years passed and FF became an annual event, few FF organisers seem to have been concerned about this situation.

A general observation is that intersections of gender, nationality, and class matter in feminist mobilisations. The different funding schemes for umbrella organisations in the Nordic countries, and the lack of substantial governmental support (except in Sweden), turned class, nationality, and language (interviews 9 and 11, organisers) into live issues in relation to participation. Interviewees missed participants from Greenland and the Faroe Islands, claiming that the reason was 'obviously' the lack of sponsorship from the Nordic Council (Focus interview 4, interview person 53). Others explained that gender equality is:

A so much bigger field in Sweden, it's like, they have hundreds of people who are getting paid for it, while we have about ten people . . . who could go to their employer and ask for funding to travel to Malmö. And I feel they didn't really understand that from a Swedish perspective. The Swedes simply didn't see how privileged they were.

(Interview 11)

Irrespective of funding, some of the (umbrella) organisations in the Nordic region that were working with issues of gender and anti-racism, migration, sexuality, and indigenousness were not involved, for different reasons. There were power struggles over who was (and who was *not*) invited or agreed to be a member of the Nordic Steering Group. Whilst members of the Nordic Steering Group have questioned its composition, they have also accepted the principle that each country had the right to decide for itself (interview 23, Focus interview 8).[1] One example is the MiRA Centre in Norway, which launched a harsh anti-racist feminist critique against the NF organisers in both public and semi-public venues. This centre, however, was one of the few organisations that succeeded in getting funding to participate in Malmö. They had several slots on the official programme and actively suggested revisions to the final document. MiRA was not, however, part of the Nordic Steering Group, and was not included, despite making a request to join. According to one interviewee, this request came too late in the planning process. However, other interviewees disagree. They lamented what they saw as a lack of diversity in the steering group (interviews 11, 34, and 35).

Who actually ended up in the Nordic Steering Group influenced the framing of the programme and generally the politics of inclusion of the event. The size of NF, and the different streams within the programme, enabled organisers to embrace both single-axis thinking and intersectional approaches, as well as different 'styles' of organising for different purposes. Consequently, the Programme of NF presented the event as inclusive:

> Our vision is that gender, ethnicity, sexual orientation and other grounds of discrimination should not limit our dreams, ambitions and life choices, but that we should all be met with respect. . . . Together, we are taking another step towards an equal world where everyone's rights are respected.
>
> (Printed Programme, Nordiskt Forum 2014, p. 5)

At the same time, the perceived lack of an intersectional approach to the composition of the steering group, the programme, or the participants was at the core of both the internal and external controversies over NF. The controversy over NF's closing ceremony, involving the presence of the right-wing Norwegian nationalist populist Minister of Equality, is one illustration of this. Should feminists foster good relations with policymakers at 'any cost,' or should they rather focus on the mobilisation of grassroots protest?

Generational conflicts and the politics of inclusion

Let us now turn to how we can combine generational and intersectional approaches in order to explain or understand the conflicts about and between NF and FF.

Generational conflicts about 'real feminism' and transnational solidarities

Generational conflicts indicate that activists are highlighting their distinctiveness from and superiority to previous or subsequent generations by defining who they are and what 'real' feminism looks like. This happens during conflictual power struggles. We have been careful not to exaggerate the conflicts that we have described previously, at least those between NF and FF. For example, frustrations arising between the organisations responsible for the two events did not restrain participants from engaging in a common march through the city, ending with a party in the park where FF took place. Moreover, the organisers of both events give quite nuanced descriptions of the dynamics between them and tend to see FF especially as developing over time into a parallel or supplementary event to NF. One of the core organisers of NF described the relationship between the two as 'totally unproblematic' and mentioned several joint meetings (Interview 39, organiser NF).

Internal and external controversies about NF seem to relate mostly to different *political generations* identifying what they consider to be 'real' feminism. Although it seemed easy for the organisers of FF to identify what they claimed 'real' feminism to be, this was more difficult for the organisers of NF (see 'Identification and dis-identification of generations' subsection, previously in this chapter). There was, however, a reason why this event was initiated, and this motivation tells us something about the feminism (or feminisms) of the NF organisers.

Since 1995, there has been no additional UN World Conference on Women due to the fear of a gender equality backlash, in the wake of an alliance of conservative and religious forces that came together to combat the UN's policy on women's sexual and reproductive rights. Feminists feared that a fifth UN conference would result in the renegotiation of the Beijing Platform for Action. Indeed, there was a general lack of confidence that the governments of member states would uphold their previous commitments and a suspicion that they would diminish women's. Therefore, the organisers stated in the programme (Printed Programme, Nordiskt Forum 2014, p. 5; confirmed in focus group interviews):

> By gathering in Malmö, we pay tribute to the arduous struggle of the women's movement during a time when women did not have the right to vote, did not have a legal age of maturity and were not considered worthy of work outside the home. We acknowledge the battles won in history by looking forward and taking the work further. It is important for the transnational women's movement to analyse the current situation, and, in an inclusive process, set the agenda for the future. When states seeking to restrict women's lives exert great influence in international negotiations, it is more important than ever for the women's movement to act.

Following Mannheim (1952, p. 291), we can understand the *generational location* of the organisers in this quote to mean that they had been exposed to modes of thought about the previous struggles of the women's movement and to experiences of success when obtaining national and human rights for women. The references to the Beijing Platform and its follow-up as a historically important legacy to address gender conservatism were explicit in the programme (Printed Programme, Nordiskt Forum 2014, pp. 6–7 on 'From Beijing to Malmö'). These modes of thought and experience made them react forcefully ('the visionary

document Beijing Platform for Action has often been reduced to a paper tiger,'
Printed Programme, Nordiskt Forum 2014, p. 5) and organise the Forum. The
threats to which they referred included the fact that 'all over the world, women's
rights are relativized, marginalized, ridiculed and threatened with varying excuses
depending upon the context . . . the principal of universality and indivisibility of
human rights is called into question' (Printed Programme, Nordiskt Forum 2014,
p. 5). Meanwhile, in Europe, the economic crisis had hit hard and in the Nordic
region 'violence and threats of violence, lower wages, fewer career opportunities
and less influence in decision-making are included in the repertoire of discrimination' (Printed Programme, Nordiskt Forum 2014, p. 5).

The description of transnational solidarity in the previous quotes contrasts to
some extent with the transnational solidarity heralded by FF. NF organisers understand a politics of inclusion to involve an international and transnational form of
feminism, focusing on women's rights as human rights, concentrating on what
happens at the UN. We take this to reflect the fact that the umbrella organisations of the steering group had met at the UN CSW/CEDAW proceedings and are
familiar with the UN system.

In contrast, FF understands a politics of inclusion to concern a local and transnational form of feminism that is intersectional, concentrating on what happens in
Malmö. In the interviews with FF organisers, there was no ambition to create an
event that reached far beyond the city. Instead, the anti-racism of FF understood
transnational solidarity as an engagement with people from all over the world who
had moved to Malmö, and the consequences of this migration.

Intersectionality as a marker for different generations?

Are these differences in understandings of feminism and transnational solidarity
a matter of generation and location? Based on our fieldwork, we might suggest
that we can identify the organisers of FF as collectively belonging to a political
generation. The actions and discourses of these organisers point to a generational
dis-identification along the lines of a need for 'real' feminism. This feminism was
described as outspokenly inclusive, primarily of anti-racist activists, issues, and
ideas, but also of, for example, LGBT*QI issues. We can use the slogan 'it's not
feminism, if it's not intersectional' to capture this identification and to label this
generation 'intersectional' (although individual anarchist and separatist participants would presumably not identify with this). In line with this self-identification
as intersectional feminists (the first use of intersectionality, in the introduction),
criticisms of NF have used intersectionality as an issue of struggle over inclusion
(the third use of intersectionality). Both internal and external critics based their
criticism on ontological complexity as opposed to single-axis thinking about gender and power. Not women, but gender and related categories were supposed to
be the focus for feminism.

From a generational perspective, many of these internal and external critics
of NF could thus potentially be identified as a *political generation* that we could

name 'intersectional feminists' in the current macro-sociological opportunity structure, or occupying a *generational location* of neoliberalism, nationalism, and conservatism (see Elomäki and Kantola 2018). Additionally, we could frame the participants at NF who preferred to engage with a predominantly single-axis analysis of women and power as belonging to a *generational unit* of what we might label state feminists or rights-based or policy-oriented feminists within this political generation of intersectional feminists. The references to CEDAW (1979) and the Beijing Platform (1995) include a focus on *women* and rights that reflects single-axis analyses that remain symptomatic of gender issues in international law and politics. Older members of this generational unit might have worked with so-called *women-friendly* or *gender-sensitive* public policies at different levels of formal politics, not least that of (Nordic welfare) states, during the times of the previous NFs in Oslo (1988) and Åbo (1994).

This suggestion has two limitations, however. Firstly, the categories of age and generation: younger members of the generational unit of state feminists do not have shared experiences of previous mobilisations with older activists. Secondly, working with gender-equality public policies does not *in and of itself* imply the need to work with a single-axis analysis of power relations between women and men. Anti-racist, queer, and indigenous feminists in the Nordic region have existed for a long time and have historically worked from intersectionality-like perspectives, as have feminists with an interest in inequalities due to gender and class. This has included strategies aiming to change public policies at different political levels during periods that have been described as the 'hey-day' of state feminism. For a long time, Sami feminists have been active in relation to human rights struggles in the intersection between gender, indigeneity, and nationality. They have always done this through a complex understanding of the notions of 'state,' 'nation,' and 'belonging' (Knobblock and Kuokkanen 2015). This empha-sises the danger of understanding state feminism as consisting only of single-axis, policy-oriented, middle-aged feminists and the only representatives of an older generation of feminists, *or* of equating state feminists with simplistic understand-ings of policy-oriented feminism.

Conclusion

Differences in power and privilege in and between the NF organisers and the FF organisers are, to some extent, a matter of generational belonging. We could relate age and generation – understood as people of the same age – to inequali-ties in power, but there are limits to how useful these categories are if we want to explain or understand the different controversies over the two feminist events. Treating the category of generation as only one category amongst others within an intersectional analysis turned out to be of little help. Based on our fieldwork, we can conclude that the controversies over a politics of inclusion do not explic-itly concern age and generation, but are rather conflicts over other intersectional inequalities, such as class, ethnicity, nationality, sexuality, and indigenousness.

Throughout the chapter, we have shown how perceptions of privilege, along with both internal and external criticisms of the reproduction of privilege in the organisation of NF, concentrated on *institutionalised privileges*. Both internal and external critics perceived access to financial resources and the ability to be part of the organising committee as privileging feminists who already had high status and significant economic resources. While FF also benefited from public resources, and eventually became an institution, it was free of charge, in contrast to NF.

Additionally, the organisers of FF used an explicit and agreed-upon strategy to include intersectional voices (see the third use of intersectionality). They intended the festival to be anti-racist and inclusive, thereby challenging the structure of privilege which they claimed characterised the other event. For the internal critics of NF, it was more controversial to implement a strategy to ensure inclusivity and to confront persisting privileges within the organisation. Whereas the organisers and participants of FF were mainly white, middle-class, cis women and young people under the age of 35, and this observation led the organisers of FF to address epistemic and political concerns over notions of privilege in their evaluations, resistance to the unsettling of privilege was in fact stronger in the organisation of NF.

Note

1 The Nordic Steering Group consisted of the Swedish Women's Lobby (founded in 1997), with 40 member organisations; Dansk kvinderåd (1899); NYTKIS (1988); Kvenfelagasambands Islands Federation of Icelandic Women's Societies (1894) and Kvenrettindafelag Islands; Icelandic Women's Rights Association (1907); FOCUS (1989/1995), with 53 organisations; and Krisesentersekretariatet (1994), an umbrella organisation for 25 shelters.

   These organisations differ significantly with respect to their histories, size, resources, organisational style, and relations to the state. Overall, the Swedish Women's Lobby stands out as the most powerful in terms of legitimacy, resources, and dedication (Seibicke 2019, p. 60). The Europeanisation of national women's organisations has 'disciplined' them due to the demands of representativeness (Strid 2009). Historically, Sweden represents the 'success of state feminism,' in contrast to Denmark, where Dansk kvinderåd suffers from the failure of state feminism (Borchorst and Siim 2008, p. 218). In Finland, partnership with the state is weak, but the women's movement has been able to mobilise in response to cutbacks and adversity – and has a radical-feminist organisational style (Seibicke 2019). Iceland and Norway were each represented by two organisations, leading to both advantages and problems in being perceived as representative.

References

Ås, Berit 1981. *Kvinner i alle land . . . Håndbok i frigjøring*. Oslo: Aschehoug.
Borchorst, Anette, and Birte Siim. 2008. "Woman-Friendly Policies and State Feminism: Theorizing Scandinavian Gender Equality." *Feminist Theory* 9 (2): 207–224.
Crenshaw, Kimberlé Williams. 1989. "Demarginalizing the Intersection of Race and Sex." *The University of Chicago Legal Forum* 140: 139–167.

Cullen, Pauline and Clara Fischer. 2014. "Conceptualizing Generational Dynamics in Feminist Movements: Political Generations, Waves and Affective Economies." *Sociology Compass* 8 (3): 282–293.

De los Reyes, Paulina, Irina Molina, and Diana Mulinari. 2002. *Maktens (o)lika förklädnader – Kön, klass och etnicitet i det postkoloniala Sverige.* Stockholm: Atlas.

Elomäki, Anna and Johanna Kantola. 2018. "Theorizing Feminist Struggles in the Triangle of Neoliberalism, Conservatism, and Nationalism." *Social Politics* 25 (3): 337–360.

Hancock, Ange-Marie. 2016. *Intersectionality: An Intellectual History.* Oxford: Oxford University Press, Oxford Scholarship Online.

Henry, Astrid. 2004. *Not My Mother's Sister: Generational Conflict and Third-Wave Feminism.* Bloomington, IN: Indiana University Press.

Hernes, Helga Maria. 1987. *Welfare State and Woman Power: Essays in State Feminism.* Oslo: Scandinavian University Press.

Hernes, Helga Maria. 1988. "The Welfare State Citizenship of Scandinavian Women." In *The Political Interests of Gender*, edited by K. B. Jones and A. G. Jónasdóttir, 187–213. London: Sage.

Hill Collins, Patricia. 2015. "Intersectionality's Definitional Dilemmas." *Annual Review of Sociology* 41: 1–20.

Kantola, Johanna and Judith Squires. 2012. "From State Feminism to Market Feminism?" *International Political Science Review* 33 (4): 382–400.

Kantola, Johanna and Mieke Verloo. 2018. "Revisiting Gender Equality at Times of Recession: A Discussion of the Strategies of Gender and Politics Scholarship for Dealing With Equality." *European Journal of Politics and Gender* 1 (1–2): 205–222.

Knobblock, Ina and Rauna Kuokkanen. 2015. "Decolonizing Feminism in the North: A Conversation With Rauna Kuokkanen." *NORA: Nordic Journal of Feminist and Gender Research* 23 (4): 275–281.

Liinason, Mia. 2018. *Equality Struggles: Women's Movements, Neoliberal Markets and State Political Agendas in Scandinavia.* London: Routledge.

Manga, Edda and Rebecca Vinthagen. 2015. *Utvägar: Feministiska allianser för en solidarisk framtid.* Stockholm: Ordfront.

Mannheim, Karl 1927/1952. "The Problem of Generations." In *Karl Mannheim: Essays. on the Sociology of Knowledge, Collected Works*, edited by P. Kecskemeti, Vol. 5, 276–322. New York, NY: Routledge.

Mügge, Liza, Celeste Montoya, Akwugo Emejulu, and S. Laurel Weldon. 2018. "Intersectionality and the Politics of Knowledge Production." *European Journal of Politics and Gender* 1 (1–2): 17–36.

Nyhagen Predelli, Line and Beatrice Halsaa. 2012. *Majority – Minority Relations in Contemporary Women's Movements: Strategic Sisterhood.* Houndmills, Basingstoke: Palgrave Macmillan.

Pietilä, Hilkka and Jeanne Vickers. 1994. *Making Women Matter.* London: Zed Books.

Reger, Jo. 2014. *Everywhere and Nowhere: Contemporary Feminism in the United States.* Oxford: Oxford University Press.

Reger, Jo. 2015. "The Story of a Slut Walk: Sexuality, Race and Generational Divisions in Contemporary Feminist Activism." *Journal of Contemporary Ethnography* 44 (1): 84–112.

Schneider, Beth. 1988. "Political Generation and the Contemporary Women's Movement." *Sociological Inquiry* 58: 4–21.

Seibicke, Helena. 2019. "Europeisering av nordisk kvinnebevegelse?" In *Europeisering av nordisk likestillingspolitikk*, edited by C. Holst, H. Skjeie, and M. Teigen, 57–77. Oslo: Gyldendal.

Springer, Kimberly. 2005. *Living for the Revolution: Black Feminist Organizations, 1968–1980*. Durham, NC: Duke University Press.

Strid, Sofia. 2009. *Gendered Interests in the European Union. The European Women's Lobby and the Organisation and Representation of Women's Interests*. Örebro: Örebro Studies in Gender Research I. Örebro University.

Van der Tuin, Iris. 2009. "'Jumping Generations': On Second and Third Wave Feminist Epistemology." *Australian Feminist Studies* 59: 17–31.

Walby, Sylvia. 2011. *The Future of Feminism*. Cambridge, UK: Polity Press.

Whittier, Nancy. 1997. "Political Generations, Micro-Cohorts, and the Transformation of Social Movements." *American Sociological Review* 62 (5): 760–778.

Primary sources

The Beijing Platform for Action. 1995. www.un.org/womenwatch/daw/beijing/platform/ [accessed 3 October 2014].

CEDAW. 1979. "The Convention on the Elimination of All Forms of Discrimination Against Women." www.ohchr.org/EN/ProfessionalInterest/Pages/CEDAW.aspx [accessed 3 October 2014].

Final document, Nordiskt Forum. 2014. "Feminist Agreements and Demands: The Nordic Women's Movement's Proposals for the Final Document of Nordiskt Forum Malmö 2014 – New Action on Women's Rights." http://nf2014.org/en/kop-biljett-3/paverka-nordiskt-forums-slutdokument/ and http://nf2014.org/wp-content/uploads/2014/05/The-Nordic-womens-movements-proposals_Nordiskt-Forum-Malmo%CC%88_New-Action-on-Women%C2%B4s-Rights.pdf [accessed 3 October 2014].

Knudsen, Grete and Berit Moen. 1989. "Evalueringsrapport. Nordisk Forum 88." *Oslo Media impact Nordiskt Forum (2014)*. http://nf2014.org/press/ [accessed 11 October 2014].

Planlægningsgruppen. 1988. *Evalueringsrapport fra planlægningsgruppen for Nordisk forum*. Oslo. PM on the background to Nordiskt Forum or 'Nordiskt Forum Malmö 2014 eng 130121' (2013); accessed at the Nordiskt Forum Malmö 2014 website http://nf2014.org/en/press-2/reportsanddocuments/ and http://nf2014.org/wp-content/uploads/2013/02/Nordic-Forum-Malm%C3%B6-2014_eng_130121.pdf [accessed 2 October 2014].

Printed Programme, Nordiskt Forum. 2014. "Nordiskt Forum Malmö 12–15/6 2014 New Action on Women's Rights." *Norra Skåne Offset*.

Conclusion

Privileges confronted?

Elizabeth Evans and Éléonore Lépinard

The wide collection of empirical case studies presented in this volume are testimony to the range of ways in which privileges manifest themselves, and the extent to which they are acknowledged and confronted by those 'with' and 'without' privilege. The chapters illustrate how intersectionality has been taken up (or indeed resisted) by activists in order to expose and resist privilege. As the various chapters demonstrate, whilst many activists across time and space, and in relation to different social movements, have, to varying degrees, sought to engage with our three intersectional approaches – collective identity, coalitional politics, and inclusivity – the desire or hope for intersectionality does not always result in the confrontation of privileges. In this concluding chapter, we tie together the key empirical findings and theoretical puzzles that emerge from the preceding chapters, in order to set out a future research agenda that brings together intersectionality, privilege, and social movement studies. We focus our concluding remarks upon three questions: (1) To what extent has intersectionality become synonymous with 'good' feminist and queer activism? (2) How and when do we understand intersectionality to have been 'achieved'? (3) What effect does the *type* of social movement organisation and form of organising have on the ability to confront privilege?

Intersectionality as good activism?

Many of the chapters presented in this book set out the ways in which intersectionality discourse is presented as the *sine qua non* of (especially) feminist and queer activism. The normalisation process that has occurred around intersectionality – and especially its use as a proxy for being inclusive – has gained legitimacy across a wide variety of countries. The 'success' of intersectional discourse has raised concerns that it has been 'whitened,' i.e. that it risks being normalised also in the sense of losing its critical edge to challenge privileges, especially racial privilege (Nash 2008; Bilge 2013; Carbin and Edenheim 2013). As illustrated in the various chapters, intersectional discourse and praxis are unevenly distributed, and gaps are clearly documented between discourses and practices. This appraisal both confirms and nuances the idea of a depoliticised and uncritical use and diffusion of the concept. Indeed, intersectionality is well established as a norm, or desirable form of feminist and queer activism in the US, Canada, and the UK (see chapters by Laperrière, Labelle, Luna, Evans, and Bonane, this volume). In these contexts, 'good' activist practices are clearly assessed in relation to this norm, and a specific set of practices are clearly implemented as a way of translating this norm into practice, especially with regards the inclusion and representation of racialised women and queer activists. Analysing these strategies of implementation, we see that they sometimes give rise to a specific expertise, for example: the organisation combatting gender-based violence studied by Marie Laperrière; practical actions to support queer Muslim groups through financial and organisational support (Bonane, this volume); distribution of guidelines for demonstration (Luna, this volume); and attempts to make meetings and activities accessible to disabled activists (Evans, this volume).

Intersectionality has also travelled to, and been locally developed in, other contexts; for example, Colombia and Ecuador (Cherubini, Garofalo Geymonat, and Marchetti, this volume), countries where intersectional collective identity strategies profoundly shape activism in the domain of domestic work, but impact differently on coalitional intersectional discourses and strategies. Intersectionality is therefore clearly used as a tool to challenge privilege, especially racial privilege, thus disrupting the idea that it has been whitened. Nonetheless, whether those practices achieve their goal often depends on the context (Martin de Almagro, this volume), the ways in which they are translated into policy and campaigns (Strid and Verloo, this volume; Laperrière, this volume), although more often than not the practices are felt to be insufficient by many minoritised activists (Luna, this volume; Labelle, this volume). What is more, even in these contexts such as the UK where intersectionality is widely used to challenge, at least discursively, privileges, its use is unevenly distributed across different privileges, with disability and religion receiving little attention. (Evans, this volume; Bonane, this volume).

In other contexts, such as Belgium and Germany (Ahrens and Meier, this volume), France (Lépinard, this volume; Quéré, this volume), Sweden (Stoltz, Halsaa, and Stormhøj, this volume), Cyprus (Kamenou, this volume), and Morocco (David, this volume), the ways in which intersectionality might be picked up and implemented remain much less clear and systematic, be it as a coalitional or inclusionary tactic. While it can be claimed by activists, it does not seem to constitute yet a shared norm. Resistances to intersectionality are also often palpable, and a lack of proper expertise and training, as well as a clear tendency to invisibilise the importance and structural dimension of racism within feminist and queer activism, lead not only to forms of whitening – although they are uneven in each of these contexts – but also to a lack of attention to other privileges and a very weak attention to issues of inclusion. Hence, where intersectionality is weak or absent, other strategies of inclusion do not replace it, which confirms the analysis that, in contemporary feminist and queer activism, intersectionality, albeit alongside homonationalism (Kamenou, this volume; Bonane, this volume; Labelle, this volume), is the main concept to frame and address inclusion issues.

Our chapters provide important insights on when, how, and why social movement actors take up intersectionality, or not, but more systematic and comparative
research is clearly needed in this area. In particular, future research should aim to
assess if the processes by which intersectionality is adopted influence its appropriation and implementation (Strid and Verloo, this volume; Laperrière, this volume). Case studies in this volume show that intersectionality might be adopted as
a reaction to transnational norms of good activism, although they may also adapt
intersectionality to better suit the local context, as in the case of Morocco (David,
this volume); this is also partly the case in Cyprus, where contestations of homonationalist trends are influenced by European activists' discourses (Kamenou, this
volume). Conversely, transnational feminist networks operating in post-conflict
societies have failed to take up intersectionality, thus relying upon strategic essentialism which reinforces privileges (Martin de Almagro, this volume).

In many other contexts, intersectionality is diffused, and adopted at least rhe-
torically, thanks to the activism of feminists and queer activists of colour. Here
a clear connection can be identified between activism which centres on intersectionality as collective identity and inclusionary intersectionality. Pressure from
self-organized feminist and queer people of colour activists trigger responses
from white and single-axis feminist and queer organisations. Confronted with
open critiques of their lack of inclusivity, mainstream and/or dominantly white
organisations try to adopt intersectionality as a new 'best practice' form of activism. However, a gap persists between rhetoric and practice, as path-dependency
mechanisms, institutional routines, and favoured activist repertoires contribute to
the reproduction of privileges, despite claimed intersectional intentions. Whether
in feminist self-help activism (Quéré, this volume), or queer coalitions (Labelle,
this volume; Bonane, this volume) inclusionary intersectionality often remains
insufficient and non-performative.

Further research should therefore explore intersectional activism as a new
activist repertoire, which normatively defines what are 'good' feminist and queer
practices in activism, and how it shapes a new activist ethos among feminist and
queer actors. How is intersectionality mobilised as an activist identity, in the
context of collective identity activism or of inclusionary and coalitional activism? Who can define their activism as intersectional, and in what context? And
how does this norm transform activists' perception of their work and identities?
Finally, the case studies in this volume suggest that the context of emergence of
intersectionality impacts on its various uses and its ability to challenge privilege.
When it is linked to the lived realities of multiple oppressions and is articulated as
a collective identity strategy, the critical power of intersectionality remains intact.
Whereas when it is diffused as a byword for good practice or funding opportunities, it may transform into an empty buzzword (Davis 2008). Hence, the tension
and confrontation between intersectionality as collective identity and as a repertoire of inclusion remains crucial, in order to ensure that intersectionality retains
its critical potential to challenge privileges. We encourage researchers working
in this field to interrogate these questions in order to understand the motivation

for engaging with intersectionality, as the motivation itself can be critical to the nature, and extent, of the intersectional activism.

How and when is intersectionality achieved?

Despite the normalisation of intersectional discourse, it is less clear how we identify *how* and *when* intersectionality has been achieved. Whilst the desire for intersectionality is clearly important, especially when demonstrated by one or more of the three approaches – identity, coalition, and inclusion – this does not always translate into forms of activism that are recognised by those at the margins as *being* intersectional. This raises questions about the affective dimensions of intersectional activism, in particular how privileged actors within social movements lay claim to intersectional organising and the perceptions of tokenism or silencing that is identified by marginalised groups (Evans, this volume; Labelle, this volume; Bonane, this volume).

Intersectionality is an emic category, as well as conceptual tool, and this raises methodological challenges for researchers seeking to capture the translation of intersectional desire into new forms of activism and discourse. Who can define and decide when intersectionality is present or achieved? Whether it should be regarded as a success or a failure? Should researchers rely on activists' own perceptions and categorizations, or should they aim at defining criteria, methods by which to measure the implementation and practice of intersectionality? Or should scholars refrain altogether from entering into this terrain which requires evaluation and normative assumptions? To what extent is scholarly neutrality even possible on such a highly political topic? Recognising the importance of feminist standpoint theory and its emphasis on epistemology, we argue that both activists' and researchers' definitions and evaluations of the achievements of intersectionality can only ever remain partial (Haraway 1988). Zakiya Luna's chapter in this volume illustrates how the positionality of activists, and also scholars, influences their perceptions and feelings about the realisation of intersectionality. Understandings of embodied intersectionality, in spaces where there are activists from visibly marginalised groups present, are shaped by the various dynamic interactions of privilege and marginalisation. They are, however, as Luna argues, perceptions which are informed both by activists' imagination about what intersectionality should feel and look like, as well as their positionality, in terms of social and geographical location.

However, this recognition does not prevent scholars from doing the work of identifying *differences* between the ways in which intersectionality is discursively defined and practiced (Lépinard 2014; David, this volume; Quéré, this volume), and inquiring about how these different repertoires of intersectional practice may challenge privilege in different ways. What is more, as we argue in the introductory chapter to this volume, focusing our critical inquiry on if and how intersectional repertoires actually address issues of privilege is an important element of evaluating and defining intersectional discourses and practices. In this perspective, one can ask if specific practices framed by particular understandings of intersectionality contest privilege. For example, to what extent does intersectionality which focuses on visible representation challenge privilege (Ahrens and Meier, this volume)? Can intersectional inclusion ever succeed (Labelle, this volume)? Or should movements which aim at critically assessing their own privileges focus rather on intersectional coalition (Bonane, this volume, see also Cole 2008)?

We propose to address, rather than answer, these complex questions about evaluation and *intersectional achievements* through a methodological lens rather than through normative assumptions. Indeed, we claim that methodological strategies are a useful way of making scholars aware of their own normative assumptions, as well as ensuring that a diversity of viewpoints are represented in research focused on what intersectionality should feel and look like. We propose here two methodological strategies. The first consists in considering feminist or queer activism as a broad field of activism rather than focusing on single organisations. More specifically, as feeling and normative assumptions about intersectional achievements inevitably vary across the dimensions of privilege that intersectionality can help contest, centring activist groups who claim an intersectional identity is a good starting point. For instance, it is clear that an important way of researching intersectionality and privilege is to pay attention to the voices of those on whose behalf intersectional claims are being made (Labelle, this volume; Bonane, this volume). Making an effort to ask 'the other question' (Matsuda 1990) also needs to be translated into specific methodological approaches that consider race but also sexuality, disability, age, religion, and gender identity and how they shape relations of privilege in activist fields. Ensuring that marginalised intersectional viewpoints are taken into account in the research can also better capture the dynamic by which intersectional identity strategies confront and contest intersectional inclusion and coalition repertoires and practices.

A second methodological strategy reverses the question of intersectional achievement to look at resistances to intersectionality. Indeed, focusing on resistances and documenting them, as they are expressed by feminist or queer activists who sometimes suggest that intersectionality is too complex to be applied or explain its slow adoption by the difficulties it supposedly raises in activist practices (Lépinard, this volume, Evans 2015), enables scholars of intersectionality to identify expression of privileges, especially in their institutional and epistemological dimensions. It is thus important to locate those discourses which widen the gap between the proclaimed 'desire' for intersectionality and the resistances to its concrete implementation as a practice challenging privileges. For instance, while race may be foregrounded in conversations about intersectionality, it does not necessarily challenge the whiteness of feminist and queer organisations.

Effect of type of organisation or tactical repertoire on intersectionality

A couple of key organisational dimensions require analysis in order to understand activist approaches toward intersectionality: (1) the type of organisation under study and (2) the types of tactical repertoires adopted. Looking more broadly at the landscape of feminist and queer activism, we can see that some forms of organisation may be more likely to adopt an intersectional praxis. Specifically, older more institutionalised types of organisation often struggle to incorporate intersectionality into their activism. A form of path dependency sets in, with some older historic organisations on the backfoot simply reacting to the 'newness' of intersectionality, as is largely the case in Belgium and Germany (Ahrens and Meier, this volume). Similarly, major institutionalised and dominant civil society organisations in Sweden (Stolz et al., this volume), Cyprus (Kamenou, this volume), and to a lesser extent the UK (Evans, this volume; Bonane, this volume), have at times sought to resist, or at least not been fulsome in their embrace of the turn towards intersectionality.

Whilst some resistance to intersectionality can be understood as being a product of generational socialisation, this only tells us part of the story (Stolz et al., this volume). The extent to which organisations, especially 'historic' or institutionalised organisations, take up intersectional discourse and the ways in which they seek to translate it into their campaign or policy focus can also act as a subtler form of resistance (Strid and Verloo, this volume). Indeed, in order to fully identify and capture resistance to intersectionality, it is critical to also take into account patterns of privilege and the variety of ways in which they are realised (Lépinard, this volume). Established actors can deploy intersectionality in such a way as to not only mask privilege but in some instances to reinforce privilege (Martin de Almagro, this volume); in fact in some cases intersectionality and intersectional discourse becomes the preserve of the professional, thus reinforcing dynamics of privilege (Laperrière, this volume). The study of resistance to intersectionality is therefore, as we identified previously, an important site for scholars interested in exploring intersectional praxis within social movements.

Conversely, many of the empirical case studies in this volume map out new types of organisation which have intersectionality as part of their founding principles. For example, feminist activists in Morocco have sought to explicitly engage with, and adapt, intersectional politics in order to create new forms of feminist praxis (David, this volume). Similarly, younger generations of activists have foregrounded intersectionality in their planning of events, in order to create new and different spaces that give voice to those typically marginalised within the wider movement (Stolz et al., this volume; Bonane, this volume). Additionally, some newer organisations have also sought to include a specific call for activists to engage with a 'pedagogy of intersectionality' (Evans, this volume). Hence, the type of organisation, and in particular whether it is a historic or newer organisation, appears to play an important role in determining when and how intersectionality is taken up, or indeed resisted.

Of course, the type of tactical repertoires taken up by activists might also affect the extent to which intersectionality is taken up and the realisation of intersectional strategies. For instance, Lucile Quéré's analysis of the self-help movement in France reveals that even when activists are explicitly committed to, and articulate their desire for, achieving intersectionality through the practice of gynaecological self-examination, the history of this form of activism has not always been one in which women of colour have been included, or have felt welcome. Similarly, Luna's analysis of the women's marches underscores the importance of the local context within which the march occurred, thereby contextualising the idea of marching as an intersectional tactical repertoire. We also see how newer and more creative forms of organising are undertaken in the name of adopting a more intersectional praxis, as is the case in Morocco (David, this volume).

Whilst coalitional organising has clear potential for pursuing intersectional activism (Kamenou, this volume; Martin de Almagro, this volume), autonomous organising spaces are critical sites in which marginalised actors can more effectively contest and confront privilege (Labelle, this volume; Bonane, this volume; Evans, this volume). Self-organising, especially when consciously framed as the pursuit of intersectional politics, provides the most significant site for activists to confront institutional privilege and to challenge resistance (Cherubini et al., this volume). Autonomous organising also facilitates discussions in which privileges can be acknowledged, named, and contested – a process central to the pursuit of intersectional praxis.

We propose that scholars interested in further exploring the entrenchment of privilege within social movements pay close attention to the ways in which different types (and histories) of organisation resist and/or engage with intersectionality in its different dimensions – as collective identity, as a coalitional strategy, and as a repertoire for inclusivity. Calling attention to the ways in which intersectionality is deployed, in which contexts, and with regards to which intersections, can reveal dynamics of privilege which ultimately serve to undermine, or restrict, the reach of intersectional praxis.

References

Bilge, Sirma. 2013. "Intersectionality Undone." *Du Bois Review: Social Science Research on Race* 10 (2): 405–424.

Carbin, Maria, and Sara Edenheim. 2013. "The Intersectional Turn in Feminist Theory: A Dream of a Common Language?" *European Journal of Women's Studies* 20 (3): 233–248.

Cole, Elizabeth R. 2008. "Coalitions as a Model for Intersectionality: from Practice to Theory". *Sex Roles* 59: 443-453.

Davis, Kathy. 2008. "Intersectionality as a Buzzword: A Sociology of Science Perspective on What Makes a Feminist Theory Successful." *Feminist Theory* 9 (1): 67–85.

Evans, Elizabeth. 2015. *The Politics of Third Wave Feminisms*. Houndmills, Basingstoke: Palgrave Macmillan.

Haraway, Donna. 1988. "Situated Knowledges: The Science Question in Feminism and the Privilege of Partial Perspective." *Feminist Studies* 14 (3): 575–599.

Lépinard, Éléonore. 2014. "Doing Intersectionality: Repertoires of Feminist Practices in France and Canada." *Gender & Society* 28 (6): 877–903.

Matsuda, Mari. 1990. "Beside My Sister, Facing the Enemy: Legal Theory out of Coalition." *Stanford Law Review* 43: 1183–1192.

Nash, Jennifer. 2008. "Rethinking Intersectionality." *Feminist Review* 89 (1): 1–15.

Index

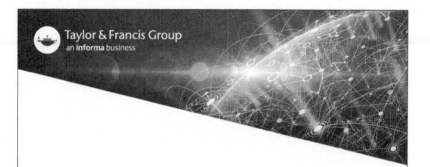